VLADIMIR NA

CONTEXT

MW00622512

EDITED BY

DAVID M. BETHEA

University of Wisconsin–Madison

SIGGY FRANK

University of Nottingham

CAMBRIDGE
UNIVERSITY PRESS

CAMBRIDGE
UNIVERSITY PRESS

University Printing House, Cambridge CB2 8BS, United Kingdom

One Liberty Plaza, 20th Floor, New York, NY 10006, USA

477 Williamstown Road, Port Melbourne, VIC 3207, Australia

314-321, 3rd Floor, Plot 3, Splendor Forum, Jasola District Centre, New Delhi - 110025, India

79 Anson Road, #06-04/06, Singapore 079906

Cambridge University Press is part of the University of Cambridge.

It furthers the University's mission by disseminating knowledge in the pursuit of education, learning and research at the highest international levels of excellence.

www.cambridge.org
Information on this title: www.cambridge.org/9781107519596
DOI: 10.1017/9781316258132

First published 2018
First paperback edition 2020

A catalogue record for this publication is available from the British Library

ISBN 978-1-107-10864-6 Hardback
ISBN 978-1-107-51959-6 Paperback

Cambridge University Press has no responsibility for the persistence or accuracy of URLs for external or third-party internet websites referred to in this publication, and does not guarantee that any content on such websites is, or will remain, accurate or appropriate.

Contents

List of Illustrations   *page* viii
List of Contributors   ix
Acknowledgements   xi
Note on Transliteration and Dates   xii
List of Abbreviations   xiii

Contextualising Nabokov   I
David M. Bethea and Siggy Frank

PART I IDENTITY   9

1 Nabokov's Life in Context I: Russia and Emigration   II
   Brian Boyd

2 Nabokov's Life in Context II: Beyond the Emigration   19
   Brian Boyd

3 Childhood   28
   Barbara Wyllie

4 Women   35
   Lara Delage-Toriel

5 Friends and Foes   43
   Julian W. Connolly

6 Academia   51
   Susan Elizabeth Sweeney

7 Authorial Persona   59
   Maria Malikova

PART II PLACES   69

8   St Petersburg   71
    Gennady Barabtarlo

9   Cambridge   80
    Beci Carver

10 Berlin   87
    Stanislav Shvabrin

11 Paris   94
    John Burt Foster, Jr.

12 East to West Coast   102
    Monica Manolescu

13 Switzerland   111
    Annick Morard

PART III LITERATURES AND ARTS   119

14 The Russian Literary Canon   121
    Alexander Dolinin

15 The Western Literary Canon   131
    Michael Wood

16 Publishing: Russian Émigré Literature   139
    Siggy Frank

17 Publishing: American Literature   150
    Duncan White

18 Detective Fiction   158
    Michal Oklot and Matthew Walker

19 Samizdat and Tamizdat   166
    Ann Komaromi

20 Nabokov's Visual Imagination   174
    Marijeta Bozovic

21 Popular Culture   182
    Nassim Winnie Balestrini

PART IV IDEAS AND CULTURES   191

22 Science   193
    Stephen H. Blackwell

23 Darwinism   201
    David M. Bethea

24 Psychoanalysis   211
    Michal Oklot and Matthew Walker

25 Faith   219
    Sergei Davydov

26 Jewishness as Literary Device in Nabokov's Fiction   228
    Leonid Livak

27 Liberalism   240
    Dana Dragunoiu

28 Totalitarianism   249
    Olga Voronina

29 The Cold War   257
    Will Norman

30 The Long 1950s   266
    Andrea Carosso

31 Transnationalism   275
    Rachel Trousdale

Further Reading   283
Index   294

Illustrations

1   Bronze statue of Vladimir Nabokov by Alexander and   *page* 60
     Phillip Rukavishnikov, Montreux. Photograph by S.Frank.
2   Nabokov writing in his car, Ithaca, NY (1958).   109
     Photograph by Carl Mydans © The Life Picture Collection,
     Getty Images.
3   First edition of *Zashchita Luzhina* (*The Luzhin Defense*)   148
     published by Slovo, 1930. Item from the collection of
     the V. V. Nabokov Museum in St Petersburg. Photograph
     by Daniel Sirgeyev.
4   Samizad copies of *Dar* (*The Gift*) and *Drugie berega*   169
     ('Other Shores') prepared by Iurii Men'shov in the
     early to mid-1970s. Items from the collection of the
     V. V. Nabokov Museum in St Petersburg. Photograph
     by Daniel Sirgeyev.
5   The Nabokovs' grave at Clarens. Photograph by S. Frank.   227
6   Book cover of *Pnin* (Doubleday, 1957). Reproduced   236
     with permission by Penguin Random House. Photograph
     by Michael Juliar.
7   Detail of Jan van Eyck, *Madonna and Child with Canon van*   238
     der Paele (1436). Musea Brugge © Lukas – Art in Flanders
     VZW, photo Hugo Maertens.
8   Vladimir Nabokov in Montreux (1967). Photograph by   239
     Philippe Halsman © Yvonne Halsman [Philippe
     Halsman/Magnum photos].

Contributors

NASSIM WINNIE BALESTRINI, University of Graz

GENNADY BARABTARLO, University of Missouri

DAVID M. BETHEA, University of Wisconsin–Madison

STEPHEN H. BLACKWELL, University of Tennessee

BRIAN BOYD, University of Auckland

MARIJETA BOZOVIC, Yale University

ANDREA CAROSSO, University of Turin

BECI CARVER, University of Exeter

JULIAN W. CONNOLLY, University of Virginia

SERGEI DAVYDOV, Middlebury College

LARA DELAGE-TORIEL, University of Strasbourg

ALEXANDER DOLININ, University of Wisconsin–Madison

DANA DRAGUNOIU, Carleton University

JOHN BURT FOSTER, JR. George Mason University

SIGGY FRANK, University of Nottingham

ANN KOMAROMI, University of Toronto

LEONID LIVAK, University of Toronto

MARIA MALIKOVA, Institute of Russian Literature

MONICA MANOLESCU, University of Strasbourg

ANNICK MORARD, University of Geneva

WILL NORMAN, University of Kent

MICHAL OKLOT, Brown University

STANISLAV SHVABRIN, University of North Carolina at Chapel Hill

SUSAN ELIZABETH SWEENEY, College of the Holy Cross

RACHEL TROUSDALE, Framingham State University

OLGA VORONINA, Bard College

MATTHEW WALKER, Middlebury College

DUNCAN WHITE, Harvard University

MICHAEL WOOD, Princeton University

BARBARA WYLLIE, University College London

Acknowledgements

First of all, we would like to thank our distinguished contributors, who not only responded in a generous fashion to our editorial suggestions and reminders of deadlines, but also showed considerable patience in the face of delays and 'hiccups' in scheduling. We feel extremely lucky to have had the opportunity to work with this group. In this latter connection, we want to thank particularly Alexander Dolinin and Jane Grayson for their thoughtful advice, buttressed by exceptional knowledge of Nabokov and his times, along the way. One person who was tapped to participate in our project but who could not complete her assignment was Catharine Nepomnyashchy: her passing was a big blow not only to Nabokov studies, in which she was making exciting strides with her typical energy and dynamism, but to Slavistics in general. She will be greatly missed!

In addition, we would like to express our gratitude to José Vergara for his fine translation of Maria Malikova's article from Russian into English. Likewise, Annick Morard would like to thank Amy Heneveld for her help with the translation of her chapter from French into English.

Note on Transliteration and Dates

Transliteration of Russian texts follows the Library of Congress system without diacritical marks, apart from common Anglicised spellings of Russian names of historical and fictional persons (e.g. Tolstoy instead of Tolstoi; Gogol instead of Gogol', Alexander instead of Aleksandr).

Unless noted otherwise, dates in brackets in the text refer to the date of first publication.

Until 1918, Russia used the Julian Calendar, which lagged in the nineteenth century twelve days and in the twentieth century thirteen days behind the Gregorian Calendar. Both Julian and Gregorian dates are given where relevant.

Abbreviations

Ada	Vladimir Nabokov, *Ada, or Ador: A Family Chronicle*, in *Novels 1969–1974* (New York: Library of America, 1996).
BS	Vladimir Nabokov, *Bend Sinister*, in *Novels and Memoirs 1941–1951* (New York: Library of America, 1996).
Defense	Vladimir Nabokov, *The Luzhin Defense*, tr. Michael Scammell in collaboration with the author (London: Penguin, 2000).
Despair	Vladimir Nabokov, *Despair* (London: Penguin, 2010).
Enchanter	Vladimir Nabokov, *The Enchanter*, tr. Dmitri Nabokov, (London and Basingstoke: Picador, 1987).
EO	Alexander Pushkin, *Eugene Onegin: A Novel in Verse*, tr. Vladimir Nabokov (Princeton: Princeton University Press, 1990).
Eye	Vladimir Nabokov, *The Eye*, tr. Dmitri Nabokov in collaboration with the author (London: Penguin, 2010).
Gift	Vladimir Nabokov, *The Gift*, tr. Michael Scammell and Dmitri Nabokov in collaboration with Vladimir Nabokov (London: Penguin, 2001).
Glory	Vladimir Nabokov, *Glory*, tr. Dmitri Nabokov (London: Penguin, 2006).
IB	Vladimir Nabokov, *Invitation to a Beheading*, tr. Dmitri Nabokov in collaboration with the author (London: Penguin, 2010).
KQK	Vladimir Nabokov, *King, Queen, Knave*, tr. Dmitri Nabokov in collaboration with the author (London: Penguin, 2010).
LATH	Vladimir Nabokov, *Look at the Harlequins!*, in *Novels 1969–1974* (New York: Library of America, 1996).

LDQ Vladimir Nabokov, *Lectures on Don Quixote*, ed. Fredson Bowers (San Diego, CA: Bruccoli Clark, Harcourt Brace Jovanovich, 1983).

Letters Vladimir Nabokov, *Selected Letters 1940–1977*, ed. Dmitri Nabokov and Matthew J. Bruccoli (London: Weidenfeld and Nicolson, 1990).

LL Vladimir Nabokov, *Lectures on Literature*, ed. Fredson Bowers (San Diego, CA: Bruccoli Clark, Harcourt Brace Jovanovich, 1980).

Lolita Vladimir Nabokov, *Lolita*, in *Novels 1955–1962* (New York: Library of America, 1996).

Lolita Screen Vladimir Nabokov, *Lolita: A Screenplay*, in *Novels 1955–1962* (New York: Library of America, 1996).

LRL Vladimir Nabokov, *Lectures on Russian Literature*, ed. Fredson Bowers (San Diego, CA: Bruccoli Clark, Harcourt Brace Jovanovich, 1981).

LTV Vladimir Nabokov, *Letters to Véra*, ed. tr. Olga Voronina and Brian Boyd (London: Penguin, 2014).

Mary Vladimir Nabokov, *Mary*, tr. Michael Glenny in collaboration with the author (London: Penguin, 2009).

NG Vladimir Nabokov, *Nikolai Gogol*, corrected edition (New York: New Directions, 1961).

NWL *Dear Bunny, Dear Volodya: The Nabokov-Wilson Letters, 1940–1971*, ed. Simon Karlinsky, revised edition (Berkeley: University of California Press, 2001).

PF Vladimir Nabokov, *Pale Fire*, in *Novels 1955–1962* (New York: Library of America, 1996).

Pnin Vladimir Nabokov, *Pnin*, in *Novels 1955–1962* (New York: Library of America, 1996).

Poems Vladimir Nabokov, *Collected Poems*, tr. Dmitri Nabokov, ed. Thomas Karshan (London: Penguin, 2013).

PP Vladimir Nabokov, *Poems and Problems* (New York: McGraw Hill, 1969).

RLSK Vladimir Nabokov, *The Real Life of Sebastian Knight*, in *Novels and Memoirs 1941–1951* (New York: Library of America, 1996).

SM Vladimir Nabokov, *Speak, Memory: An Autobiography Revisited*, in *Novels and Memoirs 1941–1951* (New York: Library of America, 1996).

SO   Vladimir Nabokov, *Strong Opinions* (New York: Vintage, 1990).

Sobr. soch.   Vladimir Nabokov, *Sobranie sochinenii russkogo perioda v piati tomakh*, 5 vols. (St Petersburg: Simpozium, 1999–2000).

Stikhi   Vladimir Nabokov, *Stikhi* (Ann Arbor: Ardis, 1979).

Stikho   Vladimir Nabokov, *Stikhotvoreniia*, ed. M. E. Malikova (St Petersburg: Akademicheskii proekt, 2002).

Stories   Vladimir Nabokov, *The Collected Stories* (London: Penguin, 1997).

TOOL   Vladimir Nabokov, *The Original of Laura (Dying is Fun)*, ed. Dmitri Nabokov (London: Penguin, 2009).

VN Berg   Vladimir Nabokov Papers, New York Public Library, Henry W. and Albert A. Berg Collection of English and American Literature, Astor, Lenox and Tilden Foundations.

VV   *Verses and Versions: Three Centuries of Russian Poetry*, tr. Vladimir Nabokov, ed. Brian Boyd and Stanislav Shvabrin (Orlando: Harcourt, 2008).

Contextualising Nabokov

David M. Bethea and Siggy Frank

> To reflect an epoch is not poetry's task, but only that poet is alive who
> breathes the air of his century, hears the music of his time. That music
> may not accord with the poet's ideas about harmony, it may even be
> repugnant to him, but his ear must be filled with that music, as one's
> lungs are filled with air. Such is the law of poetic biology.
>
> (Khodasevich, *Derzhavin*)

> I composed the Russian original exactly a quarter of a century ago in Berlin,
> some fifteen years after escaping from the Bolshevist régime, and just before
> the Nazi régime reached its full volume of welcome. The question whether
> or not my seeing both in terms of one dull beastly farce had any effect on this
> book should concern the good reader as little as it does me (*IB*, vii).

> I had been living in Berlin since 1922, thus synchronously with the young
> man of the book; but neither this fact, nor my sharing some of his interests,
> such as literature and lepidoptera, should make one say 'aha' and identify
> the designer with the design. I am not, and never was, Fyodor Godunov-
> Chernyntsev; my father is not the explorer of Central Asia that I may
> become some day; I never wooed Zina Mertz, and never worried about
> the poet Koncheyev or any other writer (*Gift*, 8).

> I do not believe that 'history' exists apart from the historian. If I try to select
> a keeper of record, I think it safer (for my comfort, at least) to choose my
> own self (*SO*, 138).

Readers can take their pick of quotations from Nabokov's forewords,
framing statements and other obiter dicta, but the result converges on
the same: 'history' is nothing more than a 'dull beastly farce', even when
one's and one's family's fate is at stake; the author '[is] not, and never was'
his most autobiographical hero, and the 'keeper of record' who identifies
the connecting strands between what happens in the world outside and the
text inside is none other than 'my own self', Vladimir Vladimirovich
Nabokov. The goal of the present volume, which we feel is an appropriate

one for maturing Nabokov studies, is to challenge such comments, but not necessarily with the typical 'hermeneutics of suspicion'. It is not our purpose as scholar-critics to assume we see things and uncover conveniently repressed moments (shades of the 'Viennese delegation' [*Defense*, ix]) that the author has swept under his psychological rug. In the present intellectual climate, we as readers are no longer – as Nabokov archly called his characters – simply 'galley slaves', nor are we 'mini-me' little Nabokovs participating in his textual games, as entertaining as the latter are. We – the historical Nabokov, his texts, and his readers – are moving to someplace else. So, let it be said from the outset: Nabokov was a genius; it is the 'solitary' part that we would like to interrogate. His play, while unique and mesmerisingly so, is not a 'violin in a void' (*IB*, ix).

At the same time, 'context' is a term and a concept suffering from overuse, at least from the perspective of some English faculties (if not Slavic faculties, which historically have been more conservative and slower to adapt). 'Context' is also the staple of 'historicist' studies, which by now are no longer 'new'. As Rita Felski expresses her critical motivation in 'Context Stinks',

> Against the grain of such critical historicism, I want to articulate and defend two related propositions: 1) that history is not a box – that conventional models of historicizing and contextualizing are notably deficient in accounting for the transtemporal movement and affective resonance of texts – and 2) that in doing better justice to this transtemporal impact, we might usefully think of texts as 'non-human actors' – a claim that, as we'll see, requires us to revise prevailing views about the heroic, self-propelling, or oppositional nature of agency and to ponder the links between agency and attachment.[1]

Our starting point is the acknowledgement that there are not enough contexts to cover the phenomenon of 'Vladimir Nabokov' sufficiently and that in our selection of connecting strands ('Nabokov and _____') some not insignificant topics have been left out. There are no separate chapters, for example, on chess or crossword puzzles, the author as poet or the author as dramatist. And while there are also no individual chapters on such defining themes as 'memory', 'translation', 'modernism' and 'language', which shaped Nabokov's art throughout his life, they are covered from multiple perspectives under different headings. We agree with Felski that 'contextualizing' Nabokov can short-change the 'transtemporal movement and affective resonance' of his texts, which is to say there are qualities in his writing, quiddities of his personal aura, that cannot be captured in

[1] Rita Felski, 'Context Stinks', *New Literary History*, 42 (2011), 574.

the 'Nabokov and _____' format. By the same token, however, as we as a democratising (and in worst case scenarios, 'levelling') literary culture move beyond notions of the romantic poet, it would behove us to develop strategies that account for texts as 'non-human actors'[2] and that require us 'to revise prevailing views about the heroic, self-propelling, or oppositional nature of agency and to ponder the links between agency and attachment'. The proverbial elephant in the room in any analysis of Vladimir Nabokov the writer is the sense of overwhelming agency, of Argus-eyed intentionality. Not for nothing did Nabokov prepare his answers to interview questions beforehand and would not be caught dead going to any real-life version of the Cremona Women's Club with the wrong lecture in tow. Our task is to interrogate the edges of this consciousness in a manner that, while still recognising the astonishing achievement, sees the traces that live on after the man's passing as part of a bigger picture.

Thus, our aim in the present volume is to mount a good-faith, but admittedly less-than-perfect, effort to anchor Nabokov more firmly in the social, historical, ideological and cultural contexts of his time. Our section headings – Identity, Places, Literatures and Arts, Ideas and Cultures – are best understood as ideational 'vectors', forces pressing in from the world in which Nabokov lived and thought that elicited the remarkable work he produced. But once again, it should be stressed that this relationship is not 'causal' in any direct sense. Explaining, say, Nabokov as a product of class – i.e. he was fortunate to be born into the privileged circumstances he was and *therefore* in some sense he was able to produce what he did – is a non-starter:

> There is also keen pleasure (and, after all, what else should the pursuit of science produce?) in meeting the riddle of the initial blossoming of man's mind by postulating a voluptuous pause in the growth of the rest of nature, a lolling and loafing which allowed first of all the formation of *Homo poeticus* – without which *sapiens* could not have been evolved. 'Struggle for life' indeed! The curse of battle and toil leads man back to the boar, to the grunting beast's crazy obsession with the search for food. You and I have frequently remarked upon the maniacal glint in the housewife's scheming eye as it roves over food in a grocery or about the morgue of a butcher's shop. Toilers of the world, disband! Old books are wrong. The world was made on a Sunday. (*SM*, 617)

---

[2] 'Nonhuman actors, then, help to modify states of affairs; they are participants in chains of events; they help shape outcomes and influence actions. To acknowledge the input of such actors is to circumvent, as far as possible, polarities of subject and object, nature and culture, word and world, to place people, animals, texts and things on the same ontological footing and to acknowledge their interdependence' (ibid., 583).

For Nabokov, work *is* life. However, this work is also play, lolling about in order to create, making a day of rest a day of intense and joyful cerebration. By the same token, this worker bee-cum-queen bee existed *in the world*, which means his professed 'lolling' was never completely free of its 'situatedness'; it had to cost something, which is also our subject.

In order to grasp this larger force field of 'Vladimir Nabokov', then, we need to understand that the relationship between life and work, or to put it crudely, the world of contexts and the world of texts, was constantly being mediated by a myriad of factors. Moreover, if the texts that Nabokov produced are indeed load-bearing and life-bearing into the future (in Felski's formulation, their 'transtemporal' qualities), then we also should consider them as 'non-human actors' in their own right. To invoke two of the thinkers who have made such a difference in late twentieth and early twenty-first century Russian studies, Mikhail Bakhtin and Yuri Lotman, the relationship between Nabokov and his surroundings is on the one hand deeply *dialogic*, which is to say, it is constantly moving in both directions, with the subject reacting to and creating from what comes his way, just as it is *semiospheric* on the other – Nabokov receives but he also shapes and defines the signs that surround him like the ambient air. The tension between text and context, agency and 'big picture', will always be there.

Each section of our volume seeks to cover the times, places and themes or issues that constitute a significant portion of the 'contextualised Nabokov'. Thus, our first section, 'Identity', focuses on aspects of biography and self-invention ('Authorial Persona') that provide a useful starting point for any understanding of this complicated man and his works. Brian Boyd initiates our path into 'identity' with a tightly woven recap of the author's 'Russian' and 'American' incarnations. Barbara Wyllie follows by demonstrating the astonishing 'paying-it-forward' patrimony of the childhood years, the 'hoarded memories' that became the mature writer's hallmark and that were preserved like butterflies under glass, while Lara Delage-Toriel brings to light Nabokov's interaction with and dependence on women, especially his wife, Véra, and the way his art remained 'masculine' even as it became increasingly absorbed with 'feminine' subjectivity and with the notion of creativity as 'androgynous'. Nabokov's capacity for friendship as well as his boxer's love of a good scrap, including his famous falling-out with Edmund 'Bunny' Wilson, is the subject of Julian Connolly's chapter. 'Professor Nabokov' and his engagement with American academia on a professional and creative level (the new subgenre of the 'campus novel') are then analysed in Susan Elizabeth Sweeney's chapter on 'Academia'. The 'Identity' section is rounded off with Maria Malikova's revisionist exploration of Nabokov's 'phantom authorial persona' of the late 1930s (as the author was considering an expansion of *The Gift* before he decided to emigrate to a different language and country) and his complex relationship with his first biographer, Andrew Field.

'Places' offers a temporal and spatial framework for Nabokov's career arc. Gennady Barabtarlo explains to the modern reader how Nabokov fits into the cultural history of his hometown; while clearly his studied elegance and reserve belong to the city's long-standing tradition, it was the suburban environs, particularly the rich opportunities for summertime butterfly-hunting on the family estate of Vyra, that tugged more at his imaginative heart-strings. Beci Carver, Stanislav Shvabrin and John Burt Foster, Jr. bring to life the three European cities that most defined, and stimulated, the writer Nabokov became between the wars. In Carver's chapter, we get a fine-grained glimpse of Nabokov, now the 'Trinity man', now the 'lab rat', now the budding poet, at Cambridge. Berlin, the 'the city of misfortunes and mishaps', is then treated by Shvabrin as the stereoscopic locale that allowed Nabokov to transit between different planes of being, to embrace his Russophone roots against the background noise of the Third Reich's march to power and to turn exile and displacement into some of his greatest art. And, as Foster writes, Paris was important for Nabokov as the émigré home of admired senior figures of the Russian diaspora (Khodasevich, Fondaminsky) and as the 'literary marketplace' he experimented with, now as a potential Francophone writer, before deciding to cast his lot with the English language and the New World. In 'East to West Coast', Monica Manolescu records the America Nabokov endeavours to invent in his writings, *Lolita* above all, and the America he loved to traverse and study with Véra at the wheel. And the 'dialogue between nature and culture' that drew Vladimir and Véra to the shores of Lake Geneva and their last home at the Montreux Palace Hotel is the subject of Annick Morard's 'Switzerland', the concluding chapter of 'Places'.

The 'Literatures and Arts' section interrogates the different terminologies – canon, publishing, genre, censorship, media/mode – by which Nabokov has been traditionally approached. Alexander Dolinin and Michael Wood initiate this section with an exploration of the meaning of 'canonical' when applied to the author's understanding of which figures and *what sort of writing* deserve to shape a tradition. Dolinin contextualises the 'un-Russianness' of Nabokov as misperceived by émigré critics (what they didn't like in Nabokov, his eschewal of moralising, was exactly what earlier critics had disapproved of in Pushkin and Chekhov – not bad company!) and his ability as time went on to 'shape his own pedigree' by 'selecting relatives and guarding against intruders'. Wood takes a different tack when analysing Nabokov's idiosyncratic use of the canonical as applied to the Western tradition: it wasn't the writer per se who defined what was 'in' or 'out', though Shakespeare, Pushkin, Flaubert, Tolstoy, Chekhov, Proust and Joyce would certainly be 'in', nor was it the writer's fully realised example of a genre, say *Anna Karenina* or *Madame Bovary*; rather it was the intense moment, the segment of the writing, that stood out and came alive against its background, perhaps like the specimen of the butterfly that was so colourfully arresting when viewed in its environment, so that 'canonical' becomes that aspect of the author's style, his specific personhood, that remains alive after he departs the scene. The next two pieces in this section address the publishing culture that prevailed first during Nabokov's émigré years in Berlin and Paris and then during his rise to fame as the author of *Lolita* in the United States: in the first, Siggy Frank reconstructs the publishing climate – the newspapers, journals, editorial practices, ideological and aesthetic alliances and material conditions – that defined everyday reality for someone of Nabokov's growing fame; in the second, Duncan White explains the shift in the American book publishing market in the direction of the 'blockbuster' that Nabokov encountered in the years following the Second World War and how the prestige of the properly promoted 'high brow' classic and book club monthly allowed the author of *Lolita* to maximise the work's cultural capital, eventually turning it into the financial capital that freed him from his teaching responsibilities. The last four chapters in 'Literatures and Arts' examine different compositional 'seams' that highlight Nabokov's mercurial positioning vis-à-vis his reading publics. Michal Oklot and Matthew Walker read Nabokov's sharply negative statements about detective fiction not as a rejection of the genre, which the author certainly turned to often in his own work (e.g. *Despair*), but of the poorly executed 'mystery' of style. Ironically, as Ann Komaromi details, it was the physical copies of his works (those published abroad and smuggled in – *tamizdat* – and those created illegally within the Soviet Union – *samizdat*) that travelled to the homeland that had expelled him and that led to his rediscovery by his most literate and appreciative readership. In 'Nabokov's Visual Imagination', Marijeta Bozovic probes the idea that the author thought 'in images', played constantly at 'painted borders' in his poems and novels, and as time went on learned how to 'mimic rival media', especially of the visual sort. And Nassim Balestrini engages the broad topic of Nabokov and popular culture: not only is *Lolita* the work most drenched in the everyday America of the 1950s, it also, after Nabokov, has taken on a life of its own in pop songs, urban parlance, video and screenplays.

Our final section, 'Ideas and Cultures', places Nabokov into the intellectual crosscurrents of his, and our, times. Several of the topics, including 'Psychoanalysis' and 'Totalitarianism', were personal *bêtes noires*, a fact which makes our readings as interesting as they are, contextually speaking, necessary. In 'Science', Stephen Blackwell tells us how art and science are deeply related in the writer's mind and how certain core concepts, such as mimicry, systematics and relativity theory, were understood – and contested – by Nabokov in his own highly idiosyncratic and aestheticised way. Following in Blackwell's footsteps David Bethea looks at Nabokov's 'Darwinism' by resituating it as a post-Symbolist reaction to the excesses of nineteenth-century positivism, empiricism and materialism. In their second chapter for the volume, 'Psychoanalysis', Oklot and Walker do a double turn worthy of their subject: rather than have Freud frame Nabokov's artistry as a function of neuroses, or have Nabokov frame Freud's myth-making as a function of perverse or 'creepy' psychology, wouldn't it be more productive to remove them both from the 'intention wars' and examine their writing instead as 'a symptom of something else: literature'? Sergei Davydov, who was one of the first to study the metaphysical and metafictional implications of 'otherworldliness' (*potustoronnost*) in Nabokov, presents the case for what 'faith' could mean to the writer. Despite being married to a Russian-Jewish woman while living in Nazi Berlin and having a number of good friends of Russian-Jewish extraction, Nabokov had a difficult time creating authentic Jewish characters in his own fiction, which is the subject of Leonid Livak's chapter.

The next four chapters in 'Ideas and Cultures' provide historical frameworks for approaching a more robust, dimensionalised Nabokov. Dana Dragunoiu fills in the back-history of V. D. Nabokov's neo-idealist, liberal, law-centred values at the turn of the century that powerfully influenced his son's sense of decency, fair play and defence of the underdog and the bullied (think of little Luzhin or slight, child-like Cincinnatus). Olga Voronina negotiates the thin line in Nabokov's writing between denying any connection to politics and ideology and building into his artistic works ingenious stylistic loop-holes – loop-holes the author himself would protest are neither 'satiric' nor 'didactic' – that function to subvert totalitarian thinking. With a deft handling of historical context Will Norman traces Nabokov's record as 'Cold Warrior', demonstrating how he went through different phases and how those phases became interwoven in his novels and their reception. In an intriguing turn of events, Nabokov's long-held disdain for Stalinist Russia placed him at odds with the American literary scene (left-leaning to begin with) in the 1940s, while Stalin was an ally in the war against Hitler, but then this same position actually worked in his favour in the post-war, anti-communist climate of the 1950s, when his long-held opposition to the Soviet Union fell on receptive ears just as *Lolita* was creating a *succès de scandale*. In 'The Long 1950s', Andrea Carosso extends Norman's discussion of politics into the highly charged area of sexual perversion, with *Lolita* again as the focus. Our last section of contextualising frames is itself framed by Rachel Trousdale's chapter 'Transnationalism': when Nabokov fuses Russian and American topographic details into a *frisson* of time-place or Russian and American words in multilingual puns, he is after something – not so much the 'commonality between unfamiliar cultures' as 'the potential for new discoveries in the conjunction of old and new worlds'.

Context does not, cannot, ever solve completely the mystery of 'Vladimir Nabokov'. But it can, when laid out carefully, help us get closer to the 'transtemporal movement and affective resonance' of his texts – those 'nonhuman actors' that continue to speak to us as though they are alive.

PART I

Identity

CHAPTER I

Nabokov's Life in Context I
Russia and Emigration
Brian Boyd

Among Vladimir Nabokov's strong opinions, none was stronger than his belief in self-determining individuality: 'there is in every child the essentially human urge to reshape the earth, to act upon a friable environment (unless he is a born Marxist or a corpse and meekly waits for the environment to fashion *him*)' (*SM*, 621). He valued individuals the more they outstripped their contexts. He did not deny that contexts could matter, but he stressed that the individual or the detail could exceed any generalisation, including those that contexts supplied. He did not choose the circumstances of his birth, but he soon began choosing his particular niches, and ended his life very largely shaping them.

Russia

Until the Bolshevik coup of 1917, Nabokov's main context was growing up in a wealthy, aristocratic, cultured, cosmopolitan, liberal, Anglophile household, where he was the oldest and favoured son. Not for him the artist as product of a tortured childhood: he adored his sensitive, imaginative mother and his self-assured, level-headed, driven, usually imperturbable father, who had a lively sense of humour but an icy anger that served as a moral guide to his high-spirited son. The outer context of Russia's political volatility impacted on Nabokov senior, who was imprisoned by both the tsarist and the Bolshevik authorities for his active opposition to both, but it did not impinge much on Vladimir until his father ordered him and his brother to flee Petrograd in November 1917.

Vladimir Vladimirovich Nabokov was born in 1899 in St Petersburg, then Russia's capital.[1] His father, Vladimir Dmitrievich Nabokov, was a liberal jurist and criminologist, teaching at the Imperial School of

---

[1] Biographical details come from Brian Boyd, *Vladimir Nabokov: The Russian Years* (Princeton: Princeton University Press, 1990) (supplemented and corrected in some cases by Brian Boyd, *Vladimir Nabokov:*

Jurisprudence, and already heralding in his law work his imminent roles as an oppositional politician and journalist. His mother, Elena, came from a millionaire family of mine-owners. Vladimir was born into rank, fortune and culture in a highly unequal society where the inequality was normalised ('about fifty servants and no questions asked' [SM, 392]) but where many saw the need for major social change.

Russia was a country unusually torn between old ways and new, rich and poor, Europe and Asia. It remained an autocracy, despite sporadic attempts at liberalisation. Under the reformist Tsar Alexander II the serfs were liberated in 1861; limited local government was set up in zemstvo councils and trial by jury instituted in 1864; and public executions were abolished, the last of these a measure introduced by Nabokov's grandfather, Dmitri Nikolaevich Nabokov, Minister of Justice under Alexander II and, after the Tsar's assassination, under his reactionary son Alexander III. The latter decades of the nineteenth century saw the emergence of both liberal and socialist movements, although with limited scope for public action.

In the political turmoil precipitated by the country's dismal performance in the Russo-Japanese War of 1904–1905, V. D. Nabokov became a leader in the movement pressing for the establishment of a constitution and a legislative assembly, and a founder of the Constitutional Democratic (CD) Party, which would become the largest party in the First Duma of 1906. That year he also discovered that his sons could read and write in English but not in Russian. He promptly had them learn from the village schoolmaster. That year, too, a French governess arrived for the boys. By the end of 1906, Vladimir would have the three languages in which he would write, and his first exposure to French literature.

In 1906 he also discovered butterfly-hunting, a passion supported by both parents, and by 1907 had begun to master the relevant science and longed to discover a new species. In this year, too, he and his brother Sergei were assigned the first of their Russian tutors, a series 'that seemed chosen to display all the variety of the Russian Empire: Orthodox, Jew, Roman Catholic, Protestant; Great Russian, Ukrainian, Lett, Pole'.[2] His father, very much a multilingual cosmopolitan, was also a Russian nationalist, but until 1917 Vladimir's own direct knowledge of Russia was confined to St Petersburg and its countryside.

Russkie gody [St Petersburg: Simpozium, 2001]); Brian Boyd, *Vladimir Nabokov: The American Years* (Princeton: Princeton University Press, 1991); *SM* and *LTV*.
[2] Boyd, *Russian Years*, 75.

In 1908 V. D. Nabokov was imprisoned for three months for signing the Vyborg Manifesto, which urged civil disobedience in the wake of Nicholas II's premature dissolution of the Duma. His capacity for work and his thirst for culture would be examples for his son, as would his courage and his high sense of honour. V. D. Nabokov's strong sense of cultural meliorism – that individuals and societies could better themselves by resolute effort – pervaded his politics. Nabokov took on his father's principles, reframing his own sense of cultural meliorism in terms of advancing art to ever-richer standards. His father, too, fostered the arts.

Russia, often a developmental laggard, had had deliberate bursts of cultural catch-up under Tsars Peter I and Catherine II but flourished robustly in literature from Pushkin on. By the late nineteenth century, Russia had tapped into Symbolism, with its strong reaction to positivism and determinism, and its stress on the imagination and invisible realms within, around and beyond. In Russian poetry, Symbolism began with Briusov and Balmont, but it was Blok, in the early twentieth century, who especially took Russian readers, and young Nabokov in particular, by storm.

In 1911, at the age of twelve, Nabokov began to attend school for the first time: the private, liberal Tenishev School, for a Russian school unusually 'democratic and non-discriminatory in terms of rank, race, and creed'.[3] Nabokov portrays himself at school as something of a loner and a snob, but although he remained his own person, challenged received opinion, and resented attempts to instil a sense of group responsibility and social consciousness, the evidence of the only Tenishev school report to discuss his character, by a teacher not reluctant to criticise pupils, shows he was in fact popular with classmates from the top to the bottom of the class, and was singled out for his unusually high moral standards as well as his achievements: a '[zealous] football-player, excellent worker, respected as comrade by both flanks (Rosov-Popov), always modest, serious and restrained (though not averse to a joke)'; 'Nabokov creates a most agreeable impression by his moral decency'.[4] His skills as a goalkeeper and in boxing, in which he had lessons at home, no doubt contributed to his popularity.

In 1914 Russia entered World War I on the Allied side. V. D. Nabokov, an ensign in the reserves, was called up, and Elena Nabokov, like other society ladies, set up a hospital for wounded soldiers. Young Vladimir continued as before. From an early age, he had been inclined to fall in love, but in the summer of 1915 began his first real love affair, with Valentina Shulgina, the

[3] Boyd, *Russian Years*, 86.
[4] Quoted in Boyd, *Russkie gody*, 130.

daughter of local vacationers. In 1916 he inherited the estate of his uncle, Vasily Rukavishnikov, and published his first book of poems, conventional love poems for Valentina, published at his own expense, and his first poem in a national magazine. By the end of the year he embarked on an affair with the married older sister of his cousin and best friend, Baron Yuri Rausch von Traubenberg – soon only one more in a seven-year-long series of serious or casual amours.

As 1917 began, Russian military setbacks and food shortages aggravated other discontents and led to mass street protests. Refusing to shoot pro-testers, soldiers mutinied, in effect launching the February Revolution. V. D. Nabokov helped draft the abdication manifesto of the last Romanov tsar. He also became Chancellor of the First Provisional Government, largely composed of CDs, but could do little within that role. Vladimir, in what would be his last year at school, resisted pressure from teachers and classmates to join in political declarations and demonstrations. Moderate socialists and Bolsheviks gained strength, and the Bolshevik coup on the night of 24–25 October / 6–7 November 1917 met little resistance. Vladimir Nabokov kept on writing poetry as he heard machine-gun fire in the street. Fearful that his oldest sons might be conscripted into the new 'Red' army, V. D. Nabokov, still struggling to further the work of the Constituent Assembly, sent Vladimir and Sergei to the Crimea on 2/15 November.

Crimea

Nabokov's main context in the Crimea was his family's precarious distance from conflicting forces. This allowed him space to write verse, study and read according to his own bent, hunt butterflies in an entirely new region, nurture a Pushkinian sense of nostalgia and pursue women.

Vladimir and Sergei took refuge in Gaspra, on the estate of V. D. Nabokov's CD colleague Countess Panin. Their mother and siblings joined them a few days later, with a few jewels hidden in talcum powder the only residue of their wealth. V. D. Nabokov remained in Petrograd, but was imprisoned and released after five days, before fleeing south the next day after reading a decree ordering the arrest of all leading CDs.

In January 1918 Bolshevik forces took nearby Yalta, massacring scores of officers. Three months later, the German army arrived, without needing to fire a single shot, and for young gentry and nobility, including Nabokov, a holiday atmosphere reigned: wine, women and song, sea, sun and moon. He continued to write poetry, composed many chess problems, performed sentry duty when tensions were high and hunted butterflies up the cliffs of

the Yaila and on the Crimean plain. He met Vladimir Pohl, who introduced him to mystical literature, which Nabokov read with curiosity in
Gaspra's large library. The poet Maximilian Voloshin introduced him to
the metrical analysis of verse by poet and novelist Andrey Bely, a method
Nabokov zealously and critically applied to his own work and to nineteenth-
century Russian verse. In September 1918, when his siblings had to resume
school, the family moved into a home in the grounds of Livadia, the old
imperial summer palace on Yalta's west flank. With Livadia's large library to
hand, Nabokov set himself a programme of reading equivalent to first-year
university study, took Latin lessons and 'completed my study of Russian
poetry and fiction'.[5]

After German forces withdrew on 2/15 November, V. D. Nabokov
became Minister of Justice in a new Crimean Provisional Government.
Its combination of CDs, Social Revolutionaries and Tatar nationalists led
to constant friction with the White Army. Early in 1919 Vladimir, who the
year before had published a poem denouncing the Yalta massacre, now
wrote a long poem in answer to the support that Blok's famous 'The
Twelve' had recently given to the Bolshevik coup. The Provisional
Government, meanwhile, felt compelled to prosecute White soldiers for
their excesses, further weakening the only army support the regional
government had. On 21 March /3 April, the Red Army broke through
into the Crimea. The Nabokov family joined the evacuation, leaving
Russia for good at Sevastopol on 2/15 April.

Cambridge

At Cambridge, Nabokov's main context was the security of old traditions
within which he could find space for his own pursuits: verse, reading and
preparation for his future as a Russian writer; butterflies; nostalgia; youth-
ful high-jinks; and women.

The Nabokovs settled in London, Vladimir choosing Cambridge over
Oxford for its more scientific bent. He soon dropped zoology for Medieval
and Modern French and Russian, to allow him more time for composing
verse yearning for Russia and for amours with young Englishwomen. His
exposure to medieval Russian would later feed into *Glory* (1931) and his
translation of *The Song of Igor's Campaign* (1960), and his encounter with
medieval French into 'Lance' (1951) and *Lolita* (1955). Nabokov's reading in
English literature was mostly poetry: among recent poets, Rupert Brooke,

---

[5] Quoted in Boyd, *Russian Years*, 150.

Walter de la Mare and A. E. Housman. His Anglophile background, his football and his English girlfriends competed with his preoccupation with his Russian verse, his Russian language (he bought Dahl's dictionary at a Cambridge bookstall and assimilated a page a day) and his Russian friends, who could understand his nostalgia and his politics.

In 1920 V. D. Nabokov took the family to Berlin, which because of its low cost of living had become the centre of the Russian emigration. There he founded and edited a Russian liberal daily, *Rul'* (*The Rudder*), where Vladimir soon began publishing verse under the name of Sirin, to distinguish his byline from his father's. In March 1922, a few months before Vladimir's final Cambridge exams, his father was killed by Russian right-wingers when he came to the aid of their intended assassination target, his CD ally, Pavel Miliukov.

Berlin

In his European émigré years – his Sirin years – Nabokov's main contexts were, first, the freedom of youth, of émigré literature and of Berlin; then, the possibilities seemingly opened by fame; and finally, the menace of Hitler, which led him to seek a way out of Germany and then Europe.

Nabokov insisted on his independence, and on his right not to be dragged into others' battles. That does not mean that in the emigration he always remained on the side-lines; as he would later write, 'Next to the right to create, the right to criticize is the richest gift that liberty of thought and speech can offer.'[6] He engaged in polemic attacks on classic, Soviet, émigré, American and German writers; on literary and cultural fashions, including Freudianism; and on communist and fascist politics and culture.

From Cambridge Nabokov rejoined his family in Berlin in June 1922. In the fluid relations between the new Soviet Union and the emigration during Lenin's New Economic Policy, Russian publishers, many aiming at the Soviet market, abounded in Berlin. In these circumstances, many established Russian writers also circulated in Berlin, including some expelled from the Soviet Union and some who would soon return there. Nabokov kept his own course, but mingled and even collaborated with other young writers of an anti-Bolshevik bent, especially historical novelist Ivan Lukash and poet, future literary critic and literary historian Gleb Struve.

---

[6] *LRL*, frontispiece.

In May 1923, just before heading for a stint as an agricultural labourer in the south of France, he met Véra Evseevna Slonim. The twenty-one-year-old Véra had long followed and collected Sirin's verse. A romance blossomed by post and poems, and was sealed in person on Vladimir's return to Berlin in September, just as the hyperinflation of the German currency began to soar. Véra became his most trusted reader and, very soon, his editor, typist, and amanuensis, happy to serve the brilliant literary career she confidently foresaw for him. She was proudly Jewish (though secular), and Vladimir, partly through his father's causes and contacts, was disposed towards philosemitism.

Although his mother had taken her younger children to Prague, where she was entitled to a pension, Vladimir remained in Berlin, living in cheap boarding houses and earning an income as a tutor of English. In the lively 1920s Berlin of cabarets and film studios, he wrote sketches with Lukash, hoped to write screenplays, and turned increasingly to fiction, first in verse mini-dramas, then the five-act verse play *The Tragedy of Mister Morn* (1997; wr. 1923–24). He had already been recognised as a writer of great promise, in Berlin and beyond, but his rapidly maturing stories of 1924 signalled still more. But that year the centre of the Russian emigration moved from Berlin to Paris, after the rise in the German cost of living when the Mark was revalued. That meant, too, that *Rul'* – whose editor, Iosif Hessen, a friend of Nabokov the father and now of the son, hugely admired and quickly published Sirin's work – became prohibitively expensive for most Russians in Paris. The impact of Nabokov's talent would therefore be subdued until the first serialisation of one of his novels in the Paris-based *Sovremennye zapiski* (*Contemporary Annals*) in 1929.

Nabokov nevertheless chose to remain in Berlin, despite his distaste for German culture. He never mastered enough German to read either fiction or verse in the language, and thought his linguistic isolation would help preserve his Russian. Apart from reading *Rul'*, he kept up with recent Russian literature by borrowing books from lending libraries or reading in snatches at bookstores, generally avoiding Soviet literature except for sudden plunges for the sake of polemic attack or derisive parody. He followed English literary and cultural news in the weekly *Observer*.

Nabokov married Véra in May 1925. During the mid to late 1920s, they belonged to a literary circle organised by Raisa Tatarinov, which included the critic Yuli Aikhenvald, Sirin's first major admirer. In Berlin, Nabokov was the émigré literary star, lionised at readings. His first novel, *Mary* (1926), was widely and well reviewed and soon translated into German. A frequent creative context for Nabokov was his most recent book, whose ground rules he would overturn in his next: in 1928 he published *King,*

Queen, Knave, with its focus on German, rather than émigré, Berlin, its adultery fulfilled rather than averted, its future apparently not open but seemingly predestined.

The sale of the German rights for *King, Queen, Knave* allowed the Nabokovs, who earned little, spent little, supported Elena Nabokov in Prague and saved nothing themselves, to travel in the spring of 1929 to the southwest of France. There Nabokov collected butterflies and caught the idea for *The Defense* (1929–30). The first of his novels to appear in *Sovremennye zapiski*, the thick journal that paid best and published much of the finest in émigré literature, *The Defense* was immediately recognised as a masterwork.

The rise in recognition also made Nabokov a target of attack from Georgii Adamovich, the most influential émigré critic, who argued that a Pushkinian mastery of form was no longer adequate to the complicated modern world, and his ally the poet Georgii Ivanov. Nabokov began to respond to these attacks with thinly veiled literary assaults of his own, especially on Adamovich's venality and his anti-Pushkinian stance. This allied him with Vladislav Khodasevich, in Nabokov's opinion the greatest Russian poet of his time. But his increasing recognition also had much more direct positive benefit. Ilya Fondaminsky, not the only editor of *Sovremennye zapiski* but its most important financial prop and most determined flag-bearer, was ready to accept and publish serially all Nabokov's novels after *The Defense*.

By 1930, Nabokov was recognised as the star writer of the Russian emigration. Through the next decade he would seek to consolidate that position, but Hitler's rise also meant that he would seek even more urgently a safer refuge beyond émigré Europe.

CHAPTER 2

Nabokov's Life in Context II
Beyond the Emigration

Brian Boyd

Like many émigrés, Nabokov hoped through the 1920s for a return to Russia; unlike others, he also hoped to achieve a permanent place in Russia's literary history. He earned that in 1929, when he composed *The Defense* (1929–30). Four years later Hitler came to power. Instead of wanting to return to the Russia he had left forever, Nabokov soon wanted to flee a new tyranny, and to find a new home beyond the continent of his birth and the language in which he had achieved mastery. But relocation would be a long trial.

In 1929 came the Wall Street Crash and, in its wake, the beginnings of the Depression, particularly severe in a Germany weakened by post-war reparations. The Nabokovs were less affected than most: Vladimir's career flourished, with *The Eye* (1930), *Glory* (1931) and *Camera Obscura* (1932–33) appearing in rapid succession, and Véra could still work as a secretary. Indeed, her having a job was a major reason for their remaining in Berlin.

In August 1932, the Nabokovs moved into an apartment with Véra's cousin Anna Feigin. That autumn, after Hitler's appointment as Chancellor became increasingly likely in the wake of his party's election success, Nabokov travelled to Paris for a reading tour and to see if he could set up a new life there for himself and Véra. Despite being feted, and despite networking as much as he could with émigré and French writers and publishers, he could find no foothold. He also began to seek publication in English and to explore a future in the Anglophone world.

Early in 1933, civil liberties shrank after Hitler came to power. Véra lost her job when the Jewish firm she worked for was closed down. Nevertheless, in the seclusion of their Wilmersdorf apartment, Nabokov was writing well, producing a series of major stories and a novel on a scale unprecedented for him, *The Gift* (1937–38). This novel would explore the contexts of both nineteenth-century Russian literature – Pushkin's high art and resolute independence versus the Russian critic Chernyshevsky's view of art as social commitment – and European modernism, challenging Proust's account of memory and lost or wasted time, Joyce's portraits of the artist as a young man and *Ulysses'* Homeric elements of the search of a son for his father.

In May 1934, the Nabokovs' own son, Dmitri, was born. Not long after this, in a rush of inspiration, and partly goaded by the rise of Nazism, even if his prime target was Soviet Russia, Nabokov broke off *The Gift* to write the nightmarish anti-totalitarian novel *Invitation to a Beheading* (1935–36).

Plunging back deep into *The Gift*, Nabokov travelled again to Paris at the end of January 1936. Again, despite extensive networking among influential French publishers and writers, and the enthusiastic acclaim of Russian audiences and fellow authors, he could find no way out of Germany financially secure enough to satisfy Véra. Back in Berlin, he continued to work on *The Gift* and, after the experience of translating *Despair* (1934), to write a short memoir in English, emphasising the Englishness in his own background in the hope this might open doors into Britain or elsewhere. When one of his father's assassins was appointed as second in command to Hitler's director of émigré affairs, Véra insisted her husband leave Germany promptly to set up a future abroad.

On his way to Paris in 1937, his friend Zinaida Shakhovskoy asked Nabokov to speak at a French club in Brussels; he quickly wrote an essay on his French governess, which, added to an essay in French on Pushkin for the centenary celebrations in Paris, and a number of French translations of his stories, led him to hope strongly for an entrée into the French literary world.[1] He also travelled to London in spring – again networking with Russians and with the English literary and publishing worlds – but here too he could obtain no entry.

From February until May 1937 (and from then until August by post) Nabokov was deep in an affair with Irina Guadanini, a Russian émigré poet who he had first met in Paris the previous year. For much of his time in Paris he was racked with severe psoriasis, apparently brought on by guilt. Because of the affair, he saw less of other Russian émigrés than previously, although his networking efforts were in any case focused on French and English literary and academic circles. Although he tried to persuade Véra to

---

[1] Several stories were translated, and apparently accepted by French magazines, but not published (see *LTV*, 298, 353, 353, 361, 369, 372, 382).

settle with him in the south of France, she refused to leave Berlin, insisting that they first needed to take Dmitri to Prague to show him to Nabokov's mother. In late May, Nabokov did travel to Prague via Switzerland and Austria, to avoid entering Germany, rejoined his wife and son, and saw his mother for the last time. The theme of the femme fatale in *The Real Life of Sebastian Knight* (1941) and the theme of Fyodor's disintegration after Zina's death, in the unfinished continuation of *The Gift*,[2] both seem oblique reflections of the affair with Guadanini.

In July, Nabokov moved with his wife and son to France, stopping first in Cannes. There he told Véra of the affair with Guadanini. Thinking it to be over, Véra settled into forbearance, until in early August she learned that he was still writing to Guadanini, and she erupted in anger. At the beginning of September, Guadanini came to see Nabokov in Cannes, despite his telling her not to. He asked her to leave, and broke off the affair. In October, the family moved to Menton, where Nabokov learned that his new translation of *Kamera Obskura* (1932–33), to be called *Laughter in the Dark* (1938), had been accepted for publication in the United States, where some of his novels, in their Russian originals, had been favourably mentioned in the press in recent years. But by 1938, without work permits, the Nabokovs were living in poverty. They moved to Paris late in the year, and there, with the incentive of a prize competition, and with Hitler's eagerness for Czechoslovakia increasing the likelihood of war, Nabokov wrote his first novel in English, *The Real Life of Sebastian Knight*, finished by January 1939.

He kept searching for a way out of France, but none materialised until the novelist Mark Aldanov passed on to him an invitation he had received to teach creative writing at Stanford University. After the declaration of war in September 1939, Nabokov became even more desperate to keep his wife and son out of Hitler's clutches, but he had to work hard to obtain a French exit visa, an American entry visa and charitable funds to cover the Atlantic crossing (these came especially from a Jewish organisation grateful for his father's role as a leading Gentile supporter of Russian Jews before the revolution). He was still not thinking of quitting Russian – he wrote the novella *The Enchanter*[3] and began the novel *Solus Rex* in that language – but he and his family were at last able to quit Europe in May 1940.

---

[2] See '*Dar*. II chast'', ed. Andrey Babikov, *Zvezda* 4 (2015), 157–75.
[3] *The Enchanter* (*Volshebnik*) was written in Russian in 1939, translated into English and published posthumously by Dmitri Nabokov in 1986. The Russian original was published in 1991.

United States

Once Nabokov reached the United States, the contexts in which he lived and worked depended increasingly on himself. His main context in his American years was the scale and wealth of the American academic and publishing worlds. These made it possible for him to use his talents as a writer, reviewer, translator, speaker, teacher, scientist and scholar to support his family, educate his son at top private schools and then Harvard, and to find the freedom to write.

Another major context was his sense of the unawareness among Anglophone audiences of the facts and the fictions of Russia, present and past. This fed into the critique of the 'communazist' regime in *Bend Sinister* (1947); into evocations, explanations, critiques and satiric barbs in his autobiography and *Pnin* (1957); and into his translations of Pushkin, Tyutchev, Fet, Lermontov, Gogol and Khodasevich, and his major translations of and commentaries to Pushkin's *Eugene Onegin* (1964) and medieval epic *The Song of Igor's Campaign* (1960).

When he arrived in America, Nabokov switched from writing in Russian prose almost exclusively to English, but he and his family kept close to and even depended on Russian family and friends. Through his cousin, the composer Nicolas Nabokov, he began to make connections with the American literary and intellectual world, especially Edmund Wilson, the best-known reviewer and critic in the United States, who as editor, briefly, of *The New Republic*, was able to commission Nabokov to compose reviews and translations in 1941. Nabokov's work also earned the admiration of Edmund Weeks, editor of *The Atlantic*; James Laughlin, of New Directions; Katharine White of *The New Yorker*, which (with Wilson's help) offered him a first-reading agreement in 1944; Morris Bishop, professor of Romance Languages at Cornell, who invited Nabokov to a professorship at Cornell in 1948; and in the 1950s, publishers Pascal Covici, of Viking, and Jason Epstein, of Doubleday.

Another couple of contexts Nabokov selected himself by his passion for Lepidoptera, especially after his discovery of apparent new species, above Moulinet in 1938 and on the rim of the Grand Canyon, en route to Stanford, in 1941. His eagerness to understand, name and describe these new catches led to his working in New York's American Museum of Natural History in his first winter in the United States and then at Harvard's Museum of Comparative Zoology from 1941 to 1948, where he became the world's leading expert in the Blues (Lycaenids) of the Americas. This research work was both the fulfilment of a life-long dream and a way of distracting himself from the pain of having to set Russian prose aside as his main literary medium.

Except when he taught creative writing at Stanford in the summer of 1941, Nabokov's addresses in the United States remained almost entirely in the Northeast, in New York City, in Wellesley and Cambridge, and at Cornell. Nabokov followed jobs, but also benefited from the proximity, in New York, of émigré friends and of publishers. But his passion for Lepidoptera was a major factor in his discovering all the contiguous forty-eight States, so essential in his quest to establish himself, in *Lolita* (1955), as an American writer.

Once in America, Nabokov was for the most part little affected by politics. The exception was the Second World War. He had to struggle to help émigré relatives and friends out of Europe. His vocal hostility to the Soviet Union when guest lecturing at Wellesley in March 1941 helped secure him the invitation to an annual appointment there later in the year, since Mildred McAfee, the president of the college, was highly political – she would soon become first director of the WAVES (Women Accepted for Volunteer Emergency Service). But when Hitler invaded Russia in mid-1941 and, within a few months, the United States entered the war and found itself Russia's ally, Nabokov's very anti-Sovietism also counted against McAfee's offering him a permanent position at Wellesley.

Nabokov's easy access to university libraries at Wellesley and Harvard affected the allusive texture of his fiction, especially *Bend Sinister*. His experience at these colleges, and especially Cornell, as well as his many guest lectures elsewhere, fed into the campus novels *Pnin* and *Pale Fire* (1962). At Cornell, his needing to teach a larger class than was possible within Russian literature courses in order to secure promotions led to his taking on a Masterpieces of European Fiction course and teaching – as he had never expected to do – Austen, Dickens, Flaubert, Proust, Kafka and especially Joyce; all but Kafka left a presence in *Ada* (1969).

Nabokov thought politics best when citizens had the freedom to ignore it. In the United States, he could afford to pay national politics little heed. He confined his active interest to his resolute anti-Sovietism – at the height of the Cold War, after Stalin's entrapment of Eastern Europe, briefly a widespread attitude even among intellectuals. But unlike many American intellectuals, Nabokov deplored the McCarthy Era in the early 1950s not because of Senator McCarthy's campaigns, but because the spuriousness of McCarthy's methods discredited what Nabokov thought to be the genuine need to deal with the dangers posed by communist influence – and loyalty to Stalin's directives – within the United States and elsewhere in the West.

He was outraged by the *New Yorker*'s censoring some of his critiques of Soviet repression. *Pnin* continued the anti-Sovietism, but also included, in passing, the first memorable fictional evocation of the Holocaust.

But politics affected his life and his art rather little.[4] More relevant to him was the new context of American literature. Through living in the United States, and partly through his friendship with Wilson, he was exposed belatedly to James, Eliot, Pound and Faulkner, all of whom he disliked heartily. Faulkner, and especially Eliot and James, he would repeatedly critique and parody. (The poem 'Pale Fire' would be a major riposte to Eliot.) He discovered and paid tribute to Melville, among older American writers; in the *New Yorker* he enjoyed John Cheever, J. D. Salinger and John Updike.

Europe

In his final European years, from 1959 to 1977, Nabokov's primary contexts were the freedom offered by the wealth that the American edition of *Lolita* had brought him in 1958, the pressures of international fame and the responsibilities he felt, given that fame, to his own present and past work.

Lolita's launches in France and England in late 1959 took Nabokov to Europe, but he was happy to remain there to be near his favourite sibling, Elena Sikorski, living in Geneva, and his son, about to study opera singing in Milan. He and Véra lingered on the Italian and French Rivieras. Only a sudden solution to the problem of filming *Lolita* – apparently, the flash forward to the killing of Quilty at the start of the film – led him to accept an earlier invitation from James Harris and Stanley Kubrick to adapt his novel for the screen, during six months in Los Angeles in 1960. After seeing the finished film in 1962, he would parody the Hollywood experience – or rather, Harris and Kubrick's subsequent rewriting of his screenplay before filming – in his next novel, *Ada*.

The Nabokovs returned to Europe, where they settled without intending to. Moving from one scenic spot to another, they found the Montreux Palace Hotel in 1961. Nabokov not only enjoyed the hotel's spectacular setting but discovered it a congenial place to write, a useful screen from intrusive, unabashed American fandom and a simplifier of daily routines. Switzerland was in efficient postal contact with US publishers, and allowed

---

[4] Recent studies have placed a stronger emphasis on the political and historical context as a pivotal influence on his art (see, for instance, Dana Dragunoiu, *Vladimir Nabokov and the Poetics of Liberalism* [Evanston, IL: Northwestern University Press, 2011]; Will Norman, *Nabokov, History and the Texture of Time* [New York, London: Routledge, 2012]).

him to remain close to his sister and his son and to remote alpine resorts where in the summer he could catch butterflies and elude even the most persistent of American tourists. Although he had expected to return to the United States to live – he had been a proud American citizen since 1945 – he never had sufficient reason to leave Montreux.

Fame allowed Nabokov the luxury of choosing his own projects, like translating *Lolita* into Russian; supervising the translation of his Russian work into English (first his novels, then his stories and poems) and other languages; revising his *Eugene Onegin* translation – after objections to its ungainly literalism in the prominent controversy surrounding it in 1965–66 – to make it even more literal and ungainly. (The main participants in the controversy were Edmund Wilson and Nabokov in reply, with Robert Lowell among those standing up for Wilson, and Anthony Burgess noting that 'small reviewers like me scuttled out of the crossfire and left it to the giants'.)[5] One project he started in 1965, a book on butterflies in art, took him to many Italian art museums, famous and obscure, an experience that soon fed into the art-saturated *Ada*. His fame, the publication of his *Eugene Onegin* and the ensuing controversy, and his revision of his autobiography, *Speak, Memory* (1967), helped make *Ada* 'the most Russian of his English works . . . [with] greater-than-usual demands on his readers, and especially more *Russian* demands than non-Russian readers would tolerate from someone not already a favorite author'.[6] *Ada* even attempted to make the most of his fame by redefining the most relevant context for literature in English as English, French and *Russian* literatures.[7]

One special consequence of Nabokov's fame presented him, as he saw it, not with an opportunity, but a compulsion. Andrew Field's 1973 draft of his biography of Nabokov, with its attempts to avoid or challenge *Speak, Memory*, became an important context for Nabokov's last completed novel, *Look at The Harlequins!* (1974), which he began to write, as a pointed inversion of *Speak, Memory*, straight after he read and corrected Field's manuscript.

The Nabokovs saw few people in Montreux beyond hotel staff and newsagents. The writer's main contacts were with visiting publishers, editors and translators, with interviewers and film crews, and with academics like Alfred Appel, Jr., Simon Karlinsky and Carl and Ellendea

---

[5] Quoted in Brian Boyd, *Vladimir Nabokov: The American Years* (Princeton: Princeton University Press, 1991), 497. See Alex Beam, *The Feud: Vladimir Nabokov, Edmund Wilson, and the End of a Beautiful Friendship* (New York: Pantheon, 2016).

[6] Brian Boyd, *"Ada" Nabokova: Mesto Soznaniia* (St Petersburg: Simpozium, 2013), 7.

[7] See Marijeta Bozovic, *Nabokov's Canon: From "Onegin" to "Ada"* (Evanston, IL: Northwestern University Press, 2016).

Proffer. Appel worried that, given Nabokov's new work was still published first and had its main audience in the United States, the novelist no longer knew enough about America in the 1960s and 1970s. But Nabokov was always keen to pump American visitors and careful to set little of his new fiction in the modern United States.

Nabokov did keep up with the American, British and French literary news, and found fresh pleasures in Robbe-Grillet, Beckett and, briefly, Borges, but contemporary political and social issues featured only rarely in his work. He took a lively and sympathetic interest in the progress of African American civil rights and a typical anti-communist stance to the war in Vietnam. Long fascinated as a reader (Jules Verne, H. G. Wells) and a writer ('Lance' [1952]) by the romance of space travel, he closely followed the space race (which launched *Ada*'s science-fiction flights of fancy), especially when the United States began winning it, and was thrilled by the Apollo moon-landing.

Of social trends in his late years, the one directly relevant to Nabokov and his work was the increase in sexual freedom. He had benefited from an earlier phase of this change in the four years between completing *Lolita* (when no American press would touch it) and his trying again to release it in America (when several publishers vied hard for the book). He took advantage of the new freedoms of the 1960s in the hectic sexual frankness of *Ada* and, albeit less centrally, in later work. He protested, though, against the sexualisation of the young, and against 'the copulation of clichés' in pornography and in recent film and fiction (*Lolita*, 295). He even parodied the success of *Playboy* – which from 1964 published much of his work, including *Ada*, in its flagship magazine – in the worldwide sexual fantasy of *Ada*'s Villa Venus. *Ada* itself was more critique than celebration of over-sexualisation.

Nabokov had an aged conservative's and individualist's distaste for the conformity of the youth rebellions of the 1960s, and an old male derisive-ness toward new-wave feminism. Through visits to the Soviet Union by his sister Elena (annually from 1972) and the Slavists Karlinsky and the Proffers, he learned of current conditions there, which he evoked in *Look at the Harlequins!* His life-long anti-communism, still evident in his late novels, kept him at odds with the long-running Marxisant stream in intellectual life, more prevalent than ever because of opposition to the Vietnam War and the youth revolt. Living in a landlocked European country, and strongly rooted in Western European traditions and stan-dards, Nabokov paid little attention to post-colonialism in life or literature.

In many ways, the contexts emerging around him in his last years ensured that he seemed more and more unfashionable, though he had always resisted and never sought fashion. But the sheer strength and individuality of his work continued not only to excite more and more readers and scholars but also to influence more and more writers, from John Updike and Andrey Bitov to Edmund White, Martin Amis, Orhan Pamuk, Michael Chabon, Zadie Smith and Aleksandar Hemon. Meanwhile, although his lepidopterological research had been largely forgotten two generations later, scientists of the next generation after his death would rediscover with excitement the depth and fertility of his work.[8] Nabokov would have been happy with only those two enduring contexts for his achievement: literature and Lepidoptera.

---

[8] See Kurt Johnson and Steve Coates, *Nabokov's Blues: The Scientific Odyssey of a Literary Genius* (Boston: Zoland Books, 1999); Roger Vila et al., 'Phylogeny and palaeoecology of Polyommatus blue butterflies show Beringia was a climate-regulated gateway to the New World', *Proceedings of the Royal Society B*, 278/1719 (22 September 2011), 2737–44 [doi:10.1098/rspb.2010.2213]; Brian Boyd, *Stalking Nabokov: Selected Essays* (New York: Columbia University Press, 2011), chapter 8.

CHAPTER 3

Childhood

Barbara Wyllie

'Everything is as it should be, nothing will ever change, nobody will ever die' (*SM*, 422). Thus Nabokov committed to memory the first twenty years of his life, following his mother's instruction to him as a young boy to take notice of the smallest, most precious details of their world: "'*Vot zapomni* [now remember]," she would say' (*SM*, 387). She could not, however, have known just how precious these memories would become, not simply as the elements of a Russia that would be lost to them all in just a matter of years, but as the resilient and irreducible foundations upon which her son would build his future creative universe.

That Nabokov grew up in an environment of immense wealth and privilege has been well documented. Accounts of his Russian childhood in his autobiography and interviews describe an atmosphere of opulence and cosmopolitanism, of summers spent at the family's three neighbouring country estates and winters at their townhouse in central St Petersburg, of pan-European travels to resorts on the French Riviera or the metropolises of Berlin and Paris, with servants on hand day and night to attend to their every need. Maids and footmen helped the Nabokov children wash and dress, nannies and governesses took them to parties or else out tobogganing and ice skating, to street fairs and puppet shows, and tutors were engaged to teach them art, languages, sciences and mathematics until Nabokov and his younger brother Sergei were old enough to start school.

In 1911, their father enrolled them at Tenishev, which was renowned for its egalitarian, liberal ethos and its non-discriminatory policy that took in boys of any class or religion. Nabokov quickly developed a reputation for stubborn non-conformism, which included arriving every morning in a chauffeur-driven Benz. When a teacher suggested, 'in a grimace of disgust', that he might be dropped off around the corner to spare the other boys this parade of extravagance, Nabokov refused: 'It was as if the school were allowing me to carry about a dead rat by the tail with the understanding that I would not dangle it under other people's noses' (*SM*, 518). From such accounts, it would be easy to conclude that the Nabokovs were just another example of the decadence, excess and social disconnectedness that characterised the doomed Russian nobility at the end of the nineteenth century. As Nabokov's cousin, Nicolas, conjectured, 'were we all, the whole upper crust of Russian society, so totally insensitive, so horribly obtuse, as not to feel that the charmed life we were leading was in itself an injustice and hence could not possibly last?'[1] The answer to this question is no, not all. Nabokov's father, Vladimir Dmitrievich, was one of a number of his class, brought up in a tradition of service to the state, who were acutely aware of the severity of the problems Russia and its people were facing, and who strove, by legal and political means, to rectify them. In doing so, he risked his career, his family's security, and at points his own life, but remained steadfast in his belief in the supremacy of democracy and individual liberties, setting an example which his son would uncompromisingly uphold, even when challenged over his use of a chauffeur-driven car.

Nabokov's privileged circumstances also meant that he was uniquely able to engage, fully and often at close hand, in the richness and diversity of late imperial Russian culture. The first two decades of the twentieth century saw extraordinary innovations in literature and the visual arts, driven by the Symbolist and 'World of Art' movements. Amongst the Nabokovs' 'many acquaintances who painted and danced and made music' (*SO*, 171) were the artists Alexandre Benois, Leon Bakst, Konstantin Somov and Mstislav Dobuzhinsky (who became Nabokov's art teacher), the conductor Serge Koussevitzky (who was to secure Nabokov's passage to America in 1939), the opera bass Feodor Chaliapin and various members of the Moscow Art Theatre, all of whom visited the family home on St Petersburg's Bolshaya Morskaya. In the theatre, Stanislavsky's pioneering productions of Chekhov's plays had brought a new kind of psychological realism to the stage,[2] while Diaghilev's Ballets Russes introduced a riot of colour and energy that drew upon the elemental qualities of Russian folklore and the spectacle of the *balagan* (fairground booth) shows. St Petersburg's Crooked Mirror, under the artistic direction of Nikolai Evreinov, staged parodies of contemporary drama and silent film,[3] while avant-garde director Vsevelod Meyerhold's reinventions of the tradition of the Italian *Commedia dell'arte* reflected a contemporary fascination for the

---

[1] Nicolas Nabokov, *Bagázh: Memoirs of a Russian Cosmopolitan* (New York: Atheneum, 1975), 45.
[2] For Nabokov's commentary on the Moscow Art Theatre, see *LRL*, 248; 301–3.
[3] See Laurence Senelick, 'Nikolay Evreinov's Inspector General', *Performing Arts Journal*, 8/1 (1984), 113–18; Brian Boyd, *Vladimir Nabokov: The Russian Years* (Princeton: Princeton University Press, 1990), 103.

masks and harlequinades of seventeenth- and eighteenth-century Europe
evident across a range of diverse forms, from street theatre to ballet, book
illustration to portraiture. The magical, colourful exoticism and grotesque
comedy of these harlequinades captured the young Nabokov's imagination, their echoes palpable throughout his work, from the farcical staging
of *Invitation to a Beheading* (1935–36), to their implied subtextual presence
in *Lolita* (1955) and overt celebration in *Look at the Harlequins!* (1974).[4]

Meanwhile, Russia was looking outwards to Western influences in
philosophy and psychology, science and politics, to which Nabokov's
father was keenly attuned. Nabokov had unrestricted access to his father's
10,000-volume library, where Russian, English, American and European
literature, history and thought sat alongside journals and pamphlets on
politics, economics, ethics, law and criminal psychology. His father introduced him to the work of William James, for example, whose writings were
formative in the development of Nabokov's own investigations into the
inscrutability of time and consciousness, and also 'the possibility, even the
probability, of another, transcendent sphere of being'.[5] James' acknowledgement of the spiritual chimed with a burgeoning interest in mysticism
and the occult in turn-of-the-century Russia which was shared by
Nabokov's mother, Elena Ivanovna, who would often describe episodes
of 'double sight, and little raps in the woodwork of tripod tables, and
premonitions, and the feeling of the *déjà vu*' (*SM*, 386–87). None of this
seemed ridiculous to Nabokov, however, who following a series of childhood fevers claimed to have developed a similar clairvoyance, such that he
was later to confess to 'embarrassing qualms of superstition', or to his being
'affected obsessively by a dream or a coincidence'.[6] This, combined with
his self-diagnosed synaesthesia (which he also inherited from his mother),
made him particularly sensitive to the 'leakings and drafts' that seemed to
penetrate so readily the not-so-solid walls of his mind (*SM*, 382). He would
later describe the nightmares he had as a child, 'full of wanderings and
escapes, and desolate station platforms' (*SO*, 132) long before these nightmares would become a reality. He even believed that James Harris and

---

[4] See Susan Elizabeth Sweeney, 'Looking at Harlequins: Nabokov, the World of Art and the Ballets
Russes', in Jane Grayson, Arnold McMillin and Priscilla Meyer (eds.), *Nabokov's World. Volume 2:
Reading Nabokov* (Basingstoke and New York: Palgrave, 2002), 73–95; Siggy Frank, *Nabokov's
Theatrical Imagination* (Cambridge and New York: Cambridge University Press, 2012), 19–21;
130–34; Barbara Wyllie, *Vladimir Nabokov* (London: Reaktion Books, 2010), 135–38; 180–82.

[5] Joan Delaney Grossman, 'Philosophers, Decadents, and Mystics', in Joan Delaney Grossman and
Ruth Rischin (eds.), *William James in Russian Culture* (Lanham, MD and Oxford: Lexington Books,
2003), 97.

[6] Quoted in Andrew Field, *Nabokov: His Life in Part* (London: Hamish Hamilton, 1977), 87.

Stanley Kubrick, who came to him in 1958 wanting to make a film of *Lolita*, were the reincarnation of his dead Uncle Ruka, who had told Nabokov in a dream that he would return as 'Harry and Kuvyrkin', bringing with him the lost fortune he had bequeathed to his nephew in 1916.[7]

The eclectic interests of Nabokov's parents extended to enthusiastic Anglophilia. Vladimir would often refer to himself as an 'English child' (*SO*, 81), defined by the trappings of Edwardian England, from Pears' Soap, Lyle's Golden Syrup and Huntley & Palmer biscuits to Rudyard Kipling, H. G. Wells and Oscar Wilde. His father would read Dickens to the children at bedtime, while his Uncle Ruka brought them Buster Brown comic-strips from America. Soon afterwards, Nabokov graduated from the tales of King Arthur and the adventures of Florence Kate Upton's Golliwogg[8] to the sleuthing of Sherlock Holmes, the travels of Phileas Fogg and the daring escapades of the heroes of Captain Mayne Reid's Wild West. These Nabokov would act out in the gardens of Vyra, the family's country home, with his cousin Yuri Rausch von Traubenberg, who was to die barely a decade later in a fitting act of gallantry during a lone charge on a Red Army machine-gun nest. Yet it is Nabokov's recollection of the midget, in Upton's *The Golliwogg's Air-Ship* (1902), 'drift[ing] into an abyss of frost and stars – alone' (*SM*, 426), that is, in its depiction of solitude and a mysterious 'elsewhere', most starkly evocative of these stories' formative impact upon his young psyche. Lying beyond the circumscribing parameters of mortal existence, this 'elsewhere' promised perfect isolation, absolute freedom and an escape from the suffocating constraint of time, which was to become an abiding preoccupation for Nabokov. It is the 'elsewhere' that Martin seeks in *Glory* (1931), that Fyodor senses but can't quite grasp in *The Gift* (1937–38) and that Cincinnatus is only able partially to enter until the final scene of *Invitation to a Beheading*.

The library at 47 Bolshaya Morskaya doubled as a sports room, and it was here that Nabokov's father taught him to box and play chess. In 1919, he and his father set about a new game as their boat pulled out of Sevastopol harbour under fire from Bolshevik guns, and the composition of chess problems begun in the Crimea became a useful source of making extra money in émigré Berlin, while the game itself became a dominant motif in his fiction, from *The Defence* (1929–30) to *The Original of Laura* (2009). At Vyra, he played tennis, on carefully mown grass courts, and at school he played football, opting to

[7] Brian Boyd, *Vladimir Nabokov: The American Years* (Princeton: Princeton University Press, 1991), 366.
[8] See Don Barton Johnson, 'Nabokov's Golliwoggs: Lodi Reads English 1899–1909', *Zembla*. URL: www.libraries.psu.edu/nabokov/dbjg01.htm.

keep goal, a position which perfectly conformed to his romanticised vision of himself as 'the lone eagle, the man of mystery, the last defender' (*SM*, 588). He carried these pursuits with him into emigration, to Cambridge where he boxed and to Berlin where he coached tennis and joined an émigré football team. His most ardent pursuit, however, was that of butterflies, which began in the summer of 1906, when a Swallowtail he captured escaped. Looking back, he would often point out that 'had there been no revolution in Russia, I would have devoted myself entirely to lepidopterology and never written any novels at all' (*SO*, 100). It is not difficult to imagine him, in such a scenario, living his dream of 'a long and exciting career as an obscure curator of lepidoptera in a great museum' (*SO*, 47), whilst otherwise blissfully ensconced at Rozhdestveno, the lavish country estate left to him by his uncle. Yet the same chance of his birth that coincided with Russia's Silver Age also shaped and defined him as a writer, affording him twenty years of intensely felt experiences of a life and a place to which he would only be able to return in the imagined worlds of his poems, novels and stories. Although in the early stages of his emigration he was certain that 'sometime in the next decade [they] would all be back in a hospitable, remorseful, racemosa-blossoming Russia' (*KQK*, v), he nevertheless carried with him, just in case, 'the careful reconstruction of [his] artificial but beautifully exact Russian world', a task which he completed during his last term at Cambridge, around Easter time, shortly before his father's assassination at a Berlin meeting hall (*SM*, 590).

The relationship of 'mutual admiration and respect' that the young Nabokov had with his father was 'truly exceptional' in the context of late nineteenth-century upper class family life.[9] Vladimir Dmitrievich took an unusually active role in nurturing his son's every interest, and especially his love of literature, such that by his mid-teens, 'besides hundreds of other books', Nabokov had 'read or re-read all Tolstoy in Russian, all Shakespeare in English, and all Flaubert in French' (*SO*, 46). That he saw himself as 'a perfectly normal trilingual child in a family with a large library' (*SO*, 43) was, therefore, far from a precocious claim. His erudition in literature was matched by his passion for poetry, for Pushkin and Lermontov, Fet and Tyutchev, but also the work of the new Silver Age poets – Blok, Bely and Briusov, Gumilev and Kuzmin. 'If I'd been born four years later, I wouldn't have written all those books', he would contend.[10] Considering the popularity of poetry in Russia in the first decade of

---

[9] Gavriel Shapiro, *The Tender Friendship and the Charm of Perfect Accord: Nabokov and His Father* (Ann Arbor, MI: University of Michigan Press, 2014), 2–3.
[10] Field, *Life in Part*, 105.

the twentieth century, it is certainly true that timing was on his side – 'I am a product of that period. I was bred in that atmosphere' (*NWL*, 246) – and in terms of his aspiration to be a writer, it is no surprise that it was with poetry that he began, composing his first tentative lines at the age of fourteen.

Nabokov's sense of artistic inspiration is deeply bound up with this initial creative act, which for him involved a fusion of place, time, sound and vision. Crucial in this combination was place – the summer house at Vyra, a pavilion with stained-glass windows, the colours of which his mother had encouraged him to appreciate in the changing light of the weather and the seasons – and sound – the interval between raindrops running off a leaf after a storm. From this instance of fusion emerged the realisation that 'while the scientist sees everything that happens in one point of space, the poet feels everything that happens in one point of time', something he would later refer to as 'cosmic synchronisation' (*SM*, 544). Nabokov's levelling out of space and time was not only central to his creative vision, but also key in overcoming the conventional perception of the past as a receding entity. By perceiving time as a series of horizontally stacked layers, rather than a sequence of events that prioritises the most recent and relegates the rest to a dim, unreachable spot in the far distance, the past remains ever present. Nabokov expressed this most explicitly in his 1974 novel, *Transparent Things* (1972), in which its ghostly narrator sustains a precarious balancing act on invisible layers of time that enables him to experience past and present simultaneously, much in the same way that Nabokov related in answer to a question from Alden Whitman from *The New York Times* in 1969:

AW: *Reflecting on your life, what have been its truly significant moments?*
VN: Every moment, practically. Yesterday's letter from a reader in Russia, the capture of an undescribed butterfly last year, learning to ride a bicycle in 1909. (*SO*, 133)

Nabokov hoarded memories, registering every 'significant moment' of his first twenty years in such a way that rendered them immune to the ravages of time. Looking back on that period, he saw himself as one of many Russians of his generation who had 'passed through a period of genius, as if destiny were loyally trying what it could for them by giving them more than their share, in view of the cataclysm that was to remove completely the world they had known' (*SM*, 373). Although conscious of the rarity and abundance of these treasured memories, Nabokov did not store them away in an exclusive, inner universe, nor did he risk their degeneration by scattering them, arbitrarily, across his work. Rather he would utilise them carefully and precisely, either by direct transfer – such as with the painting that hung above his bed at Vyra and the vision of footsteps in the snow that became the emblematic motifs of *Glory* – by transformation – as in Ganin's nostalgic evocation of his love affair with Mary or the putrid idyll that is Van Veen's Ardis – or else, and for the most part, obliquely, by constructing intricate and often barely discernible networks of imagery and allusion. Nabokov implied this process to James Mossman of the BBC in 1969:

> Items of one's past are apt to fade from exposure. They are like those richly pigmented butterflies and moths which the ignorant amateur hangs up in a display case on the wall of his sunny parlor and which, after a few years, are bleached to a pitiful drab hue. . . . a wise collector should keep specimens in the dry dark of a cabinet. (*SO*, 143)

Nabokov never attempted to go back to Russia, even though the hero of *Look at the Harlequins!* does visit, albeit briefly, an imagined version of the Soviet Union. '[A]ll the Russia I need is always with me', he would argue. '[L]iterature, language, and my own Russian childhood' (*SO*, 9–10). Nor did he try to replicate, in exile, the matchless world that remained so vivid in his memory: 'why trouble with hopeless approximations?' (*SO*, 27). But he did revisit Russia, via his art, and most intimately through the poetry in Russian that he continued to write well into his American years. These poems reveal an urgent need to maintain an unbreakable link with the Russia of his childhood, a link that proceeded from the writing itself. Nabokov's 'words' served as a fabulously ephemeral yet vital means of defying all geographical, political, physical and temporal boundaries, preventing him from retrieving this lost world, and granted him the unconditional and infinite access that he would otherwise forever be denied:

> But my word, curved to form an aerial viaduct,
> spans the world, and across in a strobe-effect spin
> of spokes I keep endlessly passing incognito
> into the flame-licked night of my native land.
>
> ('Fame' [1942], *Poems*, 109)

CHAPTER 4

Women

Lara Delage-Toriel

Nabokov famously declared that 'Lolita is famous, not I. I am an obscure, doubly obscure, novelist with an unpronounceable name' (SO, 107). The uncommon extent of the eponymous creature's emancipation from her creator can be measured by the various semantic associations evoked by 'Lolita' and 'nymphet' in many media since the 1960s, which very often clash with Nabokov's own view of Lolita as a poor debauched child and nymphets as 'girl-children, not starlets and "sex kittens"' (SO, 93). If Nabokov's novel has resonated so widely, it is not only because of the sensationalist nature of its theme – a grown man's infatuation with a girl-child – but also because of the author's narrative treatment of this theme, allowing for myriad interpretations and offering an eloquent statement on prevailing – albeit often hushed or ravelled – notions and representations of gender, in a variety of cultural contexts, ranging from America to Iran.[1] Indeed, beneath Lolita's subversive trappings, one may easily grasp the familiar *topoi* of the female imago traditionally viewed by the male artist, part demon and part innocent waif, *femme fatale* and *éternel féminin*, which have haunted literary luminaries from Poe and Baudelaire, Dostoevsky and Pushkin, down to the Arthurian legends and the Roman Elegists. How original, then, was Nabokov's conception of gender roles?

Nabokov's fictional world is often a hostile environment for mothers, few of whom are able to fully accomplish this most essential of female roles, either because they die prematurely or because they prove poor caretakers and sometimes worthless models. *Lolita* (1955) provides a particularly rich example of this, starting with the heroine's death in childbed at the novel's very threshold, then disposing of Humbert's mother in a chilling 'light-ning' parenthesis, before turning the nymphet into an orphan after her supremely vulgar and jealous mother has become an alliterative 'porridge of bone, brains, bronze hair and blood' (*Lolita*, 92). Such figures appear as

---

[1] See for instance Azar Nafisi, *Reading Lolita in Tehran* (New York: Random House, 2003).

negatives of his own mother, Elena, who lived until her son was forty and whom he presents in his memoirs as both extremely caring and responsible for nurturing the numerous facets of his sensitivity at a very early age. He thus remembers her reading spellbinding bedtime stories in English, 'accumulat[ing] a library and a museum' (*SM*, 462) around his bed when he fell severely ill in 1907, dispatching with ether his first moth and dazzling him with items of jewellery, which were to leave a lasting mark not only on his memory but also on his imagination, from which he drew the manifold harlequin and prismatic motifs that shimmer through his works. Besides sharing a passion for taxonomic biology, both mother and son were gifted with *audition colorée*, a form of synaesthesia. Moreover, some of her most deeply rooted attitudes to life seem to have shaped Nabokov's own conceptions, in particular those pertaining to religion and the importance of memory. She cultivated in her son a very subjective sense of transcendence that is echoed in his artistic creed and its belief that literature 'appeals to that secret depth of the human soul where the shadows of other worlds pass like the shadows of nameless and soundless ships' (*NG*, 149). A passionate reader of poetry, she encouraged, transcribed, learnt by heart and collated her son's poetic production for a quarter of a century. The albums she assembled in exile are considered to be 'one of the glories of the Nabokov Archive, and the prime tool for establishing the canon of his early work and the development of his art'.[2]

The dedication of many other women was also instrumental in supporting Nabokov's career: to name but a few, Raisa Tatarinov, whose literary circle, co-founded by Yuli Aikhenvald, provided the still little-known Sirin with his first audience; Zinaida Shakhovskoy, who notably organised readings for him in Brussels; Altagracia de Janelli, his first literary agent in the United States; Doussia Ergaz, his literary agent in Europe who would manage to get *Lolita* published in France after it had been turned down by five American publishers; Katharine White, his editor at *The New Yorker* and one of the few who dared stand up to him, as well as Jacqueline Callier, his secretary. But the woman who outstripped them all and was his staunchest champion in all matters, be they artistic or managerial, was his wife Véra.

In his mock autobiography, *Look at the Harlequins!* (1974), his parodic alter ego, Vadim, declares: 'my wives and my books are interlaced monogrammatically like some sort of watermark or *ex libris* design' (*LATH*, 628). One of the most conspicuous illustrations of Nabokov's uxorial inscription

[2] Brian Boyd, 'The Nabokov Biography and the Nabokov Archive,' *Biblion: The Bulletin of the New York Public Library*, 1 (Fall 1992), 15–36; 18–19.

within his own published work may be found in his dedications to Véra, whose name follows the title page of every single one of his works in English. The image of the monogrammatic interlacing is strengthened by the fact that the spouses' initials were identical, even before their marriage (Véra Slonim and Vladimir Sirin, his pen name). Such continued presence at the thresholds of his books testifies to the crucial role played by this one particular woman in the writer's life, both private and public.[3] Asked whether he could assess the scope of Véra's collaboration in his work, he answered, with eloquent laconism: 'no, I could not'.[4] A brief résumé by Nabokov's biographer furnishes the missing details: 'in her dedication to literature and to Vladimir Nabokov [note the correlation] she would be his wife, muse, and ideal reader; his secretary, typist, editor, proof-reader, translator, and bibliographer; his agent, business manager, legal counsel, and chauffeur; his research assistant, teaching assistant, and professorial understudy'.[5] During the fourteen years by which Véra outlived her husband, she was untiring in her dedication to guarding his literary legacy, be it in negotiations with publishers or in supporting scholars, for whom she proved 'a kind of walking key to the works'.[6]

Several of Nabokov's works sketch the contours of the couple's partnership. *The Gift* (1937–38), for instance, is the first of his novels in which the beloved's role is watermarked as muse as well as prime reader and interlocutor. Alongside the protagonist, narrator and writer Fyodor, another distinct presence, addressed as 'you', appears in the third chapter. This somewhat cryptic initial reference to Zina Mertz, Fyodor's beloved, points to her significance within the composition process of the novel Fyodor is writing – and which the reader is supposedly holding in his hands. Nabokov would resort to the same form of direct address in the last chapter of *Speak, Memory* – as an oblique address to Véra – and in the final pages of *Look at the Harlequins!*, a device which allowed him to hint at the permanent presence of the beloved at the writer's side without ripping the veil of connubial intimacy.

---

[3] It must, however, be noted that Véra was not Nabokov's only sweetheart: he was a notorious womaniser, conducting 'several affairs simultaneously' (*SM*, 589) when studying at Cambridge, even boasting to Véra of twenty-eight conquests before his engagement to Svetlana Siewert (see Stacey Schiff, *Véra (Mrs. Nabokov)* [New York: Random House, 1999], 36), which was broken four months before he met Véra. Their marriage itself was not without its dents, most notably owing to his affair with Irina Guadanini in 1937.

[4] Interview with James Mossman for *Review* on BBC2, published in *The Listener*, 23 October 1969. The version included in *Strong Opinions* (1973).

[5] Brian Boyd, *Vladimir Nabokov: The Russian Years* (Princeton: Princeton University Press, 1990), 215.

[6] Schiff, *Véra*, 367.

The imagery characterising Zina's relationship to Fyodor epitomises the ideal Nabokovian companion: 'cleverly and elegantly made to measure for him by a very painstaking fate' (*Gift*, 175), she is the glove that fits the guiding hand. The artist is, as the French would have it, her *patron*, in terms of both her 'boss' and the pattern upon which she is modelled. Rather than a 'creative partner' in Fyodor's poetic enterprise or a co-creator who 'processe[s], mold[s], and shape[s]'[7] the novel, *she* is the one who is moulded and shaped in order to tally with the male artist's ready-made tropes. Although Zina is intensely involved in her lover's poetic activity and is endowed with a sharp intellect, she remains on the margins of creation, echoing rather than uttering the poet's tune. Thus, '[gifted] with a most flexible memory, which twined like ivy around what she perceived, Zina by repeating such word-combinations as she particularly liked ennobled them with her own secret convolution' (*Gift*, 202). The image of the ivy conveys the slightly parasitic and ornamental nature of Zina's relation to Fyodor's craft, qualities calling to mind those of Véra, who was endowed with an 'inordinately well-developed memory', which she applied to remembering 'virtually every verse line Nabokov would write'.[8] Astute intellectual sparring partners, both Véra and Zina are praised in their roles of first and ideal readers, but never as actual writers, able to achieve creative autonomy on an equal footing with their male companions.

This is a recurrent pattern in Nabokov's fiction, in which the focal agent is almost always male, notable exceptions being his two 'German' third-person novels, *King Queen Knave* (1928) and *Laughter in the Dark* (1932–33), in which male and female points of view alternate; the story 'A Slice of Life' (1935), in which the female narrator's cloying and melodramatic style may be read as a parody of female writing; and especially *Ada* (1969), which presents an interesting perspective on Nabokov's gender politics. Indeed, although he does not allow Ada's precocity to develop into a professional activity on an intellectual par with Van's psycho-philosophical forays, Nabokov does let her perspicacity seep through by dint of numerous editorial remarks – a *sotto voce* accompaniment that often plays a contra-puntal tune to that of the lead male voice. She thus corrects his style from the very first chapter – 'Hue or who? Awkward. Reword! (marginal note in Ada Veen's late hand)' (*Ada*, 12) – and throughout the novel, deflates his self-importance, qualifies his statements, objects to his interpretations or

---

[7] Stephen H. Blackwell, *Zina's Paradox: The Figured Reader in Nabokov's Gift* (New York: Peter Lang, 2000), 1 and 3.
[8] Boyd, *Russian Years*, 215

questions the veracity of his recollections. Their verbal tussles thus instil a dialectic between male and female viewpoint which sabotages the solipsistic pre-eminence of Van's voice and discloses the partial and fragmentary nature of his vision. Moreover, their voices occasionally fuse into a mode of narrative intercourse where 'their reciprocal positions', as in the sexual act, 'become rather muddled' (*Ada*, 59, 96). For instance, during the recounting of the Burning Barn episode, commonly used editorial indications disappear and give way to a seamless *chassé-croisé* where male and female hands interlace in Escherian fashion, like their lips, that are 'absurdly similar in style, tint and tissue' (*Ada*, 83). 'Vaniada', the scrabble coinage which Lucette had discarded, is later endorsed by the narrator, as it perfectly embodies the androgynous nature of their incestuous creativity and enacts the equation Nabokov had made for his sister Elena back in 1925: 'in love you must be Siamese twins'.[9]

How equal the twins were in his mind is a matter for debate. In any case, the Nabokov partnership involved a clear division of tasks; Vladimir's mission was to develop his literary art whilst Véra took pains to serve her husband's talent rather than fulfil whatever ambitions she might have had for her own. It is impossible to ascertain whether Véra ever nursed any such ambition, but she had published some literary translations before meeting Nabokov and then seems to have stopped soon after their encounter. According to Boyd, she could have been a writer of talent, but decided instead to devote her energies to what she believed to be his superior talent.[10] In his published letters to Véra, Nabokov continuously elaborates on his literary endeavours but never encourages his wife to write anything other than letters to himself. In a similar vein, his letters to his favourite sister, Elena, fail to encourage openly expressed poetic aspirations, while he shows continued interest in the writing endeavours of his younger brother, Kirill.[11] Commenting on Nabokov's discussions with Edmund Wilson over the merits of Jane Austen, Simon Karlinsky notes – perhaps a little too optimistically – that 'it was [Wilson's] particular triumph to overcome Nabokov's typically Russian prejudice against women novelists' (*NWL*, 20). Indeed, traditionally women's – or, still more contemptuously, *lady's* – prose and poetry have, 'to a Russian ear, a belittling if not derogatory flavour', evoking sentimentality, decorativeness, triteness and lack of intellectual magnitude, in implicit opposition to the more commanding features of masculine or manly writing.[12]

[9] Quoted in Schiff, *Véra*, 46.
[10] See Schiff, *Véra*, 38.
[11] See Boyd, *Russian Years*, 362; Schiff, *Véra*, 38; *LTV*, 169.
[12] Catriona Kelly, *A History of Russian Women's Writing 1820–1992* (Oxford: Clarendon Press, 1994), 2.

The biases underlying this essentialist view are strikingly echoed by Nabokov's own pronouncements on women's writing, not only in private, but also in public, as is the case with Khodasevich's one-time companion, Nina Berberova, whose first novel, *The Last and the First* (1929), elicited the only unqualified piece of praise Nabokov ever gave in a review of a Russian woman writer's work. His reason for awarding the novel such a distinction is precisely that 'this is not lady's handiwork ... This is literature of the highest quality, the work of a genuine writer' (*Sobr. soch.*, 3, 701). Later on, in the 1950s, and in an utterly different context, Nabokov can still be found regarding writing as a predominantly male pursuit, a position that probably went largely unchallenged by his students and his peers. Stacey Schiff does write that 'a few Cornell students recoiled' at his sexist attitude to Austen.[13] In his defence of Austen, Wilson voices the same kind of prejudice against female writers, stating that 'her attitude toward her work is like that of a man, that is, of an artist, and quite unlike that of the typical woman novelist, who exploits her feminine day-dreams' (*NWL*, 270). Nabokov opens his lecture on Dickens' *Bleak House* with a sigh of relief at the prospect of leaving 'the ladies in the drawing room', that is, setting aside Jane Austen's *Mansfield Park*, the only work by a female writer he had deemed worthy of including in his lectures. The images he gathers in the cursory glance he casts upon this *mundus muliebris* before making his farewell are in keeping with the typically decorative triviality oftentimes ascribed to women writers in Russian culture: it is but 'porcelain and the minor arts', 'delicate patterns, with her collection of eggshells in cotton wool' and a 'charming rearrangement of old-fashioned values' (*LL*, 63).

Such gendered bias extended to the sphere of translation. Although Nabokov did praise the work of some of his female translators – notably Yvonne Davet and Hilda Ward – and did also lament over some of his male translators – notably Nils Kjellström, the Swedish translator of *Lolita* – his most caustic attacks were aimed at female translators, among whom Eleanor Marx Aveling and Constance Garnett were favourite targets. In 1942, he stated his position unequivocally to his publisher, James Laughlin: 'I am frankly homosexual on the subject of translators' (*Letters*, 41). Nabokov's vision of the translator's task would vary greatly over the years, but in no way did this affect his position regarding the translator's gender, as one may infer from the following declaration he made to another publisher, Walter Minton, sixteen years later: 'Two things the translator must be [note the order]: 1) male, 2) American-born or English' (*Letters*, 258).

---

[13] Schiff, *Véra*, 38.

This attitude to women's writing is largely mirrored by his fiction. Although a writer like Mary Shelley might have had a positive influence on his writing of *Lolita*,[14] and although the figure of Vivian Darkbloom, *Lolita*'s female playwright, anagrammatically hints at a form of playful cross-dressing on Nabokov's part,[15] the latter is generally more prone to drawing a clear distinction between his own writing and that of women writers, notably by displaying in his novels a string of caricatures of female hack writers, from Alla in *Glory* (1931) (like Liza in *Pnin* [1957] a failed Akhmatovian epigone whose 'poems, so sonorous, so spicy, always addressed the man in the polite form ["you," not "thou"] and were asparkle with rubies as red as blood' [*Glory*, 24]) down to *Ada*'s best-selling novelist, Mlle Larivière, 'who was a remarkably stupid person (in spite or perhaps because of her propensity for novelizing)' (*Ada*, 67). Female writing is perhaps most directly attacked in a short story, 'The Admiralty Spire' (1933), which consists of an accusatory letter written by the male anonymous narrator to a novelist writing under the name of Serge Solntsev. His avowed aim is that this letter 'might serve as a lesson of sorts not only for you but for other impetuous lady novelists as well' (*Stories*, 348). Accordingly, the letter is rife with patronising observations but the reader soon realises that the '[sheer] torture' (*Stories*, 350) the narrator experiences on reading the novel has much more to do with his own personal wound, the unrequited love which is the subject of the novel, than with the actual quality of the writing. By the end of the story, after addressing the novelist as his lost love, the narrator even wonders whether he might not have been mistaken about the gender of his addressee.

The dominant male view's recurrent unreliability in Nabokov's fiction defies simplistic notions of blunt misogyny on his part. Indeed, his most virulently misogynistic or chauvinistic narrators happen to be also his most flawed characters. Hermann in *Despair* (1934), Humbert in *Lolita*, Kinbote in *Pale Fire* and Vadim in *Look at the Harlequins!* are, despite their seductive wit, all intensely conceited, self-obsessed, short-sighted and neurotic. To David Larmour, a 'very prevalent [model] in the Nabokovian universe' is the woman who is, as Judith Butler puts it, "'always a 'being for' the masculine subject, who seeks to reconfirm and augment his identity," as well as to mask

---

[14] See Ellen Pifer, 'Her Monster, his Nymphet: Nabokov and Mary Shelley', in Julian W. Connolly (ed.), *Nabokov and his Fiction: New Perspectives* (Cambridge: Cambridge University Press, 1999), 158–176.
[15] Susan Elizabeth Sweeney shows the limits of such literary transvestism in 'Nabokov in an Evening Gown', in Elena Rakhimova-Sommers (ed.), *Nabokov's Women: The Silent Sisterhood of Textual Nomads* (Lanham, MD: Lexington Books, 2017), 187–208.

his inadequacies'.[16] However, in Nabokov's more complex novels both male
and female characters are made to perform a variety of functions that often
defy Manichean labelling and simple actantial models. *Lolita* offers perhaps
the most emblematic demonstration of the way in which a Pygmalion-like
attempt to shape and control women is doomed, as both Humbert's and
Nabokov's representations of the nymphet have been challenged and reas-
sessed by readers, female and male alike.

In many aspects, Nabokov's poetics mirror the prevailing gender structures and strictures of his time, whether his immediate environment was
Russian, European or American. Although he chose the mythological
Sirin, a bird with a woman's head, as his pen name during his Russian
years, it is mostly in his English works that his predominantly male
perspective becomes broader to include, although still rather marginally,
a closer look at women's subjectivity. Women assuredly remained an object
of intense scrutiny throughout his life, yet it is masculinity that constitutes
the centrepiece and the driving force of his verbal constructs. It is quite
unsurprising, then, that he did not identify with the success of his most
famous character. Who, indeed, could have caught him saying, in
Flaubertian style, '*Lolita, c'est moi*'?

---

[16] David H. J. Larmour, 'Leaving Eurydice in the Dark: The Absent Woman in Nabokov's Early
Fiction', *The McNeese Review*, 43 (2005), 1–16 [12].

CHAPTER 5

Friends and Foes

Julian W. Connolly

Although Nabokov himself declared that '[s]ocially,' he was 'a cripple' and had never 'joined any union or club ... or been a member of any organization whatsoever' (*Letters*, 310), he approached the world and its inhabitants with genuine curiosity and interest. In his personal and professional relationships, as in his writing, one can observe considerable depths of feeling and throughout his long life he developed a large circle of acquaintances, cultivating many lasting friendships and a few significant rivalries. While he did not go out of his way to pick quarrels with people, he would not shy away from what he perceived to be challenges to his integrity or to the interests of his family. This chapter will examine some of the more significant personal and professional relationships Nabokov had over the course of his life and career. The picture that emerges from such an examination is one of passionate engagement with 'friends and foes' alike.

It is important to recognise that some of his earliest relationships were naturally with his siblings, Sergei (b. 1900), Olga (b. 1903), Elena (b. 1906) and Kirill (b. 1910), which is particularly relevant when looking at the complex and painful relationship he had with Sergei, who was born less than a year after Vladimir. Although he would be close to his sister Elena in later years, and he would fret over his youngest brother Kirill's well-being during the 1920s and 1930s, his relationship with his other brother Sergei was less harmonious and more distant. A shy stutterer, Sergei was, as Nabokov put it, 'a mere shadow in the background of my richest and most detailed recollections ... We seldom played together, he was indifferent to most of the things I was fond of' (*SM*, 580). In fact, Vladimir was, as he himself admitted, something of a bully towards his younger brother. Sergei was passionately devoted to music, and Vladimir recalls sneaking up behind him and prodding him in the ribs as he practiced the piano – 'a miserable memory' (*SM*, 580). Vladimir's discovery of Sergei's homosexuality during their adolescence undoubtedly added to his sense of distance between them. In adulthood, their relationship continued to be strained. Nabokov's letters to his wife Véra make it clear how Sergei strove to achieve a rapprochement with Vladimir and how Vladimir in turn struggled to find a way to accept Sergei's lifestyle. A profound ambivalence shows up in the letters he wrote to Véra when visiting Paris in 1932. First he records a lunch he had with Sergei and his partner: 'The husband, I must admit, is very pleasant, *quiet*, absolutely not the pederast type, with an attractive face and manner. But I felt somewhat awkward, especially when one of their acquaintances, a red-lipped and curly-headed man, approached us for a minute' (*LTV*, 208). Three weeks later, Sergei and Vladimir met again, and this time, Nabokov noted, '[w]e had a very calm and even warm chat' (*LTV*, 229). These attempts at reconciliation were suspended when Nabokov left Europe for American in 1940. When Nabokov later learned that Sergei had died in a Nazi concentration camp, he was shocked and undoubtedly felt some remorse for the way he had treated him earlier in life. His sense of loss, and possibly of regret over the distance he could never overcome in their relationship, led to one of the most awkward and haunting lines in his autobiography. Speaking of Sergei's life, he wrote: 'It is one of those lives that hopelessly claim a belated something – compassion, understanding, no matter what – which the mere recognition of such a want can neither replace nor redeem' (*SM*, 581). Nabokov's complicated feelings towards his brother may be sensed in the story of V's quest for his half-brother Sebastian in the novel *The Real Life of Sebastian Knight* (1941), and, as Susan Elizabeth Sweeney has argued, in the story 'Scenes from the Life of a Double Monster' (1950).[1]

A more congenial companion for the young Nabokov was his cousin Yuri Rausch von Traubenberg, who was eighteen months older than he. He and Nabokov would enact versions of Mayne Reid and Fenimore Cooper stories during their childhood, and when Yuri was older, he impressed his younger cousin with a saga of amatory conquest. Killed during the Russian Civil War, Yuri left an indelible imprint on Nabokov, who wrote in his memoir that 'all emotions, all thoughts, were governed in Yuri by one gift: a sense of honor equivalent, morally, to absolute pitch' (*SM*, 531). For Nabokov, the notion of honour would be a core virtue throughout his life.

Nabokov entered literature as a poet, and, after he left Russia, his efforts to launch his career as a poet were significantly enhanced through the

---

[1] See Susan Elizabeth Sweeney, 'The Small Furious Devil: Memory in "Scenes from the Life of a Double Monster"', in Charles Nicol and Gennady Barabtarlo (eds.), *A Small Alpine Form: Studies in Nabokov's Short Stories* (New York: Garland, 1993), 193–216.

intercession and support of friends of his father's. For example, Sasha Chorny (the pseudonym for Alexander Glikberg), published Nabokov's poetry and the play *The Wanderers* (1923) (under Nabokov's penname 'Sirin') in the miscellanies he edited, and his publishing house, Grani, issued Sirin's collection *The Empyrean Path* in 1923. Even more considerable was the help provided by Iosif Hessen, a long-time friend of V. D. Nabokov's and co-editor with V. D. of the Berlin daily newspaper *Rul'* (*The Rudder*). Long after the death of Nabokov's father, the poems of Sirin would appear in *Rul'*, or, as Nabokov put it in his memoir: Hessen 'allowed me with great leniency to fill his poetry section with my unripe rhymes' (*SM*, 600). It was Hessen's publishing house, Slovo, which published Nabokov's first novel, *Mary* in 1926, to be followed by *King, Queen, Knave* in 1928, and *The Luzhin Defense* in 1930, as well as the short story and poetry collection *The Return of Chorb* at the end of 1929. Nabokov would remain life-long friends with Hessen and his son Georgii. Nabokov also found friends among writers closer in age, such as Ivan Lukash (1892–1940), with whom he wrote a series of pantomimes for the Bluebird cabaret in Berlin.

As Nabokov's career began to take off, he became tangentially involved with some of the literary debates that swirled through Russian émigré circles. Writers and critics argued about the essential characteristics of émigré literature and which earlier writers should be taken as contemporary models. One leading critic, Georgii Adamovich, advocated viewing literature as a 'human document' marked by sincerity and depth of feeling,[2] and he held that Mikhail Lermontov's work was more appropriate as a model for contemporary writers than the works of Alexander Pushkin.[3] Adamovich's advocacy of Lermontov over Pushkin was intended in part as a rebuke to a writer Nabokov very much admired – Vladislav Khodasevich. Although Nabokov did not clamorously wade into this debate, his sympathies were with Khodasevich (and Pushkin), and he had little regard for Adamovich's criticism, as he himself had been targeted by the latter. Adamovich once questioned what lay behind the 'brilliance' of Nabokov's work, finding there 'a dead world too deeply permeated by chill and indifference to be brought back to life'.[4] In contrast, Khodasevich had proved to be a sensitive reader of Nabokov's work, and wrote 'more

---

[2] The phrase 'human document' (*chelovecheskii dokument*) was the title of an article by Adamovich published in *Poslednie novosti* (Latest News) on 9 March 1933.
[3] See Sergei Davydov, 'Nabokov and Pushkin', in Vladimir E. Alexandrov (ed.), *The Garland Companion to Vladimir Nabokov* (New York and London: Garland, 1995), 485.
[4] Georgij Adamovich, 'Vladimir Nabokov', in Victor Erlich (ed.), *Twentieth-Century Russian Literary Criticism* (New Haven, CT: Yale University Press, 1975), 219; 223.

about Sirin than about any other contemporary writer'.[5] Nabokov proceeded to needle Adamovich in several ways. The literary critic Christopher Mortus in *The Gift* (1937–38) is a thinly disguised composite of Adamovich and Zinaida Gippius, another writer who disliked Nabokov and his work.[6] More ingenious is a literary mystification that was perhaps inspired by the example of a hoax perpetrated by Khodasevich – 'The Life of Vasily Travnikov'. Knowing of Adamovich's distaste for his own poetry, Nabokov penned a work by one 'Vasiliy Shishkov', and sent it to the journal *Sovremennye zapiski* (*Contemporary Annals*). Adamovich took the bait and effusively praised the work, wondering who the mysterious author might be. Nabokov then revealed the hoax by publishing in the same journal as Adamovich's review the short story 'Vasiliy Shishkov', which features an enigmatic poet who leaves Sirin with his poetry before disappearing, perhaps into the verse itself.[7]

Another well-known figure with whom Nabokov had a literary contretemps was the poet Georgii Ivanov. In the latter's case, the acrimony seemed to have a personal foundation. Nabokov had published an unfavourable review of *Isolde*, a novel by Irina Odoevstseva, Ivanov's wife, in *Rul'* on 30 October 1929. The following year, in the first issue of a new journal called *Chisla* (Numbers), Ivanov wrote a scathing critique of Nabokov's fiction, comparing him to a film character who pretends to be a count but is in reality a peasant. Nabokov responded much as he had in the Adamovich case – not with a direct assault but with fiction as a subtle weapon. His story 'Lips to Lips' transparently exposed the journal *Chisla*'s strategy of staying financially solvent by enticing a would-be litterateur to support the journal in return for publishing his novel in measured instalments. The newspaper *Poslednie novosti* (Latest News) accepted the story, but then recognised the target of the piece and broke up the type.[8]

While Nabokov had numerous friends in Russian literary circles (such as Ilya Fondaminsky, editor and promoter of the most distinguished émigré journal, *Sovremennye zapiski*), perhaps the longest and most multifaceted literary relationship Nabokov had in the 1920s and 1930s was his interaction with Ivan Bunin, the first Russian writer to win the Nobel Prize for

---

[5] David M. Bethea, 'Nabokov and Khodasevich', in *Garland Companion to Vladimir Nabokov*, 457.

[6] See Alexander Dolinin, 'Tri zametki o romane Vladimira Nabokova "Dar"', in D. K. Burlaka et al. (eds.), *Vladimir Nabokov: Pro et contra* (St Petersburg: Izd. Russkogo Khristianskogo gumanitarnogo instituta, 1997), 710–21.

[7] See Georgii Adamovich, review of *Sovremennye zapiski*, *Poslednie novosti*, 17 August 1939; Vladimir Nabokov, 'Vasilii Shishkov', *Poslednie novosti*, 12 September 1939.

[8] See Brian Boyd, *Vladimir Nabokov: The Russian Years* (Princeton: Princeton University Press, 1990), 374.

literature in 1933. Nabokov's father had initiated this relationship by asking Bunin for his opinion of his son's poetry in 1920. After some further correspondence, the younger Nabokov himself sent Bunin a selection of his poems and included effusive praise for the older writer's work, stating: 'Forgive my clumsy expressions, but this is as hard as confessing love – an old love'.[9] Later, Nabokov wrote a positive review of Bunin's poetry and dedicated both a poem and a short story ('A Bad Day' [1931]) to Bunin. At first, Bunin did not regard Nabokov as a rival, seeing in the young man's poetry traces of his own influence. Yet, as the years passed and Nabokov himself rose to prominence, Bunin became concerned with the younger writer's growing fame. Yet it was not the fame alone that Bunin resented; he was suspicious of Nabokov's stylistic finesse and dexterity that smacked to Bunin of the cold modernism he abhorred. Eventually, according to Nina Berberova, the mere mention of Nabokov's name 'sent him into a fit'.[10] As for Nabokov in the 1930s, he no longer viewed Bunin as would a young writer but felt himself to be every bit his equal. In a letter to Véra in the mid-1930s his descriptions of Bunin become quite mordant: 'he, Bunin, looks like a wasted old tortoise . . . chewing something and waving its dull-eyed head!' (*LTV*, 256). Elsewhere he offers an equally acerbic judgment: 'Upon a very close inspection Bunin turns out to be simply an old vulgarian' (*LTV*, 335). Much later he would reflect on their awkward literary and personal entanglement in his autobiography, describing a painful meal in a Paris restaurant that culminated in a farcical *pas de deux* as Bunin tried to extract a scarf of Nabokov's that the coat check attendant had stuffed into Bunin's coat by mistake (*SM*, 607).

Moving to the New World in 1940, Nabokov had in many ways to begin his career anew. It took him several years to find secure employment, and along the way he forged some solid friendships and had some less than friendly encounters. In the first category was his renewed friendship with Mikhail Karpovich, a historian at Harvard who hosted Nabokov and his family at his summer home in Vermont. Other American friends included Sylvia Berkman, a writer and colleague of Nabokov's at Wellesley College; Harry Levin, a professor at Harvard, and his wife Elena, an early fan of Nabokov's work; Katharine White, Nabokov's supportive editor at the *New Yorker*; and later, at Cornell, Morris and Alison Bishop. In some of his relationships, however, politics caused corrosive friction. For example,

---

[9] Quoted in Maxim D. Shrayer, *The World of Nabokov's Stories* (Austin: University of Texas Press, 1999), 244. The entire letter in the original can be found in Shrayer's book *Bunin i Nabokov: Istoriia sopernichestva* (Moscow: Al'pina non-fikshn, 2014), 33–4.

[10] Nina Berberova, *The Italics Are Mine*, tr. Philippe Radley (New York: Knopf, 1992), 258.

after having trouble keeping his position at Wellesley because he could not tone down his anti-Soviet sentiments during the war, at a time when the USSR had become an ally, an offer of an appointment at Cornell saved the day.[11] Similarly, a plan to collaborate with the famous linguist Roman Jakobson on a translation and commentary to the medieval Russian epic *The Song of Igor's Campaign* (1960) foundered in part because Nabokov looked askance at Jakobson's apparent sympathy with the Soviet Union. Although the two men had long had an uneasy relationship, their mutual antipathy came to a head in 1957, when Jakobson managed to block an attempt to appoint Nabokov to a teaching position at Harvard and Nabokov wrote to Jakobson that he could not work with him on the Igor tale translation as a matter of conscience because 'I am unable to stomach your little trips to totalitarian countries, even if these trips are prompted merely by scientific considerations' (*Letters*, 216).

One of the longest and, ultimately, most painful relationships Nabokov entered into in the New World was his long friendship with the writer and critic Edmund Wilson. Wilson played an invaluable role during Nabokov's first years in the United States, opening doors to potential publishers such as the *Atlantic Monthly* and New Directions, and writing a glowing blurb for Nabokov's first English-language novel, *The Real Life of Sebastian Knight*. Nabokov became a frequent guest in the Wilson home, and the two had long, bracing discussions about literature, learning from each other and correcting each other at every opportunity (especially in matters of prosody and Russian culture). Nabokov revealed authentic affection when he concluded a letter to his friend 'Bunny' in 1945: 'I like you very much' (*NWL*, 166). Over time, however, their contact became less frequent, and Nabokov chided Wilson in 1960: 'You have quite forgotten me' (*NWL*, 366). Their last meeting took place in Montreux in 1964.

The following year their friendship fatally fractured after the release of Nabokov's new, and very literal, translation of Pushkin's *Eugene Onegin* (1964). Wilson wrote a long, extremely critical review that, among other things, chastised Nabokov for using 'rare and unfamiliar words' and took on an extremely unpleasant tone: 'One knows also the perversity of [Nabokov's] tricks to startle or stick pins in the reader; and one suspects that his perversity here has been exercised in curbing his brilliance; that – with his sado-masochistic Dostoevskian tendencies so acutely noted by Sartre – he seeks to torture both the reader and himself by flattening

---

[11] See Brian Boyd, *Vladimir Nabokov: The American Years* (Princeton: Princeton University Press, 1991) 43; 124.

Pushkin out'.[12] Nabokov was surely taken aback, but he prepared a lengthy, point-by-point rebuttal in 1966. To Wilson's charge that he was addicted to rare and unfamiliar words, he archly replied: 'It does not occur to him that I may have rare and unfamiliar things to convey' (*SO*, 250). The wounds from this battle never fully healed, and although Nabokov extended an olive branch in a letter to Wilson in 1971, any rekindled warmth was extinguished when he read some disparaging remarks made about him and Véra in Wilson's memoir *Upstate* the same year. This impelled him to send another strong rebuttal to *The New York Times Book Review* in November 1971. Wilson died the following year.

Other relationships that seemed to begin on a positive note but that ended badly include Nabokov's dealings with the first publisher of *Lolita* (1955), Maurice Girodias, and his first biographer, Andrew Field. Desperate to place *Lolita* after it had been turned down by a series of American publishers, Nabokov agreed to let Girodias have the book for publication in Paris, not knowing that Girodias' publishing house did a vigorous trade in pornographic novels for an English-language audience. Soon he found himself entangled in contractual and financial disputes, and it took several years to rid himself of Girodias and his misrepresentations. Perhaps more complex was his relationship with Field. Favourably impressed with Field's interest in the work Nabokov had written in Russian as well as in English, Nabokov agreed to let Field begin a biography to follow his first book, *Nabokov: His Life in Art* (1967). Soon, however, it became clear that Field was not exacting in his handling of facts, and to make matters worse, he began to indulge in wild speculations that caused the Nabokovs great distress. Nabokov's repeated attempts to correct Field's misstatements and misrepresentations took a toll on him during the last years of his life.

As if in compensation, however, Nabokov took great comfort from the establishment of new friendships during his final years in Montreux. He welcomed the intelligence, acumen and enthusiasm of such people as Alfred Appel, Jr., who provided a richly annotated version of *Lolita*; Carl and Ellendea Proffer, who brought news of recent developments in unofficial Soviet literature and sought to reissue Nabokov's Russian-language works through their Ardis Press; and Simon Karlinsky, a shrewd and congenial scholar with an extensive knowledge of Russian literature.

Nabokov possessed a robust sense of self-worth, an acute sensitivity to perceived slights against his family and a deep regard for those who could

---

[12] Edmund Wilson, 'The Strange Case of Pushkin and Nabokov', *New York Review of Books*, 15 July 1965, 3.

appreciate his intellect and humour. This combination of traits led him to be a fierce defender of what he held dear and an implacable foe to those who demonstrated values that seemed sharply at odds with his own. Seen as irascible by some, and warmly engaging by others, Nabokov seldom left people in a state of indifference, nor was he himself indifferent to those with whom he had close contact.

CHAPTER 6

Academia

Susan Elizabeth Sweeney

As soon as Nabokov started teaching at American colleges and universities –
in the summer of 1941, a year after his arrival in New York – he began
setting his novels in college towns and populating them with professors,
faculty wives, administrators and students.[1] He also referred to his protagonists, often ironically, by their academic titles. In *Bend Sinister* (1947),
Nabokov's first American novel and only the second that he composed in
English, officials address Adam Krug as 'Professor', usually with a sneer; a
policeman warns, for example, that 'the best a professor could do (if Krug
was a professor) would be to keep his mouth shut' (249). In *Lolita* (1955),
Humbert assumes that most Americans perceive him as a comic figure,
'bespectacled, round-backed Herr Humbert' or 'comedy father Professor
Humbertoldi' (52, 229). The narrator of *Pnin* (1957) gently mocks its hero's
academic rank: he is 'none other than Professor Timofey Pnin', 'the great
Timofey Pnin, scholar and gentleman, teaching a practically dead language
at the famous Waindell College', and, sadly, the still untenured 'Assistant
Professor Pnin' (301, 359, 397). The narrator of *Pale Fire* (1962) – whom
others call 'Dr. Kinbote' – is apparently an obscure individual listed in the
index as '*Botkin, V.*, American scholar of Russian descent' (659). Even as
Nabokov entered the academy, he worried about the status of faculty,
especially from elsewhere, teaching foreign languages and literatures.

His own education had included a parade of governesses, tutors and
drawing-masters; attendance at St Petersburg's Tenishev School; and
studies in French and Russian literature at Cambridge. As an émigré in
Berlin and Paris, he augmented the meagre income from his pen by giving
lessons in English, French, tennis, boxing and Russian prosody. Once he
arrived in America, Nabokov re-invented himself as a professor – despite
having no advanced degrees – thanks to his literary talent and social
connections. With Ivan Bunin's endorsement and help from two friends,

[1] Nabokov's first professorial protagonist appeared in his story 'Revenge' (1924).

51

Mark Aldanov and Henry Lanz, he secured a temporary position at Stanford University. Meanwhile, he prepared for a possible future in the classroom by composing two thousand pages' worth of lectures in advance.

Nabokov worked in academia for two decades, virtually his entire time in the United States. He taught Russian literature and creative writing at Stanford (summer 1941); comparative literature, introductory and inter-mediate Russian, and Russian literature at Wellesley College (1941–42, 1943–48); Russian and European literature at Cornell University (1948–59); and European literature at Harvard (spring 1952).[2] Although Nabokov received tenure at Cornell, he was denied a permanent position at Harvard, supposedly because (as Roman Jakobson put it) he might be a great writer, but one would not offer the elephant a chair in zoology.[3] During those decades he encountered other American educational institutions, too, from the elite Northeastern preparatory schools his son Dmitri attended – Dexter, Saint Mark's and Holderness – to the Southern and Midwestern women's colleges, black colleges and universities he visited on a 1942 lecture tour. Nor was Nabokov's participation in the academy limited to teaching and lecturing. Besides studying lepidoptera at Harvard's Museum of Comparative Zoology (1941–1948), he pursued extensive literary research: a critical biography, *Nikolai Gogol* (1944); translations of Russian poetry (1945), of Lermontov's novel *A Hero of Our Time* (1958), and of the medieval epic *The Song of Igor's Campaign* (1960); and a monumental edition of Pushkin's *Eugene Onegin* (1964). Although Nabokov has been portrayed as an anti-intellectual who taught only to support his art,[4] his scholarship profoundly influenced his fiction. He probably would not have created *Pale Fire*'s mock pedantry, for example, had he not been engaged in editing *Onegin*.

During these years, he transformed himself from V. Sirin, or Vladimir Nabokoff-Sirin, into Professor Nabokov. At Cornell, in particular, his opinions, habits, classroom performances, and reliance on his wife's deft assistance became the stuff of legend.[5] Nabokov's lectures candidly

---

[2] On Nabokov's academic employment, including course loads, course titles, and sabbaticals, see Charles Nicol, 'Teaching,' in Vladimir E. Alexandrov (ed.), *The Garland Companion to Vladimir Nabokov* (New York and London: Garland, 1995), 705–6.

[3] See Galya Diment, *Pniniad: Vladimir Nabokov and Marc Szeftel* (Seattle: University of Washington Press, 2007), 59.

[4] See Mark McGurl, *The Program Era: Postwar American Fiction and the Rise of Creative Writing* (Cambridge, MA: Harvard University Press, 2009), 1–12.

[5] On Nabokov in the classroom, see Nicol, 'Teaching', 705–9; Ross Wetzsteon, 'Nabokov as Teacher', in Alfred Appel, Jr. and Charles Newman (eds.), *Nabokov: Criticism, Reminiscences, Translations, and Tributes* (Evanston, IL: Northwestern University Press, 1970), 240–6; Hannah Green, 'Mister

expressed his likes and dislikes – on matters ranging from an author's merit to a book cover's offensiveness – while urging students to notice details of a work's aesthetic patterning (*LL; LRL; LDQ*). His examinations posed notoriously specific questions about just such minutiae, as when he asked students to describe 'Emma's eyes, hands, sunshade, hairdo, dress, shoes' in *Madame Bovary* (*LL*, 385). Anecdotes about Nabokov's apparent absent-mindedness – for example, when he entered the wrong classroom, began addressing another class, and explained his mistake as a preview of coming attractions – suggest that he enjoyed performing 'that good-natured German platitude of [the] last century, *der zerstreute Professor*' (*Pnin*, 305). Charles Nicol speculates that teaching was 'central to his experiences' in America, since many of his protagonists are teachers.[6] Samuel Schuman proposes that Kinbote and Pnin may even reflect Nabokov himself, because both characters are immigrants 'seen as oddities by their students'.[7] This interpretation seems reasonable, although Nabokov's fictional self-portraits include celebrated academic figures as well: a 'fascinating lecturer' (*Pnin*, 420); 'Professor Nabonidus of Babylon College, Nebraska' (*Ada*, 128), a lepidopterist who discovers a rare case of mimicry; and 'Professor Noteboke, the best translator of Gogol's immortal *The Carrick*' (*LATH*, 659).

How, then, did Nabokov's experience as a professor affect his writing? First, it led him to contribute to a brand-new genre, the academic or campus novel: that is, fiction 'set primarily in a college or university community in which the main characters are academics', featuring closed environments, idiosyncratic personalities and an air of 'comic inconsequentiality'.[8] Mary McCarthy is generally credited with having written the first such novel. Nabokov apparently devoured her book, *The Groves of Academe*, soon after its 1952 publication; when McCarthy's ex-husband, Edmund Wilson, urged him to read it, Nabokov replied by return mail that he had already done so, thought it 'very amusing and quite brilliant in parts' (*NWL*, 304), but noticed errors in her use of Russian words and names to characterise a Russian-born professor. There is no evidence that

---

Nabokov', *New Yorker*, 17 February 1977, 32–5; Robert Roper, *Nabokov in America: On the Road to Lolita* (New York: Bloomsbury, 2015), 57–8; 129–30; and Nabokov's own remarks (*SO*, 41, 104).

[6] Nicol, 'Teaching', 705.

[7] Samuel Schuman, '"I May Turn Up Yet, on Another Campus": Vladimir Nabokov and the Academy', in Merritt Moseley (ed.), *The Academic Novel: New and Classic Essays* (Chester: Chester Academic Press, 2007), 180.

[8] *A Glossary of Literary Terms*, ed. M. H. Abrams and Geoffrey Galt Harpham, 11th ed. (Stamford, CT: Cengage Learning, 2015), 3. See also Moseley, *The Academic Novel*, 3–19; 99–113.

Nabokov ever read the second academic novel, Randall Jarrell's *Pictures from an Institution* (1954), but he knew the author – indeed, he met him through Wilson and McCarthy – and probably heard the literary gossip about its connections to *The Groves of Academe*: it was based on Jarrell's experiences at Sarah Lawrence College, where McCarthy had also taught, and included a sardonic female novelist whom most readers assumed was a caricature of her.

Pnin first took shape as four stories published in *The New Yorker*, beginning in November, 1953 – that is, after McCarthy's novel and before Jarrell's. As David Lodge explains, reading *The Groves of Academe* 'may have planted in [Nabokov's] mind, if only unconsciously, the thought of making similar fictional use of his own academic experience'. Lodge traces 'personal and literary connections' among these three novels, including their satiric tone, stylistic virtuosity and thinly veiled portraits of institutions and individuals.[9] Indeed, all three explore ethical dilemmas that arise from misleading people, gossiping about them, or mining them as sources for fiction. In the case of *Pnin*, certain aspects – the hero's characterisation, the narrator's identity, the blend of comedy and pathos, and the hopeful ending Nabokov grafted onto the novel – suggest that its protagonist was based on Nabokov's colleague Marc Szeftel, as many at Cornell, including Szeftel himself, suspected.[10]

Without a doubt, *Pnin* helped to establish the template for subsequent academic fiction. (Nabokov's own followers in the genre include Richard Fariña, his former student at Cornell, who wrote *Been Down So Long, It Looks Like Up to Me*, and David Lodge, a Nabokov scholar and the author of five academic novels.) Lodge and Schuman also identify Nabokov's next book, *Pale Fire*, with this genre. Merritt Moseley even calls it a 'Doubly Academic Novel', since it includes both a satire on college life and a parody of scholarship.[11] Aspects of Kinbote's commentary, such as the 'jesting and teasing . . . among American intellectuals of the inbreeding academic type' (*PF*, 449), do resemble scenes in McCarthy's and Jarrell's books. Yet it is difficult to categorise either *Pnin* or *Pale Fire* simply as academic fiction. *Pnin* is not a 'straightforward' case, because it contains a novel about exile as well as one about the academy,[12] while *Pale Fire* is both 'a campus novel, and a murder-mystery'.[13] Both books can be read not only as academic novels but also as moral fictions, whose characters 'suffer tangible

[9] David Lodge, 'Nabokov and the Campus Novel', *Cycnos*, 24/1 (2007), 235; 231.
[10] See Diment, *Pniniad*.   [11] Moseley, *The Academic Novel*, 112.   [12] Lodge, 'Nabokov', 239.
[13] Aida Edemariam, 'Who's Afraid of the Campus Novel?' in *The Academic Novel*, 155.

consequences for their morally reprehensible actions'.[14] Indeed, Nabokov's works are too original and too complicated to be safely pigeonholed.

His experiences in academia did not lead him to write academic fiction, then, so much as they prompted him to draw on university life for settings, characters, plots and devices, no matter what genre he was exploring. *Bend Sinister*, for example, is hardly an academic novel, yet this dystopian tragedy, set in an imaginary totalitarian state, features faculty meetings, absentminded professors, students (even a college football player and his sweetheart) and a potpourri of Shakespearean scholarship. *Lolita* may be a romance, a road novel or a detective story, but it also lampoons education in America, from 'the campfire racket' to research in the social sciences (*Lolita*, 125). In addition to addressing higher education, Nabokov muses on secondary schools – and mocks progressive experiments, in particular – when describing an Institute for Abnormal Children in *Bend Sinister*, Beardsley School in *Lolita* or St. Bart's in *Pnin*. He also alludes to academic matters in shorter works. 'The Vane Sisters' (1959), for example, is a puzzle story that exemplifies Nabokov's interest in the otherworld even as it depicts final examinations, grading and a fatal faculty-student affair. Or consider 'An Evening of Russian Poetry' (1945), a poem that imitates a visiting professor's slide lecture – complete with instructions to adjust the image, questions from the audience and polite compliments from the host. Academia thus seems inextricably connected to the themes and stratagems of Nabokov's four American novels and other works from this period. Indeed, his English-language texts emphasise scholarly research so much that they practically assume an academic reader, one familiar not only with classic works of literature in several languages but also with philosophy, the social sciences, the study of lepidoptera, the history of Western painting and many other fields.

Why did the academy have such a profound influence on a mature writer who had already published poetry, drama, short fiction, nonfiction and nine novels? Although universities offer good libraries, a steady income and time to write during the summer, Nabokov may have benefited even more from the unique social environment they provide. During his long European exile, he had written primarily for and about the small, highly educated Russian émigré communities of Berlin and Paris. Once he became an American professor, his colleagues served a similar function: that is, they provided both context and inspiration for his art.

[14] Kenneth Womack, *Postwar Academic Fiction: Satire, Ethics, Community* (New York: Palgrave, 2002), 43.

This development is not surprising, since many of Nabokov's fellow émigrés also ended up in academia. In *Pnin*, the narrator describes the scores of Russian expatriates congregating each year at 'The Pines' – a summer home modelled on Harvard professor Mikhail Karpovich's Vermont cottage, where Nabokov himself stayed.[15] Later, the narrator remembers having seen Pnin in Paris, post-emigration, at 'one of those informal gatherings where old-fashioned terrorists, heroic nuns, gifted hedonists, liberals, adventurous young poets, elderly novelists and artists, publishers and publicists, free-minded philosophers and scholars would represent a kind of special knighthood, the active and significant nucleus of an exiled society' (*Pnin*, 430). For both Pnin and the narrator, participation in this 'special knighthood' led to an affiliation with American colleges and universities. For Nabokov, too, the academy offered another exalted fraternity of like-minded peers, ending but also extending his earlier exile. 'The intellectual life suits me better than any other country in the world', he remarked of the United States. 'I have more friends there, more kindred souls than anywhere'.[16]

As a place where Nabokov might finally belong, academia contrasted poignantly with the apartments and sabbatical homes his family rented in Wellesley, Cambridge and Cayuga Heights (which reappear as Humbert's, Pnin's or Kinbote's borrowed lodgings). Indeed, it existed as an actual location: '. . . the streets / Of College Town . . .' (*PF*, 466), the pastoral campus, the classrooms, the buildings assigned to various disciplines. But even here, Nabokov's position was ambiguous. Cornell had no Russian Department, for example, although Nabokov had been hired to chair it. Instead, other faculty taught Russian in the Modern Languages Department, in Morrill Hall, while he taught Russian literature under the auspices of Romance Literature, housed in Goldwin Smith Hall – which explains why he once called himself, in a letter to the *Cornell Daily Sun* about the teaching of Russian, 'strictly a Goldwin Smith man' (*Letters*, 267).

Nabokov was apparently aware of institutional politics from the moment he entered the academy, given his portraits of a weak president and an ingratiating assistant in *Bend Sinister*. That novel's protagonist esteems his colleagues, however, 'because they are able to find perfect felicity in specialised knowledge' (*BS*, 214–15). Indeed, *Bend Sinister* identifies Krug's fellow professors primarily by their disciplines; thus

---

[15] See Diment, *Pniniad*, 50–51.
[16] Vladimir Nabokov, interview by Douglas Davis, *National Observer*, 29 June 1964, 17.

'Economics, Divinity, and Modern History stood talking near one of the heavily draped windows' (201). The theme of categorising one's colleagues continues with 'Professor Chem' in *Lolita* (195); the 'versatile Starr couple', who exhibit mutable first names, genders, departments and research projects, in *Pnin* (396); and assorted professorial Doppelgängers throughout Nabokov's four American novels. In *Bend Sinister*, for example, an indeterminate presence divides into 'Gleeman, the frail professor of Medieval Poetry, and the equally diminutive Yanofsky, who taught Slavic scansion' (200); *Lolita* juxtaposes 'two professors of English, . . . Miss Lester and . . . Miss Fabian' (168); Pnin repeatedly confuses two colleagues in Ornithology and Anthropology; and in *Pale Fire*, Shade is tragically mistaken for Goldsworth.

These ambiguous distinctions among faculty suggest Nabokov's continued concern about the status of those entering the academy from elsewhere. In *Bend Sinister*, Krug, a philosopher trapped by a tyrannical regime, tries in vain to escape to America. Other protagonists manage to immigrate, but struggle to establish themselves in academia: Humbert has a temporary position teaching French at Beardsley College; Pnin, a Russian émigré, is denied tenure at Waindell; Kinbote, another émigré, is apparently an adjunct professor at Wordsmith University. For such protagonists, encountering colleagues at faculty meetings, faculty parties or discussions in 'the lounge of the Faculty Club' (*PF*, 630) often causes anxiety. Some characters, like Krug and John Shade, are campus celebrities; others are obscure or ignored. Friendships – between Krug and Ember, Gaston Godin and Humbert, the narrator and Pnin, Shade and Kinbote – seem oddly unbalanced. Nabokov may have experienced such fraught relationships himself: despite his popularity at Cornell, he remarked that Morris Bishop was 'my only close friend on the campus' (*SO*, 294). In addition to these ambivalent portraits of other professors, Nabokov's imagined academic community of insiders and outsiders includes faculty wives, staff and students, from 'earnest Betty Bliss' and 'prodigious' Charles McBeth (*Pnin*, 302) to troubled souls like Sybil Vane or Hazel Shade.

Despite his evident affinity for academia, Nabokov resigned from Cornell in September, 1959, in the aftermath of *Lolita*'s success. He returned to Europe but remained an American citizen and a self-proclaimed American writer. Although he still wrote about the academy – even planning a chapter on Cornell for his proposed sequel to *Speak, Memory* – its manifestations in his fiction grew dimmer and more distant. In *Ada* (1969), for example, Van Veen holds the Rattner Chair of

Philosophy at the University of Kingston, but only gives ten lectures annually for 'a score of dull years' before retiring to Europe, 'an obscure figure around which no legends collected in the university' (405). The narrator of *Look at the Harlequins!* (1974) offers another distorted reflection of Nabokov's own career: becoming a lecturer at 'Quirn University on the strength of [his] European reputation', 'expand[ing] into a Full Professor' (*LATH*, 660), then retiring. *The Original of Laura* (2009), Nabokov's unfinished final manuscript, describes how 'Philip Wild[,] Lecturer in Experimental Psychology' at the University of Ganglia (147), tries to mentally eliminate his aging body rather than retire.

In these novels, Nabokov's depiction of his protagonists' academic lives seems theoretical, fanciful and remote, and yet the increasing abstraction also suggests that concepts relating to academia had become fundamental to his thinking. Wild's experiments, for example, involve erasing his image from an imaginary blackboard, a teaching aid that Nabokov no longer used but which still lingered powerfully in his memory: 'It is strange to think that never again shall I feel between finger and thumb the cool smoothness of virgin chalk or make that joke about the "gray board" (improperly wiped), and be rewarded by two or three chuckles' (*SO*, 294). Long after he left, the academy remained integral to Nabokov's imagination and to how he thought of himself – as outsider or insider – in relation to the world.

CHAPTER 7

Authorial Persona

Maria Malikova

The theme of 'authorial identity' or, more precisely, of the public, textual 'authorial persona' is one of the most important in Nabokov's work. In Nabokov's oeuvre, the authorial persona manifests itself in such peculiar phenomena as the creation of fictional artist-protagonists (in particular writers) who possess both striking similarities with and differences from their author and sometimes sense the presence of a higher authorial consciousness; the use of autobiographical codes in the portrayal of both primary and secondary characters (e.g. synesthetic experiences, chess, entomology, physiognomy, Russian language, anagrams of the names Vladimir Nabokov and Sirin); a half century's work on his autobiography (from the first essays of the mid-1930s to the planned continuation, *Speak On, Memory*) as the ultimate metatext and compendium of elements that make up Nabokov's textual 'persona'; and the post-factum creation of the 'Nabokov myth' (as well as a 'Sirin myth') in non-fictional, largely late public statements (interviews, forewords, afterwards, articles). The theme of 'authorial identity' is also closely tied to Nabokov's interest in the genre of literary biography where he was searching for a single formula to describe both life and art, focusing on the figure of Pushkin as a type and archetype for a national public construction of a poet's biography and, in his final years, as a personal reflection on his own biography the writing of which, by the young Slavist Andrew Field, Nabokov was trying to control.

This wide-ranging theme has already been extensively examined from various perspectives. Beginning with Jane Grayson's book, which traces recurring autobiographical motifs in Nabokov's work, many studies of Nabokov's poetics have focused on *Speak, Memory* (1967).[1] It would be difficult to find a study that does not mention one of Nabokov's many Hitchcockian appearances – casually camouflaged as a stout man with a

---

[1] See Jane Grayson, *Nabokov Translated: A Comparison of Nabokov's Russian and English Prose* (Oxford: Oxford University Press, 1977).

Illustration 1 Bronze statue of Vladimir Nabokov by Alexander and Phillip
Rukavishnikov, Montreux.

butterfly net or a 'philosophical friend' hidden under an anagram – in his
late English-language texts and English translations of Russian works. This
chapter will trace the meaning and function of the authorial persona in
Nabokov's creative evolution as it comes to the fore in two moments of
crisis – in the late 1930s when he was taking stock of his 'Sirin' literary past

and metamorphosing into the English-language writer of Russian extraction, and in the 1970s during the infamous Nabokov–Field conflict about the biographer's version of the writer's life.

The first crisis came when Nabokov reached the apex of his Russian literary career. Having abandoned the planned sequel to *The Gift* (1937–38), he began composing in English, staging his own eclipse (the disappearance of the mature Russian writer Sirin) and transforming himself into the American writer Nabokov. This unprecedented metamorphosis fell into a contextual void both in the Russian émigré community, where Nabokov's later Russian texts, very different from his 'Sirin oeuvre', were available only partially or remained unpublished, and in America, where Nabokov was still an obscure author. Thus poorly understood and finding little response, this metamorphosis of the Nabokovian authorial persona on the very boundary of his Russian and American years generally slipped away from the attention of later scholars. One major reason it did so was because the planned sequel to *The Gift* (let's call it the 'large' *Gift*), which would have determined the final shape of Nabokov's central text during this period, remained incomplete and – until recently – unpublished.[2] Nabokov's second moment of crisis revolved around the notorious disagreement in the 1970s between him and Andrew Field over the latter's biographical study, *Nabokov: His Life in Part*, published in 1977. This conflict revealed vividly the highly idiosyncratic and 'strongly opinionated' public persona that the author had carefully created throughout his American years.

In the latter half of the 1930s, Nabokov started playing with the concept of authorial control in his texts by delegating not just narrative but also authorial function per se to several invented character-creators, for whom he crafted fragments of texts and literary biographies. The fictional artists Vasiliy Shishkov (from the eponymous short story) and Fyodor Godunov-Cherdyntsev, the protagonist of *The Gift*, find themselves in complicated relationships with their creator; they partly represent the potential development and alternative sources of his poetics and biography and they partly parody – not in the comedic sense, but in one of emulation – both Nabokov himself and other literary styles and lifestyles. Vladislav

---

[2] See Jane Grayson, 'Washington's Gift: Materials Pertaining to Nabokov's *Gift* in the Library of Congress', *Nabokov Studies*, 1 (1994), 21–68; Vladimir Nabokov, 'Father's Butterflies: Second Addendum to *The Gift*', transl. Dmitri Nabokov, in *Nabokov's Butterflies*, ed. Brian Boyd and Robert Michael Pyle (Boston, MA: Beacon Press, 2000), 198–234; Vladimir Nabokov, 'Vtoroe dobavlenie k "Daru"', ed. Alexander Dolinin, *Zvezda*, 1 (2001), 85–109. The recent publication of the second part of *The Gift* prepared by Andrey Babikov (*Zvezda*, 4 [2015]) has led to controversy (see Alexander Dolinin, 'O pagubah diletantizma', *Zvezda*, 9 [2015]).

Khodasevich warned Sirin against depicting his writer-protagonists as 'true artists' or 'positive types', who invariably come out 'pompous and sugary', and advised him instead to give 'a merciless satiric portrayal of a writer'.[3] Nabokov proceeded along a somewhat different path, combining parodic distance with the full gravity of the creative task and keeping 'everything ... on the very brink of parody' (*Gift*, 197). Thus, in *The Gift* the implied author of the entire text occupies the role of 'true artist', while the hero-writers represent his masks. Nabokov's primary strategies for producing an authorial presence through 'autobiographical codes' and fictional characters' presentiments of the author's higher reality during his American period can be traced back to works written during his Russian years or, more exactly, before the appearance of *Conclusive Evidence* (1951). However, in his Russian works such strategies are less noticeable and function differently. In *The Gift*, readers familiar with Nabokov's autobiography can draw parallels between several recurring motifs: Fyodor's childhood at the family's Leshino estate (based on the Nabokovs' Vyra), his *audition colorée* or his adoration of his father. At the time of the text's composition and in its contemporaneous reception, however, only a small circle of friends and relatives could have identified these autobiographical references. Although in the novel these references point to the implied presence of the author Nabokov, they do not act as autobiographical markers per se. Rather, as Alexander Dolinin notes, they regularly appear within descriptions of Fyodor's creative epiphanies and function as autobiographical markers of a metaliterary order, which highlight and explicate some mechanism of inspiration lying behind the creation of *The Gift*.[4]

Judging by the sequel to *The Gift*, the fragmented 'authorial persona' device within Nabokov's Russian-language fictional world would have become more multi-layered, reflecting an unprecedented complexity of authorial consciousness and the instability of 'reality' associated with it. Notably, Nabokov allows the fictional author Fyodor Godunov-Cherdyntsev to generate his 'own' fictional creators of the second and third order along with their texts. For instance, in the sequel, after losing Zina, Fyodor invents the 'no longer independent artist' Sineusov (*Stories*, 526), who is also widowed and who is commissioned to illustrate a poem about the king of a 'melancholy and remote island' (*Stories*, 510) in the far North that he comprehends only in general outline, as it is written in an

[3] Vladislav Khodasevich, 'On Sirin', in Norman Page and Paul Kegan (eds.), *Nabokov: The Critical Heritage* (London: Routledge, 1982), 61–64.
[4] See Alexander Dolinin, '*The Gift*', in Vladimir E. Alexandrov (ed.), *The Garland Companion to Vladimir Nabokov* (New York and London: Garland Publishing, 1995), 135–69 [152].

unfamiliar language (this part of the sequel to *The Gift* was later published separately as two short stories, 'Solus Rex' [1940] and 'Ultima Thule' [1942]). The incomprehensible language points to the higher narrative level of the novel, a level that remains inaccessible (foreign and unintelligible) for the hero-artist. The hierarchy between different narrative planes illustrates the ontological and metaliterary status of the implied author's higher consciousness in comparison to which the hero-artists' perception is by definition limited. In an equally telling scene in the sequel to *The Gift*, Fyodor reads a book which is 'difficult and strange, and its pages seemed mixed-up'.[5] Its title, which Fyodor unexpectedly 'recalls' prompted by a reference to Pushkin's line 'vain gift, chance gift', obviously refers to the 'real' book authored by Vladimir Nabokov.

The stereoscopic and multi-layered structure of the artistic world as presented in the two parts of the 'large' *Gift* actualises the author's presence behind this gigantic and diverse construction. The purpose of this device is to show that the writer's overall creative energy and versatility can be represented only through the fragmentation of his superior talent: literary skill is designated to one hero, naturalistic philosophy to a second and the artist's imagination to a third. A similar process of fragmentation appears in Nabokov's first novel intended for an English-speaking audience, *The Real Life of Sebastian Knight* (1941), written at the same time as the sequel to *The Gift*. Following Alexander Dolinin, who called the unpublished sequel to *The Gift* 'a phantom text' akin to the second volume of Nikolai Gogol's *Dead Souls*, it is possible to speak of a 'phantom authorial persona' of the Russian writer Nabokov, who, succeeding Sirin, appeared briefly towards the end of the 1930s, only then to metamorphose into the American writer Nabokov.[6] *The Real Life of Sebastian Knight* presents the transition of the authorial 'I' which is marked by bifurcation into two languages, Russian and English, and is presented literally in the images of the two half-brothers: (1) the recently deceased, famous English author, Sebastian Knight, who was born half-Russian; and (2) V., the Russian narrator who writes a biography of Sebastian and attempts to understand his life primarily through his books. In a 1942 letter to his close friend Georgii Hessen, Nabokov describes the linguistic-psychological substrate of this device: 'It is as though I created the person who composed *The Real Life of Sebastian*

---

5 Nabokov, 'Vtoroe dobavlenie k "Daru"'.
6 Alexander Dolinin, *Istinnaia zhizn' pisatelia Sirina: raboty o Nabokove* (St Petersburg: Akademicheskii proekt, 2004), 291.

Knight . . ., but it's not I who am creating'.[7] That somebody's 'real life' should be a doubly fictional narrative says a good deal about the reality of fiction and the fictiveness of reality. This motif of the biographical reconstruction of the poet's life through his works – the description of his life as a 'pastiche' of his work – goes back to Nabokov's central argument about the poet's biography made in the 1937 essay 'Pushkin, or the Real and the Plausible' ('Pouchkine ou le vrai et la vraisemblable'), the title of which is echoed in *The Real Life of Sebastian Knight*. Moreover, V., the attentive reader and biographer who experiences a kindred empathy of such depths that even his own life becomes a pastiche of Sebastian's works, might be a 'creation' of Knight in the literal sense: he is a character thought up by Knight as a device for the composition of his own autobiography. Nabokov thus once again declares the impossibility of writing a real poet's biography 'without contaminating' it 'with a kind of secondary poetization'.

However, this device did not work when in his later years Nabokov made a similar attempt to use a biographer as a scribe for composing his own autobiography. Instead, Andrew Field, who was by definition not fictional, proved to be both real and ambitious. In the course of his work on Nabokov's biography, he came to realise what was expected of him and challenged Nabokov with exasperated irony to 'try very hard to imagine a biography which was not written by himself'.[8]

Following his post-*Lolita* fame, Nabokov had taken great pains to ingrain the image of the domineering, strongly private and linguistically extraterritorial presence behind his 'strong opinions' into the minds of his audience and critics. Attacks on the 'Viennese quack' Freud, declarations of total indifference to politics, other writers, all critics and any music, club or creed, all expressed in an eccentrically dictatorial manner that included sweeping aesthetic judgments and declarations of American patriotism, were directly oriented toward his American audience and were instrumental in establishing the difference between 'good' and 'bad' readers. However, this 'persona' displeased some admirers of his novels and

---

[7] Quoted in Andrew Field, *Vladimir Nabokov: His Life in Part* (Harmondsworth: Penguin Books, 1977), 249.

[8] Field, *Life in Part*, 14. Before his biography of Nabokov, Field wrote a voluminous monograph on Nabokov's work (see Field, *His Life in Art*) that was highly valued by Nabokov; he also compiled a bibliography of Nabokov's works with the author's help (*Nabokov: A Bibliography* [New York: McGraw-Hill, 1973]). In his final book on the writer Field mentions the riches of his private Nabokov archive, most of them still unpublished (*VN: The Life and Art of Vladimir Nabokov* [New York: Crown, 1986], 377–78).

even provoked comparisons with Andrey Zhdanov and President Richard Nixon.[9] Among other things, Nabokov presented himself to the public as a writer whose appropriate 'literary' biography would be the absence of any biography other than the 'story of his style': 'the only rational and artistic way to write the history of an individual of my dismal kind (whose only human and entertaining side is the gift of inventing clouds, castles, lakes) would be to follow his development as a writer from his first opaque poems to *Transparent Things*'.[10] Field understood these idiosyncratic requirements – 'Vladimir Nabokov insists that he exists **only** as a writer, in his written words' – [11] but he dared to disagree: 'Vladimir Nabokov values most highly the discovery of ... patterns of repetition in telling of a life. But I would hesitate – not that I could not do it – to write Nabokov's own life according to this speculative prescription. These are merely the question sparks of reality'.[12]

Pekka Tammi suggests that Nabokov wanted his biographer to see 'an author's life as a consciously crafted fiction comparable to any other'.[13] Among other things, this desire explains Nabokov's strong objection to Field's quite legitimate biographical practice of using information from other sources, even those authorised by Nabokov himself, such as his sister Elena Sikorski or Hessen, and of scrutinising facts Nabokov fed to him. Field suggested that Nabokov had 'an ingrained conviction that all *facts* ... are basically extrinsic to his self if they do not come from himself'.[14] The root cause for Nabokov's scepticism seems not so much that other people's reminiscences of him had the potential to be garbled, tasteless or revealing, but rather that the view of his authorial self from an outside perspective was naturally illegitimate in his strongly 'anti-Bakhtinian' world. Field's project, as long as he refused to be a 'docile secretary' with eyes thoroughly 'Nabokovized', was doomed to dissatisfy his subject.

The part of the Nabokov–Field conflict relevant for the discussion of authorial identity is Nabokov's conviction that his biographer must accept '*the radiant, glacial, and final truth* of *Speak, Memory*'.[15] Otherwise his study

[9] N. G. Mel'nikov, *Klassik bez retushi. Literaturnyi mir o tvorchestve Vladimira Nabokova: Kriticheskie otzyvi, esse, parodii* (Moscow: Novoe literaturnoe obozrenie, 2000), 508–17.

[10] Quoted in Brian Boyd, *Vladimir Nabokov: The American Years* (Princeton: Princeton University Press, 1991) 606.

[11] Field, *Life in Part*, 28 (bold print in Field's book indicates Nabokov's own words).

[12] Field, *Life in Part*, 48.

[13] Pekka Tammi, *Problems of Nabokov's Poetics: A Narratological Analysis* (Helsinki: Suomalainen Tiedekatemia, 1985), 239.

[14] Field, *Life in Part*, 35.

[15] Field, *Life in Part*, 28.

would be doomed to be nothing but 'rot and nastiness'.[16] However, considering the Nabokov–Field conflict from an academic perspective, Field's book is much more than mere 'rot and nastiness'. It is, for instance, interesting to note that Field's approach was closely modelled on Nabokov's autobiography, imitating its structure and mannerisms with the long digression on genealogy, a Sterne-like report of his hero's birth in the middle of the story and the pastiche of Nabokov's early poetry to describe his first romance.[17] Field's poetic license (considered by Nabokov tasteless and illegitimate) is also akin to Nabokov's own biographical experiments in the vein of the Anglo-American tradition of Lytton Strachey, who invented 'a new kind of creative and artistic biography – strictly keeping to the facts but avoiding all the props of footnotes, sources and lengthy quotations . . ., – in a word, striving to create a complete, self-contained, concise work of art'.[18] This description of Strachey's biographical method is applicable not only to Field's work but even more so to Nabokov's own attempts at the biographical genre in Chernyshevsky's life story in *The Gift*, which combines vast factual material into aesthetic patterns. In other words, Field's approach to life-writing in many ways reflected that of Nabokov.

There seems to be a general consensus in Nabokov studies that Field's book teems with countless distortions and errors. While there is no doubt that factual errors crept into Field's book, some of the 'exhibits' Brian Boyd provides for those who 'may wish to know what was wrong with Field's work'[19] are vital for understanding Nabokov's own method of combining, deforming and contaminating facts of his real life in creating his public persona.[20] For instance, Boyd criticises Field for the casual manner in which he inserts Nabokov's corrections into his text, retaining at the same time his own initial wrong assessments such as the description of Bunin as 'a very little man (he was of average height)'.[21] Nabokov's correction in parentheses that makes the phrase self-contradictory was introduced after he remarked to Field that Bunin was 'not of small stature'.[22] In reality, Bunin, being 170 cm. tall, as is indicated in his Nansen passport, could

---

[16] Nabokov's letter to his lawyer, 28 May 1973, quoted in Boyd, *American Years*, 616.
[17] See Field, *Life in Part*, 89.
[18] Dmitrii Mirskii, 'Iskusstvo biografii (Litton Strechi)', in *O literature i iskusstve: Stat'i i retsenzii 1922–1937*, ed. O. A. Korostelev and M. V. Efimov (Moscow: Novoe literaturnoe obozrenie, 2014), 73–77 [75–76]. First published in *Zveno* (Paris), 52 (28 Jan 1924).
[19] See Boyd, *American Years*, 723, fn. 23.
[20] See a more detailed analysis of Field's alleged mistakes in: Maria Malikova, 'Zashchita Filda, ili Zapozdalaia retsenziia na pervuiu biografiiu Nabokova', *Russkaia literatura*, 1 (2016), 220–38.
[21] Field, *Life in Part*, 227; Boyd, *American Years*, 618.
[22] Quoted in Boyd, *American Years*, 618.

barely get to Nabokov's chin (Nabokov was 188 cm).[23] Bunin was a poet whom young Sirin adored, imitated and likened to the mountain peak and himself – to a hill in a 1922 poem ('As the mountain waters your voice is proud and clear . . .') dedicated to the older writer. The poem was sent to his mentor with a letter saying 'I just want you to understand with what pure rapture I am looking from my hill at a shining peak where you have carved in stone eternal, incomparable words'.[24] From the perspective of Nabokov's poetic truth, therefore, Bunin could not even physically be a man of 'small stature'. Retaining in his text this obviously paradoxical phrase, Field made visible the conflict between Nabokov's specific notion of real poetic truth and false realistic plausibility.

The dominant feature of the many-faceted manifestations of Nabokov's authorial self in both his Russian and American period, in fictional and non-fictional texts, is his marked position of higher authorial presence, of the one who does not necessarily always speak (the narrative voice could be temporarily delegated either to a fictional semi-parodic character-writer or to a real-life biographer) but who sees and judges. Ultimately, Nabokov's tombstone conclusively declares this authoritative position beyond any possible further contradiction: 'Vladimir Nabokov. Ecrivain'.

---

[23] See [Ivan Bunin's] Passeport Nansen (1941), Leeds Russian Archive, Ivan Alekseevich Bunin Collection, MS 1066/1273.

[24] Nabokov's letter to Ivan Bunin, 26 Nov 1922, quoted in Maxim Shrayer, *Nabokov: Temy i variatsii* (St Petersburg: Akademicheskii proekt, 2000), 134.

PART II

Places

CHAPTER 8

St Petersburg

Gennady Barabtarlo

In the spring of 1899, perhaps days before Nabokov was born, Alfred Eberling, then a young painter who went on to make a large number of celebrity portraits (Russian courtiers and ballerinas at first, then a gallery of Soviet leaders, his Lenin appearing on early Soviet banknotes), produced a dozen remarkable photographic pictures of St Petersburg street scenes. These are nothing like the typical old photographs of people standing at attention, faces petrified; rather, decades before Cartier-Bresson, they look like frozen frames of a motion picture: another instant, and they will resume jerkily walking, getting off a horse-drawn tram, folding the umbrella, unfolding a newspaper. In the philosophical opening of his memoirs, Nabokov marvels at the mind-tingling strangeness of seeing filmed images of his parents and his empty pram weeks before his arrival onto the setting. Eberling's pictures, all taken close to Morskaya St., Nabokov's place of birth, would have kept him mesmerised for hours.

He derived a prosodic pleasure from seeing in later years that his life's rhythm yielded nearly perfect twenty-year-long stanzas, all defined by the unity of place: Russia, then the move west to Europe, then further west to America, then back to Western Europe – as if half-hoping against mad hope that the last, nonagenarian stretch might, as in a well-composed novel in which the ending rhymes with the beginning, bring him back to St Petersburg. As it happened, the fourth, incomplete, stretch double-barred at seventeen years, and his last novel, also the seventeenth, remained unfinished.

His first eighteen years was the longest Nabokov resided in any city. The turn of the century made the three-dimensional stony space of a European *urbs* an object of a very special artistic adoration, a theme cultivated by the French and Belgian Symbolists (of the latter particularly Verhaeren and Rodenbach) and eagerly admitted into the Russian aesthetic consciousness by Briusov and Blok, especially. At thirteen, Nabokov could already have learned by heart the latter's spellbinding short poem about a hopeless view from a window in St Petersburg, which begins and ends with a chiastic string of stark subjects with no predicate: 'Night. Street. Lamppost. Apothecary'. At twenty-eight, from an insurmountable distance, in a poem about an imagined fatal slipping across the border, he invokes the spastic pulse of Blok's iambic tetrameter and the staccato of its nominatives: 'Russia, the stars, the night of execution' ('Rossiia, zvezdy, noch' razstrela ...') ('The Execution', *PP*, 46–47).

In the Russian version of his memoirs, *Drugie berega (Other Shores)* (1954), among the many added passages not found in the English original, there is one of particular poignancy. In 1904–05, the family spent a whole year abroad, and in a wistful, paragraph-long sentence, Nabokov ponders the workings of an artistically thoughtful fate: '. . . at six, I was given a chance for the first time to experience the real, charcoal-smoke-smelling rapture of coming back to one's homeland – which was another of fate's mercies, one in the series of beautiful rehearsals which have replaced the actual performance that, as far as I am concerned, may not now take place after all, even though a musical resolution of life seems to call for it'.[1]

Something of a Pity

Nabokov is unique even in his contexts. A great many distinguished writers lived in St Petersburg, but one will be stumped to name another Russian writer of stature, apart from Blok, who was born there. None among its famous inhabitants and paeanists could call the imperial capital his place of birth – neither Pushkin, nor Lermontov, nor Nekrasov, nor Dostoevsky, nor Gumilev, nor Mandelstam, nor Akhmatova. It is a curious fact that of the eleven authors of the trend-setting *Petersburg's Physiology* and *Petersburg's Almanac* (1844–46) only one was the city's native (Ivan Panaev). It is as if the marshy soil, under always-pale skies, was more attractive than it was fecund.

Flat as a pitch and therefore regularly flooded, built up like a masterpiece monument on a shaky pedestal, the city flaunted its dichotomies, which

---

[1] *Drugie berega* (New York: Chekhov Publishing House, 1954), 20. My translation.

Pushkin captured, on a large scale, in *The Bronze Horseman* and, compactly, in one of his trademark two-part miniatures:

> City sumptuous, city squalid,
> Air of elegance and thrall,
> Vault of skies all green and pallid,
> Boredom, cold, and granite walls.
>
> Still, it's something of a pity
> That you miss the furtive sight
> Of her slender foot and pretty
> Golden locks, all mussed in flight.[2]

This curiously non-jarring contradiction can be best observed in Dostoevsky's pre-imprisonment *White Nights*, when he sees 'something ineffably touching' in St Petersburg; a score of years on, these limpid white nights would turn under his pen into the yellow-grey, filthy, febrile days and nights of *Crime and Punishment*, the former 'beautiful canals' now dirty ditches that lure suicides. That city might entrance but it did not enchant, and for Nabokov its notorious phantasm was annually dispelled and overcome by the organic realism of his country estate, setting up a bias that became so great in the retrospect of exile. *Peterburg* is no place to chase butterflies.[3] The urban, dank to the core chill of 'the icy ripple on the channel' ('ledianaia riab' kanala') of Blok's poem is replaced by the countryside scenery in Nabokov's tragic 1927 sequel – a fragrant gully, at the edge of which the nostalgic trespasser is to be shot: '... and full of racemosas the ravine' ('... i ves' v cheremukhe ovrag') ('The Execution', *PP*, 46–47).

As if to compensate for the perfectly level terrain of his Russian years, his forced displacement would take him, a butterfly net in hand, first up the easy slopes of the Crimean mountains, then to timberline altitudes in the Alps and the Pyrenees, the Rockies, and the Alps again.

---

[2] A. S. Pushkin, *Polnoe sobranie sochinenii* (Moscow: AN SSSR, 1948), vol. 3 (1), 124. The foot and the locks belonged to Anna Olenine, the daughter of the director of the St Petersburg Imperial Library, one of the four young ladies he unsuccessfully proposed to marry between 1826 and 1830. The translation is mine.

[3] Not with a net, in any event; however, 'On the Nevski Avenue, during the last days of March, when the wooden blocks of the spacious street pavements gleamed dark blue from the damp and the sun, one might see, flying high over the carriages, along the façades of the houses, past the city hall, past the lindens in the square, past the statue of Catherine, the first yellow butterfly' (*Gift*, 102); and 'a Camberwell Beauty, exactly as old as our romance, sunning its bruised black wings, their borders now bleached by hibernation, on the back of a bench in Alexandrovski Garden' (*SM*, 564).

A Portable Homeland

In later years, Nabokov and his best Russian heroes would revisit the park alleys of that estate much more often, more vividly and tenderly than the avenues of the city. St Petersburg and the vicinity south of it, where Vyra and Rozhestveno were situated, encompassed the curiously small terrain of Nabokov's 'on the ground' experience of Russia, an unprecedented compression of the notion of fatherland. The hero of Nabokov's last Russian novel, *The Gift* (1937–38), gives, in a poem, bitter thanks to his native land for the 'cruel mist' ('pain' in the original) of an unrequited love, rhyming the word *otchizna* (fatherland) with *toboi ne priznan* (by you unnoticed). What of the immense Empire did Nabokov manage to see while he could? Too young to travel far and, of course, unable to foresee the travel routes pre-charted for him, he never went to Moscow ('a city which I had never seen in my life and which interested me about as much as, say, Birmingham', says V.V.N., the narrator of his last English novel, *Look at the Harlequins!* [1974]) or Odessa, Pskov, Tiflis, Nizhni or Orenburg – to name just a few from Pushkin's itinerary. (Pushkin, of course, started on his incessant travels across Russia at the age Nabokov began his peripatetics outside it; in a curious converse symmetry, Pushkin, born in Moscow, never set foot abroad.) The southern tip of the Crimean peninsula was an exotic prologue to life in exile, its receding shore the very last image of Russia.

Impressions of live images abandoned forever in his youth were to stock Nabokov's fiction for decades to come. He carefully avoided placing his characters in settings untrodden by him; even *Ada*'s (1969) Terra is but a fanciful reproduction of familiar topography. It is utterly extraordinary for a Russian writer not to have a single story, or a chapter of a novel or memoirs, set in Moscow. The fact that in Russia he lived exclusively in St Petersburg and Vyra (with the Crimean sojourn at the exit) and travelled domestically almost exclusively between those two locations, determined the quality and scope of the content of Nabokov's Russian visual memory. For a Russian artist, it was a very rare, perhaps one-of-a-kind, case of stenotopia. His Russia, sensually limited to the city of his birth and its vicinity, was for Nabokov a tremulously beautiful, but also a tremendously condensed, terra, with the specific gravity of a black hole. In a sense, this made it perfectly portable.[4]

---

[4] One of the essays comprising Alexander Herzen's *From the Other Shore*, a collection whose title, a hundred years on, would cross over to the Russian version of Nabokov's memoirs, was called 'Omnia Mea Mecum Porto'.

'I reserve for myself the right to yearn after an ecological niche:

> ... Beneath the sky
> of my America to sigh
> for *one* locality in Russia.' (*SM*, 419)

This '*one* locality for which he yearns is not the imperial city of Saint Petersburg itself but not far to its south, the few square miles of the Oredezh River valley around Vyra and Batovo'.[5] The emphasis in this wistful recast of Pushkin's lines is Nabokov's.

Of course, St Petersburg was not like Russia – and, just as indisputably, vice versa; nor was it intended to be like Russia at its conception.

Imaginary Revisiting

Was Nabokov attached to the memory of his native city? One wonders. In his prose, one finds no real trace of a deep-seated feeling, in striking contrast to the inexhaustible ardour and pain of his life-long recollections of the lost paradise of his country estate and its environs. His description of St Petersburg in the memoirs and elsewhere range from unromantic backdrop for romantic trysts – 'The Hermitage, St Petersburg's Louvre, offered nice nooks, especially in a certain hall on the ground floor' (*SM*, 561) – to mildly poetic impressions – ice cracking up on the river in Lent, yachts creaking in the harbour at Easter[6] – to slight mocking – 'Le Jardin d'Eté, a public park on the Neva embankment, with avenues of crow-haunted shade trees (imported elms and oaks) and noseless statues of Greek deities (made in Italy); there, a hundred years [after Onegin], I, too, was walked by a tutor' (*EO*, II, 41). St Petersburg receives very scant treatment in *The Defense* (1929–30), where the boy Luzhin is walked invariably along the same St Petersburg streets, in a narrow triangle: Nevski Avenue, the Embankment near the Winter Palace, and back home. It is remarkable that Nabokov's biographer sketches a picture of St Petersburg's architecture and cultural life that is richer in visual and factual detail than anything Nabokov himself wrote on the subject in prose, counting even his commentaries to *Eugene Onegin*.[7] Perhaps the largest space he accords the city's wondrous layout is in

---

[5] Victor Fet, 'A Few Notes on Nabokov's Childhood Entomology', in Stephen H. Blackwell and Kurt Johnson (eds.), *Fine Lines: Vladimir Nabokov's Scientific Art* (New Haven, CT and London: Yale University Press, 2016), 221.

[6] See esp. the beginning of *Pnin*'s ch. 7.

[7] See Brian Boyd, *Vladimir Nabokov: The Russian Years* (Princeton: Princeton University Press, 1990), 36. In verse, however, Nabokov set his fresh and fierce nostalgia in the picturesque iambic tetrameters

chapter 9 of his memoirs, where he gives a three-quarters-of-a-page detail of his daily quarter-of-an-hour ride by motorcar from home to school (this account rings more lyrical in the Russian version).

The hero of *Look at the Harlequins!*, a writer of genius with a chronic disease, shares with his maker more than all three initials of his Russian name and most of his books' plots: their childhood memories overlap almost completely. He makes a brief incognito sally behind the Iron Curtain in the late 1960s and finds himself wandering about Leningrad, 'idly trying to derive some emotional benefit from my being born there almost three-quarters of a century ago' (*LATH*, 718). What follows is a most remarkable confession, full of deliberate exaggerations and diminuendos, that explains why in the final version of his autobiography, *Speak, Memory* (1967), the country-to-city descriptive ratio is about twenty to one, while the emotional, beyond comparison. It explains also why the narrator of 'The Visit to the Museum' (1939), on being transported magically across the forbidden terminus, shudders from cold terror on finding himself in the streets of the former St Petersburg, whereas the hero of the 1927 poem mentioned above struggles with lump-in-the-throat love of recognition even as he is led to be shot at the edge of a ravine near his estate; or why the hero of the untitled 1926 story who risks his life venturing into the USSR to catch a glimpse of his country manor apparently does not care to see his city house.[8]

> Either because it could never get over the presence of the bog on which a popular bully had built it, or for some other reason (nobody, according to Gogol, knows), St Petersburg was no place for children. I must have passed there insignificant parts of a few Decembers, and no doubt an April or two; but at least a dozen winters of my nineteen pre-Cambridge ones were spent on Mediterranean or Black Sea coasts. As to summers, to my young summers, all of them had bloomed for me on the great country estates of my family. Thus I realized with silly astonishment that, except for picture postcards ..., I had never seen my native city in June or July. Its aspect, therefore, evoked no thrill of recognition; it was an unfamiliar, if not utterly foreign, town (*LATH*, 718).

Nabokov liked, *po staroi pamiati* ('by the old memory,' a Russian saying implying an indulgent view of things long past that one might now judge

---

of a longer poem 'Peterburg' (1921) – see note 16 – and in a beautiful *dinggedicht* 'Ut Pictura Poesis' (1926), which can be read as an epilogue to 'The Visit to the Museum'.

[8] The original was published in *Esquire* (Moscow), no. 110 (May 2015), 70–73. An English translation had appeared slightly earlier as 'The Man Stopped', tr. Gennady Barabtarlo, *Harper's Magazine*, March 2015, 62–64.

differently), Andrey Bely's *Peterburg*, but himself never lets his fiction dwell in St Petersburg for long. He does revisit it in his first and last novels. But in *Mary* (1926) the city does not appear even as a sketch, only as an implied back scenery: in chapter 9, his hero's and heroine's addresses are mentioned in passing '(he lived on the English Quay, she on Caravan Street)', followed, as soon as the parenthesis closes, by a fresh recollection of the past summer in the country: '. . . both recalled the paths through the park, the smell of fallen leaves, as being something unimaginably dear . . .' (*Mary*, 72). In *The Defense*, he devotes a few pages to the description of St Petersburg's grid that fit well young Luzhin's mapping mind, with the Admiralty as the focal point and the Fortress of SS Peter and Paul a place to be far from at noon, when its cannon went off, booming the time.

Wartime Blok

'The Petersburg dandy in aesthetic and intellectual matters', Edmund Wilson remarked disapprovingly.[9] A childhood memorable more for the summers spent in the countryside and the winters abroad than for the demi-seasons in the city; the school years overcast, just as were Pushkin's a hundred years earlier, by a great war, but unlike Pushkin's cut short by a cataclysm that ousted Nabokov to the south and overseas – these biographical facts scarcely agree with the image of a metropolitan dandy in any matters, least of all aesthetic.

In the summer before Russia was plunged into a war from which it never emerged, Nabokov began to compose his first verses. Blok's poem of September 1st 1914, rated recently as 'perhaps the main Russian poem about WWI',[10] was rejected by *Rech* (Speech), a leading liberal Petrograd (St Petersburg's name was Russified on 18/31 August that year) daily, co-published by Nabokov's father, who in wartime was a militia ensign and for the three summer months in 1915 served as an aide-de-camp. The poem was evidently deemed unpatriotic even by the left-leaning. Fyodor, the hero of *The Gift*, closest to his author in aesthetic and intellectual matters, failed to impart his enthusiasm for Blok to his father, whose tastes were staidly classical and who considered '*avant-garde* verse' rubbish (*Gift*, 146). This episode could well have had a biographical echo, of which there are many in the novel. In chapter 11 of *Drugie berega*, in yet another part that differed from the English version, Nabokov writes that already in the

[9] From an unpublished manuscript, quoted in Gennady Barabtarlo, *Aerial View* (New York: Peter Lang, 1993), 278.

[10] Maria Stepanova, *Kommersant-Weekend*, 22 August 2014, 14.

summer of 1915 one could discern 'distant backstage rumblings of thunder in the poems by Alexander Blok'.[11] Blok was one of the exceptionally few eminent writers who were born, bred and buried in St Petersburg.

A View from the Oriel

The full firestorm soon erupted, sending Nabokov, along with millions of Russians, on a life-long wandering. One dull Wednesday two months before he left St Petersburg forever, he penned a letter to a classmate in light verse remarkable not for its poetic quality but for its date: 25 October 1917. The breezy jocularity of much of the letter gives way to graver matters: scattered gunshots were coming from the street under the poet's oriel window in 47 Morskaya, shells ricocheting off the lampposts, the apothecaries shuttering up. It is perhaps idle, if tempting, to charge these facile lines with unbidden significance. And yet for Nabokov the day of Russia's doom was forever connected with this bit of ill-at-ease versifying, sitting three storeys above the battle scene, like a romanticised king about to abdicate and escape in the midst of a raging sedition, an awkward prototype in the series of Nabokov's *solorum regum*. Many years on, he recalled that overture to the dreadful cacophony of the riot staged by the 'gray ragtag people'.[12] And it was the crackle of the random gunfire in the port of Sevastopol that would be the last sound of Russia that Nabokov heard, while playing chess with his father on board the freighter *Nadezhda* (Speranza). This detail is absent from both English versions of the memoirs, too.[13] The ship was aptly and cruelly named, as hope was to become the refugees' only remaining investment in Russia, reviewed annually with ever-diminishing returns.[14]

"Nadezhda, I Shall Then Be Back When the True Batch Outboys the Riot"

The swallowtail of *Speak, Memory*, dislodged from its habitus, one of its spurs missing, skimming and hopping over the continents and straits and

---

[11] *Drugie berega*, 197 (my translation). Cf. *SM*, 554.
[12] 'Nabokov's Reliquary Poem', published in the original and in English in *Aerial View*, 245–53.
[13] See *Drugie berega*, 217.
[14] One wonders whether Nabokov recalled the ship's name when in 1966 he translated, as an exercise in metric-semantic exactness, Bulat Okujava's 'Sentimental Ballad' which begins: 'Speranza, I'll be coming back / The day the bugler sounds retreat' (*VV*, 359–65) (a trickier homophonic rendition of these lines was entered in *Ada*, 330).

mountain ranges could make a good emblem for a new Nabokov coat of arms. *Patriam meam mecum porto*, could be its neatly alliterative device. In the 1950s, the edge of the memory of the loss began to dull, the memory itself transfusing into a masterful image of it – a memory committed to memory commandeered by imagination. Occasionally, the crunch returned, as when the blurry grayscale pictures of remembered places, snapped by an admirer whose skills were no match to Eberling's, reached Nabokov from the USSR. The pictures arrived exactly fifty years after he had left his rioting hometown for good, and in what turned out to be one of his very last Russian poems he pensively shuffles those photographs, recognising in the last two the family estates, the two points of the triangle whose sides limned the Russia he took along and remembered, and the map of which he put on the flyleaf of every edition of *Speak, Memory*: 'This is Batovo. This is Rozhestveno' ('S serogo severa', *PP*, 148–49) – not 'this is Morskaya street, that – Mokhovaya' – even though there were probably pictures of his former St Petersburg house and the former Tenishev School in the batch as well. The third and dearest point, his estate Vyra, had been burnt down.

In November of 1964, he recorded a dream in which he was dictating to his wife a new version of *The Gift*, where he 'subtly introduced' a 'secret strain' into the theme of nostalgia like none had done: '. . .*before* anybody had left forever those avenues and fields, a sense of never-returning was already inscribed into them'.[15]

As mentioned earlier, Nabokov was one of the very few prominent artists who happened to have been born in St Petersburg. Yet most of the writers who came to reside there, died there. Nabokov, reversing that tradition as well, was to be buried two thousand versts away from the city, then long redubbed, defiled, forbidden, strange.

> I'm not alone. Sleepless we wander
> the earth, yet know: though buried now,
> it'll rise again, and all about it
> will be harmonious, joyous, new . . .
> But our old city, our very own,
> we'll never see again.[16]

---

[15] *Insomniac Dreams: Experiments with Time by Vladimir Nabokov*, compiled, edited, and with commentaries by Gennady Barabtarlo (Princeton and Oxford: Princeton University Press, 2017), 66.

[16] 'Peterburg', *Rul'* (Berlin), 17 July 1921, 2. My translation.

CHAPTER 9

Cambridge

Beci Carver

In 1904, when Nabokov was being read Frances Hodgson Burnett's *Little Lord Fauntleroy* (1885) by his English governess, Miss Clayton, he would have been less likely to identify with Fauntleroy's apprehension in being transplanted from America to England than to treat the story as a canvas for his own fantasies of becoming English. Not only was he surrounded by the 'products of Anglo-Saxon civilization' in St Petersburg in the 1900s and early 1910s – including, in addition to *Little Lord Fauntleroy* and Miss Clayton, Pears Soap, Golden Syrup, blazers and 'talcum-white tennis balls' (*SM*, 423) – he was also, at the time, fascinated by the sheer unRussianness of the English language. In *Speak, Memory* (1967), he remembers a version of himself 'repeating, in a kind of zestful, copious, and deeply gratifying incantation, the English word "childhood"' (*SM*, 374), as if the sound were uniquely performative of his condition. Then, when his family fled from revolutionary Russia in 1919, England recommended itself as a refuge from political extremism. Circumstances engineered themselves in such a way that he should have been as 'intellectually at home' in England as he later imagined himself to be in America (*SO*, 10). Nevertheless, the accounts of his college years at Cambridge in his essay, 'Cambridge' (1921), his poem, 'The University Poem' (1926), his autobiography, *Speak, Memory* (1967) and in Brian Boyd's biography cast him as a misfit in England. In this essay, I will provide grist for an alternative viewpoint.

Nabokov was certainly outnumbered by Englishmen when he arrived at Trinity in 1919, but the view that he spent his degree consumed by an 'exile's sadness' – as he puts it in 'The University Poem' (*Poems*, 31) – is troubled by the description of him under 'Nabokoff, V.' in *The Trinity Magazine*'s 'Who's Who' of June 1922 as: 'A welcome visitor who has made the College his home and our language his own.'[1] In the context of this directory, Nabokov differs from the Russian student 'Mrosovsky, P.', who advertises his

---

[1] 'Who's Who', *The Trinity Magazine* (June 1922), 80.

anomalousness either by opting out of college life and 'draw[ing] his curtains' or by 'play[ing] bowls the wrong way up . . . '[2] Mrosovsky may have been the inspiration for Sebastian Knight's confusion as to whether tennis requires a 'stick' in *The Real Life of Sebastian Knight* (1941) (*RLSK*, 35), whereas Nabokov's own flair for tennis and football aligned him with his English peers. Nabokov also arguably betrays his familiarity with the sports pages of *The Trinity Magazine* by filching the image of the tennis champion E. C. Francis' 'dog-like devotion to seemingly impossible balls' in 'The Lawn Tennis' section of May 1921; in *Lolita* (1955), Humbert Humbert reflects on Lolita's 'inordinately prehensile' tennis stroke (*Lolita*, 217).[3] Moreover, in addition to being typically Trinitarian in his enthusiasm for ball games, Nabokov was relatively typical in his foreignness in pre-war Trinity, when the prestige of internationally renowned dons like the mathematician and philosopher A. N. Whitehead and the electrophysiologist E. A. Adrian 'acted as a magnetic force to attract gifted men from all over the world'.[4] Both Trinity's fellowship and its undergraduate corpus were losing their old homogeneity in the 1920s, as the application process was adapted to accommodate overseas scholars and students.[5] Trinity offered the young Indian mathematician S. Ramanujan a job on the basis that he was a 'genius of an untrained and self taught kind', as if his very unexaminability were proof of his distinction.[6] Something of the romance of identifying ability regardless of background also seems reflected in the variety of surnames in 'Who's Who',[7] while the introduction of Anthropology and Oriental Studies as academic subjects hints at a broader curiosity about cultural difference.[8] Nabokov opens his account of his Cambridge years in *Speak, Memory* with an anecdote that presents his tutor E. Harrison and himself as novices at cultural integration; Nabokov upsets Harrison's tea and Harrison tactlessly pronounces 'it a fine idea to have one "White Russian" lodge with another' (*SM*, 582). But Harrison's role as Senior Tutor and his tendency to overcommit himself – he was owed more than any of the other tutors by the Tuition Fund of 1920–21,[9] and was overdue a holiday – meant that he was at least sufficiently exposed to different kinds of 'White Russians' to have no excuse for philistinism.

[2] Ibid.
[3] 'Lawn Tennis', *The Trinity Magazine* (May 1921), 92.
[4] R. Robson, 'Epilogue', in G. M. Trevelyan, *Trinity College: An Historical Sketch* (Cambridge: Cambridge University Press, 2011), 112.
[5] See 'Dominion and Colonial Exhibitions, November 1921', *Trinity College Council Reports*, 117.
[6] *Trinity College Council Reports*, 122.
[7] See 'Who's Who', 75–84.
[8] See 'Private: For the Master and Fellows Only', *Trinity College Council Reports*, 111.
[9] *Trinity College Council Reports*, 96.

Nabokov cites his first tea with Harrison as one of the 'weird theatricals' at Cambridge which he made a habit of 'embarrass[ing]' himself by failing to perform smoothly (*SM*, 581), but it was by no means unusual to find oneself stumbling over the bizarre customs of Trinity's older members. *The Trinity Magazine* has a section called 'Interviews with Famous Men' devoted to the comedy of awkward meetings with dons – including the Senior Dean, who would confound his student guests as well as the staff at High Table by 'mov[ing] restlessly from one chair to another in search, as he said, of a clean place . . .'[10] and the historian G. T. Lapsley, who renders his interviewers doubly redundant by asking his own questions and answering on behalf of everyone. Lapsley's conversational methods may have derived from Harvard, where he did his PhD, but his sense of 'appearing to the younger generation as rococco' is Trinitarian in its awareness of the tension between behavioural archaisms and the manners of incoming undergraduates.[11] However, that Nabokov was prepared to be convinced by some Trinity traditions is suggested by the appearance of one of his English poems in *The Trinity Magazine*.

'Home' appears in the issue in which the magazine 'reviv[es]' itself from obsolescence,[12] and is characteristic of other poetic contributions of the early 1920s in its regular rhyme and rhythm and slightly old-fashioned syntax (e.g. 'lonesome was my soul').[13] There is an irony to the statement: 'My home magnificent is but a word' in the context of an English poem by a Russian émigré writer that potentially hints at a wryness in his attitude towards the odd, arbitrary necessity of writing in English for English readers,[14] but the fact that he also took the magazine seriously is implied by a letter of November 18th 1920 to his mother, in which he basks in the 'hero[ic]' sensation of seeing his work in print.[15] Moreover, if we read the poem in conjunction with the Russian essay he wrote the following year, entitled 'Cambridge', the intense nostalgia for Russia which forms the basis of both may seem counterbalanced in the poem by his decision to write in English. Where the essay pictures him 'mumbling' in English and 'per-plexedly smiling',[16] the poem shows him capable of modelling himself on A. E. Housman – the Trinity professor and author of *The Shropshire Lad*

[10] 'Interviews with Famous Men: Mr Simpson', *The Trinity Magazine* (November 1920), 14.
[11] 'Interviews with Famous Men: Mr Lapsley', *The Trinity Magazine* (November 1921), 12.
[12] 'Editorial', *The Trinity Magazine* (November 1920), 1.
[13] Nabokoff, 'Home', *The Trinity Magazine* (November 1920), 26.
[14] Ibid.
[15] Brian Boyd, *Vladimir Nabokov: The Russian Years* (Princeton: Princeton University Press, 1990), 179.
[16] Vladimir Nabokov, *Rasskazy, Priglashenie na kazn', esse, interv'iu, retsenzii* (Moscow: Kniga, 1989), 339.

(1896). Nabokov's exact rhymes (e.g. 'gems'/'stems', 'waves'/'knaves', 'kissed'/'mist'),[17] his marching beat and his rustic setting repeat the formulae of Housman's aesthetic, while they lack Housman's signature lilt and fluency, with the effect that, as V writes of Sebastian Knight, 'Nabokoff' reads as 'trying to out-England England' and making a fool of himself in the process (*RLSK*, 35). But the conscientiousness of his imitation of Housman, especially when juxtaposed with the literariness of the article he published in *The Entomologist*, 'A Few Notes on Crimean Lepidoptera' (1920), point to an investment in or at least an appetite for flexing his muscles as an English writer, which runs counter to the pessimism of 'Cambridge' and to the obscure reflection in 'The University Poem' that 'to think of poetry was harmful in those years' (*Poems*, 33). The article revels in the sonorousness of partial rhyme-sounds – like, 'lime, elm, ash, mountain ash' in a list of tree names; or, 'lunules', 'on', 'margin', 'hind', 'wings', 'hinged' and 'orange' in the beautiful formulation: 'two upper lunules on the outer margin of hind wings are hinged with orange.'[18] Here, Nabokov may be said to use the English language to propel himself away from England's 'Venetian languor' ('Cambridge')[19] and 'perpetual murk[iness]' (*Poems*, 32) into the more congenial scenes of his youth, but he also reveals his capacity to think imaginatively in English as well as his consciousness of the cachet attached to defining himself as a Trinity man; he ends with the unusually involved identifier: 'Trinity College, R. Great Court, Cambridge.'[20]

Nabokov began his career at Trinity as a scientist, and the analytic precision of his article arguably reflects the pedagogical emphasis given to histology at Cambridge in the 1920s. For instance, some contemporary lepidopterists complained that Nabokov prioritised 'description' over 'synthesis',[21] but this priority would have seemed appropriate to his lecturers at Cambridge. Trinity had led the way in biological taxonomy since the late nineteenth century with the work of Michael Foster, whose use of microscopy to analyse the mechanics of frogs' muscles potentially provides a context for Nabokov's account of the dissection of a frog's 'hidden muscle' in the Russian poem, 'Biology' (1921) – which he wrote in a Cambridge laboratory. Foster had long gone by the time Nabokov matriculated, but his

[17] Nabokov, 'Home', 26.
[18] Nabokov, 'A Few Notes on Crimean Lepidoptera', *The Entomologist*, 53/681 (February 1920), 29 and 33.
[19] Nabokov, *Rasskazy*, 338.
[20] Nabokov, 'A Few Notes on Crimean Lepidoptera', 33.
[21] Robert Michael Pyle, 'Between Climb and Cloud', in *Nabokov's Butterflies*, ed. Brian Boyd and Robert Michael Pyle (Boston, MA: Beacon Press, 2000), 63.

legacy remained strong. His obituarist and successor at Trinity, John Newport Langley, also gives central prominence to a frog's cells in his much reissued textbook, *Practical Histology* (1901); and Langley's most influential book, *The Autonomic Nervous System* (1921), draws its main evidence from microscopic slides, and understands itself as a contribution to nomenclature. Langley writes: 'I felt the need of a new term for the system of nerves I was dealing with',[22] and the term 'autonomic' meets the case by proposing a rationale for why the particular sets of nerves responsible for controlling involuntary mechanisms (like sneezing and sexual arousal) 'have a different degree of effect on the different cells on which they act.'[23] The example that crystallises his theory derives from a series of experiments with the effects of nicotine, and reveals a self-contained sequence of nervous reactions running from the mouth to the heart.[24] That Nabokov had heard of Langley is implied by the random appearance of a Professor Langley in *Looking at the Harlequins!* (1974), whom Vadim Vadimovich N. 'dislike[s]' (*LATH*, 662), but whom Nabokov vaguely favours by partnering him with one of Lolita's proxies, Dolly Borg – as if to invoke the coincidence by which Trinity's Langley was married to a namesake of Véra Nabokov (namely, Vera Kathleen Forsythe-Grant). The most vivid instance of Nabokov's debt to Trinity's Langley is the nervous circuit with which *Lolita* begins; Humbert exults: 'Lolita, light of my life, fire of my loins. My sin, my soul. Lo-lee-ta: the tip of the tongue taking a trip of three steps down the palate to tap, at three, on the teeth' (*Lolita*, 7). 'Lo-lee-ta' defines a nervous energy moving from Humbert's mouth to his loins, which affects him like nothing else.

That Cambridgean science failed to secure Nabokov's committed attention in 1920 is suggested by his decision to switch to Russian and French in his second year, though this restlessness is also symptomatic of his uncertainty in choosing a career. When his Oxonian friend Gleb Struve advised him to apply to Cambridge in 1919, it was because he pictured himself as an entomologist, but he was never clear in his mind about where his vocation lay.[25] A positive spin on his change of direction might emphasise the freedom that Trinity gave him to backtrack, as well as the range of options that awaited him when he did. His choice of Modern and Medieval Languages was relatively conventional, but his awareness of the widening scope of Trinity's curricula is reflected in Sebastian Knight's decision to study English Literature – a new course which seemed radical to

---

[22] Langley, *The Autonomic Nervous System* (Cambridge: W. Heffer & Sons Ltd, 1921), 6.
[23] Langley, *The Autonomic Nervous System*, 57.
[24] Ibid.
[25] See Boyd, *Russian Years*, 166.

undergraduates and academics alike in neither requiring nor conferring traditional forms of expertise: English students were neither scientists nor linguists. Trinity specifically set out to 'encourage the study of English Literature' by 'paying the stipend of a Clark Lecturer' and funding 'research . . . towards the publication of books'.[26] In 1922, this appointment was made to the English poet, Walter de la Mare, with whom Nabokov admits to Edmund Wilson in a letter of 24 August 1942 he was 'much fascinated' (*NWL*, 87) while writing the poems that comprise *The Empyrean Path* (1923). In *Speak, Memory*, he imagines 'various contemporaneous ("Georgian") English verse patterns' running amok in his Russian verse structures 'like tame mice' (*SM*, 587), but these 'patterns' were not only contemporaneous *but coincident* with him while he remained at Trinity, in the form of de la Mare and Housman's poems; it is thus hard to imagine him not wanting to study English. Nabokov's ultimate decision to read Russian and French led to his discovery of the medieval chantefable *Aucassin and Nicolette*, and the poetry of Chretién de Troyes, with the exception of which it seems to Brian Boyd that his 'formal studies' left him cold.[27] And yet, the scholar whom Boyd credits with the feat of administering 'nearly all the Russian teaching at Cambridge'[28] appears to have fundamentally shaped his conception of fictional characters. Alexander Goudy writes of Leo Tolstoy's *Sevastopol* (1855) in a preface of 1916: 'The absence of a "hero" in the conventional literary sense, as a figure having the full sympathy of the author and serving as the focus of vision from which the whole is to be regarded, is not a mere accident; it is the symptom of a mental attitude.'[29] For years after the publication of *Lolita*, in interviews and essays, Nabokov sought to explain the trick by which he withheld his 'sympathy' from Humbert, leaving his novel empty at centre stage.

Nabokov's years at Cambridge were overshadowed by his nostalgia for Russia, while the death of his father in 1922 cast a further pall over the episode, both emotionally and practically. Contingency had lumbered him with a second class degree, in spite of his success in the first part of Tripos. However, by the time he left France for America in 1940, he was ready to reinvent himself as an Anglophone writer and thinker. Russia had drifted into the remote past; his exile remained a 'private tragedy' (*Lolita*, 298), but the shock of the first rupture had subsided. America's slightly warmer climate was also an inevitable draw for so outdoorsy an outsider. When he

---

[26] 'Ordinance XXI: The Clark Fund and Lectureship', *Trinity College Council Reports*, 95.
[27] Boyd, *Russian Years*, 174.
[28] Ibid.
[29] Alexander Goudy, 'Preface', in Leo Tolstoy, *Sevastopol*, ed. Alexander Goudy and E. Bullough (Cambridge: Cambridge University Press, 1916), xviii.

visited California in 1942, Wilson warned him: 'I have a fear ... you may become bewitched out there and never come back ... You know, it is like getting into Yeats's fairyland or under the Venusberg. The weather is fine every day, and the rest of the world seems very unreal' (*NWL*, 49). 'Getting into ... fairyland' is an impossible dream in Yeats' poem, 'The Man Who Dreamed of Fairyland' (1916), and to be 'under the Venusberg' is to be under Venus' spell: neither condition implies a solid grasp of reality, though both are synonymous with a rejection of 'the world' as 'unreal.' Nabokov was never sufficiently 'bewitched' to settle in California, but his tendency to insist on America's perfections – particularly from the distance of Montreux in the 1960s – had the effect that Wilson anticipates of rendering other homes unviable, including England. If Massachusetts became his Venusberg and Yeatsian fairyland, then, Nabokov's Cambridge suggests another kind of alternative dimension, where he flourished as a sportsman and found his feet as a writer and entomologist, but which he could not or would not romanticise in looking back.

Berlin

Stanislav Shvabrin

Essential as a privileged Russian childhood and British education were for Vladimir Nabokov, it was Berlin where he came of age as a writer and spent fifteen eventful, indeed formative, years. The studied detachment with which he regarded his German surroundings, however, belies this convenient linearity, confounding attempts to contextualise him with the aid of readily available geographical and cultural markers. Labelled by his émigré peers a quintessential 'Berliner', he resented the exigencies that confined him to 'the city of misfortunes and mishaps' where he attempted to encase himself in a cocoon of Russophone 'linguistic occlusion' until Hitler's ascent to power prompted Nabokov to trade his indifference for disgust. And yet what is customarily referred to as Nabokov's 'Russian' years – the 'antithetic' coil of his life's spiral, the most productive period of his Russian literary activity – might just as well be called the 'German' chapter of his biography. The time Nabokov spent in England and France before finding a safe haven in the United States is not reflected in his writing with anything resembling the comprehensiveness he affords his German environment. From *Mary* (1926) to *The Gift* (1937–38), every one of his novels and a good deal of his short stories, poems and plays dating from 1919 to 1940 teem with manifestly German minutiae. To some extent this may be attributed to the acuity of his perception. Unable and unwilling to turn a blind eye to his Berlin 'locus', this writer, exiled for eternity, fixed the existence of his dislodged compatriots against a variety of astutely observed and vividly captured German backdrops. So high is the fidelity of Nabokov's record of his Berlin surroundings, it has invited parallels with such connoisseurs of this city's demeanour and spirit as the painter Eduard Gaertner, the photographer Max Missmann and the novelist Alfred Döblin.

Small wonder then that a closer reading of Nabokov's Germany helps us catch a glimpse of a nuanced enough notion of this country while suggesting a greater degree of his involvement with its culture at large. To be sure, the torments visited upon the writer by his first-hand encounters with

Nazism were harrowing: aspiring Russian fascists killed his father; his brother, relatives by marriage and friends died at the hands of the Nazis; the regime directly threatened his Jewish wife and their son. In his introduction to *Bend Sinister* (1947), Nabokov acknowledged that the 'worlds of tyranny and torture' featured in the bleakest of his creations were inspired by his close observation of the natural habitat of 'jack-booted baboons' that was Nazi Germany; in *Speak, Memory*'s (1967) chapter 14, the meticulous capital punishment aficionado Dietrich lends Nabokov's utterly realistic, if most certainly composite, portrayal of a sadistic delectation in violence its unmistakable local colour. Grim and unforgettable as these impressions would have been, the variety of German contexts pertaining to Nabokov's personal circumstances indicates that his idea of the country could not be limited to his well-known, well-articulated loathing of Hitler's Third Reich. A Slavic scion of Teutonic Crusaders and Saxonian musicians, all his life Nabokov nurtured fond memories of pre–First-World-War Berlin, where he not only had his teeth straightened, but sensed his first sexual arousal – this event is commemorated by the 'double somersault with a Welsh waggle' that serves as a 'curtain raiser' on the theme of erotic desire in the memoir's chapter 10. As we gauge Nabokov's involvement with Berlin, it seems prudent not to ignore the wider spectrum of his German attitudes.

In Nabokov's case, the general modernist propensity towards supplanting realistic depiction of urban settings with multifaceted individual visions inspired by that milieu acquired particular relevance – and poignancy. The conundrum-like existence at the crossroads of transitory and elusive identities (its absurdity successfully rivalled that of Franz Kafka's Prague and James Joyce's continental exile) did not become for Nabokov a mere source of nostalgia, but rather that of inspiration which ensured the eventual triumph of his creativity. The best proof of this is in Nabokov's ability to observe, reflect and instil with individual significance his depictions of such evanescent socio-cultural loci as Russian Berlin and Weimar Germany during their heyday and disintegration.

Coupled with his cosmopolitan upbringing and polyglossia, Nabokov's inquisitive and imaginative mind equipped him with the means of distilling loss and displacement into art. While there is little doubt that the rarefied atmosphere of St Petersburg's linguistically and spatially mercurial upper classes was a perfect point of origin for someone like him, a different extinguished universe became his true birthplace as a writer. Given his interest in the interplay of disparate planes of being, it seems appropriate that his truly consequential compositions began to appear in the atmosphere of an intellectual construct rather than an actual place, as was the case with the parallel universe known as 'Russian Berlin'.

Much has been made of the chimerical quality of Nabokov's cityscapes. The validity of such interpretations appears to be borne out by Nabokov's own retrospective summation of his exilic experience in *Speak, Memory*:

> As I look back at those years of exile, I see myself, and thousands of other Russians, leading an odd but by no means unpleasant existence, in material indigence and intellectual luxury, among perfectly unimportant strangers, spectral Germans and Frenchmen in whose more or less illusory cities we, émigrés, happened to dwell. (*SM*, 594)

In his interviews, Nabokov repeatedly stressed the relative nature of subjectively experienced reality; in *Speak, Memory* this irony asserts itself when he shows that those same 'spectral' natives had most tangible means of imposing their will on presumptuous transients. What may seem unusual for those who derive their idea of Nabokov's attitude towards his surroundings exclusively from the interviews selected in *Strong Opinions* (1973) is his willingness and readiness to speak on behalf of his fellow émigrés, to employ not his signature first person singular, but rather that 'we' which effectively places him in the position of a spokesman for his community. That by the time Nabokov began his work on the earliest version of his memoir this community had long ceased to exist may make it sound doubly surreal, but this cannot distract us from recognising in this shift in his narrative voice a retrospective declaration of allegiance, a signal helping us contextualise this reference to his past as an evocation of an intellectual atmosphere he had every right to consider his true native element.

While the author of *Mary* may not have become 'a chronicler of the Russian diaspora' as the novel's critic Mikhail Osorgin wished, it is difficult to find a writer whose work encompasses a more durable portrait of that universe in all its misery and pathos. While such early stories as 'The Dragon' and 'A Guide to Berlin' (1924) may be said to articulate pointedly individual visions of their German background, the bulk of his Russian fiction features outstandingly true-to-life portrayals of the émigré predicament the author shared with his protagonists and members of his primary target audience alike. Not only Lev Ganin (*Mary*), Martin Edelweiss (*Glory*, 1931) and Fyodor Godunov-Cherdyntsev (*The Gift*), but also Alexander Luzhin (*The Defense*, 1929–30), Vanya Smurov (*The Eye*, 1930) and even Cincinnatus C. (*Invitation to a Beheading*, 1935–36) comprise a gallery of utterly believable portraits of the inhabitants of displaced communities caught in the act of trying to make sense of their destiny with regard to their kindred past and not-so-germane present. The same is true of a vast number of lesser-known characters, such as Olga, the heroine of the short story 'A Russian Beauty' (1934), or a flock of Russian Jews in 'Breaking the News' (1935). The unity of style alone cannot account for this impression of underlying consistency. What is it, then, that furnishes this multitude of different personalities with its unifying principle and provides it with a sense of shared purpose discernible in all of Nabokov's writing of the Berlin years?

With utmost candour, Nabokov defines it in his extra-literary pronouncements dating from the Berlin period. Thus 'The Jubilee' (1927), ostensibly a private opinion piece marking the first decade since the Bolshevik coup, crescendos into a formulation of a shared identity that provides the essayist, his fellow émigrés and, one senses, his Russian protagonists with a common reason for being:

> we have spilled ourselves all over the world – yet our wanderings are not always doleful, and a manly yearning for our motherland does not always interfere with our enjoying an alien country ... And although today it is obvious how different we all are, and although sometimes it seems to us that not one, but a thousand upon thousand Russias roam the world – now pathetic and bitter, now at war with each other – there exists, however, something that unites us, some kind of shared ambition, shared spirit that a future historian will comprehend and appreciate ... In that special Russia which invisibly surrounds, nourishes, upholds us, permeates our soul and colours our dreams, there is not a single law apart from the law of our love for her and there is no power apart from our own conscience ... Our dispersed country, our nomadic nation is fortified by this freedom, and some day we will be grateful to the blind Clio for giving us an opportunity to partake of that freedom and in exile obtain a particularly trenchant understanding and feeling for our native land. [*Sobr. soch.*, 2, 646–47; translation is mine]

This self-contained universe did not merely provide Nabokov with a congenial audience for his compositions or a market for his publications. It empowered him with a sense of belonging denied him by his nominal homeland and gave him a once-in-a-lifetime opportunity to take an active part in shaping it not only on his own, personal, but also on his community's behalf. Nabokov's habitual use of the first person plural in his pronouncements on the nature of his exilic experience indicates that he relished those occasions on which he could connect his own individual emotions with those felt by his readers and listeners. Addressing his fellow 'Berliners' in a 1931 public talk devoted to Alexander Pushkin, he deliberately abstained from the use of 'I' with the aim of conveying to his audience a sense that his deeply personal vision of the poet's legacy and its importance has universally Russian proportions and significance. This notion acquired particular urgency at a time when that once-lively encampment of nomads was about to be swept away and dispersed forever.

In comparison with the tangible historical continuity of its host city, Russian Berlin may well seem little more than an imaginary community that came in and out of existence within a brief period of time. It was its charged and polarised atmosphere, the unprecedented intellectual freedom enfolded in this shard of a recently imploded Russian universe, however, that summoned to life the writer and thinker Vladimir Sirin. Once he gained a foothold in it, Russian Berlin granted him an opportunity to take part in shaping its evolution and perpetuation well beyond its spatial and temporal boundaries ('Recruiting', a short story of 1935, reflects on the act of claiming artistic dominion over this world by an author-narrator who himself inalienably belongs to it). This may well be the most important aspect of the Russian-German context of his career and an explanation of why he found it so difficult to part with a metropolis for which he seemed to care so little.

Grounded in the certainty of his cultural bearings, from the convenient vantage point of an outsider Nabokov conducted his first extensive foray into the intimate spheres of his German characters in *King, Queen, Knave* (1928). A display of his growing capacity for overcoming the limitations of a solitary, culturally determined, consciousness by means of artistic imagination, this drama of foreign mores is rendered credible by the specificity of its historical context. The state of Kurt Dreyer's business affairs, his knack for capitalising on the opportunities offered by the economic tribulations of the early 1920s and his subsequent difficulties in navigating his way through the second half of the decade are proof of Nabokov's attention to the life of his alien abode and his deftness in putting his observations at the service of his overarching concerns and intuitions. His sensitive treatment of Dreyer's humour, curiosity and ingenuity – along with an awareness of this character's flaws – points towards his creator's readiness to appreciate the humanity of the German other without compromising his aversion to the sad circus of the Weimar-era *Polizeipräsidiums* as depicted in *Mary* and beyond. *Despair* (1934), with the would-be con artist and leader of the gullible Hermann at its centre, proves that Nabokov needed no crystal ball to foresee Germany's near future.

Nabokov's unsparing portrayals of proto-Nazi barbarity are set against its breeding ground in the Germany of his day ('The Leonardo' (1933), 'Cloud, Castle, Lake' (1941) and *Speak, Memory* are not the only exemplars of this theme), but the writer also dissects fascism's highbrow underpinnings further afield, for instance in the casual moral relativism of Professor Hagen's duplicitous geniality in *Pnin* (1957), whereas 'Conversation Piece, 1945' (orig. 'Double Talk' [1945]), sounds an alarm on fascism's ability to cling on to life despite its defeat on the battlefield. While Nabokov's revulsion at the sight of 'Hitler's grotesque and ferocious shadow' was capable of engendering such consummate depictions of cruelty and vulgarity, it would be an oversight to think that the creative energy that brought such visions to life was restricted to the solely 'negative' aspects of this capacity. It seems fitting that the writer who in his childhood derived so much pleasure from excellent German *Schmetterlingsbücher* should have created a moving paean to the kindred soul of a butterfly enthusiast hidden in the body of an ordinary Berlin shopkeeper ('The Aurelian' [1930]); in *The Gift* he gave his plenipotentiary Fyodor a lesson in how easily anti-German Russian sentiments may distract one from appreciating the grace and kindness of a slyly and delightfully arranged life.

During his stay in Berlin, Nabokov certainly paid heed to major German cultural events of his day. Freudianism's ascent to the forefront of contemporary intellectual discourse is but one striking example of this alertness; at least one major work of German literary expressionism left a lasting impression on the writer (D. Barton Johnson has shown that Nabokov's disgust at Leonhard Frank's *Bruder und Schwester* [1929] mutated into a cornerstone upon which the fictional premise of *Ada or Ardor* [1969] is raised). Are we to infer, then, that Nabokov's persistent protestations of indifference towards all things German are not to be taken at their face value?

While the extent of Nabokov's engagement with German culture has not been studied with exhaustive fullness, it would not be an overstatement to say that his art and thought could not and did not remain unaffected by his exposure to German literature and philosophy. A life-long admirer of the Russo-German metaphysical poet Afanasy Fet (1820–92), Nabokov came in close contact with the thought of Arthur Schopenhauer through Fet's mediation. Nabokov eagerly acknowledged his familiarity with Heinrich Heine; echoes of Heine's lyrics he read and translated prior to his departure from Russia persist well into *Look at the Harlequins!* (1974) and *The Original of Laura* (2009). At a crucial moment in Nabokov's early career Heine provided him with inspiration as he was confronted with the necessity to forge his identity as a poet of exile; after the dissolution of his engagement with Svetlana Siewert, he could not help but notice parallels between his plight and that of the author of 'Junge Leiden'.

In *The Gift*, Fyodor makes a caustic comment concerning the extinction of those German 'originals who used to teach natural history to Russian children' and wonders whether they had not been 'a special breed of Germans, for export to Russia' (*Gift*, 100). Fyodor's failure to encounter these fabulous creatures on Berlin streets suggests a tacit parallel with Nabokov's own view of the anti-evolutionary essence of the 'struggle for life'. As witnessed by Fyodor, German 'originals' would have been ill-equipped to meet the evolutionary challenge posed by the Schultzes and Schramms ('Cloud, Castle, Lake'), who were clearly outbreeding their meeker compatriots in the anticipation of one massive triumph of 'the grunting beast'. In a diversion from some of the harsher of Nabokov's pronouncements concerning Germany and its post–Second-World-War future, however, the apparently recessive gene of unassuming curiosity manages to emerge from the rubble and shame of the German twentieth century. It is epitomised by Paul Hentzner, an 'eccentric farmer of German extraction' and 'atavistic throwback to the curious German', who becomes John Shade's confident in *Pale Fire* (1962).

This instance of the survival of the weakest appears to be aligned with the twist Nabokov puts on the Hegelian triad in *Speak, Memory*. The possibility of such a synthesis, however, may be said to be predicated on Nabokov's integration into a broader context of German thought, on his first-hand familiarity not only with 'Nazist pseudo-efficiency' or his unwillingness to ignore the bathetic effects of Faustian passions, but also with the Goethean celebration of artistic memory and the Heinean brand of lyricism in a perfect fulfilment of the major Nabokovian dictum according to which there is no unseeing something once it has been seen.

CHAPTER II

Paris

John Burt Foster, Jr.

Over the period in Western literature from Pushkin's time onwards that meant the most to Nabokov, artists and writers thronged to Paris, drawn by its unmatched prestige for cultural innovation. The painters from all parts congregating in Montmartre or Montparnasse come to mind, followed by the American 'Lost Generation' of Gertrude Stein and Hemingway. Among analysts of Paris' magnetism one thinks of Walter Benjamin's sense of Paris as capital of the nineteenth century and of Pascale Casanova on its role in creating a 'world republic of letters'. Nabokov, however, with his resistance to myth-making, did not share this grand vision of the 'City of Light'.

On a personal level, the biggest crisis in his marriage came from a Parisian love affair, and the periods between October 1938 and May 1940 that he and his family lived there were difficult. Lodgings were hard to find, pricey and cramped, and the French bureaucracy could be frustrating for stateless émigrés. *The Real Life of Sebastian Knight* (1941), his first novel in English, which he wrote during these years in France, mentions the graffiti 'Death to the Jews' and '*Vive le front populaire*' in a Paris phone booth (*RLSK*, 154), signs of the venomous ideological conflicts in the 1930s, with worse to come. Nabokov's brother Sergei, who had not managed to flee Paris before the Germans arrived in 1940, eventually perished in a concentration camp. The author, when free to choose francophone places to live, preferred the Riviera; eventually he settled in Montreux, in the French-speaking part of Switzerland.

Still, Nabokov did know French well, and Flaubert and Proust were favourites. However, other French novelists like Balzac and Stendhal were 'detestable mediocrities' (*SM*, 511), and he was impatient with trends like realism and surrealism that had flourished in Paris. Given the demands of his writing and his discomfort with groups, he preferred to remain aloof from or respond polemically to many of the city's literary coteries, Russian as well as French. Yet at three turning points in his career, Nabokov discovered that he needed Paris. Overall, his mixed attitude towards this city bears out Patrice Higonnet's contention that during the twentieth century Paris still attracted attention as 'the mythological focal point of the present', but that its appeal was dwindling.[1]

At specific junctures, whether he was writing in Russian, French or English, Nabokov worked closely with Paris as a literary market place. His first writings appeared in Berlin, home to many Russians who left the Soviet Union, where his father had edited a Russian newspaper and where Nabokov moved after leaving Cambridge University. But by the later 1920s Paris was the dominant centre for the emigration. In October 1929, when his third novel *The Defense* (1929–30) began to be serialised in *Sovremennye zapiski* (*Contemporary Annals*), the leading Russian journal in Paris, Nabokov had responded to the shift, and this novel helped establish his stature as the emigration's best young writer. Throughout the 1930s he continued to publish there (though many works still had German settings), and he also came to Paris for public readings. He befriended several Russian writers there, especially the poet Vladislav Khodasevich, but he resisted trends, known as the 'Paris School', that were aligned with Dostoevsky and related mystical-spiritual currents.

When visiting Paris, Nabokov often stayed with Ilya Fondaminsky, the patron of *Sovremennye zapiski* and one of its editors, a Russian Jew Nabokov memorialised as 'a saintly and heroic soul' (*SM*, 607). They had different literary tastes, however, which surfaced when the journal refused to serialise chapter 4 of *The Gift* (1937–38), Nabokov's best Russian novel. The irreverent, parodic tone of this long biography of Chernyshevsky, a hero for generations of Russian radicals, collided with the politics of the journal's left-leaning but non-communist editors. Fondaminsky's death at Auschwitz, which brought his Paris-based support of émigré cultural activities to a lamentable end, coincided with the general demise of émigré Russian literature during the Second World War.

Nabokov had sensed this looming crisis for his continued work in Russian. Encouraged by translations of his fiction into French, he began exploring the option of writing in that language. Here he joined a Franco-Russian tradition beginning in the eighteenth century with Catherine the Great, the poet and translator Vasily Trediakovsky and some aristocratic sojourners in old-regime Paris. Among later exemplars of this trend, Nabokov singled out Mme de Ségur, born Rostopchine, who was a prolific

---

[1] Patrice Higonnet, *Paris: Capital of the World*, trans. Arthur Goldhammer (Cambridge, MA: Belknap Press, 2002), 434.

author of nineteenth-century children's books in French (*SM*, 421). Focusing on the period between the world wars, Elizabeth Beaujour has discussed both Nabokov and Elsa Triolet (1896–1970) and, more briefly, several other figures in the 'Paris Emigration'. With *Sebastian Knight* in mind, however, she concedes that if Nabokov 'did dabble in French', it was more significant that in these years he 'wrote his first novel in English'.[2]

Nabokov's French output may have been modest, but it did appear in significant venues. Marking the centennial of Pushkin's death, he placed a lengthy essay, 'The Real and the Plausible', in the *Nouvelle revue française* (*NRF*), France's premier literary journal.[3] Another journal, the short-lived *Mesures*, printed the story 'Mademoiselle O', an autobiographical piece on the Swiss governess who taught him French. In an April 1937 photograph of some of this journal's associates, Nabokov stands (though at some distance) from three notable French writers – Jean Paulhan (editor of the *NRF*), poet Henri Michaux, and anthropologist and autobiographer Michel Leiris.[4] The separation may be emblematic of Nabokov's situation vis-à-vis literary circles in Paris. At the time, during the longest of his three visits to the city from Berlin (*LTV*, 280–381), he was combining public readings before both Russian and French audiences with frantic and overly optimistic efforts to develop contacts with French editors and publishers.

In general, though Nabokov's time as an author in French was brief, it would prove fruitful after he moved to the United States in 1940. The memoir of his governess and the Pushkin essay were foundations for his much-admired autobiography *Speak, Memory* (1967) and for his controversial translation of Pushkin's *Eugene Onegin* (1964). Thus, though his Russian novels are impressive for their many innovations in style and subject, his language crisis in Paris during the waning 1930s went on to inspire two major projects from outside fiction entirely in the decades to come.

Other connections with this period are evident in Nabokov's later strong exceptions to Jean-Paul Sartre and André Malraux, who had written for the *NRF* in the 1930s and went on to win major reputations outside France. As with the Paris émigrés, Nabokov condemned Dostoevsky's

[2] *Alien Tongues: Bilingual Russian Writers of the 'First' Emigration*, (Ithaca, NY, and New York: Cornell University Press, 1989), 88.

[3] See Vladimir Nabokoff-Sirin, 'Pouchkine, ou le vrai et le vraisemblable,' *La nouvelle revue française*, 48 (1937), 362–78. For the English translation, see Vladimir Nabokov, 'Pushkin, or the Real and the Plausible', tr. Dmitri Nabokov, *New York Review of Books*, 31 March 1988, 38–42.

[4] For the photograph, see Brian Boyd, *Vladimir Nabokov: The Russian Years* (Princeton: Princeton University Press, 1990), following p. 446.

influence on these two novelists/intellectuals, now for inspiring novels of mere 'ideas'; he also denounced their sympathies with the Soviet Union. When Sartre reviewed *Despair* (1934) in French translation in 1939, he had linked the deluded protagonist Hermann to the author as a displaced Russian. Nabokov's preface to the novel's English retranslation (1965) targeted this 'remarkably silly' thesis along with Sartre's ties to both existentialism and communism (*Despair*, viii). In 1949, reviewing *Nausea* (1938), he condemned this first novel of Sartre's for drawing on 'Dostoevski at his worst' and placing 'arbitrary philosophic fancy' before the creation of 'a work of art' (*SO*, 229, 230). Malraux's *Man's Fate* (1933) prompted a disagreement with Edmund Wilson, the influential critic who helped promote Nabokov in the United States. In 1946, to Wilson's letter calling Malraux 'probably the greatest contemporary writer' (*NWL*, 201), Nabokov replied that he was 'a very decent fellow' but no true novelist (*NWL*, 202). Dostoevsky's role in fostering novels of ideas was again an issue along with Malraux's cliché-laden style and his mistakes about Russian politics. However, Nabokov missed a convergence relevant in 1946, since even as he sent his own *Bend Sinister* to the printer, his letter to Wilson used Dostoevsky's *The Devils* to critique Malraux (*NWL*, 202–03) but did not note the searing depictions in all three novels of lethal, ideology obsessed politics.

For Nabokov, these writers fell short of Flaubert and Proust from earlier generations, whose novels were genuine works of art. His mixed views of Paris, however, show up in his seeming neglect of the city's role in their writings. With Flaubert's *Sentimental Education* (1869), he bypasses the richly evocative scenes of Paris that compensate for the provincial narrowness of *Madame Bovary*. Instead, he savours a curt sentence summing up its protagonist's eventual disillusionment, 'Il voyagea' ('he travelled').[5] To be sure, the mastery of style in the abrupt shift of sentence rhythm and radical elision of descriptive detail probably meant the most to Nabokov. Yet in this appreciation, Flaubert's complex vision of Paris fades into the remote distance just as the St Petersburg of Nabokov's past was sealed off from the much-displaced adult. In Proust, the adult narrator's melancholy sense that his obsessions with Parisian high society have stifled the freshness of perception he had once known in the country and by the ocean may play into Nabokov's preference for 'the first half of *In Search of Lost Time*' (*SO*, 57), with its vivid evocations of those earlier experiences. A similar regret for lost immediacy accounts for his contention that, in the moonlit scene in *War and*

---

[5] See the first sentence in part III, chapter 6, of Flaubert's novel.

Peace where Andrey overhears Natasha singing at an open window, Tolstoy was Proust's precursor (*LL*, 220). Not only do the passage's vivid sense impressions generate figurative meanings as in Proust; Andrey's jaded worldliness set against Natasha's joyous receptivity to the night parallels the contrast between the Proustian narrator's social anxieties in Paris and his earlier openness to experience, at both the village of Combray and the seaside resort of Balbec.

Fifteen years after leaving France, Nabokov was again negotiating with a Paris publisher, this time about a manuscript that was too edgy for American firms. This work, of course, was *Lolita* (1955), whose predecessor in turning to France to circumvent Anglophone scruples had been Joyce's *Ulysses*. The novel initially appeared with Olympia Press, which (as Nabokov soon learned) lacked the reputation and the integrity of his earlier Paris contacts. Advertised with off-colour titles, *Lolita* had the unusual distinction, for a book in English, of being banned in France, but three years later, when it finally came out in the United States, it was a best-seller. In October 1959, Nabokov returned to Paris for the first time since 1940, to be honoured at a grand reception for the novel's French translation.

He had come full circle, since pre-war Paris was where he had the disturbing idea of a man marrying a mother to gain access to her daughter and wrote (in Russian this time) the novella *The Enchanter* (1991). Now, after a detour via the United States and a French publisher of dubious merit, that idea's growth into a novel had granted Nabokov an entry into the mythic Paris of daring innovation in the arts. Yet even as *Lolita* sparked debates about literary freedom of expression, its deeply Russian elements alongside its recent Americana set limits to Paris' standing to bestow international recognition.

Nabokov's creative work casts added light on his ambivalence towards Paris, which can be concisely tracked in *Nabokov's Dozen* (1958), released a month after *Lolita*. Here is not the place to discuss how its stories and memoirs acquired their forms in this book, after being written, rewritten and revised at several places and in two or three languages.[6] Overall, they give a composite sense of modern Paris up to 1940 and beyond: the comfortable Belle Époque city around 1910, the controversial centre for avant-garde movements in the 1920s, and the anxious French capital before World War II, with the author's post-war outlook peeping through.

---

[6] Citations will refer to *Stories*, but the Paris date-lines mentioned below appear in *Nabokov's Dozen: A Collection of Thirteen Stories* (Garden City, NY: Anchor/Doubleday, 1984), 38 and 196.

'Spring in Fialta' (1936), the book's opening story, ends with a 1938 Paris date-line, but consists of vignettes set in Russia and all over Europe between 1917 and 1931. It shuttles between two groups of memories, the most recent ones in Fialta, a fictitious resort on what gives the impression of being the Dalmatian coast. This is where the narrator Victor has his final meeting with Nina, another displaced Russian, just before her death in an automobile accident. A group of older memories ranges over chance meetings in previous years. As in Nabokov's life, scenes in Russia and Germany precede the ones in Paris, which present the elusive yet emotion-laden sensations expressing Victor's emerging regret at a relationship that promised much but was leading nowhere. At the hotel where they make love the only time, they close the French window, and the billowing curtains drop 'with something like a blissful sigh' (*Stories*, 419). With only this image to evoke their encounter, the sentence jumps to Victor on the balcony afterwards, breathing 'a combined smell of maple leaves and gasoline' (*Stories*, 420). If the episode's hotel corridor and breakfast tray by the door might be anywhere, the window and city street feel explicitly Parisian. But for Victor in retrospect the jarring mix of smells outside infuses a 'growing morbid pathos' (*Stories*, 420) of blocked feelings for Nina. Years later, in a nondescript Parisian home, he greets her briefly, and then wanders among the guests trying to catch her eye. His sadness crystallises on overhearing a chance remark about a 'burnt leaf' smell (*Stories*, 428), which for attentive readers evokes the dead-end latent in the combustible mix of gasoline and maple leaves.

Paris as way-station for the evanescence and melancholy of émigré life becomes the capital for avant-garde posturing once Victor meets Nina's husband Ferdinand. Ensconced in a café off the beaten track for visitors to Montparnasse, he holds forth before a group loosely connected to trends like cubism and surrealism, but also sympathetic to the Soviet Union, due to what Nabokov's narrator regards as a mistaken linkage between upheavals in art and politics. Ferdinand's writing typifies this 'ultramodern' fallacy, and Victor – anticipating the tone of Nabokov's *Strong Opinions* (1973) – scornfully attacks his creation of 'ideological trash' that exploits 'a ripple of stream of consciousness' and 'dismembered symbols' (*Stories*, 427). With Parisian avant-gardes, as with Sartre and Malraux, Nabokov is quick to pillory radical allegiances in the arts, but the scene also exposes the emptiness of reputations dependent on publicity. However, if judged by his own standards, as illustrated by his subtle treatment of Victor's inner life, this polemic with the avant-garde can itself seem inartistic and ideological.

Next-to-last in *Nabokov's Dozen* is 'Mademoiselle O', which is also chapter 5 in *Speak, Memory*. It enlarges on the sketch in *Mesures*, and its tribute to the 'lovely' sound and rhythm of the governess's French when reading aloud (*Stories*, 490) may have been a bid for a French audience. Paris only appears by name in the 1939 date-line at the end, but it should be regarded as the provisional end-point for the theme of exilic displacement running through the piece: in the governess's total ignorance of Russia, in her isolation because of poor hearing, but then – more directly and doubly so – in the author. If his narrated persona returns to Berlin after seeing her in Lausanne, the date-line places the narrating self in Paris, due to flight now from Germany as well as Russia. The exile theme culminates with the sight of a swan trying to clamber into a boat; absurdly out of its element, it echoes with a twist the awkward bird lost in Paris in Baudelaire's 'Le Cygne'. The similarly displaced author's last words cut more explicitly to his own experiences, as he mourns 'the things and beings' in his past that were 'turned to ashes or shot through the heart,' experiences soon to be repeated (*Stories*, 493).

To justify such self-revelation, the sketch opened by defending the memoir as a narrative mode against fiction, affirming that 'the man in me revolts against the fictionist' (*Stories*, 480). For the French, with a tradition that includes Rousseau's *Confessions*, this declaration would not seem startling. But in the United States, as Nabokov continued with this breakthrough, his interest in literary autobiography was a novelty. Only with the growing attention to 'life writing' over the last couple of decades has *Speak, Memory* been recognised as a major work of literature in its own right.

The collection's other story/memoir is 'First Love' (chapter 7 in *Speak, Memory*). It opens on a note of vanished Belle Époque luxury, with the 'then great and glamorous' Nord Express (*Stories*, 604), which connected Paris and St Petersburg. The French capital figures at first as just the transfer point for the Riviera or Biarritz. But then, during a two-month vacation at the latter destination, the writer meets Colette, daughter of '*des bourgeois de Paris*' (*Stories*, 609), and at age ten has his first taste of romantic love. His plan to save her from supposed mistreatment by her parents falls flat. But then, while returning to Russia, he meets her one last time in a Paris park. As he watches her dash around a fountain pushing a hoop, something in her clothes reminds him of a 'rainbow spiral in a glass marble', and the adult author adds, 'I still seem to be holding that wisp of iridescence' (*Stories*, 611). Parisian glamour has flickered throughout the story but only at a distance: in a few French phrases, transfers between stations and love for a Parisian who is merely middle-class and too young to fit with scripted expectations.

That farewell sight of Colette ultimately expands to become the emblem of an older Nabokov's attitude towards Paris. Late in *Speak, Memory*, while comparing his life to 'a colored spiral in a small ball of glass' (*SM*, 594), he values the spiral for avoiding 'vicious,' all-too-confining circles. He goes on, quite schematically, to relativise his time in Paris by absorbing it into a longer 'European' period from 1919 to 1940, itself presented as just one arc in a larger, uncoiling spiral. He has thus resolved his puzzlement at 'not knowing exactly where to fit' that wisp of iridescence on Colette (*Stories*, 611).

But the final words of 'First Love' had actually suggested a richer emblem of cultural dynamism and diversity to contrast with 'Parisian' centrality. As Colette races around the fountain with her hoop, circling girl and spinning toy appear to fade into 'the interlaced arches' of an enclosing fence. For her, fountain and hoop may still represent circularity, but for the narrator the scene has begun to resemble an anthemion. This arcane term designates an ornament with 'elaborate interlacements and expanding clusters' (*SM* 362), which Nabokov mentions as a title he proposed for the book, until it was rejected, in the 1966 Foreword to *Speak, Memory*. But in 'First Love', where the park's details started to generate a vision of interconnecting arcs, he glimpsed an image that surpasses the spiral in evoking the overlapping network of connections that marks a life like Nabokov's, lived in and among several cultures, with Paris included but not supreme.

CHAPTER 12

East to West Coast

Monica Manolescu

In 1940, Vladimir Nabokov and his family left France for the United States to escape the advancing German troops. Having arrived in the New World, Nabokov was faced with the challenge of securing a job to support his family, finding a new readership, reinventing himself as a writer in another language and recreating America itself as a setting for his work. Nabokov held teaching positions at Wellesley College and Cornell University, and was first a volunteer curator, then part-time research fellow in entomology at the Harvard Museum of Comparative Zoology. He taught for eighteen years in the United States and, although he resented his time-consuming academic obligations, was deeply appreciative of the lavish libraries on American university campuses.

This dynamic pattern that is a hallmark of his life is manifest in his American years as well. He changed homes frequently, preferring to rent homes vacated by colleagues on leave rather than acquire a permanent place to stay. He also travelled extensively across the United States, either on lecture tours or on butterfly collecting trips. As a lecturer, he visited numerous university campuses, including black colleges on a tour of the South in 1942, which allowed him to become familiar with social and historical issues typical of the United States, notably racial segregation. Nabokov spent most of his time on the east coast but travelled through the West almost every summer. Between 1941 and 1959 he undertook ten trips west in all, two from coast to coast. His first cross-country odyssey from New York to California constituted his first encounter with American motels and highways, as well as his first entomological trip, resulting in the capture of a butterfly specimen that belonged to an undescribed species of *Neonympha*. Nabokov analysed the forms of the North American members of the Blues genus *Lycaeides* in two major papers published in 1944 and 1945, and also wrote a treatise on the North American *Lycaeides* in 1949.[1]

---

[1] See Vladimir Nabokov, 'Notes on the morphology of the genus *Lycaeides* (Lycaenidae, Lepidoptera)' *Psyche*, 50 (1944), 104–138; 'Notes on Neotropical Plebejinae (Lycaenidae: Lepidoptera)', *Psyche*, 52

Nabokov himself never learned to drive, but Véra served as his chauffeur, and Dmitri nurtured a strong passion for cars and racing. In 1948, the Nabokovs bought a car, a Plymouth, and Nabokov estimated that between 1949 and 1959 Véra drove him more than 150,000 miles all over the United States mostly on butterfly collecting trips.[2] Their travels coincided with the now widespread use of the car and the emergence of an increasingly functional and ramified system of cross-country highways. It is to a great extent through travelling that Nabokov steeped himself in this 'cultured and exceedingly diverse country',[3] as he called it, whose fundamentally easy-going manner he cherished,[4] where he found his 'best readers' (*SO*, 10) and whose geography, linguistic specificity and popular culture became vital sources for his art.

Studying Nabokov's texts in relation to their geographical contexts may seem problematic given the author's claim that his works and all great literary works are 'fairy tales' (*LL*, 2) devoid of any referential dimension. Nabokov presents fiction as an autotelic world mapped by the demiurgic author: 'We should always remember that the work of art is invariably the creation of a new world, so that the first thing we should do is to study that new world as closely as possible, approaching it as something brand new, having no obvious connection with the worlds we already know. . . . The writer is the first man to map [the new world of the book] and to name the natural objects it contains' (*LL*, 1–2). This cartographic metaphor reflects Nabokov's fascination with exploration and the discovery of new worlds, which left its mark on many of his texts, just as it supports his claims about the autonomy of fiction, but such claims deserve to be read against the grain. They should not prevent us from identifying a scale of mimesis that spans his *oeuvre*, with varying degrees corresponding to distinct representational strategies and to specific aesthetic projects. In novels such as *Lolita* (1955), *Pnin* (1957), *Pale Fire* (1962) and *Ada* (1969), Nabokov would probe the limits of America as a 'new world' of fiction offering different visions and versions that range from the recognisable 'quilt of forty-eight states' (*Lolita*, 141) to a radically reconfigured North American continent that merges American and Russian/European spaces, cultures and languages in *Pale Fire* and *Ada*.

(1945), 1–61; 'The Nearctic members of the genus *Lycaeides* Hübner (Lycaenidae, Lepidoptera)', *Bulletin of the Museum of Comparative Zoology*, 101/4 (1949), 477–541.
[2] See Kurt Johnson and Steve Coates, *Nabokov's Blues. The Scientific Odyssey of a Literary Genius* (Cambridge: Zoland Books, 1999), 9.
[3] Brian Boyd, *Vladimir Nabokov: The American Years* (Princeton: Princeton University Press, 1991), 21.
[4] Ibid., 12.

In the afterword to *Lolita*, Nabokov comments on his attempt to 'invent America' (*Lolita*, 294) through an alchemical process whereby the individual imagination distils elements gleaned from reality. This can be read as a more balanced account of how both documentation and invention contribute to the emergence of America, a place that is both recognisable (referentially valid) and uniquely personal (produced in writing and involving artistic transformation). This strategy is apparent in the first of Nabokov's texts to use an American setting, the short story 'Time and Ebb' (1945), which introduces a defamiliarising perspective from which the present is remembered as a remote past. American cityscapes, sites and objects (skyscrapers, a soda fountain, Central Park, trains, cars) are rendered obsolete and unreal by a peculiar use of retrospective vision. Other texts confront the reader with a palpably real America situated in the present (*Lolita* and *Pnin* in particular), which investigate and reflect on American landscapes, language and cultural fabric. *Ada* shifts the referential focus away from our planet to construct a 'dream-bright America' (*Ada*, 467) situated on Antiterra, whose texture and contexts are mainly literary and artistic, while *Pale Fire* brings together on the same world map Appalachia, a recognizable version of New York State, and Zembla, 'a distant northern land' that has no existence outside the text and whose representational vividness is inseparable from Kinbote's madness.

Nabokov's America is first and foremost a space that is endlessly crossed, explored and (re)named. The theme of travelling, which is particularly prominent in Nabokov's novels that involve an American setting, cannot be dissociated from the understanding of fiction as having the power to redefine cartography, especially in *Ada* and *Pale Fire*. *Ada*'s ambitious reconfiguration of the world translates travelling into a form of transatlantic doubling, resulting in a vast compensatory fantasy, a demonstration of the power of fiction to rethink the world in hybrid transnational terms. *Pale Fire* constructs a specular, dynamic geography and textual structure in which the poem and the commentary are separate but connected by recurrent to-and-fro movement, and John Shade's Appalachia constantly recalls Kinbote's Zembla without merging with it.

However, restless movement is not always eagerly embraced or conducive to a strategy of metamorphic renaming and shifting of boundaries. In *Pnin*, the theme of displacement is grafted onto a meditation, both comic and tragic, on exile, linguistic inadaptability and cultural disorientation. The novel closes on Timofey's departure from Waindell College for an unknown destination, an emblematic image that reminds one of Nabokov's repeated change of location and renting of homes.

Travelling in Nabokov's fiction also reflects his interest in geographical exploration, which is closely linked to his passion for entomology, the two coming together in his American trips in search of butterflies. One important entomological discovery Nabokov made on his American excursions left its mark on *Lolita* in the crucial epiphany scene, in which Humbert, on a mountain trail overlooking a valley, hears the melody of children at play and laments the absence of Lolita's 'voice from that concord' (*Lolita*, 290). In the 'Afterword' to *Lolita*, Nabokov brings together autobiography, geography and fiction by identifying the trail as the place where he caught 'the first known female of *Lycaeides sublivens* Nabokov' (*Lolita*, 297). Such moments when geography, entomology and fiction overlap also point to the question of the correspondence between real and fictional spaces, and invite us to consider the role of toponymic invention in Nabokov's representation of America, especially in *Lolita* and *Ada*, which offer particularly interesting examples.

Ada treats toponymy as a lexical playing field, in which places and place names dislocated on Antiterra are shadows and combinations of terrestrial originals. Based in Switzerland at the time when he wrote *Ada*, Nabokov situates this particular version of America in a rich literary and artistic context, but seems to divorce it from any explicit historical or political contexts contemporary with the writing of the novel.[5] *Lolita*, however, is manifestly anchored in a familiar geography and its travels cover the United States from East to West in meandering fashion. Yet, even this familiar geography involves both real and invented place names disseminated across the American grid, thus complicating any straightforward connection between real and represented spaces. A process of 'camouflage' affects toponymy: both the fictional editor John Ray Jr and the narrator Humbert claim to have modified certain place names in order to protect the 'real' people in the memoir (*Lolita*, 3, 251). Some of the imaginary towns in the novel have intertextual and metaphorical implications, but certain invented toponyms are haunted by their referential doubles, entertaining the illusion of a possible cartographic identification. Thus, Coalmont is described as 'a small industrial community some eight hundred miles from New York City' (*Lolita*, 251), a precision that has led to speculation regarding the real place behind the camouflage. Referential approaches to Nabokov's texts, especially *Lolita*, attempt to uncover the real geography behind the literary one and to highlight the importance of documentation.[6] Such painstaking investigations are encouraged by the fact

[5] Will Norman has judiciously proved that *Ada* does reflect history and politics in his *Nabokov, History and the Texture of Time* (London: Routledge, 2012), 130–54.
[6] See, for instance, Dieter H. Zimmer, 'Lolita, USA. A geographical scrutiny of Nabokov's novel *Lolita*'. URL: www.d-e-zimmer.de/LolitaUSA/LoUSpre.htm

that Nabokov's toponymic creativity relies both on poetic suggestion and the illusion of cartographic verisimilitude.

Moving through real and invented geographies, Nabokov's characters are exiles, tourists or explorers. The character of the explorer appears in many of Nabokov's works (*The Pole* [1924], 'The Aurelian' [1930], 'Lance' [1952], 'Terra incognita' [1931], *The Gift* [1937–38], *Lolita* and *Ada*) and is sometimes inspired by an existing explorer (Robert Falcon Scott in *The Pole*; Marco Polo, Nikolai Przhevalsky and Pyotr Semyonov-Tian-Shansky in *The Gift*; Vasco da Gama in *Ada*). The explorer is often a tragic figure celebrated for his heroic attempts to discover and name the unknown. As a discoverer and name-giver, he appears as an *alter ego* of the writer and his vulnerability stands in stark contrast to the invincibility and arrogance usually associated with the Nabokovian figure of the author. Humbert Humbert is a shallow version of the genuine explorer: he narrates his embellished 'arctic adventures' (*Lolita*, 41) and presents himself as 'Edgar H. Humbert ..., "writer and explorer"' (*Lolita*, 70) for a local newspaper, suggesting a grandiose connection with Poe's *Narrative of Arthur Gordon Pym*. Humbert blindly explores two indistinguishable entities: what he calls 'the nymphet' and the American continent, ignorant of the former's inner world and of the latter's scientific minutiae. One finds in *Lolita* echoes of the nineteenth-century tradition of the Transcendentalists and the Hudson River School of painting that presents America as an 'unsung' Adamic space still awaiting a prophetic bard to celebrate it. The mystique of revelation and wonder that surfaces occasionally in Humbert's reactions can be placed alongside Emerson's in *The Poet*, although a strong sexual undercurrent is present in Humbert's appraisal of the American scenery as an unsuitable place for open air trysts: 'They are beautiful, heart-rendingly beautiful, those wilds, with a quality of wide-eyed, unsung, innocent surrender that my lacquered, toy-bright Swiss villages and exhaustively lauded Alps no longer possess' (*Lolita*, 157); 'Our logrolling, our stumps and their politics, our fisheries, our Negroes, and Indians, our boasts, and our repudiations, the wrath of rogues, and the pusillanimity of honest men, the northern trade, the southern planting, the western clearing, Oregon, and Texas are yet unsung. Yet America is a poem in our eyes; its ample geography dazzles the imagination, and it will not wait long for metres'.[7] Humbert is a parodic version of the American bard, whose occasional sensitivity to the landscape is marred by the bitter confession that he and Lolita 'had been everywhere' but 'had really seen nothing' (*Lolita*, 164).

---

[7] Ralph W. Emerson, '*The Poet*', *Self-Reliance and Other Essays* (New York: Dover, 1993), 80.

In contrast to the explorer as a superior discoverer, the tourist is a risible figure and a victim of the mirages of advertising and tour books. Nabokov's representation of tourism should be understood in the context of the massive development of recreational tourism in 1950s America, but also in the context of travel writing as a genre that projects the tourist as a shallow, gregarious creature who reduces culture to a series of sites and monuments to be dutifully consumed. Elements of the universe of American tourism that Nabokov encountered on his road trips and on his lecture tours find their way into the second part of *Lolita*, which condenses traditional and contemporary American discourses of mobility and leisure, and reflects on what constitutes American 'authenticity' that tourism seeks to promote. America seen through Humbert's eyes is translated into lists and nominal sentences that testify to his keen sense of observation and to the standardisation of American mass culture. His numerous descriptive vignettes of restaurants, hotels and attractions mimic and mock the rhetoric of tourism. Humbert projects a clear-cut opposition between himself and Lolita in terms of high and low culture when he casts himself as the cynical critic of popular culture operating with European references and Lolita as the 'ideal consumer' to whom 'ads were dedicated' (*Lolita*, 138). This opposition between high and low, albeit undoubtedly accurate, serves to elude the fact that Humbert consumes Lolita even as she consumes the tourist culture around her.[8]

Lolita documents not just the variety of services and attractions in the tourist industry, but also offers an implicit investigation into what constitutes American authenticity, since markers of cultural authenticity are what tourists usually seek to collect.[9] In *Lolita*, American authenticity seems to be a heterogeneous concept, synonymous with natural wonders, but also with popular culture itself, in which the mythology of the West meets replicas of European monuments. If Humbert is admiring of American landscapes and their unique beauty, a satirical dimension is manifest in the treatment of the material culture of tourism and its discourses. In his interviews, Nabokov voiced great annoyance when accused of satirical intentions and retorted that philistinism (which he called 'poshlust') knows no national boundaries. He also added jokingly that *Lolita* should have been published in the Soviet Union because it was 'thought to condemn bitterly the American system of motels' (*SO*, 97).

---

[8] Rachel Bowlby, '*Lolita* and the Poetry of Advertising', in Ellen Pifer (ed.), *Vladimir Nabokov's Lolita: A Casebook* (Oxford: Oxford University Press, 2003), 166.
[9] See Jonathan Culler, 'The Semiotics of Tourism', in his *Framing the Sign: Criticism and Its Institutions* (Norman: University of Oklahoma Press, 1988), 153–68.

The discourses of tourism parodied by Humbert are symptomatic of certain historical realities and social attitudes. Thus, a quote from the tour book mentions that in New Orleans 'pickaninnies ... will ... tap-dance for pennies' (*Lolita*, 145), hinting at the racial divide typical of the South of the United States and implying that tourism thrives on the exploitation of racial tropes and performances. Several instances of latent anti-Semitism are also presented: *The Enchanted Hunters* advertises its location as being 'near churches' (*Lolita*, 245) and its desk clerk treats Humbert with suspicion, taking his name to be Jewish (*Lolita*, 110). Humbert briefly records these recurring instances, sketchily depicting tourism as a sociological microcosm that bears the imprint of larger social concerns.

As a travel narrative, *Lolita* reflects the rising American automobile culture at the beginning of the 1950s, when growing affluence made it possible for most Americans to own cars. The car occupies a central place in the vast and varied migratory logistics present in Nabokov's work, which includes the bicycles of the summers spent on the Vyra estate, the trains taking the Nabokov family across Europe and rocking the drowsy child to sleep, the ship that carried the Nabokovs to the United States away from Nazi Europe, the train and the car in *Pnin*, the car in *Lolita*, the magic carpet in *Ada*, the unspecified means of transportation used for the interplanetary voyage in *Lance*. The car is definitely associated with America, with its open spaces and shifting life patterns, and also with the composition of *Lolita*. Nabokov amassed notes for the novel on his 1951 trip to Wyoming and Colorado, and wrote parts of it on the road, on his 1952 trip to the Continental Divide in Wyoming, and on his 1953 trip to Arizona, when he was working on the final draft. In 1958, *Life Magazine* published a photographic reconstruction of the writing of *Lolita* and immortalised Nabokov scribbling on index cards in his car. One year after *Lolita*'s publication, in 1956, President Eisenhower signed the National Interstate and Defense Highways Act, a landmark legislation designed to consolidate a network of national highways initiated in 1916. The car, seen as the quintessentially American mode of locomotion embodying the pioneer spirit and opening up endless possibilities of migration and leisure, changed the fabric of the landscape at a fast pace.[10] It becomes for Humbert such an inseparable companion that at the end of *Lolita*, when he chooses to park his car and walk to dentist Ivor Quilty's house in Ramsdale, he realises he has exposed himself to inevitable

---

[10] See James R. Akerman, 'Twentieth Century American Road Maps and the Making of a National Motorized Space', in James R. Akerman (ed.), *Cartographies of Travel and Navigation* (Chicago, IL: University of Chicago Press, 2006), 152.

public scrutiny, since 'in an American suburban street a lone pedestrian is more conspicuous than a lone motorist' (*Lolita*, 271). The rivalry between Humbert and Quilty is couched in the automobile language of a dark highway drama: Humbert and Lolita consume 'those long highways' (*Lolita*, 141) in Charlotte's 'Dream Blue Melmoth' sedan (*Lolita*, 213), with Gothic undertones, taunted by Quilty, who turns into 'a veritable Proteus of the highway' (*Lolita*, 213). Humbert uses a Tour Book of the Automobile Association, which is an actual guide, probably in its most recent edition of 1947. Road maps abound in the novel, serving navigational purposes, but also functioning as relics of the characters' trips across the United States and as mnemonic devices for the writing of Humbert's memoir in prison.

Illustration 2 Nabokov writing in his car, Ithaca, NY (1958)

As a road novel, *Lolita* can be placed in the literary context of the American road trip tradition, along with Whitman's 'Song of the Open Road' (1855), Twain's *Roughing It* (1872), Kerouac's *On the Road* (1955) and Steinbeck's *Travels with Charley* (1962), while its transatlantic component invites connections with Henry James' international theme. *On the Road* was published in the United States a few months before *Lolita*. Kerouac (another bilingual writer) read *Lolita* in 1962 and expressed his admiration.[11] The two texts are obviously dissimilar stylistically, with Nabokov's carefully polished prose standing in stark contrast to Kerouac's raw, freewheeling vernacular. Yet, both novels represent characters drifting endlessly across the United States, with the automobile and the highway seen as forms of evasion making possible the rejection of norms and the consecration of a state of social marginality, with criminal undertones in Humbert's case. Nabokov's protagonist stands apart from Kerouac's characters since his odyssey echoes with imprisonment and is reconstructed from prison. Humbert's irony and detachment prevent him from fully embracing the road for the sake of its revelatory potential, although he uses it as a means of spatial seduction of the nymphet and deferral of the inevitable end. Kerouac's prose deals with openly celebrated excesses that the road makes possible and accentuates, and that define the ethos of a group and an era, while Humbert's crime remains an intensely solipsistic enterprise from whose entrapment he contemplates and annexes both Lolita and America.

[11] See Jack Kerouac, *Selected Letters 1957–1969* (Harmondsworth: Penguin, 2000), 342.

CHAPTER 13

Switzerland

Annick Morard

Even though he spent the last fifteen years of his life in Switzerland, Nabokov – generally seen as a Russian, American or even a European author – is rarely imagined in relation to his last country of adoption. A more or less providential series of circumstances seems to have made Montreux his calling ground, his default home, more by chance rather than by choice. Nevertheless, Nabokov's ties to Switzerland reach much further back beyond the time he lived in Montreux (1961–77), appearing as early as 1905, embodied by the figure of his Swiss governess, Cécile Miauton. Switzerland not only reappears at different stages of his life, but it also emerges throughout his multilingual works: as the geographical background for his later English texts (*Pale Fire* [1962], *Ada* [1969], *Transparent Things* [1972], and *Look at the Harlequins!* [1974]) and several Russian novels (*Laughter in the Dark* [1932–33], *Glory* [1931]) as well as in 'Mademoiselle O' (1936), one of his rare works written and published in French. The pathways that linked Nabokov to Switzerland are more complex than they might at first appear: they developed on several levels, inviting us to leap from reality to fiction as lightly as a chamois.

In response to the question 'Why Montreux?', Nabokov had a plethora of answers, including the proximity to his family (his son in Milan, his sister in Geneva) and the opportunity to hunt rarely studied mountain butterflies, as well as other more professional and emotional reasons. In January 1964, he told the Radio Suisse Romande: 'It is a city that I love tenderly, for several reasons: it is beautiful, sweet, and one can work very well there'.[1] On a famous French television programme, he also stressed the fact that, unlike its neighbours, Switzerland did not suffer from strikes and had an extremely reliable postal service, which 'makes the life of an author

---

[1] Henri Jaton, 'Interview with Vladimir Nabokov (January 1964)', in *L'horloge de sable*, Radio Suisse Romande, 6 June 2004, timeline 46'50". URL: www.rts.ch/archives/radio/culture/l-horloge-de-sab le/4185926-facettes-de-nabokov.html.

much easier'.[2] In short, the country provided ideal working conditions for both the writer and the lepidopterist, and its central location greatly facilitated the Nabokovs' trips throughout Europe. The Nabokovs' last place of residence thus allied practicality with beauty, the useful with the pleasurable. In addition, ever since the success of *Lolita* (1955), the Nabokovs had enjoyed financial security. At the time, of course, Switzerland already had the reputation of openly, and discretely, welcoming foreign fortunes. But Switzerland was not only a country of economic refuge; the strong anti-Soviet stance that characterised public opinion in Switzerland during the twentieth century surely gave this country, in Nabokov's eyes, the allure of a political refuge.

Yet the principal reason for choosing Montreux, which Nabokov reiterates in all his interviews, is essentially aesthetic: describing the 'fabulous sunsets . . . spangling the lake, splitting the crimson sun' (*SO*, 192) and the 'floral arrangements along the promenade from Territet to Clarens', which, he adds, 'is really the work of a great artist',[3] the author seems truly thrilled with the landscapes of the Swiss Riviera. In particular, this last quote underscores the dialogue between nature and culture that Nabokov imagines as soon as he thinks of the shores of Lake Geneva. In a letter written in 1966 to Roman Grinberg, he regrets: 'It is too bad that you missed Montreux! . . . There is not much art here, but the birds on the lake are beautiful.'[4] It seems a commonplace: the gifts of nature compensate for the absence of culture. Most significantly, this lack of culture is also one of the main characteristics attributed to his Swiss governess in his various portrayals of her: the narrator systematically insists on the physical as well as social awkwardness of Mademoiselle, on her lack of distinction and basic manners.[5] With a condescending tone, Nabokov caricatures the uncouth manners and uncultured language of his governess who, in addition to insufficiently airing out her room, has no elegance and only speaks in dictums. Her 'nightingale voice',[6] however, with its brilliant, stimulating tone effaces all her flaws. From one textual variant to another, water, as an element, best defines Mademoiselle: her eyes are always wet, her fine voice

---

[2] *Apostrophes. Special program dedicated to Vladimir Nabokov*, hosted by Bernard Pivot, Antenne 2, 30 May 1975. URL: www.ina.fr/video/CPB75050355/vladimir-nabokov-video.html.

[3] Jaton, 'Interview'.

[4] 'Druz'ia, babochki i monstry: Iz perepiski Vladimira i Very Nabokovykh s Romanom Grinbergom (1943–1967)', ed. Rashit Yangirov, in Vladimir Alloi (ed.), *Diaspora: Novye materialy*, vol. 1 (Paris, St Petersburg: Athenaeum – Feniks, 2001), 549.

[5] See Vladimir Nabokov, 'Mademoiselle O', in Vladimir Nabokov, *Nouvelles complètes* (Paris: Gallimard, 2010), 662–67; *SM*, 443–50.

[6] *SM*, 455; Nabokov, 'Mademoiselle O', 674.

'runs through books without ever tiring' in 'a kind of cold and brilliant stream'.[7] Moreover, 'O', which the narrator presents as the 'real name' of Mademoiselle, is in French the homophone of *eau*.[8] Later, Nabokov would remember 'her tongue's limpidity and luster', which compensates for 'the shallowness of her culture' and 'the banality of her mind' (*SM*, 455). Nabokov's first French teacher thus failed to impress him with the content of her lessons, her intelligence or her culture; she did so rather with her voice, which he describes using terms from the register of nature. In the foreword to the final version of his autobiography, *Speak, Memory* (1967), Nabokov insists on the crucial role 'Mademoiselle O' played, along with Lake Geneva, in his autobiographical writing and in the organisation of his memories:

> That order [of the chapters in *Speak, Memory*] had been established in 1936 [the year of the publication of 'Mademoiselle O'], at the placing of the cornerstone which already held in its hidden hollow various maps, timetables, a collection of matchboxes, a chip of ruby glass, and even – as I now realize – the view from my balcony of Geneva lake, of its ripples and glades of light, black-dotted today, at teatime, with coots and tufted ducks. (*SM*, 362)

One of many biographical markers, the Swiss lake thus appears in the midst of other realia taken from different periods. It is the element that ties the present moment of writing ('as I now realize', 'today') to the period described (the Russian years), through the French interlude of his emigration ('1936'). The lake stands out from the other chosen objects in that it is physically elusive: reinforced by the watery characteristics of Mademoiselle, who also ties together these different periods, the lake accentuates the moving, fluctuating character of autobiographical writing itself.

The creative and artistic gesture, the very act of writing, thus becomes subsumed within the debate between nature and culture. Here again, there is nothing arbitrary about Nabokov's choice of the shores of Lake Geneva to represent the relationship between the two: since the eighteenth century, the region has been a particularly privileged place of residency for artists and writers, who often prolonged their stay there when on their Grand Tours of Europe. Lord Byron with his *Prisoner of Chillon*, as well as Jean-Jacques Rousseau's *Nouvelle Héloïse*, which takes place in Clarens, made Montreux and its surroundings famous.[9] Numerous writers have explored

---

[7] Nabokov, 'Mademoiselle O', 666 and 674. Translation is mine.

[8] Nabokov, 'Mademoiselle O', 658. Translation is mine.

[9] This Swiss thinker and writer caught the attention of Nabokov from an early age. In January 1917, he wrote a poem entitled 'A Stroll with J.-J. Rousseau'. See 'Progulka s J.-J. Rousseau', in *Sobr. soch.*, I, 570.

and continue to explore these very same shores, finding different sources of inspiration there, including the British writers William Wordsworth, Mary and Percy Bysshe Shelley, John Ruskin, Leslie Stephen and Arthur Conan Doyle, as well as the Russian authors Nikolai Karamzin, Vasily Zhukovsky, Petr Vyazemsky, Nikolai Gogol, Fyodor Dostoevsky, Fyodor Tyutchev and Lev Tolstoy. All of them have left written reports of their travels in Switzerland, be they letters, poems, travel narratives or fictional works. From Nabokov's perspective, the Swiss landscape itself bears the mark of the passage of these famous travellers:

> I like to think of all the English and Russian poets and prose writers who wandered here, leaving the imprint of their imagination on the landscape, after having taken it in themselves.[10]

Nabokov considers the region's environment a place of cultural sedimentation, shaped by the writings that describe and praise it. Though Nabokov's repeated entreaties not to search for reality in his works of fiction are well known, his appeals to look for literature in reality are less so. Nabokov's life and work, however, constantly invite the reader to move back and forth between landscapes and texts, between nature and culture, not as between two conflicting, hierarchical or even opposing pairs, but as between two complementary ways of moving through the world, which together aid in the comprehension of it, in all of its complexity. *Ada* contains an explicit reference to this invitation to read the imprints of literature left on the landscape:

> Van with his tutor going first to Gardone on Lake Garda, where Aksakov reverently pointed out Goethe's and d'Annunzio's marble footprints, and then staying for a while in autumn at a hotel on a mountain slope above Leman Lake (where Karamzin and Count Tolstoy had roamed). (*Ada*, 124)

If the landscape around Lake Geneva carries the imprint of the authors and artists who have wandered through it, Nabokov undoubtedly also wished to leave his mark there, however futile, precarious and unreadable his trace would prove to be, the more so as Switzerland is the place where he grew old and died – where he played, so to speak, his last cards. Death is a menacing and persistent presence in Nabokov's last writings: many of his protagonists die, but they put up a stubborn resistance in the face of death. The inevitability of death is only counterbalanced by the survival of texts, which, as much in *Pale Fire* as in *Ada*, seem to exist in order to stave off the death of their authors. Writing thus seems to be a way of fighting off one's

[10] Jaton, 'Interview'.

demise, of leaving one's trace, or one's mark, on reality. In this way, the changing flux of Nabokovian writing resembles the streams, glaciers and lakes that carve out the alpine valleys, dropping in layers their alluvial deposits. Indeed, the movement is also one of coming and going: his collection of 4300 butterflies given to the Museum of Zoology in Lausanne is a record of the footprints Nabokov left literally and meta-phorically in these places. In turn, the landscape marked his literary production. The dominance of the pastoral genre,[11] in his last works, proves this, as well as the obvious, thematised, presence of Switzerland. As Brian Boyd writes: 'for Gradus's journey in *Pale Fire* [Nabokov] needed a little of Switzerland as well as the France he had assimilated sufficiently in Nice, and he needed to create Zembla "out of other countries" in Europe'.[12] There is no doubt that the Swiss alpine landscapes continued to inspire Nabokov's imagination beyond *Pale Fire*. Finally, on a more intimate level, reserved for his readers, Nabokov's texts, like all literary works, leave their impressions on the landscape, in the sense that the Nabokovian imagination undoubtedly enriches one's perception of reality, one's reading of the world. Thus literature intervenes in reality, leaving its trace in turn; culture and nature, like reality and fiction, constantly commingle, and neither one comes out untouched.

This notion of leaving a trace inherently contains also its opposite, that is, the concept of disappearance or erasure, present in all of Nabokov's writings. There too, Switzerland offered Nabokov an ideal playground for those mystifying undertakings so dear to him. A tiny country lost in the middle of Europe, Switzerland is made up of an astonishing patchwork of cultures: four national languages, numerous dialects, administrative divisions into cantons, strong regional identities with a large diversity of customs and traditions. Switzerland is heterogeneous by definition and by history, despite a political tendency towards consensus. The country is marked by a search for unity within diversity, which may appear impos-sible. Ever-changing and kaleidoscopic, a fixed image of Switzerland, perhaps more than of any other country, is also hard to grasp due to the numerous myths and clichés largely propagated by travellers, especially during the romantic era. All of these characteristics combined place the country solidly in the realm of the indefinite, where one can ideally dis-appear, but also reinvent oneself. It should be noted that in Nabokov's work,

---

[11] On the function of the pastoral in Nabokov's work, see Norman, *Nabokov, History and the Texture of Time*, 130–54.

[12] Brian Boyd, *Vladimir Nabokov: The American Years* (Princeton: Princeton University Press, 1991), 422.

Switzerland is most often a place of passage or transit (as in *Pale Fire*, *Transparent Things*, *Look at the Harlequins!*), when it isn't purely and simply a place of evaporation: it is in Switzerland that Martin Edelweiss (*Glory*) and Bel (*Look at the Harlequins!*) plan their escape. And what if Switzerland itself was a kind of reflection – shimmering, mirror-like – of the émigré experience:

> During the sumptuous Swiss autumn [Martin] felt for the first time that he was, after all, an exile, doomed to live far from home. That word "exile" had a delicious sound: Martin considered the blackness of the coniferous night, sensed a Byronic pallor on his cheeks, and saw himself in a cloak. (*Glory*, 52)

Despite the evident irony of this romantic vision of exile, one cannot help remembering that like his character, Nabokov's view of his émigré status was quite different from that of the majority of Russian émigrés. Nabokov took a particular, denationalised stand in the socio-cultural and literary debates that, at the beginning of the 1930s, had opposed a young generation of émigré writers to the older one. He was neither on the side of those who felt they would always be duty-bound to the fatherland, nor with those who saw France as a new literary homeland. Neither 'uprooted',[13] nor 'extraterritorial',[14] Nabokov, in his life and his writings, suggests a third, by far more joyous, way, which is the putting down of roots in multiple places. Far from any type of lamentation, Nabokov has learned to transform forced exile into an interesting, advantageous and even charming experience: an experience in which one could continuously reinvent oneself in one culture or another, at the same time reinventing the world. Monica Manolescu sees in Nabokov 'an author who explores this world and all of the new worlds that emerge in his fiction', concluding that 'precisely because he knows well how to open this reality onto others, Nabokov proves his familiarity with the here and now, with history and its ruptures, with geography and the inadequacies of cartographic representations'.[15] And there too, Switzerland, with all of its plurality, probably gave him some inspiration: *Transparent Things* brings the reader to 'Diablonnet, near Versex', the first name, which, for French-speaking Swiss, brings to mind the devil (*diable*), and Les Diablerets, a mountain village where the Nabokovs bought a piece of land, while it sounds like '*yabloni*' (apple-

---

[13] Sartre was the first person to apply this term to Nabokov. Jean-Paul Sartre, 'Vladimir Nabokov: "La Méprise"', *Europe*, 15 June 1939, 240–42.

[14] George Steiner, 'Extraterritorial', *TriQuarterly*, 16 (1969), 119–24.

[15] Monica Manolescu, *Jeux de mondes. L'ailleurs chez Vladimir Nabokov* (Bordeaux: Presses Universitaires de Bordeaux, 2010), 358.

trees), to Armande's mother, who speaks Russian. Regarding Versex, it is a combination of Versoix and Bernex, both real places situated near Geneva, and evokes even more Vernex, the original site of the Montreux Palace. Besides, Nabokov draws all these toponyms ending in *–ex* (incidentally at the very heart of *text*), so frequent in his later writings, from local geography: the château at Ex in *Ada*, Hex and Trex in *Look at the Harlequins !*, Trux in *Transparent Things* recall Château-d'Œx, Bex, Vex or Champex, not to mention Sex Rouge and Sex Noir, that Nabokov does not even modify in *Ada*. The word *sex*, which is of Franco-Provençal origin and signifies *rock*, is all but obsolete in French, except in the cantons of the Valais and Vaud. What a gift for Nabokov![16] Finally, while following the characters from Trux to Thur, then from Chur to Thurn in *Transparent Things*, how could one ignore that Swiss cities are living in several linguistic realities, especially in the bilingual cantons. Thus Thun is also Thoune, Chur is Coire, Sierre is Siders, etc. And when, for *Ada*, Nabokov mixes Sierre and Orsières to create 'Sorcière, in the Valais' (*Ada*, 422) it gives the impression that the writer has played by the rules imposed by the very places themselves.[17]

And what if Nabokov had not only found *his* sister in Switzerland, but also *a* sister in Switzerland? Multicultural, pluralistic, diversely rich, cultivating a certain discretion without any false modesty, the country defines its collective identity around the notion of *Sonderfall*, that is the conviction of having a particular fate, of being like no other.[18] The author of *Strong Opinions* (1973) would certainly never have denied such a definition of his work or his person.

[16] The toponym Sex reappears in *The Original of Laura* as 'a delightful Swiss resort' (*TOOL*, 223). Such a repetition is unusual for Nabokov.

[17] *Sorcière* means *witch* in French.

[18] See François Walter, *Histoire de la Suisse*, 5 vols. (Neuchâtel: Éditions Alphil-Presses universitaires suisses, 2010), vol. 5, 145.

PART III

Literatures and Arts

CHAPTER 14

The Russian Literary Canon

Alexander Dolinin

In the 1930s when Nabokov's (aka Sirin's) domineering presence in Russian émigré literature became a well-established though disconcerting fact, contemporary critics answered the challenge with a concept alleging his 'un-Russianness.' Not only Nabokov's open enemies like Georgii Adamovich and Georgii Ivanov but also some of his admirers would claim that he posited himself as an author alien to the Russian classical tradition, a literary defector who had betrayed his Russian roots. Introducing a new talent to British Slavists, Gleb Struve, a friend of Nabokov, wrote in 1934:

> Sirin's un-Russianness has been pointed out by several critics. This is certainly true of his technique. His interest in the plot, his careful construction, his inventiveness and 'artificiality' make up a whole that is very un-Russian, though separately these elements can be found in individual Russian writers. Besides, Sirin has no interest in ideas, in the social background, so characteristic of the Russian traditional novel. Finally, Russian literature has always been notorious for its interest in, and sympathy with, men, for its *humaneness*. According to the Russian philosopher Berdiaev, Gogol alone of the major Russian writers lacked that trait. I think Pisemsky and among the moderns Sologub can be placed on the same line. Sirin certainly belongs to it. . . . From his works you will not learn what are his own views, ideas and feelings. His attitude to his heroes is artistically objective and ruthless . . . [1]

What the critics called the 'Russian traditional novel' was, in fact, a lopsided construct not unlike the notorious 'great tradition' of F. R. Leavis, who defined it by a 'contrasting reference to Flaubert'. According to Leavis, all the great British novelists (Jane Austen, George Eliot, Henry James, Joseph Conrad and D. H. Lawrence) share 'moral seriousness', 'moral insights' and a 'profoundly serious interest in life', while Flaubert

---

[1] Gleb Struve, 'Current Russian Literature. II. Vladimir Sirin,' *The Slavonic and East European Review*, 12 (January 1934), 443–44.

and Flaubertians idolise literary form and style, ignore moral issues, stay away from life and therefore lack human and artistic significance. Similarly, Russian critics construed their 'great tradition' on the same premises, extolling the moral awareness and humaneness of Dostoevsky, Tolstoy and their followers, and disparaging those writers who seemed to be indifferent to big ideas and unsympathetic towards the plight of their characters. Yet, if we compile a list of writers whom the émigré critics found akin to Nabokov at least in some respects, we'll see that he was far from a loner. As well as relating him to Gogol and two other Russian masters of the grotesque, Aleksei Pisemsky and Fyodor Sologub, Gleb Struve stated that in his yearnings for form, measure and order Nabokov was very close to Pushkin, the most revered figure in the national canon.[2] Petr Bitsilli, whom Nabokov called 'his most intelligent critic', connected 'the deathly weirdness and grotesque deformity' of Sirin's images to the writings of Saltykov-Shchedrin.[3] Responding to Nabokov's detractors who accused him of inanity, a New York Russian critic, Vladimir Mansvetov, noted that it reminded him of attacks against Chekhov, who was also blamed for the lack of substance.[4] A tradition that boasts of Pushkin, Gogol and Chekhov among its adherents can hardly be dismissed as a minor one.

Of course, Nabokov, a staunch Flaubertian, understood that he didn't measure up against the yardstick of the Russian 'great tradition' and ridiculed its supposed humanistic virtues. 'Literature is love for mankind' ('literatura – eto liubov' k liudiam' – *Sobr. soch.*, 3, 467) is a motto of his most repulsive character, the murderer and madman Hermann in *Despair*. Nabokov insisted that the criteria applied to any Russian novelist of the past, even to Tolstoy and Dostoevsky, should be strictly aesthetical, not philosophical or moral. In his lectures on *Anna Karenina*, he argued that Tolstoy is a great writer only in those chapters where 'he attains that dispassionate ideal of authors which Flaubert so violently demanded of a writer: to be invisible, and to be everywhere as God in His universe is' (*LRL*, 143). Nabokov's flippant critique of Dostoevsky in his American years can be explained as a response to philosophical and religious inter-pretations of the writer prevalent in the American academy of the 1950s and 1960s. In a different Russian context of the 1930s, he took a much more favourable view of the 'author of *The Double* and *The Possessed*' (*Gift*, 339),

[2] [Gleb Struve], 'Vladimir Nabokoff-Sirine, l'amoureux de la vie,' *Le Mois*, 6 (June–July 1931), 141–42.
[3] Petr Bitsilli, 'The Revival of Allegory,' in Alfred Appel, Jr. and Charles Newman (eds.) *Nabokov: Criticism, Reminiscences, Translations and Tributes* (London: Weidenfeld and Nicolson, 1971), 108–9.
[4] See Vladimir Mansvetov, 'Literaturnyj bloknot: Sirin,' *Novoe russkoe slovo*, 2 February 1941.

praised the masterfully constructed narrative of *The Brothers Karamazov* and called Dostoevsky a 'writer of keen perception' – one of the highest compliments on his scale of aesthetic appraisal.[5]

Just as any major writer, Nabokov shaped his own literary pedigree, carefully selecting relatives and guarding against intruders. In fact, no one Russian novelist of his generation paid so much attention to his predecessors and contemporaries, responded to so many texts in various ways or alluded to other authors so often. Nabokov's Russian oeuvre is circumscribed by two Pushkin references: his first novel, *Mary*, (1926) opens with an epigraph from *Eugene Onegin*, and *The Gift* (1937–38), his last one, ends with an imitation of the Onegin stanza and an allusion to the final scene of Pushkin's novel in verse. Actually, every Russian novel of Nabokov contains several echoes of Pushkin's writings. Thus German characters of *King, Queen, Knave* (1928) unknowingly re-enact a scene of Pushkin's play *The Stone Guest;* Martyn in *Glory* (1931) recites Pushkin's verse and replicates exploits of Ruslan, a hero of his playful epic poem; Hermann in *Despair* (1934) sacrilegiously compares himself to Pushkin, misquoting one of the poet's most poignant elegies, but does not notice that he is a parody of Pushkin's madmen: his namesake in 'The Queen of Spades' and Evgenii in *The Bronze Horseman*; the name of Cincinnatus (which means 'curly haired' in Latin) in *Invitation to a Beheading* (1935–36) points at Pushkin's proverbial curly hair, while the protagonist modestly identifies himself with Vladimir Lensky, Pushkin's half-ironic and half-loving portrait of a romantic poet as a very young man.

It is in *The Gift* that Nabokov's worship of Pushkin finds its full expression. The protagonist, Fyodor, an aspiring émigré writer in Weimar Berlin, 'fed on Pushkin, inhaled Pushkin ... studied the accuracy of the words and the absolute purity of their conjunction ... Pushkin entered his blood. With Pushkin's voice merged the voice of his father' (*Gift*, 95). He believes that one ought to 'measure the degree of flair, intelligence and talent of a Russian critic by his attitude to Pushkin' and scorns Chernyshevsky and his school of 'progressive' ideological criticism that is unable to '[discard] its sociological, religious, philosophical and other textbooks, which only help mediocrity to admire itself' (*Gift*, 252). Fyodor's (and Nabokov's) filial love for their literary progenitor, however, does not exclude disagreement, competition and active engagement. The audacious young writer not only learns from Pushkin and admiringly

---

[5] On Nabokov's changing views of Dostoevsky see Alexander Dolinin, 'Nabokov, Dostoevsky, and 'Dostoevskyness', *Russian Studies in Literature*, 35/4 (Fall 1999), 42–60.

quotes and paraphrases his writings but finds fault with lapses in his prosody and style, imagines his post-mortem existence as a brief exercise in uchronia and even finishes one of his unfinished plays Pushkin's *Rusalka* (*The Mermaid*). This 'irreverent Reverence' for the founding father of Russian literature will later characterise Nabokov's mammoth commentary to *Eugene Onegin* in which he, on the one hand, explores and extols Pushkin's poetic originality but on the other, takes issue with instances of what he considers a cliché, a trite Gallicism or a borrowed banal image.

Two other important figures in Nabokov's Russian pantheon were Tolstoy and Chekhov and, again, his attitude towards them was double-edged. Together with his characters he would admire, for example, 'the pages on the zemstvo elections and the dinner ordered by Oblonski' in *Anna Karenina* (*Defense*, 113); or Tolstoy's 'violet shades and the bliss of stepping barefoot with the rooks upon the rich dark soil' (*Gift*, 70); or a scene in Chekhov's 'The Lady with the Little Dog' when the heroine 'lost that lorgnette in the crowd on the pier at Yalta' (*Glory*, 74). Portraying a faint-hearted man in *Camera Obscura* (*Laughter in the Dark*, 1932–33), he uses the mannerisms of Tolstoy's Aleksei Karenin (the protagonist cracks his finger joints like the latter), and the complaining cadences of an unhappy woman in *Mary* clearly mimic the inflections of Chekhov's *Three Sisters* (*Mary*, 54–55). Yet, at the same time he bemoaned 'all kinds of howlers in ... Tolstoy's hunting scenes and descriptions of nature' (*Gift*, 71) and, playing with the plot of Tolstoy's novella 'The Devil' in *Camera Obscura*, questioned and subverted its anti-sexual message.[6] With respect to Chekhov, Nabokov was more lenient and eager to partake of his 'hamper, which contains enough food for years to come' (*Gift*, 70) but still could mock his poor humorous story 'The Double-Bass Romance' (*Eye*, 12; 18; 84–85) and parody the same rambling monologues of Chekhov's heroines that he tried to imitate in *Mary* (*IB*, 103–5).

In the 1920s and 1930s the writer most palatable to Nabokov was Gogol. His early essay on *Dead Souls* (1927) panegyrises Gogol's unexpected similes and 'rambling metaphors', the detailed portrayals of peripheral characters, the incredible feel of colours, the magnificent 'flight of fantasy', the beautiful rhythm of lyrical digressions.[7] It seems that the young writer has just discarded a high-school idea of Gogol as a realist author, a critic of serfdom and autocracy, and discovered instead a weird artist with the

---

[6] On Tolstoy motifs in *Camera Obscura* see G. M. Hyde, *Vladimir Nabokov: America's Russian Novelist* (London: Marion Boyars, 1977), 59–63 and A. Yanovsky's annotations to the novel in *Sobr. soch.*, 3, 742–54.

[7] Vladimir Nabokov, 'Gogol', *Zvezda*, 4 (1999), 14–19.

uncanny sense of the absurd and the unreal, the master of the vivid grotesque from whom he could learn a lot. In the third chapter of *The Gift*, Fyodor rereads Gogol and, like Nabokov, enjoys his artistry but remarks: 'and at the same time, on his walks in Switzerland, the man who could write *thus*, used to strike dead with his cane the lizards running across his path – "the devil's brood" – as he said with the squeamishness of a Ukrainian and the hatred of a fanatic' (*Gift*, 177). The expression in quotation marks (in Russian: *chertovskaia nechist*) is taken not from Gogol's letters that Fyodor is reading but from a low-brow patriotic play, *Ivan Riabov: An Archangel Fisherman* by Nestor Kukol'nik, a prolific hack-writer popular in the 1840s.[8] Mocking Gogol's bizarre behaviour and ascribing the words of the disreputable author to him, Nabokov seems to distance himself from the forefather he had worshipped and hence to undermine Adamovich's favourite idea that Sirin continued the sterile, cold and inhuman streak of Gogol's writings. In Nabokov's American book on Gogol (1944), and especially in his university lectures, reservations about Gogol's genius become stronger and stronger.

It is clear that Nabokov's view of continuity within the context of a classical Russian tradition involved disputation, dialogue and reinterpretation. He believed that a modern Russian writer should incessantly question and test the canon, debunking stale notions and developing potentialities that have been overlooked or untried. Otherwise the heritage of Russian classical writers would get ossified and they would turn into 'rag dolls for schoolgirls' like those meaningless toys on which Cincinnatus C. used to work (*IB*, 14). His strategy of re-examination, reshuffling, appropriation and rejection was made explicit in *The Gift*, whose heroine, as he quipped in the English foreword, was not Zina, Fyodor's lover and muse, but Russian Literature. The protagonist begins his literary evolution under the influence of Symbolist poetry but soon rejects it and tries to find his own neoclassical style that stresses visual ingenuity and derives mostly from Russian post-Symbolist poetry and Ivan Bunin's colourful descriptive language. Then he discovers Pushkin's prose and, inspired by its 'divine stab', sets to write a biography of his father, a prominent naturalist and explorer, in which he demonstrates that the Pushkinian precise laconic diction overshadowed by the Russian nineteenth-century novel could be revived and elaborated in the modern context. His next step is the move 'from Pushkin Avenue to Gogol Street' (*Gift*, 143) when Fyodor begins to study Gogol's imagery and devices to use in his iconoclastic *Life of*

---

[8] Nestor Kukol'nik, *Sochineniia dramaticheskie*, vol. 2 (St Petersburg: Ivan Fishon, 1852), 549.

Chernyshevsky – a devastating critique of utilitarian, materialistic aesthetics of the 1860s that, in Nabokov's view, mangled Russian literature and prepared the way for socialist realism. Having exorcised the evil spirit of Russian literature in his book, he is ready to tackle a new challenging task – to write ' a classical novel, with "types", love, fate, conversations' (*Gift*, 347), that is to venture out into the territory of Dostoevsky, Tolstoy and Turgenev. The last chapter of the novel abounds with echoes of the 'great tradition' but almost all of them have an ironic or parodic twist.

In his hostile newspaper reviews of *The Gift*, a Riga critic, Petr Pilsky (who probably recognised himself in a scathing caricature of a Warsaw reviewer, Valentin Linyov, 'famous not only for not being able to make sense of the book he reviewed but also for not having, apparently, read it to the end' – *Gift*, 166), accused Nabokov of being 'fed up with all the recognized literary forms, both of the past and of the present, especially Russian.'[9] Sirin, in Pilsky's words, is 'a point person of protest and any kind of insubordination' who 'doesn't want to write like the others before him'; he 'feels no serene and joyful veneration of the tradition and the writers of the past' and 'all his writings display scorn and contempt toward every-thing celebrated in literature'.[10]

Pilsky's indignation is, of course, preposterous but his main point is not. Nabokov's treatment of the Russian classical tradition was indeed a far cry from a 'serene veneration'. His ambition as a writer was to earn a leading position within its context, but to be accepted into the club he had to change the very rules of admittance. For him, 'any genuinely new trend is a knight's move, a change of shadows, a shift that displaces the mirror' (*Gift*, 236–37). Like many other modernists, Nabokov believed in the truth famously formulated by T. S. Eliot:

> No poet, no artist of any art, has his complete meaning alone. His signifi-cance, his appreciation is the appreciation of his relation to the dead poets and artists. You cannot value him alone; you must set him, for contrast and comparison, among the dead ... The existing monuments form an ideal order among themselves, which is modified by the introduction of the new (the really new) work of art among them. The existing order is complete before the new work arrives; for order to persist after the supervention of novelty, the *whole* existing order must be, if ever so slightly, altered; and so the relations, proportions, values of each work of art toward the whole are read-justed; and this is conformity between the old and the new.[11]

---

[9] *Segodnia* (Riga), 29 April 1937.
[10] Ibid., 26 October 1938.
[11] T. S. Eliot, *The Waste Land and other Writings* (New York: Modern Library paperback, 2001), 101.

So, each of Nabokov's major Russian writings was strongly related to the tradition and at the same time tried to alter the canon and to introduce different standards of evaluation. In *The Gift*, Fyodor (whom Nabokov's Russian publishers called 'an *alter ego* of the author')[12] offers a set of instructions on how to tell literary right from literary wrong. The cardinal sins in this prescriptive system are as follows:

- the predominance of the general and abstract over the individual and concrete concurrent with serious flaws in the authorial sensory perception of the world – '[a] blissful incapacity for observation (and hence complete [uninformedness] about the surrounding world – and a complete inability to put a name to anything)' (*Gift*, 313);
- the utilitarian view of art that turns it into an 'eternal tributary to this or that Golden Horde' (*Gift*, 199);
- the indifference to (or the fear of) the irrational;
- the disregard for the artistic form and for the originality and precision of language, the use of clichés, stock plots and banal imagery.

On the opposite side, the cardinal virtues include the prevalence of the individual and concrete over 'general ideas' of any kind; an acute sensory perceptiveness, especially a visual one, and an ability to name any specialised element of the physical world; the view of art as an autotelic activity creating a 'second reality'; the yearning for the beyond; the originality of language and structure. In this system, Chernyshevsky is the greatest sinner, Pushkin is the greatest saint and all the other Russian writers of the past and the present are situated somewhere between the two poles. That is why Nabokov, throughout his Russian years, would present himself as an heir apparent of Pushkin and apply a 'Pushkin check' to both his contemporaries and predecessors.

With Nabokov's switch to English and, correspondingly, to a different literary context, the role of the Russian classical tradition in his writings faded. As he put it in the sly essay 'On a Book Entitled *Lolita*', his English books, in contrast to the Russian ones, are devoid of 'the implied associations and traditions – which the native illusionist, frac-tails flying, can magically use to transcend the heritage in his own way' (*Lolita,* 298). It means that the umbilical cord through which Nabokov's Russian oeuvre had been connected to the classical heritage was severed and the tradition itself became an object of contemplation from afar (and often the butt of hollow mockery, like in the first sentence of *Ada* [1969]) rather than a

---

[12] In an unpublished English synopsis of the novel hitherto attributed to Nabokov. See Yuri Leving, *Keys to The Gift: A Guide to Nabokov's Novel* (Boston: Academic Studies Press, 2011), 46.

battlefield of constant engagement. Some echoes of the past can be discerned only in *Pnin* (1957) with its Pushkin quotes and an insightful discussion of the double time frame of *Anna Karenina* copied from Nabokov's own lectures, though the very distance between the playful narrator-cum-doctor and his hapless 'patient' seems to imply that these inlays are there to characterise the mind of Timofei Pnin but not to transcend the heritage of the author's Russian forefathers.

In some cases, however, Russian references that go beyond the limits of a unilingual character's individual encyclopaedia and a unilingual English reader's common encyclopaedia make up a substratum of the text indicating the presence of the omniscient bilingual author. Thus in the poem of John Shade, an American poet par excellence in *Pale Fire* (1962), there are at least two allusions to Pushkin's poems he is not supposed to know: '*A watchman, Father Time, all gray and bent*' (*PF*, 470) seems to borrow an image of 'gray-haired time' ('sedoe vremia') from 'The Cart of Life' ('Telega zhizni'), while '... sensual love for the *consonne / D'appui*, Echo's fey child ...' (*PF*, 484) derives from 'The Rhyme' ('Rifma') and an unfinished 'Rhyme, my faithful friend ...' ('Rifma, vernaia podruga ...'), poems about origins of rhyme. If the first example can be explained away as a modification of the conventional formula 'old Father Time', the second one refers to nothing but Pushkin's subtexts because it was Pushkin who invented a unique pseudo-classical, quasi-Ovidian myth of the nymph Echo giving birth to a 'feisty daughter' named Rhyme, contrary to the common knowledge that classical Greek and Latin poetry did not use rhymes. The very idea of *Pale Fire* seems to come from Nabokov's Herculian (and slightly Kinbotean) labour of annotating *Eugene Onegin* and rekindling Pushkin's feud with clichés of the romantic imagination.

Similarly, *Lolita* (1955) can be read as a continuation of Nabokov's polemic against certain 'life-creating' (*zhiznetvorcheskie*) aspects of Russian Symbolism begun in *The Eye* (1930) and *Despair* (1934). Humbert Humbert's callous aesthetisised paedophilia, his utter disregard for other human beings whom he treats as docile dolls, parody daring pronouncements and representations of sexual desire in notorious writings of the Silver Age – Liudmila's playing cruel games with the naked body of an underage boy, Sasha Pyl'nikov, in Fyodor Sologub's *Petty Demon*,[13]

---

[13] See David M. Bethea, 'Sologub, Nabokov, and the Limits of Decadent Aesthetics', *The Russian Review*, 1/63 (2004), 48–62.

erotic poems of Valery Briusov, Konstantin Balmont and Viacheslav Ivanov,[14] Alexander Blok's manifesto 'About the Contemporary State of Russian Symbolism', in which the poet proclaimed that his aim was to turn the world into 'the arena of [his] personal actions, [his] anatomical theater or puppet theater' where he would act alongside his puppets.[15] The Russian roots of *Lolita* are hidden under the layer of explicit references to French Symbolism since Humbert Humbert, like John Shade, has no Russian background but in spite of that his 'confession' is interspersed with various Russian allusions for which the Francophone narrator cannot be responsible.

'On a Book Entitled *Lolita*' provides a list of ten episodes (one, 'pale, pregnant, beloved, irretrievable Dolly Schiller dying in Gray Star', non-existent) which, in Nabokov's words, are 'the nerves of the novel', 'the secret points, the subliminal coordinates by means of which the book is plotted' (*Lolita*, 297). It begins with the image of Maximovich, a 'stocky White Russian ex-colonel' (*Lolita*, 25) who is a cabdriver in Paris. His very name immediately evokes Maxim Maximych, an unpretentious officer in Lermontov's *A Hero of Our Time* and Aleksei Maximovich Gorky, a famous writer. When he is helping the narrator's unfaithful wife, his lover, to pack her things, Humbert sits 'with arms folded, one hip on the window sill' (*Lolita*, 26), thus unknowingly repeating the Napoleonic pose of Hermann in Pushkin's 'The Queen of Spades'. Each of the subsequent scenes on the list with the exception of the last one similarly has a name or detail that refers to some Russian subtext – to Pushkin's unfinished *Rusalka* and 'magic crystal' ('magicheskii kristall') in the finale of *Eugene Onegin*, to Diaghilev's company *Les Ballets Russes* and its productions, to Russian fairy tales, to a short story by Ivan Bunin about a huge dog saving a teen girl from being raped by a foreigner and to Dolly Oblonsky watching a doubles tennis match in *Anna Karenina*. The series culminates in a Hitchcockean cameo appearance by the author in the Elphinstone hospital under disguise of a 'bald brown-headed patient' who speaks with an obvious Russian accent. 'Now, who is nevrotic, I ask?' (*Lolita*, 232), he asks Humbert and the change of 'u' for 'v' not only suggests a bawdy Russian pun (*nevrotic=ne*

[14] See Alexander Dolinin, 'Nabokov's Time Doubling: From The *Gift* to *Lolita*', *Nabokov Studies*, 2 (1995), 18; Savelii Senderovich and Elena Schwarz, 'Zakulisnyi grom: o zamysle Lolity i o Vizcheslave Ivanove', *Wiener Slawistischer Almanach*, 44 (1999), 23–47.

[15] Alexander Dolinin, 'Nabokov's Time Doubling: From *The Gift* to *Lolita*', 22–23; Savelii Senderovich and Elena Schwarz, 'Lolita: Po tu storonu pornografii i moralizma', *Literaturnoe obozrenie*, 2 (1999), 63–72.

v rotik=not into the mouth) but also smuggles Nabokov's famous monogram VN.

Numerous echoes of Russian classics in most of Nabokov's English novels as well as his translations of *Eugene Onegin* (1964), *The Song of Igor's Campaign* (1960) and *A Hero of Our Time* (1958) show that he kept close ties with the tradition until the end of his life. Once his growth medium, in the American period it turned into an important part of his intertextual repertoire, a secret personal code and a backlight of his public persona. At any rate, it is safe to say that without Pushkin, Tolstoy, Gogol, Chekhov, Lermontov, Dostoevsky and scores of other nineteenth-century Russian writers there would have been neither Vladimir Sirin nor Vladimir Nabokov as we know these rare semi-identical twins.

CHAPTER 15

The Western Literary Canon

Michael Wood

Nabokov's Canon

At first glance, Nabokov's views of the western literary canon seem simply dismissive, or to be more precise, they seem selective, subtractive. He admires the writers others admire – there are few outliers or surprises among his preferences – but regularly wants to drop a few from whatever the given list is. If Thomas Mann appears in the company of Proust and Joyce, Nabokov asks 'What on earth is this ponderous conventionalist, this tower of triteness, doing between two sacred names?' (*Letters*, 242). In his notes to his translation of *Eugene Onegin* (1964) he places Cervantes and George Eliot among 'the plaster idols of academic tradition', although the chief one in this context is Dostoevsky, 'one of those megaphones of elephantine platitudes (still heard today)' (*EO*, III, 192). Baudelaire was not a mediocrity but he 'admired Balzac, Sainte-Beuve, and other popular but essentially mediocre writers' (*EO*, II, 354).

More gravely perhaps, Nabokov gives the appearance of not believing at all in the idea of a canon. He has no time for 'great books' (*SO*, 57) or 'great literature' (*SO*, 102), and declares his refusal 'to be guided by a communion of established views and academic traditions' (*SO*, 266). The word 'canon' is not a favourite of his. He doesn't appear to use it at all, although the story 'Tyrants Destroyed' (1938) offers a series of portraits of one of the title figures showing '[e]xperimental variety . . . followed by a canonized uniformity' in the man's look. The final result of the sequence is, rather surprisingly, a gaze that is 'stony' and 'lusterless' but also 'somehow unbearably eerie' (*Stories*, 439).

Eeriness in a tyrant's look is not attractive, but it does make the notion of political canonisation more interesting than disapproval or safely distant opposition will ever imagine it could be, and it finds an analogy in Harold Bloom's definition of his literary canon as marked by 'strangeness': 'a mode of originality that either cannot be assimilated, or that so assimilates us that we cease to see it as strange'.[1] Bloom's rather lurid enthusiasm for his pantheon of twenty-six authors clearly puts him at odds with the Nabokov who totally rejects consensus, but there are intriguing points of contact all the same. Bloom writes at one point of the 'seven deadly moral virtues', and is as adamantly opposed to sermonising in art as Nabokov is. Bloom celebrates singularity in terms that closely echo Nabokov's own. All his chosen works 'have in common is their uncanniness, their ability to make you feel strange at home', and 'all that the Western Canon can bring one is the proper use of one's own solitude'.[2]

If Nabokov had a literary canon, it would not differ from Bloom's in its broad outline. Shakespeare and Dante would be there, Dickens, Tolstoy, Proust, Joyce, Kafka. Even Borges and Beckett might make it. Asked about the linking of their names with his 'as the three figures of *probable* genius in contemporary fiction', Nabokov said

> That playwright and that essayist are regarded nowadays with such religious fervor that in the triptych you mention, I would feel like a robber between two Christs. Quite a cheerful robber, though. (*SO*, 184)

He did admire both writers, and he accepts the company, even if he mildly mocks the inflation of the rumour, and carefully separates the genres. This is a long way from (repeatedly) kicking Thomas Mann off the pedestal.

A presence and an absence in Bloom's list mark the real difference between his canon and what might have been Nabokov's. Freud is present in Bloom's book as a modern mythologist, 'the mind of our age';[3] psychoanalysis is a form of literature. Nabokov repeatedly evoked and dismissed 'the Viennese witchdoctor' ('Why should I tolerate a perfect stranger at the bedside of my mind?' [*SO*, 115]), and although these banishments are not quite the terminal affairs they appear to be, no amount of nuance is going to bring Freud into the circle of Nabokov's overt favour.[4]

The absence is more important. Bloom makes laudatory remarks about Flaubert and includes him among the 'canonical' novelists, but devotes no chapter to him,[5] or to any French novelist before Proust. Nabokov would be happy to let Balzac and Stendhal go, but, for him, there would be no modern literature without Flaubert: 'there would have been no Marcel Proust in France, no James Joyce in Ireland. Chekhov in Russia would not have been quite Chekhov' (*LL*, 147). Flaubert may even have rivalled his successors. Of

---

[1] Harold Bloom, *The Western Canon* (New York: Harcourt Brace, 1994), 3.
[2] Ibid., 28; 3; 28.
[3] Bloom, *Western Canon*, 348.
[4] See chapter 24 by Michal Oklot and Matthew Walker in the present volume.
[5] Bloom, *Western Canon*, 298.

a certain chapter in *Madame Bovary*, Nabokov says he does 'not think that, despite superficial innovations, Joyce has gone any further' (*LL*, 160). Flaubert was the first to treat the novel entirely as an art form; he thought prose should be at least as well written as poetry. He invented, if not the death of the author, then the author's stylistic disappearance, and he is the one writer in Nabokov's lectures on literature who is cited as a theorist of his own practice – because the theory is very much Nabokov's own.

> In several passages he lists all the romantic clichés dear to Emma's heart; but his cunning choice of these cheap images and their cadenced arrangement along the curving phrase produce an effect of harmony and art. (*LL*, 138)

Or in Flaubert's own words as Nabokov quotes them, 'irony does not impair pathos – on the contrary, irony enhances the pathetic side' (*LL*, 149). We have only to substitute the name Charlotte for the name Emma to transport ourselves into *Lolita* (1955).

If Nabokov had a canon, Flaubert would be at the heart of it, along with Pushkin and Tolstoy. The Russians would be part of the western canon, of course.[6] Indeed it is in large part because he thinks Russian literature is both western and poorly understood in the self-centred non-Russian west that Nabokov distinguishes so carefully between books and what we think of them, a distinction often reflected in the one we need to make between books and what he says of them. With this provision in mind we can consider what makes a canon without attributing a particular canon to Nabokov, and we can respect what may seem to be a startlingly democratic interest in literary moments as distinct from Literature.

'A Veritable Encyclopedia of Cruelty': *Don Quixote*

Nabokov is not sceptical about great books themselves; he thinks there are many of them. He does suspect 'fabricated notions about so-called "great books"' (*SO*, 57). It's the so-calling that matters. He says he feels he 'must fight a suspicion of conspiracy against my brain when I see blandly accepted as "great literature" by critics and fellow authors Lady Chatterley's copulations or the pretentious nonsense of Mr Pound, that total fake' (*SO*, 102). It is in the name of actual, particular instances of great work that he resists routine or ready-made claims for greatness. Even Dostoevsky can be 'extraordinarily amusing' (*SO*, 42), and one often feels that the undoubted virulence of Nabokov's attacks on him has to do not with the work but

---

[6] See chapter 14 by Alexander Dolinin in the present volume.

with what the later writer sees as an American infatuation and a Russian sentimentality:

> Non-Russian readers do not realize two things: that not all Russians love Dostoevski as much as Americans do, and that most of those Russians who do, venerate him as a mystic and not as an artist. (*SO*, 42)

Nabokov spoke most clearly about this distinction between texts and reputations in his lectures on *Don Quixote* (1983), and the argument is worth following out in some detail, not least because Nabokov later went to some lengths to travesty it. In a 1966 interview, he said (or rather read out from his notes), 'I remember with delight tearing apart *Don Quixote*, a cruel and crude old book, before six hundred students in Memorial Hall, much to the horror and embarrassment of some of my more conservative colleagues' (*SO*, 103). The placing of 'with delight' points us both ways: towards the memory and towards the tearing apart.

The occasion was a course Nabokov taught as a visitor at Harvard in 1952: six lectures on *Don Quixote* were followed by a further set on Dickens, Gogol, Flaubert and Tolstoy. He is not remembering wrongly; he had a great deal to say about cruelty in the lectures. But he had other things to say as well, and it is important to remember the time frame. In 1947, Nabokov had published *Bend Sinister*, his own masterpiece on the horrors of cruelty. In 1948, he moved from Wellesley to Cornell, and 'around 1949', as he later said, he picked up work on *Lolita*, which he had started in Paris. In 1953, he began to publish the stories that constituted *Pnin* (1957) in *The New Yorker*. When Pnin tells a colleague that 'the history of man is the history of pain' (*Pnin*, 419), the end of the phrase comes directly from the *Don Quixote* lectures (*LDQ*, 56).

Nabokov has two objections to the 'cheerful physical cruelty' (*LDQ*, 51) he finds in *Don Quixote*: the cruelty and the cheer. The reader, Nabokov thinks, is expected to react with 'wild merriment' to pictures of suffering and torture – with 'a shriek of hilarity' at one episode and a 'moan of mirth at another'. 'What a riot, what a panic!' (*LDQ*, 53). The 'mental cruelties' (*LDQ*, 51) are even worse, and here we see a 'detached cruelty ... driven to ... a diabolically sharp point' (*LDQ*, 48). 'Both parts of *Don Quixote* form a veritable encyclopedia of cruelty' (*LDQ*, 52), but that is only in keeping with 'the irresponsible, infantile, barbed and barbarous world of the book' (*LDQ*, 88). How could scholars have thought, so comfortably and for so long, that this is a 'humane and humorous' (*LDQ*, 110) work?

There is no doubt that Nabokov is having a good time, and no doubt either that Philip II's Spain was in many ways a cruel place. But it's a little difficult to distinguish between Nabokov's 'delight' in his description and the novel's supposed delight in pain. What has happened, I think, is not that Nabokov has 'surprised himself in his final opinion of *Don Quixote*', as Guy Davenport suggests (*LDQ*, xviii), but that he is talking about (at least) three different books: the *Don Quixote* traditionally read as a matter of good clean fun, sane mockery of illusion; the *Don Quixote* so full of violent trickery and mishaps that this tradition simply fails to see; and the romantic *Don Quixote* whose suffering hero invites repeated comparison with Christ,[7] and without whose presence we would not care about the torture and the pain.

Nabokov fully credits Cervantes with the creation of the figure of Don Quixote, and that is why he is able to call the book a 'scarecrow masterpiece' (*LDQ*, 27) and to contrast 'the Don Quixote masterpiece' with the 'trash' (*LDQ*, 37) of other parts of the book. He speaks lyrically about whole sections of the novel, and when he defines 'the artistic sense' as 'a sense of pity and beauty' (*LDQ*, 123), he is talking about the reader's sympathy for Don Quixote. He ends his lectures on just this note:

> His blazon is pity, his banner is beauty. He stands for everything that is gentle, forlorn, pure, unselfish, and gallant. The parody has become a paragon. (*LDQ*, 112)

We should briefly note how wonderfully partial and old-fashioned this summary is. Don Quixote is all of these things, and also angry, snobbish, bullying and deluded. Only in critical mythology can Cervantes' book be seen simply as either a jolly romp or a sacrificial tale of sorrows.

But our subject here is Nabokov's thinking and his argument takes an interesting turn precisely through his distinguishing between the book's myth and its world. The myth is what endures, and the world, which paradoxically enlarged the myth by giving it such a hard time, is what can be blamed. Can Cervantes be blamed for creating this world? Logically, this ought to be the case, or ought to be discussable. But mainly Cervantes just disappears from view. What interests Nabokov here is not the writer but what he calls 'the long shadow cast upon receptive posterity of a created image which may continue to live independently from the book itself'. 'Shakespeare's plays, however', Nabokov thinks, 'will continue to live, apart from the shadow they project' (*LDQ*, 8), while *Don Quixote* will not, does not. It *is* its shadow, or its different shadows, and we have to decide which shadow to watch.

---

[7] See *LDQ*, 55, 63, 73, 100, 102.

By shadow Nabokov in part means influence or recurrence, the echoes of *Don Quixote* in Dickens, Gogol, Flaubert and Tolstoy. But when he evokes 'books that are, perhaps, more important in eccentric diffusion than in their own intrinsic value' (*LDQ*, 111), he seems to have something more in mind, and when he describes 'Freedom from Pain' as 'one of the few things that may save our world' (*LDQ*, 75), he is speaking, as the narrator of *Bend Sinister* speaks, and as Pnin speaks, from the heart of a modern shadow, where a character in a novel can be saved from unbearable torment only by the charity of an author who will tweak him out of his fictional universe, where another has 'taught himself ... never to remember' his childhood sweetheart who died in Buchenwald (*Pnin*, 394). These impossibilities – freedom from pain, escape from fiction, controlled forgetting – are forms of hope for Nabokov, moral enchantments, ways of not giving in to the insensibility of consensus. When he remembers tearing apart *Don Quixote* and when he calls Cervantes a plaster idol – the dates of these acts are quite close, 1966 and 1964 – he is talking about reputations rather than a book and a writer, certainly, but above all he is resisting a view of literature and history that cannot acknowledge pain, and therefore cannot dream of freedom from it, cannot know what it means to be trapped in someone else's story or to have inconsolable memories.

The 'Thrill' of Reading

In the *Don Quixote* lectures, Nabokov offers us '*sensuous thought*' as 'another term for authentic art' (*LDQ*, 13). 'Sensuous' points us to Nabokov's recurring metaphors on this subject: shiver, quiver, tingle, thrill, throb (*LL*, 382; *Lolita*, 293) '[A] wise reader reads ... not with his heart, not so much with his brain, but with his spine' (*LL*, 6). One could imagine a canon made of remembered meetings with such sensations in reading, and it would in one sense be entirely private, an experience in solitude in Bloom's sense. No 'communion of established views and academic traditions' would be required. But of course we cannot be surprised if it turns out that almost identical thrills have been provoked in other readers by the same reading moments. This is not exactly what a classic is, but a classic would hold quite a few such moments for quite a few people.

Still, the slightly anarchic individual instance is important, and Nabokov turns it into a critical principle. Writing in 1972 in the *Saturday Review* about inspiration, a term he assumes others see as 'tasteless and old-fashioned' (*SO*, 309), he does what he so often does; he conflates the writer and the reader. If the writer knows what inspiration is – 'can readily distinguish it from the froth of a fit, as well as from the humdrum comfort of the "right word"' – then he or she is likely to 'seek the bright trace of that thrill in the work of fellow authors' (*SO*, 311). That trace, Nabokov says, can be found

> in this or that piece of great writing, be it a stretch of fine verse, or a passage in Joyce or Tolstoy, or a phrase in a short story, or a spurt of genius in the paper of a naturalist, of a scholar, or even in a book reviewer's article (*SO*, 312).

'This or that' is beautifully casual, as is the unfolding of the possible occasions. It is important that no complete work is evoked, not even a short story or a paper or an article, only a stretch or a passage or a phrase or a spurt of genius. These are modernist moments of the kind we find in Proust and Joyce, but the range of writing on offer is extraordinary, and is all generously covered by the word 'great'.

Nabokov's prose assumes the perfect meeting of thrills: the reader traces just the thrill the writer experienced. But the implied theory of reading could do without this magic. Precisely because of the brevity of the instances and the range of chances, we no longer have to think, to borrow another image from Nabokov, of 'the master artist' and 'the panting and happy reader' meeting on the mountain top, having each climbed from their different sides (*LL*, 2). The artist is not a master, and no one has to scale a mountain. The writer and the reader may thrill at the same phrase, at the writing and reading of it, and doubtless often do. But the only sure thing for either is the thrill, the unmistakable encounter with sensuous thought in words.

'Modern Atrocity' and the Western Canon

We have now met with pity, beauty and sensuous thought in relation to the artistic sense and art itself. How does Nabokov conjugate these abstractions – even sensuous thought is an abstraction as a concept – with his endless devotion to the concrete and the particular? We can throw his terms from the afterword to *Lolita* into the mix. Curiosity, tenderness, kindness, ecstasy are presented to us as either synonyms for art or elaborations of art's possibilities – it is hard to determine what it means simply to place them in parentheses after the word, as if the relation took care of itself. However we read them, they will help us to understand the notion of 'states of being where art . . . is the norm' (*Lolita*, 296).

The *Don Quixote* lectures contain a practice run for this kind of thinking that illuminates the argument of the *Lolita* afterword considerably.

Nabokov first demolishes the notion of 'reality' as itself an abstraction: what we call 'reality' is just that, not the thing itself but our name for a simplification of the thing. Then he acknowledges that there must be 'some correspondence' between 'certain generalities of fiction and certain generalities of life' (*LDQ*, 4). Which generalities? Pain, dreams, madness, kindness, mercy, justice are the instances Nabokov gives. It's a strange and also exemplary list, partly because of everything it leaves out, and partly because the terms invite the act of pairing: pain/kindness, dreams/mercy, madness/justice. We could travel a long way into Nabokov's fiction just by thinking about these twins. More locally, though, and connecting Nabokov's theory of art to the time frame I evoked earlier, we see that pain comes first, and we may want to imagine art and all the benign words associated with it (pity, beauty, thought, curiosity, tenderness, kindness, ecstasy) as caught up in a permanent relation with pain, neither denial nor transfiguration nor escape, but a sort of utopian balancing act, the projection of a world where something else 'is the norm'.

This is not our world, and Nabokov underlined the thought by frequently telling his students that novels were fairy-tales.[8] But it is a world we forget at our peril, and there is a remarkable moment in *Pnin* that combines irony and pathos in just the way Flaubert advised. Pnin is talking eagerly about the courses he would like to teach at Waindell College ('On Tyranny. On the Boot. On Nicholas the First. On all the precursors of modern atrocity'), and makes his remark about the history of pain. His kindly colleague taps him on the knee and says, 'You are a wonderful romantic, Timofey' (*Pnin*, 419). It's not clear whether Pnin is a romantic because he naively believes he can insert these horrors into a benign American curriculum, or because the colleague in question thinks all such things are just old stories, museum pieces from Old Europe. It is clear that for Pnin himself, and for Nabokov, 'modern atrocity' is just what a western canon would have to face, if it was not to be betrayed by the 'canonized uniformity' of those who prefer the idea of great books to the books themselves.

---

[8] See *LL*, 2, 10, 125; *LDQ*, 1.

CHAPTER 16

Publishing
Russian Émigré Literature
Siggy Frank

In a breathless tribute to Nabokov, the Russian émigré writer Nina Berberova would later remember her reaction on reading Nabokov's third novel, *The Luzhin Defense* (1929–30): 'A tremendous, mature, sophisticated modern writer was before me; a great Russian writer, like a phoenix, was born from the fire and ashes of revolution and exile. Our existence from now on acquired a meaning. All my generation were justified. We were saved'.[1] Nabokov's work indeed left an indelible mark on Russian émigré literature. And conversely, Nabokov's fate as a Russian writer was closely tied to the artistic, political and economic contingencies of Russian émigré literature which he chronicled carefully in his last Russian novel, *The Gift* (1937–38). Despite Nabokov's later perception that '[among] the young writers produced in exile [Sirin] was the loneliest and most arrogant one' (*SM*, 607), his work and aesthetics developed not in isolation but in direct response to two factors of émigré literature: the ideological debates which dominated the literary life of the Russian emigration in the interwar period and the economic uncertainties of Russian émigré publishing.

The October Revolution set in motion an unprecedented exodus of Russians to Western Europe, America and Asia, which became known as the First Wave emigration. Besides the many military men who had fought on the side of the White Guard in the Russian civil war, a large proportion of the refugees were members of the intellectual, cultural and political elite of pre-revolutionary Russia. The major political and cultural centres of the Russian emigration in Europe in the 1920s and 30s were Paris, Berlin and Prague (alongside Harbin in Manchuria and New York). Berlin, which due to its weak currency and low living costs had initially attracted a large number of Russian refugees, was – following the recovery of the German Reichsmark in 1924 – superseded by Paris as the unrivalled capital of the

[1] Nina Berberova, *The Italics Are Mine*, tr. Philippe Radley (New York: Knopf, 1992), 314–15.

Russian emigration. In all these centres, émigré communities endea-voured to recreate the cultural and political life of pre-revolutionary Russia with its attendant hierarchies, networks and institutions such as Russian schools, university departments, churches, libraries, newspapers, periodicals, publishing houses, theatres, uncountable cultural, social and professional clubs and associations as well as restaurants, shops and enterprises. In retrospect, Nabokov detected a certain pathos in these artificial worlds which could only ever be inadequate replicas of a lost homeland, suspecting that 'it would be easy for a detached observer to poke fun at all those hardly palpable people who imitated in foreign cities a dead civilization, the remote, almost legendary, almost Sumerian mirages of St Petersburg and Moscow, 1900–1916 (which, even then, in the twenties and thirties, sounded like 1916–1900 B.C.)' (*SM*, 601).

Legitimised by the authority of established Russian writers (Mark Aldanov, Ivan Bunin, Zinaida Gippius, Vladislav Khodasevich, Dmitri Merezhkovsky, Boris Zaitsev) and invigorated by the emergence of the next generation of Russian writers (Ekaterina Bakunina, Lidiia Chervinskaia, Iurii Fel'zen, Gaito Gazdanov, Vasily Ianovsky, Boris Poplavsky, Sergei Sharshun), the literary life of the Russian emigration manifested itself in prolific literary production, frequent public and private readings and talks, the establishment of literary associations and writers' unions, and incessant debates and polemics about the specific nature and purpose of émigré literature which continued throughout the interwar period. Russian émigré literature was part of the cultural nationalism which underpinned the émigrés' political project of national restoration. The initially firm belief in a speedy return home together with the 'emigration's founding myth of heroic anti-Soviet struggle' provided a common denominator for a community which lacked political cohesion and was riven by factionalism.[2] Perhaps because of the singularity of its extraterritorial position, Russian émigré literature of the First Wave was driven by a sense of its own significance in the defence of national culture. Against what was perceived as the Soviet corruption of authentic Russian literature and culture, Russian émigré writers articulated their own mission as the conservation and continuity of an authentic Russian literature and language. The anti-Soviet consensus was translated into an aesthetic impera-tive which rejected Soviet literary experiments, including the avant-garde movements of the 1920s, as well as the later state-imposed aesthetics of socialist realism.[3] This anti-Soviet stance became literally visible in the stubborn refusal of the major émigré periodicals and newspapers to adopt the new Soviet orthography. This peculiarity of émigré publishing became an integral part in Nabokov's short story 'The Visit to the Museum' (1939), at the end of which the Russian émigré narrator realises that he has been miraculously transported from France to the Soviet Union because the hard sign is missing from the shop sign of a cobbler, indicating the use of the new Soviet orthography. The dazzling effect of the story which invites the reader to recognise the absence of the sign as a sign in itself, relies entirely on its being printed in the Russian émigré press, which still adhered to the old orthography.

Although the agreed values of 'anti-Soviet' and 'authentically Russian' by which émigré literature was judged remained largely unchallenged, their exact definition was contested. While writers such as Bunin or Khodasevich continued to work in a pre-revolutionary literary tradition that leaned towards aestheticism, many writers of the older generation held up the nineteenth-century literary canon with its ideal of civic art as a touchstone of authentic Russian literature. Challenges to the realist model by the Soviet literary avant-garde or modernist writers were quickly dismissed as 'artificial' and inherently alien to the 'sincerity' and 'spiritual depth' of genuine Russian literature and its concern with pressing social and human questions. The close engagement with French modernism by the younger generation of writers, for instance, was seen as 'foreign' and 'un-Russian', so that an essentially aesthetic debate became couched in the rhetoric of national betrayal.[4]

Insisting on their legitimate position as heirs to the great Russian tradition, the younger generation, in a strategic move, deposed of Pushkin as the father of Russian literature. Instead they considered Lermontov's romantic exploration of spiritual ennui as a more suitable psychological model for their own work and recast Dostoevsky's realist novels as the direct predecessors of a modern literature of alienation and spiritual exile. This modernist reading of one of the major realist writers in the Russian canon allowed them to reinvent the existentialist strand of modernism as quintessentially 'Russian' and eschew the civic duty of art.[5] The sense of crisis which impressed itself deeply on modernist sensibilities was easily assimilated by this group of writers, for whom exile had been a formative experience. Their work became associated

---

[3] See Leonid Livak, *How It Was Done in Paris: Russian Émigré Literature and French Modernism* (Madison, WI and London: University of Wisconsin Press, 2003), 14–44.

[4] Livak, *How It Was Done*, 28–38.

[5] Livak, *How It Was Done*, 38–40.

with the adaptation of the French 'human document' (*chelovecheskii doku-ment*), a literary genre in the confessional mode defined by the merging of autobiographical and fictional elements, deliberate stylistic simplicity, political disengagement and introspective preoccupation with themes such as alienation, anxiety and crisis (e.g. Bakunina's *Body*; Sharshun's *Long Face*, Ivanov's *Disintegration of the Atom*).[6] This specific form of modernism defined by a pessimistic worldview and a striving for the paradoxical ideal of literary sincerity came to be known as the 'Paris note', promoted by the influential literary critic Georgii Adamovich and the literary journal of the younger generation, *Chisla* (*Numbers*).

In its self-conscious rejection of the realist tradition and the civic duty of art Nabokov's work converged to some extent with the literature of the younger generation of writers. More specifically, Nabokov shared the younger generation's interest in questions of (authorial) identity, the border between (auto-) biography and fiction, the relationship between life and art and the merging of different literary genres. Yet his work has none of the earnestness and existentialist anxiety which characterised the literature of the younger generation, and in works like *Despair* (1934) and *The Gift* he openly parodied the programmatic requirements of the 'Paris note', poking fun at Dostoevsky and the confessional style of the 'human document'. Keeping a clear distance from the younger generation, Nabokov oriented himself towards writers of the older generation without subscribing to their conservative aesthetics. To some extent, Nabokov's work, like that of the older generation, continues pre-revolutionary literary traditions, but the playfulness, the irony and the metafictional experiments which distinguish his work reach back to Pushkin's irony and authorial personae and Gogol's phantasmagorias rather than the giants of Russian realism (although he deeply admired Tolstoy). The implicit (and sometimes explicit) challenge his work presented to the realism of the older generation then was smoothed by the tribute he paid to the conventional canon of nineteenth-century Russian literature. Illustrative of this two-fold strategy is Nabokov's last Russian novel, *The Gift*, which caused a small scandal among the editors of *Sovremennye zapiski* (*Contemporary Annals*) who refused to print the fourth chapter, an irreverent biography of the nineteenth-century literary critic Nikolai Chernyshevsky, whose aesthetic and ethical programme of civically minded literature continued to have currency for the older generation. At the same time, *The Gift*, with its myriad allusions to Russia's literary

---

[6] See Maria Rubins, *Russian Montparnasse: Transnational Writing in Interwar Paris* (Basingstoke: Palgrave, 2015), 15–46.

legacy, was Nabokov's declaration of love to Russian literature, the uncontested 'heroine' of the novel (*Gift*, viii). It was this intriguing combination of aesthetic challenge and conservatism which helped facilitate his rise to fame in the Russian emigration.

The mixed reception of Nabokov's work within the emigration has to be seen as part of the generational struggle over the question of what constituted a national literature in exile. The rhetorical binaries (content versus form; sincerity versus artificiality; authentic Russian versus foreign) which shaped the literary discourse of the Russian emigration were also used to determine the value of Nabokov's writings. Frequent criticism of his work included notions of 'coldness', 'un-Russianness' and 'insincerity', while positive reviews noted his stylistic precision and formalist innovation.[7] Nabokov's later recollections of his reception in the emigration are structured by the same critical paradigms: 'the mystagogues of émigré letters deplored [Sirin's] lack of religious insight and of moral preoccupation ... Conversely, Sirin's admirers made much, perhaps too much, of his unusual style, brilliant precision, functional imagery and that sort of thing. Russian readers who had been raised on the sturdy straightforwardness of Russian realism ... were impressed by the mirror-like angles of his clear but weirdly misleading sentences' (*SM*, 608). The question of Nabokov's national and cultural allegiance continued to frame perceptions of him even after he had departed from Russian émigré literature. His linguistic transition from Russian to English at the end of the 1930s was interpreted as an 'act of cultural betrayal'[8] – a serious condemnation but also an implicit recognition of the vital contribution he had made to the legacy of Russian literature.

Nabokov was not as aloof from the émigrés' literary debates as his later recollections suggest. Combative and sharp-tongued, he engaged closely with the happenings in the literary world and sometimes became embroiled in their polemics. He was a member of several literary associations in Berlin and later in Paris attended sessions of Ilya Fondaminsky's literary 'Circle'.[9] He regularly wrote book reviews for émigré newspapers, in which the normative values underpinning his judgements positioned

---

[7] See Alexander Dolinin, 'Nabokov as a Russian Writer', in Julian W. Connolly (ed.), *The Cambridge Companion to Nabokov* (Cambridge: Cambridge University Press, 2005), 59–60.

[8] Alexander Dolinin, 'The Gift', in Vladimir E. Alexandrov (ed.), *The Garland Companion to Vladimir Nabokov* (New York and London: Garland, 1995), 137.

[9] Alexander Dolinin, 'Doklady Vladimira Nabokova v berlinskom literaturnom kruzhke', in *Istinnaia zhizn' pisatelia Sirina* (St Petersburg: Akademicheskii proekt, 2004), 369–75; Dolinin, 'Nabokov as a Russian Writer', 53–54.

him clearly within ongoing debates. For instance, his enthusiastic praise for Khodasevich and Bunin alongside his acerbic condemnation of some younger poets and their 'formless', existentialist work[10] made him a natural ally of Khodasevich in the latter's dispute with Adamovich and the 'artless' poetry of followers of the 'Paris note'. He invented intricate literary hoaxes which were designed to humiliate his opponents, in particular Adamovich. The short story 'Lips to Lips' (1956) is a cunning pastiche of the scandal that erupted around the corrupt publishing policies of *Chisla*, a journal Adamovich was involved with. In 1931, when the magazine was close to folding, it printed a short excerpt of a poorly written romantic novel entirely unsuitable for publication in a literary journal. The author, just like the protagonist of Nabokov's story, turned out to be a Russian businessman who had offered to subsidise the magazine. Nabokov's story was accepted by the émigré newspaper *Poslednie novosti* (Latest News), but withdrawn by the editors at the last minute and appeared only in translation more than twenty years later. In the late 1930s, a complex hoax based on the fictional poet Vasiliy Shishkov was another successful ploy to expose Adamovich's dubious literary judgement. The publication of a poem by the until then unknown poet Shishkov in *Sovremennye zapiski* elicited great praise from Adamovich, usually one of Nabokov's harshest critics, which turned into a wry smile when Nabokov published his short story 'Vasiliy Shishkov' (1939), claiming both the poem and Shishkov as his own creation. Beyond providing ammunition in another skirmish with Adamovich, the hoax also invoked a complex network of references to Khodasevich and became a poignant contemplation of his death and by extension that of émigré poetry.

Nabokov's fiction continued the literary debates by addressing topical questions head-on. *The Gift*, for instance, set in the Russian literary scene in Berlin, is on one level a direct response to the pressing questions which were discussed among Nabokov's literary contemporaries. Here he advances an alternative concept of literature, expressed in his 'programmatic statement, a Magna Carta of exilic creative behavior'.[11] Against the utilitarian function of literature which is inherent in both the younger generation's cultural pessimism and the older writers' notions of civic literature, *The Gift* sets an ideal of formalist aesthetics and commitment to pure art. Subverting realist

---

[10] Vladimir Nabokov, 'Vladislav Khodasevich. Sobranie stikhov', *Rul'*, 14 Dec 1927; 'Novye poety', *Rul'*, 31 August 1927; 'Iv. Bunin. Izbrannie stikhi', *Rul'*, 22 May 1929; 'Irina Odoevtseva. Izol'da', *Rul'*, 30 Oct 1929; 'Molodye poety', *Rul'*, 28 Jan 1931; 'Boris Poplavskii. "Flagi" Izd. "Chisla"', *Rul'*, 11 March 1931.

[11] Dolinin, 'The Gift', 146.

temporal and narrative structures, playing with different genres and literary traditions and creating a palimpsest of different texts, the novel is an unapologetic celebration of self-sufficient artifice. Alexander Dolinin has elegantly argued that 'Nabokov's intent [was] to reshuffle the Russian classical canon, to reconsider the accepted criteria of selection, and thereby to construe his own literary lineage'.[12] This redrawing of the literary tradition was part of an attempt to define a different critical field within the Russian emigration, the values and categories of which would accommodate his aesthetics. Long after he had switched to English, Nabokov would continue to define critical contexts which suited his own works, using forewords to his novels, the afterword to *Lolita* (1955), university lectures and most importantly a collection of interviews in *Strong Opinions* (1973), to control the critical reception of his work.

The fierce debates over the fate of Russian émigré literature concealed a deeper generational conflict within the literary field. The older generation's resistance to modernism, justified by their national mission to preserve Russian literature, served to maintain the hegemony of the nineteenth-century realist canon and by extension to legitimise the prime position of established writers in the hierarchy of émigré literature. It was the older writers who, embedded in the networks of the pre-revolutionary political elite, controlled distribution and access to the most important journals of the Russian emigration, including the Paris-based 'thick journal' *Sovremennye zapiski* (whose editorship included members from the right-wing of the Socialist Revolutionary Party such as Vadim Rudnev, Mark Vishniak and Fondaminsky). Younger writers were by no means barred from the major émigré publications but their perceived cultural and social exclusion allowed them to create a distinct group identity in opposition to the older generation.

Within this generational divide, Nabokov positioned himself aesthetically apart from but socially in close proximity to the literary establishment. From the very beginning, his professional network was tied to the older generation, partly because he could draw on his father's contacts within the political and cultural elite of the Russian emigration. He would later fondly remember that the 'editor of the daily *Rul'* [where Nabokov's father also served as editor until his death in 1922] (and the publisher of my first books), Iosif Vladimirovich Hessen [who was, like Nabokov's father, a member of the Kadet Party], allowed me with great leniency to fill his poetry section with unripe rhymes' (*SM*, 600). Nabokov went on to

---

[12] Dolinin, 'Nabokov as a Russian Writer', 59.

develop and maintain close personal relations with some of the key figures in the emigration's cultural and literary establishment. He felt a close affinity in all literary matters with Khodasevich, the literary critic of the émigré newspaper *Vozrozhdenie* (Resurrection), whom he described as 'the greatest Russian poet that the twentieth century has yet produced' (*Gift*, viii). He was also generally on good terms with Bunin, who was awarded the Nobel Prize for Literature in 1933, although initial flattery and good will would soon turn into a complex rivalry.[13] Other literary allies included Yuli Aikhenvald, an eminent literary critic of the Russian emigration in Berlin (up to his untimely death in 1928); Fondaminsky, who as editor of several journals strongly supported Nabokov's literary career; and Aldanov, a major writer of the older generation and later editor of the New York émigré journal *Novyi zhurnal* (New Review). Hessen also published Nabokov's first three novels, *Mary* (1926), *King, Queen, Knave* (1928) and *The Luzhin Defense* in the publishing house Slovo, which he had founded in Berlin in 1919. With financial backing from the German publisher Ullstein, Slovo focused on the reprinting of Russian classics, but also published some contemporary émigré writers, including, apart from Sirin, Aldanov and Bunin. Nabokov's later novels and short stories appeared regularly in the most prestigious publishing venue of the older generation, *Sovremennye zapiski*.

The literary emigration's vocal insistence on their own national importance ultimately betrayed a deep-seated sense of insecurity and the implicit recognition that the cultural elites of the émigrés' host countries, despite the occasional flaring up of interest, overall remained indifferent to the émigrés' cultural and literary production and mission.[14] This sense of 'working in an absolute void' (*SM*, 600), as Nabokov described the experience, was deepened by émigré writers' isolation from readers in their homeland. Books by Russian émigrés as well as their newspapers and journals were officially boycotted by the Soviet government for obvious ideological reasons, but also with a view to increasing the economic pressure on struggling émigré publishers.[15] Although by 1924 there were still an estimated eighty-six Russian publishers in Berlin, the majority of them were Soviet enterprises, while many Russian émigré publishers folded once the Mark stabilised and prices for paper and printing

[13] See Maxim D. Shrayer, *Bunin i Nabokov: Istoriia sopernichestva* (Moscow: Al'pina non-fikshn, 2014).
[14] See Alexander Dolinin, 'Clio Laughs Last: Nabokov's Answer to Historicism', in Julian W. Connolly (ed.), *Nabokov and His Fiction: New Perspectives* (Cambridge: Cambridge University Press, 1999), 197–215.
[15] See Efim A. Dinerstejn, '"Feindbeobachtung": Russische Verlage in Berlin im Blick der Sowjetmacht', in Karl Schlögel (ed.), *Russische Emigration in Deutschland 1918–1945: Leben im europäischen Bürgerkrieg* (Berlin: Akademie Verlag, 1995), 411–38.

increased.[16] It was their economic isolation and financial unfeasibility which made them weirdly artificial enterprises in Nabokov's eyes: 'The number of titles was more impressive than the number of copies any given work sold, and the names of publishing houses – Orion, Cosmos, Logos, and so forth – had the hectic, unstable and slightly illegal appearance that firms issuing astrological or facts-of-life literature have' (*SM*, 600). The continuously shrinking émigré readership did not form a stable literary marketplace which could have sustained Russian émigré literature in the long term. The literary capital Russian émigré writers could accumulate in this situation could never be transformed into financial gain, as Nabokov recognised: 'Owing to the limited circulation of their works abroad, even the older generation of émigré writers, whose fame had been solidly established in pre-Revolution Russia, could not hope that their books would make a living for them' (*SM*, 602).

In the end it was not only a question of whether the books could make a living for the writers, but even more profoundly, whether these books could save their writers from oblivion. Among the few sentimental objects with which his mother Elena surrounded herself in emigration were, as Nabokov would later remember, 'a cast of my father's hand and a water-color picture of his grave [which] . . . shared a shelf with émigré writers' books, so prone to disintegration in their cheap paper covers' (*SM*, 395). The brittle books, positioned here in close proximity to death, point to a deeper sense of impermanence which pervaded both creative and material aspects of the émigré literary production. Nabokov's entire Russian oeuvre, including poems, reviews, articles, short stories, novellas, plays and novels, was printed by Russian émigré publishers, periodicals and newspapers, none of which survived beyond the outbreak of the Second World War. Starting with *The Luzhin Defense*, all of Nabokov's novels were initially serialised in *Sovremennye zapiski* before being published in book form (with the exception of *The Gift*, which was not printed before 1952 by the Chekhov Publishing House in New York) by various Russian publishers (Russkie zapiski, Petropolis and Dom Knigi). Although within the context of the emigration Nabokov's prolific publishing constituted a prestigious achievement, the books, produced in soft covers on cheap paper and in small print runs, were printed for immediate dissemination in the small community of Russian émigré readers rather than for posterity.

While offering him a number of creative and financial advantages, Nabokov's switch to English must also be read as an attempt to write

---

[16] See Robert C. Williams, *Culture in Exile: Russian Émigrés in Germany 1881–1941* (Ithaca and London: Cornell University Press, 1972), 133–34.

Illustration 3 'Émigré books so prone to disintegration': First edition of *Zashchita Luzhina (The Luzhin Defense)* published by Slovo, 1930.

himself into a more permanent literary culture. In the process he also managed to consolidate and guard his legacy, ensuring that Sirin's delicate books were given a second life in the reprints of his Russian works by the Chekhov Publishing House, including the first unabridged publication of *The Gift*, as well as the subsequent English translations of his Russian books. Nabokov's later habit of recording exact bibliographical data for each Russian work in the forewords and commentaries to their English translations provides 'conclusive evidence' of their previous material existence and anchors them firmly in the transient literature of the Russian emigration. Even after he had departed from Russian literature, Nabokov continued to believe that despite the 'hectic, unstable and slightly illegal appearance [of émigré publishing]', when 'judged by artistic and scholarly standards alone, the books produced *in vacuo* by émigré writers seem today, whatever their individual faults, more permanent and more suitable for human consumption than [Soviet literature]' (*SM*, 600). The privileging of the intangible and abstract over the concrete and material is an integral part of Nabokov's idealist notions of reality, but it is also an essential belief for a writer who came of age in a literary culture which depended on 'books, so prone to disintegration'. Nabokov would immortalise Russian émigré literature and its never-ending debates over its own fate and nature in *The Gift*. Carried across the Atlantic and rehoused in an American émigré edition and an English translation, *The Gift* is also Nabokov's attempt to guard the legacy of the Russian emigration, his gift, as it were, to the literary culture which made him.

CHAPTER 17

Publishing
American Literature

Duncan White

When Vladimir Nabokov arrived in New York in May 1940, the US publishing industry was in the midst of a radical change. The economic privations of the previous decade had provoked a period of self-examination by an industry that had until then existed in a commercial microclimate. Publishers started to think of readers as consumers and realised that, by meeting their needs, they could compete in an increasingly crowded cultural marketplace. O. H. Cheyney's *Economic Survey of the Book Industry 1930–31* (1931) was followed by numerous other surveys of the industry producing research that, in Gordon Hutner's words, was 'crucial to the reshaping of the publishing business and the concomitant rise of the blockbuster'.[1]

The economic pressures of the Great Depression made expensively produced hardbacks unaffordable for large parts of the American population, stimulating the development of paperbacks and the parallel rise of so-called pulp fiction.[2] The success of Allen Lane's Penguin Books in Britain had not gone unnoticed and was emulated in 1939 by Robert de Graff and Simon & Schuster. Through their founding of Pocket Books affordable paperbacks became a fixture of the American literary marketplace. At the end of the Second World War, American publishing, like the larger American economy, entered the long boom. The 1946 American Book Publishers Council brought publishers together in the cause of their common commercial interest and forged stronger industry-wide alliances. With the end of war-time paper rations, the added value of lucrative movie tie-ins and new markets being opened up by paperbacks, publishing was flourishing and, by 1959, the year after Nabokov published *Lolita* in the United States, *Publishers Weekly* reported that the industry was 'approaching

[1] Gordon Hutner, *What America Read: Taste, Class and the Novel, 1920–60* (Chapel Hill, NC: University of North Carolina Press, 2009), 141.
[2] Hutner, *What America Read*, 124.

a billion dollar level'.[3] Nabokov's career as an American writer was coterminous with what John Tebbel has called 'The Great Change' in the history of American publishing.[4]

These economic changes in the publishing industry were far from universally welcomed. The champions of high modernism, from the Frankfurt School to the New York Intellectuals and the New Critics, argued that the culture industry was corrupting genuine literary art. The New Critic John Crowe Ransom, in his 1937 manifesto essay 'Criticism Inc.' attacked the idea that,

> art comes into being because the artist, or the employer behind him, has designs upon the public, whether high moral designs or box-office ones. It is an odious view in either case, because it denies the autonomy of the artist as one who interests himself in the artistic object in its own right, and likewise the autonomy of the work itself as existing for its own sake.[5]

By introducing the demands of a public, Ransom argued, the aesthetic integrity of the artist was compromised. This was an argument developed in the best-known attack on encroaching mass culture from the period, Clement Greenberg's 'Avant-Garde and Kitsch', published in *Partisan Review* in 1939. Greenberg warned that '[a]mbitious writers and artists will modify their work under the pressure of kitsch, if they do not succumb to it entirely' and that the consequences for succumbing to the temptations of the 'enormous profits' on offer was not just bad art but art that participated in the cultural imposition of totalitarianism. 'Kitsch', Greenberg argued, 'is merely another of the inexpensive ways in which totalitarian regimes seek to ingratiate themselves with their subjects.'[6]

Nabokov might not have shared Greenberg's Marxism but he shared his cultural politics. In 'The Proletarian Novel', a lecture he gave at Wellesley in 1941, Nabokov warned his undergraduate audience that, 'at the present moment this country is facing a grave danger: that danger is the best-seller'.[7] In a lecture on Pushkin delivered in Paris four years earlier, Nabokov had argued that ubiquity diluted the power of a literary work and that only after 'its literary fame has tarnished' can its 'true character' be revealed. 'The

[3] Quoted in Evan Brier, *A Novel Marketplace: Mass Culture, the Book Trade and Postwar American Fiction* (Philadelphia: University of Pennsylvania Press, 2010), 8.

[4] John Tebbel, *Between Covers: The Rise and Transformation of Book Publishing in America* (New York: Oxford University Press, 1987), 335.

[5] John Crowe Ransom, 'Criticism, Inc.', in his *The World's Body* (New York: Scribner's, 1938), 334.

[6] Clement Greenberg, 'Avant-garde and Kitsch', in *The Collected Essays and Criticism*, ed. John O'Brian, vol. 1 (University of Chicago Press, 1986), 10–13.

[7] Quoted in Will Norman, *Nabokov, History and the Texture of Time* (London: Routledge, 2012), 88.

greater the number of readers', he said, 'the less a book is understood, the essence of its truth, as it spreads, seems to evaporate.'[8] This was not a problem Nabokov had to contend with in his early years as an American writer. The challenge for Nabokov was to find a way to square his commitment to high modernist aesthetic autonomy with the life of a professional writer in the literary marketplace of 1940s and 50s America.

Nabokov expended a lot of energy chasing around Paris and London in the latter half of the 1930s trying to find American, British and French publishers for translations of his Russian novels, with limited success. In Britain, he published *Camera Obscura* (John Long, 1936) and *Despair* (John Long, 1937), in France translations of *The Defense* and *Despair* as *La course du fou* (Fayard, 1934) and *La Méprise* (Gallimard, 1939), and in the United States a revised version of *Camera Obscura* as *Laughter in the Dark* (Bobbs-Merrill, 1938). He arrived in New York, therefore, with almost no literary reputation to speak of outside the émigré community. After working in the Russian émigré environment where he had established good connections with the major journals and publishers, he was now competing in a much more open market. This meant less stability in Nabokov's relations with publishers, with the result that his first five novels published in America all came out with different houses: *Laughter in the Dark* (Bobbs-Merrill, 1938), *The Real Life of Sebastian Knight* (New Directions, 1941), *Bend Sinister* (Henry Holt, 1947), *Pnin* (Doubleday, 1957) and *Lolita* (Putnam's & Sons, 1958). *Conclusive Evidence*, his other major work of this period, came out with a sixth publisher, Harper & Brothers, in 1951.

Fortunately for Nabokov, he was not completely without allies in the United States. His cousin Nicolas Nabokov, a composer and formidable networker on the American cultural scene, introduced him to America's most influential critic, Edmund Wilson, who in turn secured Nabokov a gig writing book reviews for *The New Republic*. Wilson also helped put Nabokov in touch with James Laughlin, a publisher whose mission it was to save high modernist writers from the encroachment of mass culture.

Laughlin, the heir to a steel fortune, had wanted to be a poet and had gone to Europe in 1933 to pursue that dream but instead ended up as Ezra Pound's factotum. Pound, evidently not convinced of Laughlin's poetic talent, told him to 'do something useful . . . Go back and be a publisher'.[9] Laughlin used his family money to found New Directions, which was to be

---

[8] Vladimir Nabokov, 'Pushkin, Or the Real and the Plausible', tr. Dmitri Nabokov, *The New York Review of Books*, 31 March 1988, 41.

[9] Gregory Barnhisel, *James Laughlin, New Directions, and the Remaking of Ezra Pound* (Amherst and Boston, MA: University of Massachusetts Press, 2005), 51.

a publishing venue for serious writers without commercial appeal; he became an evangelist for literary modernism. In February 1937, New Directions published its first book, *White Mule* by William Carlos Williams, and in a postscript, Laughlin argued that it was,

> time to damn the book publishers as hard as you can damn them. They're traitors and enemies of the people. They have made literature a business. They have made the writing of books the production of cheap-goods [sic]. They have made a book a thing no more valuable than an automobile tire.[10]

While Laughlin offered Nabokov a way to get his first American novel out (after three years of rejections), he paid only a $100 advance for *The Real Life of Sebastian Knight* and while it garnered some positive reviews, it was ultimately a commercial failure. Publishing with New Directions brought Nabokov to a highbrow American readership, and increased his store of cultural capital in this new field, but it did very little for his *actual* capital. Another advocate of modernist difficulty, the poet and New Critic Allen Tate, championed Nabokov's second English-language novel. In his role as editor of *belles lettres* at Henry Holt, Tate advocated for *Bend Sinister* even when many of his colleagues were sceptical about its appeal. When Tate left Holt shortly before the novel appeared, the publisher seemed to lose faith in the project and failed to promote it, which resulted in very poor sales figures. This was frustrating for Nabokov, who wanted to be freed from his reliance on university teaching for income, but also confirmed him in the rectitude of his cultural politics, in which authentic literary value was defined by its autonomy from the demands of the marketplace rather than by something as crass as sales.

There was, however, a double game being played by publishers, one that Nabokov was drawn into with *Lolita*. The great divide between modernist literature and the demands of the market was not quite as profound as it was made out to be. As Evan Brier points out, in the post-war period publishers realised that 'announcing the novel's distance from commerce and especially mass culture could quickly pay commercial dividends'.[11] This was not new: between the wars, modernist works had been carefully marketed to capitalise on their capacity for enriching the reader's cultural status, and James Joyce's *Ulysses* and Gertrude Stein's *Alice B. Toklas* became bestsellers.

In the case of *Ulysses*, the appeal of the novel to a wider audience was driven not just by this idea of cultural self-improvement but also by its

[10] Barnhisel, *James Laughlin*, 64.
[11] Brier, *A Novel Marketplace*, 13.

notoriously explicit sexual content. Bennett Cerf, of Random House, not only challenged the book's censorship in a 1933 court case but also prepared an edition to go on sale to capitalise on the publicity of winning the case. This was a pattern – accusations of obscenity, the struggle against censorship, marketable notoriety – that had been initiated by the publication of Gustave Flaubert's *Madame Bovary* (1856) and Charles Baudelaire's *Les Fleurs du mal* (1857) and it was one repeated through the evolution of modernist literature. The success of this covert marketing strategy depended, of course, on the publisher's ability to either successfully overturn censorship or narrowly avoid it; otherwise the publicity would go to waste. This is exactly what had happened to Nabokov's friend Wilson, who lost his case to have the ban on *Memoirs of Hecate County* (1948) lifted.

By the time Nabokov began looking for a publisher for *Lolita* at the end of 1953 he had begun to develop his reputation in the American literary marketplace by publishing poems, short stories and excerpts from his memoir in *The New Yorker*, introducing him to an influential and wealthy readership. He was also publishing work in *Partisan Review*, the foremost intellectual journal of the moment. Nabokov could not, however, find an American publisher willing to take a risk on *Lolita* and so he contacted Doussia Ergaz, his French agent, about trying to place it with a publisher in Paris. Nabokov suggested Ergaz approach Sylvia Beach, who had published *Ulysses* in 1922 but the manuscript eventually found its way to Maurice Girodias' Olympia Press. Modelled on the Obelisk Press, which had been run by Girodias' father Jack Kahane, Olympia published avant-garde writers whose work could not get past the censors in the United States and Britain, along with more straightforward pornographic fiction (what Nabokov called 'obscene novelettes').[12] In September 1955, *Lolita* came out in the 'Traveller's Companion' series, aimed at tourists visiting Paris who wanted to read books that were banned back home. Fortunately for Nabokov, one of those readers turned out to be Graham Greene, who selected it as one of his favourite books of the year in *The Sunday Times*.[13]

With *Lolita*'s notoriety established, the time was ripe for American publication, and the battle was on to prevent it being censored. Jason Epstein, who had originally wanted to publish *Lolita* with Doubleday, but had been overruled by the company president, suggested to Nabokov that a substantial excerpt be published in the second edition of *The Anchor*

---

[12] Quoted in Brian Boyd, *Vladimir Nabokov: The American Years* (Princeton: Princeton University Press, 1991), 266.

[13] 'Books of the Year: Chosen by Eminent Contemporaries', *The Sunday Times*, 25 December 1955, 4.

Review, packaged with essays by the respected literary critic F. W. Dupee and Nabokov himself. *Anchor Review* came out in June 1957, the same month that the Supreme Court diluted the powers of obscenity laws in *Roth* v. *United States*.[14]

While the threat of censorship in the United States appeared to recede, Girodias' recklessness regarding copyright law and the sale of copies to American buyers created headaches for Nabokov. In a further complication, Girodias threatened to ruin Nabokov's chance at securing an American publisher with his demand for 50 per cent of the author's royalties. Walter Minton, of Putnam's, did not give up in his pursuit of the novel, however, and after protracted negotiations, Nabokov secured an American publisher for *Lolita* in early 1958, more than four years after he had finished writing it.

On 28 September 1958, *Lolita* climbed to the top of *The New York Times* bestseller list. It held that position for seven weeks, until Boris Pasternak's *Doctor Zhivago* supplanted it. The successful sales of *Lolita* were not entirely a result of its scandalous reputation. *Lolita* was included in the Reader's Subscription book club, which, in the words of one of its founders, Jacques Barzun, had been created in 1951 to build 'an audience for books that the other clubs considered to be too far above the public taste'.[15] The editorial board of the book club consisted of Barzun, W. H. Auden and Lionel Trilling, who would write critical essays to accompany a book's publication in the series. For *Lolita*, Trilling wrote his influential essay 'The Last Lover', which was published in the August 1958 edition of *The Griffin*, the subscriber's pamphlet. The paradox inherent in the very notion of a highbrow book club was a reflection of the double game publishers were playing with their marketing of serious fiction, advertising its status as elite culture but also advertising this fact as widely as possible. The trick was to acquire a large readership without seeming to want to.

By September 1959, after spending more than a year on the bestseller list, *Lolita* had sold 236,700 copies in bookshops and a further 50,000 through book clubs. Sales spiked again when the Stanley Kubrick film adaptation hit the cinemas in 1962 and by the mid-1980s the novel had sold fourteen million copies around the world.[16] The scale of this success radically changed the power dynamic between Nabokov and his publishers. With the royalties from *Lolita*, the film rights and the prospect of large advances

[14] See *The Anchor Review: Number Two* (June 1957).
[15] Quoted in Arthur Krystal, *A Company of Readers: Uncollected Writings of W. H. Auden, Jacques Barzun, and Lionel Trilling from The Readers' Subscription and Mid-Century Book Clubs* (New York: Free Press, 2001), x.
[16] See Boyd, *American Years*, 387.

for future works, Nabokov could afford to leave his university post at Cornell and become a full-time writer. There was now such demand for his work that he could publish not only new novels in English but also translations of his Russian novels. Furthermore, he began to exert control over the *way* his books were published; his extensive correspondence from the period attests to the attention he paid to cover art, blurbs and other peritextual material. He conceived of the parts of the book as being integral to the literary work of art rather than merely packaging to help foster sales. In effect, Nabokov used the success of *Lolita* as leverage to publish books on his terms.

To some critics, Nabokov's writing after *Lolita* exhibited a deliberate refusal to conform to the market expectations his bestseller had created. Dwight Macdonald argued that in *Pale Fire* (1962) there was 'a perverse bravado' on Nabokov's part, 'as if the author, with a superior smile, is saying to the large public that read "Lolita": "So you think I'm a manufacturer of best-sellers? Try *this* on your pianola!" I must confess I find this attitude, if not its product, attractive.'[17] His next novel, *Ada* (1969), was, if anything, even more inaccessible, yet on its publication Nabokov was pictured on the cover of *Time* magazine. Both these novels were designed to encourage non-linear recursive readings, defying the logic of consumption inherent in the idea of books as commodities. These were not books to be consumed and disposed of after a single reading and their value as cultural object bore little relation, by this way of thinking, to the cost of purchase.

By then Nabokov was established as a literary celebrity and his value to a publisher was as much his cultural 'brand' as any promise of sales. He appeared on the cover of *Newsweek* on 25 June 1962, and the following year he was nominated for an Oscar for best-adapted screenplay for Kubrick's *Lolita* (he lost to Horton Foote, for his adaptation of *To Kill a Mockingbird*) despite the fact that the final script bore little resemblance to the one he had submitted.[18] He attended glamorous parties at which he met stars like Marilyn Monroe and Billy Wilder, and he corresponded with Alfred Hitchcock about writing a screenplay for a Cold War thriller.[19] In 1967, McGraw-Hill decided to prise him away from Putnam's, offering $250,000 for eleven books, with generous royalty agreements. As well as providing financial security, this deal guaranteed the integrity of Nabokov's oeuvre for posterity, something that must have seemed an unlikely prospect when he arrived in New York as an obscure Russian novelist at mid-century.

---

[17] Dwight MacDonald, 'Virtuosity Rewarded', *Partisan Review* (Sept 1962), 439.
[18] Barbara Wyllie, *Vladimir Nabokov* (London: Reaktion, 2010), 144.
[19] See *Letters*, 361–64.

Nabokov's oeuvre continued to grow after his death in 1977. He had insisted that he did not want any unfinished manuscripts published but retaining posthumous control of his literary production proved challenging. Nabokov had written a note in 1972 insisting that his 'chaotic and sloppy' lectures 'must *never* be published. None of them!'[20] This note was filed separately from the manuscripts of the lectures so neither Véra, Nabokov's widow, or his son Dmitri saw it until long after they had consented to the publication of the lectures. Some extant fiction was also discovered and published, including the novella *The Enchanter* (1986) and the story 'Easter Rain' (1997). In 2009, Dmitri Nabokov decided to publish *The Original of Laura*, the novel Nabokov had been working on at the time of his death and which he wanted destroyed. The demand for a 'new' Nabokov novel proved too strong to resist.

[20] Quoted in Boyd, *American Years*, 173.

CHAPTER 18

Detective Fiction

Michal Oklot and Matthew Walker

In considering the question of Nabokov and detective fiction, we might begin with his Cornell lectures on Robert Louis Stevenson's *Dr. Jekyll and Mr. Hyde*, which open with an 'injunction' for his students:

> Please completely forget, disremember, obliterate, unlearn, consign to oblivion any notion you may have had that 'Jekyll and Hyde' is some kind of mystery story, a detective story, or movie. It is of course quite true that Stevenson's short novel . . . is one of the ancestors of the modern mystery story. But today's mystery story is the very negation of style, being, at the best, conventional literature. Frankly, I am not one of those college professors who coyly boasts of enjoying detective stories – they are too badly written for my taste and bore me to death. Whereas Stevenson's story is – God bless his pure soul – lame as a detective story . . . It has, however, its own special enchantment if we regard it as a phenomenon of style (*LL*, 179–180).

'Style', of course, is always Nabokov's paramount concern in his literary criticism. As he argues elsewhere in his lectures, style 'is not a tool, it is not a method, it is not a choice of words alone. Being much more than all this, style constitutes an intrinsic component or characteristic of the author's personality. Thus when we speak of style we mean an artist's peculiar nature' (*LL*, 59–60). Style, in other words, is shorthand for the organising principle of the artwork, what synchronises its origin with its end. We might therefore conclude from Nabokov's injunction that detective fiction, being the 'very negation of style', ought to occupy one of the lower rings of his artistic inferno, somewhere between psychoanalysis and book clubs, and, furthermore, that it ought to stay there for good. The situation, however, is more complicated. Certainly, detective fiction supplies Nabokov with a slew of entries for his encyclopedias of *poshlost*[1] – his protagonists mock its clichés, his fools consume it 'with the zest of . . . model prisoner[s]' (*LATH*, 607) – but, paradoxically, considered as a

---

[1] See Oklot and Walker, 'Psychoanalysis', in the present volume, 214.13 for Nabokov's definition of *poshlost*.

genre, or perhaps more precisely as an epistemological problem, detective fiction also seems to present Nabokov with nothing less than a cosmic schema for tracing 'style' as such; the reader follows clues back to the authorial crime, as it were. As if to confirm this, there is the line posted as an epigraph by Nabokov's posthumous editor, Fredson Bowers, at the very beginning of *Lectures on Literature* (1980) itself: 'My course, among other things, is a kind of detective investigation of the mystery of literary structures.' A mystery and an investigation: we may be required to forget considering 'Dr Jekyll and Mr. Hyde' as a detective story, but at the same time we are being asked to read it as if it were, at least if we want to follow it down to its root, to its style.

All of this is one way of stating that in contrast with some of his other enemies, Freud obviously, or Marx, Nabokov's relation to detective fiction is somewhat more ambiguous. An object of repulsion and attraction, detective fiction may be denounced as the very negation of art, but Nabokov nevertheless allows us to entertain the notion that it plays a decisive role in his own. *Lectures on Literature* is not the only place we encounter this dialectic. *Strong Opinions* (1973), for one, that other gospel of Nabokov criticism, on this note seems no less contradictory: in one interview Nabokov remarks that, 'with a very few exceptions, mystery fiction is a kind of collage combining more or less original riddles with conventional and mediocre artwork' (*SO*, 129), but in another, asked to comment on the *nouveau roman* as 'the detective story taken seriously', Nabokov does not reject the suggestion that he takes it 'seriously' too, though one can also argue that he is nothing if not coy in his response. 'My boyhood passion for the Sherlock Holmes and Father Brown stories may yield some twisted clue' (*SO*, 174), he says, invoking the heroes of Arthur Conan Doyle's and G. K. Chesterton's mysteries, but then this is still but a puzzle-piece, not the last one in the puzzle itself. Even when detective fiction is savaged in his work – perhaps most expressly in *The Prismatic Bezel*, the novel within the novel described in *The Real Life of Sebastian Knight* (1941) – it does so as 'a clown developing wings, an angel mimicking a tumbler pigeon', that is, as parody, 'a springboard for leaping into the highest region of serious emotion' (*RLSK*, 70) – though of course the chiasmus of the prior metaphor suggests that any leap might well be followed by a fall. Thus if we are to approach the theme of detective fiction in Nabokov's art properly we will need to navigate between an urge on one hand to consign the genre to oblivion and, on the other, an adept's fondness for its 'twisted clues', bearing in mind that, with Nabokov, our own attempts to unravel them are always in danger of unravelling as well.

Contrary to his protestations before his students, there is evidence that Nabokov was in fact a willing reader of detective fiction as an adult, not just in his youth. In a letter of 1946 to Edmund Wilson, he discusses rereading Conan Doyle (*NWL*, 185–86), and in another from 1943, written in the aftermath of a visit to the dentist, we even find him reading detective stories for what we might call light entertainment – but still critically, paying attention to the smallest details of the narrative

> I was laying on my bed groaning as the frost of the drug gradually gave way to the heat of pain – and as I could not work, I lay there yearning for a good detective story – and at that very moment the *Taste for Honey* sailed in. Mary [McCarthy, Wilson's then wife] was right, I enjoyed it hugely – though the entomological part is of course all wrong (in one passage he confuses the Purple Emperor, a butterfly, with the Emperor moth). But it is very nicely written. Did Mary see the point of the detective's *name* at the very end? I did. (*NWL*, 123)[2]

In a different letter, written in late 1944 in response to an essay on crime fiction that Wilson had just published in the *New Yorker*, Nabokov refers to Agatha Christie, but also gives us some more clues about his overall attitude toward the genre:

> I liked very much your article on detective stories. Of course, Agatha is unreadable – but Sayers, whom you do not mention, writes well. Try *Crime Advertises*.[3] Your attitude towards detective writing is curiously like my attitude towards Soviet literature, so that you are on the whole absolutely right. I hope that one day you will tackle the quarter of a century-old literature *sovetskovo molodnyaka* [of the younger Soviet generation] – and then I shall have the exquisite pleasure of seeing you reel and vomit—instead of the slight nausea you experienced with:

Here there follows a long inventory of genre automatisms (culled from a 1929 anthology identified as *The World's Best One Hundred Detective Stories*), at the end of which Nabokov presents Wilson with what he calls 'the gem of my collection, – note the beautiful coincidences':

> 'I stared at him in complete bewilderment. "Do you mean to say" – I began. "That she'd never been murdered" he supplied.' (J. D. Beresford, 'The Artificial Mole')

> 'He whipped out the photograph in question and confronted the astounded Chief Inspector with it. "*Beresford*, man! Beresford's the murderer, of his own wife."' (Anthony Berkeley, 'The Avenging Chance') (*NWL*, 159–160)

---

[2] A *Taste for Honey*, as Simon Karlinsky notes in his commentary to the Nabokov-Wilson letters, is a 1941 novel by H. F. Heard that also appeared under the title *A Taste for Murder* (see *NWL*, 124).

[3] This is *Murder Must Advertise* (1933) by Dorothy L. Sayers, as Karlinsky also points out in his commentary (see *NWL*, 160).

This 'gem' stands out not only because a random, 'avenging' coincidence ends up implicating the author of one story as the murderer of another. It also highlights what rings most false in the genre for Nabokov beyond its gimcrack language, what it most has to answer for: when detective fiction obeys its rules, chance becomes nothing but a slave to fate, always on hand to ensure that the moment of revelation comes when it must and equally quick to make itself scarce lest things become obscure again. Wilson's essay in the *New Yorker* that Nabokov endorses makes a similar point, but takes it further and interprets the mass appeal of detective fiction as a disguised reaction to the uncertainties of modernity itself. Between the world wars, detective fiction became 'more popular than ever before', Wilson writes,

> ... and there is, I believe, a deep reason for this. The world during those years was ridden by an all-pervasive feeling of guilt and by a fear of impending disaster which it seemed hopeless to try to avert because it never seemed conclusively possible to pin down responsibility. Who committed the original crime and who was going to commit the next one? ... Everybody is suspected in turn, and the streets are full of lurking agents whose allegiances we can never know. Nobody seems guiltless, nobody seems safe; and then, suddenly, the murderer is spotted, and – relief! – he is not, after all, a person like you or me. He is a villain ... and he has been caught by an infallible Power, the supercilious and omniscient detective, who knows exactly how to fix the guilt.[4]

It is not hard to guess why Nabokov might have encouraged Wilson to draw a connection between detective fiction and socialist realism: in both cases when the genre's conventions are rehearsed successfully there can be no doubts about who is to blame, what is to be done and what will happen in the end.

Some of the parodies of detective fiction that we find in Nabokov subvert it precisely by challenging this sense of an ending. Consider 'The Passenger' (1927), in which the narrator, a writer in conversation with a critic, laments how false art turns life into an 'entertaining film' that unfolds 'without a hitch' and is 'furnished with an unexpected but all-resolving outcome' (*Stories*, 183). In the anecdote that lies at the heart of the story, however, life defies convention: the writer, traveling on an overnight train, is awoken by a newly boarded passenger climbing into the bunk above him – all he sees is a hideous toe protruding from a hole in his sock – and then has to listen as the man begins to sob to himself in the dark. When the writer's stop comes he gathers his things, still without getting a glimpse of the man, and makes to disembark, but is prevented from doing so by the

---

[4] Edmund Wilson, 'Why Do People Read Detective Stories,' *The New Yorker* (14 October 1944), 76.

police – they are searching for a murderer. Documents are checked one by one, and the suspense dutifully builds as the detective finally comes to the man in the upper bunk, wakes him and asks for his passport (surely he is the culprit!), only for the detective to calmly return his papers and continue on. The critic counters: 'The Word is given the sublime right to enhance chance and to make of the transcendental something that is not accidental. Out of the present case, out of the dance of chance, you could have created a well-rounded story if you had transformed your fellow traveler into a murderer'. The writer responds: 'Yes, yes, that did occur to me ... The trouble is that we are in the dark – maybe Life had in mind something totally different, something much more subtle and deep. The trouble is that I did not learn, and shall never learn, why the passenger cried' (*Stories*, 187). Of course, the reader who attends to small details will see how Nabokov has rounded off his own story – in its first sentence, the writer absent-mindedly tosses a match into the critic's empty wine glass, and it is still there at the end, as the writer refills it for him. Yet in giving us the tools to solve this little mystery Nabokov has not resolved his writer's larger one: life might be pure chance, or it might just have more imagination than average human fictions can muster, but in either case, the question of one's ability to narrate it adequately and account for all its details has to remain an open one for the true artist. Hermann, Nabokov's villain in *Despair* (1934), fails precisely for this reason.

Tzvetan Todorov, in an essay from 1966, 'The Typology of Detective Fiction', argues that the hallmark of the genre is its 'duality', insofar as its representatives necessarily contain 'not one but two stories, the story of the crime and the story of the investigation'. The first is 'what really happened', whereas the second explains 'how the reader (or narrator) has come to know about it'.[5] On the face of it, this seems to conform to Russian Formalism's distinction between *fabula* (story) and *siuzhet* (plot), between a signified 'real' and the manner in which a narrative represents it. Yet according to Todorov, what sets detective fiction apart from other literature is the peculiar, tenuous relation between the two stories, for the story of the crime 'is in fact the story of an absence: its most accurate characteristic is that it cannot be immediately present in the book'.[6] Todorov of course is not the first to make this argument – indeed, knowledge of this fissure might well lie at the crux of all serious modernist evaluations of the

[5] Tzvetan Todorov, 'The Typology of Detective Fiction', in *The Poetics of Prose* (Ithaca, NY: Cornell University Press, 1977), 44–45.
[6] Ibid., 46.

genre. Gertrude Stein, for instance, in her 1936 essay 'What are Master-
Pieces and Why Are There So Few of Them', writes:

> It is very curious but the detective story which is you might say the only
> really modern novel form that has come into existence gets rid of human
> nature by having the man dead to begin with the hero is dead to begin with
> and so you have so to speak got rid of the event before the book begins.[7]

Ernst Bloch too sees this as the 'most decisive criterion'. In detective
fiction, he argues,

> . . . the crime has already occurred, outside the narrative; the story arrives on
> the scene as a corpse. It does not develop its cause during the narrative or
> alongside it, but its sole theme is the discovery of something that happened
> *ante rem*. Everywhere else the narrative was genetically present: the Alberichs
> rob the gold before our eyes and Raskolnikov kills the pawnbroker just as
> epically and visibly as he conceals everything that follows.[8]

Certainly, no small number of Nabokov's plots arrive as corpses: in the first
chapter of *Despair*, when Hermann stumbles upon the vagrant he thinks is
his double, he recognises in him – mistakenly, it will turn out – 'my own
face, my mask, the flawlessly pure image of my corpse' (*Despair*, 10); in the
Real Life of Sebastian Knight, the biographer V.'s quarry is dead from the
beginning; from the foreword of *Lolita* (1955) we learn that Humbert
Humbert and all the principal figures in his confession are already dead;
from the foreword of *Pale Fire* (1962), that the author of a poem we are about
to read by the same name is already dead; and, from the brief note at the
opening of *Ada* (1969), that, with the exception of the editors, 'a few
incidental characters, and some non-American citizens', *everyone* mentioned
by name in the novel is dead. This is not an exhaustive list, and the motif
goes beyond plot structure. To wit: if we take as a model for Nabokov's own
art that of Sebastian Knight, which is said to originate from an 'uncanny
perception of secret decay', then the dead body might just as well figure
everything in culture that has lost meaning or begun to rot; after all, for
Knight, 'the merest trifle, as, say, the adopted method of a detective story,
became a bloated and malodorous corpse' (*RLSK*, 70). The constant question in Nabokov's oeuvre thus becomes how to go about reanimating it.
Knight's *Prismatic Bezel* makes a joke of this by unmasking its chief murder
suspect (a certain 'Nosebag') as the alleged murder victim, alive and well in

---

[7] Gertrude Stein, 'What are Master-Pieces and Why Are There So Few of Them', *Writings and
Lectures 1911–1945* (London: Peter Owen, 1967), 149.
[8] Ernst Bloch, 'A Philosophical View of the Detective Novel,' *Literary Essays* (Stanford, CA: Stanford
University Press, 1998), 219.

the cheap disguise of a palindrome ('G. Abeson'), but his biography seems to repeat the same movement in a more tragic key, at least for the biographer: 'I am Sebastian, or Sebastian is I, or perhaps we both are someone whom neither of us knows' (*RLSK*, 160). As in *Pale Fire*, in *The Real Life of Sebastian Knight* an investigator works through a set of clues in order to discover the real truth about the object of his investigation: the life of the investigator's brother; a poem left behind by the investigator's 'friend' who has been suddenly murdered. But rather than discover a hidden truth, the investigation is exposed as a projection of the detective, and, moreover, we recognise that our reading of said projection may be no more secure from error.

On Todorov's reading, the task of the second story in detective fiction is one of mediation: the investigative line draws into presence the absence it is charged with recuperating. However, if the standard detective novel goes out of its way to render the labour of this mediation effortless and imperceptible (the eavesdropped phone-call, the address scribbled on the inside of a matchbook, etc.), Nabokov's forays into the genre always seem to strive for the opposite effect – the second story, the text of the narrative, becomes a hostile witness and starts to insist on its own immediacy rather than cooperate and, like all law-abiding attempts at mimesis, feign transparency. As an exemplary instance of this we might finally consider Nabokov's novella *The Eye* (1930), one of his few works that he openly associates with the detective genre in his auto-commentaries. 'The texture of the tale mimics that of detective fiction', he writes in the foreword to the English translation, 'but actually the author disclaims all intention to trick, puzzle, fool, or otherwise deceive the reader' (*Eye*, 4). Deceiving, one assumes we have to add, is what the genre typically does, but *The Eye* will be more forthright than what it copies: its hero-investigator, Smurov, literally arrives as a corpse himself, presenting himself as a suicide narrating from beyond the grave, and he ends the novella as nothing but a mirror-reflection in the minds of others, with no substantial or immediate relation to his own being: 'I do not exist: there exist but the thousands of mirrors that reflect me' (*Eye*, 88). A reader familiar with Chesterton's Father Brown mysteries might recognise this set-up as a Proustian elaboration of the story 'The Man in the Passage', wherein all the witnesses to a murder misrecognise their own reflection in a mirror and identify it as another, as the perpetrator of the crime. In Smurov's case, however, the only crime he has committed is 'the mere fact of living' (*Eye*, 88), and even then he is unable to prove it. According to Nabokov, '*The Eye* is the pursuit of an investigation which leads the protagonist through a hell of mirrors and ends in the merging of twin images' (*Eye*, 4), so at first glance it would seem to obey

Todorov's 'two-story' model. Yet the merging of these images does not take us beyond the image as such, to an *ante rem*, but simply presents us with another image. Understood from this standpoint, as this problem, we might say that the detective novel provides the generic template for most of Nabokov's major works; its only serious competition would be the *Bildungsroman*, or rather a specific sub-species of it, the novel of the artist. In any case it is from the predicament of the detective genre that Nabokov devises his traps for his villains, and it is the same predicament that his heroes, in one way or another, have to escape. This is no simple task, insofar as it requires accepting mystery as the norm rather than dispelling it. In the case of Cincinnatus, the hero of *Invitation to Beheading*, it even becomes a crime: 'gnostic [or, in the Russian original, 'epistemological' *gnoseologiches-kaia*] turpitude'. But in the final analysis it is a problem of signification, and Chesterton, in a 1901 essay entitled 'A Defence of Detective Novels', makes this quite clear. Crediting detective fiction with introducing into popular literature a 'sense of the poetry of modern life', he writes:

> A city is, properly speaking, more poetic even than a countryside, for while Nature is a chaos of unconscious forces, a city is a chaos of conscious ones. The crest of the flower or the pattern of the lichen may or may not be significant symbols. But there is no stone in the street and no brick in the wall that is not actually a deliberate symbol – a message from some man, as much as if it were a telegram or a post-card.[9]

Of course, in the worlds Nabokov devises in his fiction 'the poetry of modern life' may just as easily slip into the paranoia of 'Signs and Symbols' (1948). But for Chesterton, whose world still corresponds with an 'infallible Power', this 'romance of details' can only be 'a good thing', and the Nabokov of *Lectures on Literature*, for his part, will ask his students to fall in love with novels in much the same way. Yet to conceive of literature simultaneously as both a matter of style *and* detective work might require suspending the very contradiction that gives Nabokov's engagement with the detective genre all its pathos: it betrays the tension in his art between present and past, between narrative and event. In other words, it requires us to think of the author's style as immanent or genetically present, and of the work of fiction as an organic, living thing – and not as a corpse, that is, as an unsolved riddle. Critics accustomed to reading Nabokov for the magic of discovery may object to such a formulation, but lest we forget, this is an author who seriously contemplated titling his last novel *Dying is Fun*.

---

[9]   G. K. Chesterton, 'A Defence of Detective Fiction,' *The Defendant* (Mineola, NY: Dover, 2012), 75.

CHAPTER 19

Samizdat and Tamizdat

Ann Komaromi

As a graduate student in geological sciences at Tashkent University in the late 1960s, Alexander Gorianin went on several study trips to Moscow, where instead of spending his time on geological research he enjoyed the company of friends who shared with him their copies of illegal literature, in the form of samizdat (self-published works) and tamizdat (uncensored western editions). Immediately upon arriving in Moscow in January 1967, Gorianin was given two of Nabokov's novels, *Dar* (*The Gift*, 1937–38) and *Priglashenie na kazn'* (*Invitation to a Beheading*, 1935–36). The frost was terrible, Gorianin had a single room in the dormitory and rather than pursue a romantic tryst as some might have done, he spent the next three days in trembling communion with Nabokov's prose. Remembering this moment later, Gorianin recalled that while the outstanding quality of the works moved him, the form in which they came to him also motivated him to read with special intensity: 'Tamizdat books stood out for this particular condition: you had to give them back immediately'. Such editions were in short supply and high demand. He remembered reading with such passionate attention to detail that he would later be able to recall whole passages by heart. A year and a half later, when he consulted a version of *Dar*, published in the émigré journal *Sovremennye zapiski* (*Contemporary Annals*) and held in the special collections (*spetskhrany*) of the Latvian State Library in Riga, he was able to note a missing word in the journal edition.[1]

Gorianin's description of this intense and solitary reading experience corresponds to a significant degree with Nabokov's own statements about how his works should be read. Nabokov asserted, for example, that '[the] only valid method of study is to read and ponder the work itself, to discuss it with yourself but not with others, for the best reader is

[1] See Alexander Gorianin, 'Kak pervuiu liubov . . . ', *Zvezda*, 7 (2007), 200.

still the egoist who savors his discovery unbeknownst to his neighbors'.[2] That conception of private, even secret, reading resonates also with the mythologised image of the lone samizdat reader furtively gleaning precious truths from the forbidden text. Writer Andrey Bitov, for instance, like others who speculated about a Nabokov 'cult', referred to a sect of 'Nabokovians' in the Soviet Union. Unwitting members of this secret society did not even suspect one another's existence, he claimed. Bitov dated the foundation of this 'group' in the late 1970s when Ardis editions of Nabokov's works made their way into the USSR.[3]

In fact, the ranks of Nabokov's enthusiastic readers began to fill earlier, and their reading, like all reading of samizdat and tamizdat, was neither free of material constraints nor wholly solitary. This reading occurred within an intensely social context of sharing and discussing texts. Mikhail Aizenberg recalled being part of a book-sharing network at the beginning of the 1970s when Nabokov's *Lolita* (1955) enjoyed particular popularity. So many people read it that the copy in which Aizenberg had invested got blackened by finger smudges, it lost its binding, briefly reappeared crudely glued together and at last disappeared altogether. Instead of returning the original copy of *Lolita*, the final reader of the Ardis/samizdat edition sent Aizenberg a photographed copy.[4] Slava Paperno and John V. Hagopian reported that in Leningrad in 1969, 'the price for one night with Lolita was five rubles – if the reader promised not to take pictures'.[5] To consider Nabokov's work in samizdat and tamizdat means to address its often messy social and historical context. Nabokov the author could not entirely control the interaction with his Soviet readers – those readers, like all readers, were conditioned by their particular context, and they interacted with one another to develop meaningful engagement with Nabokov's works.

Nabokov wrote in his Afterword to the Russian edition of *Lolita*, dated 1965, that the question of Russian readers belonged to the sphere of 'metaphysics and humour'.[6] Only in some other imagined world or reality

---

[2] Vladimir Nabokov, 'Pushkin, or the Real and the Plausible', tr. Dmitri Nabokov, *New York Review of Books*, 31 March 1988, 38–42 [41]. For the original article see Vladimir Nabokoff-Sirin, 'Pouchkine ou le vrai et le vraisemblable,' *La nouvelle revue française* 48 (1937), 362–78.

[3] Andrey Bitov, 'Iasnost' bessmertiia (Vospominaniia nepredstavlennogo)', in Vladimir Nabokov, *Krug* (Leningrad: Khudozhestvennaia literatura, 1990), 17.

[4] See Mikhail Aizenberg, 'Vania, Vitia, Vladimir Vladimirovich', *Znamia*, 8 (2001), 140.

[5] Slava Paperno and John V. Hagopian, 'Official and Unofficial Responses to Nabokov in the Soviet Union', in George Gibian and Stephen Jan Parker (eds.), *The Achievements of Vladimir Nabokov* (Ithaca, NY: Center for International Studies, 1984), 113.

[6] Vladimir Nabokov, 'Postskriptum k russkomu izdaniiu', *Lolita* (Ann Arbor: Ardis, 1976), 298.

would Soviet readers be able to obtain and appreciate his work. In fact, Nabokov knew that his books were being smuggled back into the Soviet Union. According to his wife, he was aware that at least 500 copies of *Lolita* had already reached the Soviet Union by 1968, but he was wary of, and for, his Soviet readers. His wife Véra cautioned one American scholar who passed along a letter from enthusiastic young readers in Leningrad: 'The people you write about risk very much in seeking even indirect contact with VN' (*Letters*, 431). Véra was emphatic: 'VN has made it a rule not to enter into contact with people living beyond the iron curtain, for their sake' (*Letters*, 432). For his own sake, too, Nabokov was cautious: even if these readers' letter did not represent some KGB provocation, he had doubts about the political orientation and literary preparation of his unfamiliar Soviet readers. It seemed better to let his books speak for him. Responses to his works which Nabokov received through Radio Liberty were more easily verifiable and seemed more reliable. The Nabokovs especially appreciated one articulate letter they received from a Soviet reader in his twenties who talked about *Dar* and *Priglashenie na kazn'*: 'We really did not know that readers in this age bracket, nurtured on Sholohov and his likes, could judge literature from the purely aesthetic point of view', wrote Véra on this occasion.[7]

Post-war editions of Nabokov's works in Russian included *Dar* in 1952 and the Russian version of his autobiography, *Drugie berega* (Other Shores, 1954), published by Chekhov Publishing in New York. The novel *Priglashenie na kazn'* appeared in 1966, from Éditions Victor, Paris. Similarly, *Zashchita Luzhina* (*The Defense*, 1929–30) came out under the imprint Éditions de la Seine, Paris, in 1967. Also in 1967, the Russian *Lolita* made her debut, with Phaedra, in New York. In rare cases, Soviet readers might have had occasion to see early émigré editions of Nabokov's works in special library collections. According to Gorianin's account, in the 1960s, the *spetskhrany* had become slightly more accessible to a wider readership.[8] Gorianin was able to make use of such a collection. Lazar Fleishman also recalled seeing *Priglashenie na kazn'* in its serialisation in the émigré journal *Sovremennye zapiski* (1935–36) in a *spetsfond* in Riga.[9] Beginning in 1974, Ardis Publishers, based in Michigan (Ann Arbor) and run by Carl and Ellendea Proffer, undertook to reprint the full run of Nabokov's

[7] Quoted in Brian Boyd, *Vladimir Nabokov: The American Years* (Princeton: Princeton University Press, 1990), 524.

[8] See Gorianin, 'Kak pervuiu liubov', 196; 200.

[9] The author gratefully acknowledges the responses of Lazar Fleishman and other former Soviet readers to her survey on their encounters with Nabokov's works.

Illustration 4 Samizad copies of *Dar* (*The Gift*) and *Drugie berega* ('Other Shores') prepared by Iurii Men'shov in the early to mid-1970s.

Russian works, starting with *Mashen'ka* (*Mary*, 1926) and ending with another reprint of *Priglashenie na kazn'* in 1979.[10] All of these post-war Russian editions of Nabokov's works were published primarily for readers in the Soviet Union. They were taken into Soviet Russia secretly by visiting foreign academics, students, tourists and diplomatic staff, shown at Book Fairs (slipping by design into visitors' hands) and probably mailed to people as part of the massive Book Program, which sent books to recipients in Eastern Europe and the USSR. The CIA Book Program, run by George Minden, worked in concert with a variety of established and specially created publishing houses to mail books to readers of the communist bloc to foster a 'spiritual understanding of Western values' through psychology, literature, the theatre and the visual arts.[11] People in the Soviet Union would photograph these and other Western editions, printing off copies for further circulation. Less frequently, they would retype the books using carbon paper for multiple copies. Occasionally, they would produce their own beautiful samizdat editions to keep like the lovely volumes of two of Nabokov's novels produced by V. Men'shov in Moscow in the 1970s. The Nabokov Museum possesses Men'shov's editions of *Dar* and *Drugie berega* – these are carefully hand-bound volumes with Xeroxed texts. The museum also has photographic samizdat copies of western editions of *Dar* and *Lolita*, as well as samizdat typescript versions of *Lolita*. In addition, a

[10] See Ann Komaromi, 'Ardis Tamizdat Publishing: Giving Back Russian Literature', in Friederike Kind-Kovács and Jessie Labov (eds.), *From Samizdat to Tamizdat: Transnational Media During and After Socialism* (New York: Berghahn Books, 2013), 27–50; 334–37.

[11] See John P. C. Matthews, 'The West's Secret Marshall Plan for the Mind', *The International Journal of Intelligence and CounterIntelligence*, 16 (2003), 418.

typescript version of *Priglashenie na kazn'* was found in the archive of the Memorial's NIT (Nauchno-informatsionnyi tsentr), Moscow. A handful of Russian readers began translating Nabokov's English novels for samizdat in the late 1960s, although it is not clear whether such samizdat translations circulated widely. Predictably, Nabokov did not encourage the creation or dissemination of these unauthorised translations (see *Letters*, 432).

In the late 1930s, Nabokov's Russian audience was dwindling to almost nothing. It was then that the author tossed his novel *Dar* like a bottle into an ocean in the hopes it would travel across the gulf separating him from Russian readers, whom Nabokov needed as much as they needed him, as Gorianin imagined it. Like other Soviet readers of the late Soviet period, Gorianin dreamed of Russian writing again occupying its rightful place in contemporary international letters. Nabokov fulfilled that desire.[12] As Nina Berberova wrote, 'Nabokov is the only Russian writer (both within Russia and in emigration) who belongs to the *entire* Western world (or the world in general), not Russia alone.'[13] For their part, once the Nabokovs felt more secure about their Soviet interlocutors they reached out to strengthen that connection. The Proffers of Ardis acted as intermediaries, travelling from the United States to the USSR and to the Nabokovs in Montreux. One of the Proffers' Soviet acquaintances, a book collector, offered to forward a copy of Nabokov's *Stikhi* (*Verses*) from 1916. Another had a copy of the book written by Nabokov's father, V. D. Nabokov, *Iz voiuiushchei Anglii* (*From England at War*), which Véra said would be particularly welcome.[14] The gifts and fan letters suggest that Nabokov's Soviet readers were anxious that Nabokov know about their existence and their regard for his works. These offerings were a first attempt to reinstate Nabokov as part of the Russian literary tradition and reclaim him as their very own Russian writer. The Nabokovs in turn sent gifts of money and clothes (including jeans from Sears and Roebuck for Joseph Brodsky)[15] to writers and dissidents in the Soviet Union.

Before the period of *perestroika*, Nabokov's works circulated clandestinely and against the odds on the basis of reader enthusiasm. Those readers took a certain amount of risk: producing and sharing copies of uncensored literature was potentially (if not always actually) punishable by Soviet authorities. The samizdat bulletin *Chronicle of Current Events* (*Khronika tekushchikh sobytii*) recounts ten instances of seizures of works by Nabokov

[12] See Gorianin, 'Kak pervuiu liubov', 197.
[13] Nina Berberova, *The Italics Are Mine*, trans. Philippe Radley (New York: Knopf, 1992), 316.
[14] See 'Perepiska Nabokovykh s Profferami', *Zvezda*, 7 (2005), 135; 138.
[15] See 'Perepiska', 142.

between 1973 and the end of the bulletin's publication in 1982. In 1983, Mikhail Meilakh was arrested and imprisoned in connection with a samizdat collection that included Nabokov's works.[16] Despite this threat, readers invested great effort in preparing Nabokov's work for wide dissemination. Evgeny Shikhovtsev, an instructor at the Kostroma Higher Military Officers' School for Chemical Defense, copied out *Otchaianie* (*Despair* [1934]) and *Podvig* (*Glory* [1931]) from the Lenin library, where he probably enjoyed privileged access to special collections. Shikhovtsev added his own notes and preface to the two works, and released them in this enhanced samizdat edition.[17]

The record of judicial proceedings in the *Chronicle* helps substantiate individual recollections of the relative availability of Nabokov's works in Soviet samizdat circulation of the 1970s. Most people remember seeing them in post-WWII Western editions. *Lolita* in all editions enjoyed particular popularity. The Ardis editions of Nabokov occupied a privileged place in the memory of late Soviet readers. The Proffers had become familiar with the Nabokovs thanks to Carl Proffer's work on his study, *Keys to Lolita*, published in 1968. They regarded it as their mission to help return repressed or unavailable Russian literary works to Russia. Aside from Ardis and the Proffers' labour of love, there was the Chekhov publishing house in New York in the 1950s, and the Parisian editions of the mid-1960s, which actually came from Radio Liberty in Munich. Both Chekhov publishing and Radio Liberty activities comprised part of the Cold War cultural battle being waged from the United States and Europe to win the hearts and minds of Soviet readers as well as Western non-communist intellectuals. Nabokov's cousin Nicolas Nabokov led the Congress for Cultural Freedom's efforts in continental Europe, while Vladimir's brother Kirill worked for Radio Liberty. Nabokov's works fit the bill as materiel for this cultural war because they represented high-quality émigré cultural production that was not communist but was also not overtly political. However much Nabokov knew or did not know about the 'secret' American government funding for such operations, he was happy to offer his books for the nascent Chekhov Publishing venture in 1951, and for Radio Liberty's projected publications in the mid-1960s.[18] While the

---

[16] One finds information on seizures and criminal cases relating to uncensored literature documented in *Khronika* using the search tool developed by Gennady Kuzovkin and Josephine von Zitzewitz. URL: http://hr2.memo.ru/wiki

[17] See Igor Dedkov, 'Novyi tsikl rossiiskikh illiuzii: Iz dnevnikovykh zapisei 1985–1986 godov', *Novyi mir*, 11 (2001), 119. I am indebted to Gabriel Superfin for this reference.

[18] Boyd, *American Years*, 204; 504.

mission of Cold War politics might seem to jibe uneasily with the devotion to autonomous literary values professed by the author and his readers, there was obviously a convergence of practical interests at the time: all concerned wanted to make Nabokov's books available to readers in Soviet Russia.

Discussion of the works – *pace* Nabokov on 'the egoist who savours his discovery unbeknownst to his neighbours' – proved crucial to their successful reception. The writer Raisa Orlova confessed to the Proffers that she had tried reading *Lolita* in 1956 or 1957 and put it down, exasperated. Not until meeting them (and reading Proffer's *Keys to Lolita*) more than a decade later, did she understand what she termed the novel's 'depth' and 'purity'. Having learned to appreciate Nabokov's writing, she also loved his *Speak, Memory* (1967).[19] In the late 1970s, Orlova gave Alexander Dolinin the Ardis edition of *Lolita* along with Proffer's *Keys* to help spark his appreciation of Nabokov's works. In a recent article, Dolinin recalls his introduction to Nabokov, and reflects on the role of readers in discovering and creating the significance of Nabokov's works. Nabokov had acknowledged that there were many keys and combinations readers found in his works which had not occurred to him, but some of which he nevertheless found entirely plausible (see *Letters*, 391). In this rare gesture of surrendering authorial control, Nabokov acknowledged the primacy of the text over authorial intention. Such a concession makes the productive dialogue between reader and work (and author) possible.[20]

This give-and-take between author and readers at the site of the text helps justify the considerable claim Nabokov's works have to being 'great' literature with layers of meaning to be unfolded through passages across political borders and eras.[21] It also belies the caricature of Nabokov as severe master author and sole interlocutor of the obedient silent reader. On the contrary, the dialogue with Soviet readers shows Nabokov as author recognising – and even rejoicing in – the passion readers brought to his works, even as those Soviet readers strove to read them into their context.

'The surest way not to read a book is to buy it', observed Gorianin. Experiencing works in samizdat and tamizdat produced an entirely

---

[19] See *Perepiska*, 142.
[20] See Alexander Dolinin, 'Karl Proffer i Vladimir Nabokov: k istorii dialoga', *Novoe literaturnoe obozrenie*, 1/125 (2014).
[21] Mikhail Bakhtin wrote about the life of works by great writers (like Shakespeare) that grow over time both because of what is in them and through the efforts of readers to disclose semantic potentials not immediately accessible to the author ('Response to a Question from the *Novyi Mir* Editorial Staff', in *Speech Genres and Other Late Essays*, trans. Vern McGee [Austin: University of Texas Press, 1986], 4–5).

different type of reading, in which one invested more than money – one invested oneself. Aizenberg memorialised that kind of reading in a poem:

> Who remembers now the 'cratic fox' [*giliarnaia lisa*]?
> Those were the days, my friend.
> We referred to that book often, kissing every page,
> we swore oaths not in words, but in quotations.[22]

The '*giliarnaia lisa*' appeared on page twenty-three of the Phaedra edition of *Lolita*, where a line was transposed from the bottom of the page to the middle. The edition appears to have been typeset on a Linotype machine, on which whole lines were cast at once and then arranged vertically to produce the page.[23] The grotesque fox, exhibiting both polar (*poliarnaia*) and fatal (*gibel'naia*) characteristics, was born neither from Nabokov's pen nor from the intellectual effort of the reader. However, we might see it as a symbol of the material vehicle of the text that brings author and reader together in a shared (if somewhat quixotic) quest to transcend historical contingency. For that service, perhaps the 'cratic fox' merits a place in the story of Nabokov's oeuvre – somewhere marginal, of course, maybe wandering above Nabokov's 'Arctic no longer vicious circle'.

---

[22] Mikhail Aizenberg, *Ukazatel' imen* (Moscow: no publisher, 1993), 99. I have borrowed from Jim Kates's translation in Mikhail Aizenberg, 'Who Now Remembers . . . ', *Say Thank You* (Brookline, MA: Zephyr Press, 2007), 23.
[23] Komaromi, 'Ardis', 41.

CHAPTER 20

Nabokov's Visual Imagination

Marijeta Bozovic

Transnational, Transmedial

In his youth, Nabokov had aspired to become a landscape artist; throughout his life, he placed great emphasis on the visual orientation of his imagination. One of the most famous of synaesthete-writers, Nabokov insisted that, 'I don't think in any language. I think in images' (*SO*, 14). He even suggested that his oeuvre might be conceptualised *as* visual art, describing the desired final effect of his novels as something like viewing 'a picture in a picture: *The Artist's Studio* by Van Bock' (*SO*, 73).

It behooves the émigré writer, reliant not only on a foreign language but on readers' perception of his mastery over that language, to think in images. Nabokov was so often perceived as 'not very Russian', or not Russian enough, by fellow émigrés in large part because he refused to be at home only in the Russian language. Instead, he maintained that English might as well have been his first language and that he could have easily become a great French writer. Nabokov's masterful and often outrageous fashioning of his public persona is evident throughout his interviews, introductions and lectures, as is his positioning of himself and his oeuvre outside the bounds of the marginalised émigré and Russian abroad. If he could slide between languages and national literary traditions, crossing borders with no need of a Nansen passport, he was free.[1]

It is even more liberating to think in images than equally well in three languages. In numerous novels and poems, Nabokov spoke of stepping across and into the alluring images he so admired. He persistently probed that painted border: his writings, from the earliest Russian-language works to the final fragments of *The Original of Laura* (2009), are replete with artworks and artists, ranging from Pnin's genius surrogate son Victor Wind

---

[1] For Nabokov's transnational literary canon, see Marijeta Bozovic, *Nabokov's Canon: From Onegin to Ada* (Evanston, IL: Northwestern University Press, 2016).

to the sociopathic Axel Rex. Scholars have counted over 150 references to painters in Nabokov's oeuvre, even limiting the count to references 'explicit or recognizable'.[2] Yet painting is far from the only visual technology permeating Nabokov's prose (and poetry): as subject matter, sister art, resource for appropriation and parody, and metaphor for memory and artistic creation, film is as present and closely linked to painting. According to Dmitri Nabokov, his father's writing 'was all there, inside his mind, like film waiting to be developed'.[3] Albinus, the doomed protagonist of *Laughter in the Dark*, dreams of animating Old Masters; his author fulfils the fantasy at an ekphrastic remove, in the medium of language.

While all of Nabokov's works are saturated with visual arts, the three novels that most overtly engage in a paragone contest with them are *Kamera Obskura/ Laughter in the Dark* (1932–33), *Lolita* (1955) and *Ada or Ardor: A Family Chronicle* (1969). All three feature heroines who dream of, and fail to achieve, stardom on the silver screen. All three heroines are caught in the gaze of art-critically minded protagonists and narrators who recognise them first as living works of art and then as film noir *femmes fatales*. Margot has long Luini eyes; Lolita's tear-stained face turns Botticelli-pink; Ada, along with her mother Marina and sister Lucette, steals beauty from too many classics to count. All three novels are preoccupied with blindness and sight – and all three were made, or very nearly made, into film adaptations. Film directors, it seems, could not resist the implicit challenge.

Nabokov was acutely aware of the advantages available to other media: for example, of the wide international audiences that Tchaikovsky's or Repin's adaptations of *Evgenii Onegin* could reach. Paintings are accessible to viewers regardless of linguistic background: in visual media, it is evident that stylistic practices and innovations cross national borders. In turn, the international language of cinema, as it was proclaimed by Dziga Vertov and other early practitioners in the 1920s, aspired to create a visual Esperanto with the potential to unify the world culturally.[4] As a transnational and increasingly experimental novelist, Nabokov sought to mimic both the effects and possibilities of rival media.

---

[2] Gerard de Vries and D. Barton Johnson, *Nabokov and the Art of Painting* (Amsterdam: Amsterdam University Press, 2006), 19. Cf. Gavriel Shapiro: 'Nabokov's turning to the works of the Old Masters ... enabled him to view himself as part and parcel of European cultural continuity and to rightly claim his rich cultural ancestry' (*The Sublime Artist's Studio: Nabokov and Painting* [Evanston, IL: Northwestern University Press, 2009], 189).

[3] Quoted in Brian Boyd, *Vladimir Nabokov: The American Years* (Princeton: Princeton University Press, 1991), 585.

[4] Pascale Casanova's *World Republic of Letters* trans. M. B. DeBevoise (Cambridge, MA: Harvard University Press, 2007), for example, deals only with literature for a reason: film and the visual arts cross language borders in ways that interact with but complicate the cultural capital of powerful literary traditions.

Media Ecologies

Building on the work of Frederic Jameson, Julian Murphet reminds us in *Multimedia Modernism* that literary works do not compete for resources and audiences with literary works alone, much less quietly coexist with other media. In periods of transition when new species 'emerge to contest . . . with the existing life forms', media ecologies display what Murphet casts in metaphors of evolution: 'savage competition for resources, sudden mutations, survival of the fittest, extinction of unsuccessful species'.[5] Cinema strongly affected all other media in the twentieth century: with the introduction of film, in a matter of decades, novels were displaced 'from the position of unquestioned dominance which they enjoyed for four centuries in the West'.[6] Competition with other media forces literature, especially, into self-consciousness and a quest for meaningful materiality.[7]

The absorption and appropriation of other media serves a host of functions in Nabokov's work. Visual media suggest an alternative route out of the language quagmire faced by the émigré writer with their tempting claims of international accessibility. *Ada* above all is written and not painted or shot, but in a hybrid cosmopolitan's English that seems to have absorbed Nabokov's other beloved languages. By leaning on an internal gallery of internationally recognised art, he moves further away from the limitations of national literary canon. Moreover, he attempts to reimagine and renovate the novel through an open competition with the dominant forms of the twentieth century.

In *Remediation: Understanding New Media*, Jay David Bolter and Richard Grusin argue that refashioning (allusion, parody, appropriation) within a single medium is

> the one kind of refashioning that literary critics, film critics, and art historians have acknowledged and studied with enthusiasm, for it does not violate the presumed sanctity of the medium . . . Refashioning within the medium is a special case of remediation, and it proceeds from the same ambiguous motives of homage and rivalry – what Harold Bloom has called "the anxiety of influence" – as do other remediations.[8]

---

[5] Julian Murphet, *Multimedia Modernism: Literature and the Anglo-American Avant-garde* (Cambridge: Cambridge University Press, 2009), 13.
[6] Julian Murphet and Lydia Rainford (eds.), 'Introduction', *Literature and Visual Technologies: Writing After Cinema* (New York: Palgrave Macmillan, 2003), 23.
[7] See Murphet, *Multimedia Modernism*, 30.
[8] Jay David Bolter and Richard Grusin, *Remediation: Understanding New Media* (Cambridge, MA: MIT Press, 2000), 49.

By expanding our understanding of refashioning, the interventions of narrative and media theory, transnational and world literatures can help to set aside exhausted critical dichotomies and evaluative judgements to open new modes of reading Nabokov's work.

Ut Pictura Poesis

Nabokov's fascination with new ways of understanding word and image was hardly singular in the late 1960s. Much of the twentieth century's most interesting and experimental art fused and confused the sister arts, rebelling against a classical understanding of which medium was appropriate for what type of exposition. In 1969, the same year as *Ada*'s publication, Rudolf Arnheim, a pioneer of film theory, released his treatise *Visual Thinking*. Like Nabokov, Arnheim believed that the linear sequence of language expressed only a fraction of the workings of the mind and argued for the primacy of the visual.[9] In the same decade, Marshall MacLuhan – credited by some for predicting the World Wide Web thirty years in advance – published his *Gutenberg Galaxy* (1962) and *Understanding Media* (1964). Marie-Laure Ryan summarises the key thought from MacLuhan that helped to shape media theory: medium affects the message, and 'print culture favors logical, abstract, and controlled thought, at the expense of spatial perception and of the artistic, holistic, metaphorical, or musical types of imagination'.[10]

Taking Arnheim and MacLuhan as examples, we can imagine an underexplored context for Nabokov's intuitions and less systematically formulated claims. Visual thinking highlights the innovative turns of Nabokov's verbal art in the late period of his career, beyond the documented attempts to master and subsume literary heritage. Nabokov seems to practice what Bolter and Grusin call 'aggressive remediation', incorporating elements of other media into the seamless and tightly controlled whole of the novel, and insisting on the text as a heterogeneous space pieced together out of explicitly mediated borrowings. Indeed, Nabokov's works abound with remediations and stress representation 'not as a window on to the world, but rather as "windowed" itself – with windows that open on to other

---

[9] See Rudolf Arnheim, *Visual Thinking* (Berkeley: University of California Press, 1969), 246.

[10] Marie-Laure Ryan, 'Introduction', in Marie-Laure Ryan (ed.), *Narrative Across Media: The Languages of Storytelling* (Lincoln: University of Nebraska Press, 2004), 27. Cf. Marshall MacLuhan and Bruce R. Powers, *The Global Village: Transformations in World Life and Media in the Twenty-first Century* (New York: Oxford University Press, 1989), 56.

representations or other media'.[11] *Pale Fire* (1962) and *Ada* in particular
resemble nothing so much as print culture hypertext.

Nabokov uses the device of ekphrasis in the narrow sense to describe
well-known works of art in detail, but also to conjure invented or hybri-
dised works, and to create tableaux through mixed painterly and literary
allusions. Demon Veen recalls Lermontov's as well as Vrubel's demons,
and dies in celestial flames like the mythological Icarus (son of Dedalus, the
maker of living sculptures, with murmurs of Joyce's Stephen Dedalus),
suggesting also Pieter Breughel's *Landscape with the Fall of Icarus* (1558).
Lucette drinks alone at a bar, reminding Van of Blok's 'The Stranger', but
her dress and posture are borrowed from Toulouse-Lautrec's *Divan
Japonais* (1892–93), through the intervention of Barton & Guestier's advertisement for wines in *The New Yorker*.[12] Francesco Parmigianino's frescos
of Adam and Eve inspire the image of Marina leaving her bath, as does the
painting *Bath of the Nymph* described in *Ulysses*. All the Veens are children
of Venus, rising from the sea or associated with mermaids in countless
literary and visual representations from Pompeii to Proust. It is easy to see
why *Ada* has been read as 'the most serious attempt since *À la recherche* to
combine the aesthetics of painting and the aesthetics of literature'.[13]

The lushly curated *Ada* mimics the erotic *Forbidden Masterpieces* that Van
and Ada discover in the Ardis library, 'the kind of voluptuous and tender
stuff that Italian masters allowed themselves to produce in between too many
pious Resurrections during a too long and lusty Renaissance' (*Ada*, 113). The
original volume is lost, stolen or never existed, and thus offers no competition to the novel but only a myriad of inspirations: Nabokov can describe in
detail his favourite artworks (Bosch), combine and re-imagine pieces to come
up with new but vividly 'real' images (Parmigianino's sketches); or he can
invent his own *Forbidden Masterpieces*. As a New Master of prose and a
belated student in the school of Caravaggio, he glides further away from the
restrictions of history and geography.

Cinema by Other Means

The potential rivals presented by Nabokov's preferred paintings were long
gone if, as he claimed, immortal. His novels betray a more agonistic

[11] Bolter and Grusin, *Remediation*, 34.
[12] See *The New Yorker*, 23 March 1963.
[13] de Vries and Johnson, *Nabokov and the Art of Painting*, 22. See J. E. Rivers, 'Proust, Nabokov and
Ada', in Phyllis A. Roth (ed.), *Critical Essays on Vladimir Nabokov* (Boston, MA: G. K. Hall,
1984), 144.

struggle with the all-consuming twentieth-century medium of film. The two arts intersect in prose, for the verbal ekphrasis of painting inevitably introduces the dimension of time, animating images on the wings of action. Nabokov explicitly contrasts the magic of film with photography's frozen time: Humbert and Van both destroy photographs of their beloveds for betraying their mind pictures, but dream of and pursue their images in film.[14] Even more radically than painting, film affords Nabokov an opportunity to experiment with prose: he describes invented films in great detail, or else borrows their techniques to zoom, pan, double-take and conjure explicitly cinematic scenes. Such effects engage the visual imagination directly, while at the same time utilising the peculiar pyrotechnics and multivalent meanings available only to language.

Alfred Appel, Jr. suggests that Nabokov's oeuvre 'abounds in images and scenes that are cinematic by design'.[15] Barbara Wyllie points out that Nabokov's interest in film started early, lasted his entire life and 'extended into a desire to participate in the industry': in Berlin, Nabokov not only earned money as an extra but 'auditioned as a movie actor, wrote scenarios and screenplays, and negotiated with film directors and producers over potential screen adaptations of his work'.[16] Unlike the modernist writers with whom he is frequently associated, Nabokov – born in 1899 and writing actively until his death in 1977 – was a perfect contemporary of the developing medium.

Much of Nabokov's fascination with cinema centres on commercial culture and its automaton consumers. Appel notes that, as a film critic, Nabokov was 'loosely speaking, a Marxist, as he will be happy to learn'.[17] Nabokov preferred silent films to the talkies that succeeded them, and in general favoured films that made self-conscious use of the medium's idiosyncratic possibilities. Nabokov loosely echoes Adorno and Horkheimer's critique of the culture industry in the movie-madness of Margo or Lolita.[18] On the whole, however, he was actually a more forgiving viewer, finding charm and brilliance in mainstream productions. (Adorno makes a cameo appearance in *Ada* – as a movie star, best known for his film *Hate*.)

[14] See Elena Gualtieri, 'The Grammar of Time: Photography, Modernism and History', in Julian Murphet and Lydia Rainford (eds.), *Literature and Visual Technologies: Writing after Cinema* (New York: Palgrave Macmillan, 2003).

[15] Alfred Appel, Jr., *Nabokov's Dark Cinema* (New York: Oxford University Press, 1974), 195.

[16] Barbara Wyllie, *Nabokov at the Movies: Film Perspectives in Fiction* (Jefferson, NC: McFarland, 2003), 5.

[17] Appel, *Nabokov's Dark Cinema*, 57.

[18] See Theodor Adorno and Max Horkheimer, *The Dialectic of Enlightenment* (Stanford, CA: Stanford University Press, 2002).

Even before he translated *Lolita* into a (long and virtually unusable) screenplay for Stanley Kubrick, Nabokov wrote the original with the movies in mind.[19] For the screenplay, rather than pare down his novel to bare plot or rely on literary language in voice-over narrations, Nabokov laboured to find cinematic equivalents for his narrative frame and estranging devices, lush prose and distinctive humour.[20] He thought highly enough of the experiment to publish the screenplay once he realised that Kubrick would use very little for the actual film.[21] For, despite his sole screen-writing credit and an Oscar nomination, the majority of Nabokov's wittiest transfigurations were cut. Kubrick also flatly refused to allow Nabokov a Hitchcock-like cameo.

Incredibly, Nabokov had even hoped to see *Ada* make it to the screen. Producers circled around the unfinished novel, and the screen rights were optioned, but in the end no one dared to try and make a movie of *Ada*. Aside from the obvious reasons as to why not (length, production costs, infernal complexity), the novel already thoroughly appropriates and refracts cinematic practice. Its many internal films are all adaptations and reflections of the storyline. Besides *Don Juan, Les Enfants Maudits* and *Letters from Terra*, there are two minor references to film: Marina's *Torrid Affair*, which she conflates with her affair with Demon; and the final incarnation of *Les Enfants Maudits* as a 'painted Western', *The Young and the Doomed*, in which all but the shadow of Ada's elbow ends up on the cutting-room floor. Van's memoir proposes a literary alternative, but the professionals' moving images prove contagious to his style.

Likewise, Van's eternal beloved Ada embodies not only two centuries of literary heroines and painted nymphs but a noir *femme fatale*, 'shot' in black and white (Lucette is in colour) although inexplicably doomed as an actress. Van witnesses the disintegration of the last remaining reel of *Don Juan's Last Fling* and Ada's only real role.[22] Just as the volume of *Forbidden Masterpieces* has been lost or destroyed, so Ada's 'magic gambols' on celluloid are doomed. Her star performance is reserved for Van's memoir. Nabokov imagines rival artistic productions in other media, describes them intricately, demonstrates that he can conjure them mentally for his readers through words alone and then incinerates the originals.

---

[19] See Nabokov's comparable struggles with stage directors in Siggy Frank, *Nabokov's Theatrical Imagination* (Cambridge: Cambridge University Press, 2012).

[20] Appel, *Nabokov's Dark Cinema*, 195–256. See Julia Trubikhina, 'Struggle for the Narrative: Nabokov and Kubrick's Collaboration on the *Lolita* Screenplay', *Ulbandus* [special issue: 'My Nabokov'], 10 (2007), 149–72.

[21] See Appel, *Nabokov's Dark Cinema*, 232.

[22] See Wyllie, *Nabokov at the Movies*, 187.

Beyond Inbreeding Literary Masterpieces

Once he successfully broke out of the provincialism of a (marginalised, interrupted) national tradition, Nabokov faced the same dilemma as had Samuel Beckett: how to write novels after Joyce and Proust? Frederic Jameson and others have read Nabokov as a misplaced modernist, spinning out his last 'unseasonable forms' from the lofty and isolated perch of Swiss retreat.[23] Viewed from another angle, his late works seem less the last in a series than forerunners of emergent forms. His exaggeratedly dense and allusive prose not only mimics but reflects back on modernist practices; in the clash of high and low cultures and styles, of Parmigianino and pornography, *Ada* shares a family resemblance with David Foster Wallace's *Infinite Jest* (1996). Nabokov's trick of distancing himself from his foreign or mad narrators – a sly strategy for his English-language works – even approaches conceptualism in its extreme exposures of the device and experiments with readability. While his unreliable narrators produce increasingly hysterical and wildly derivative prose, the conceptual constructions and artistic imagination of their author sketch worlds of meaning beyond the text.

---

[23] Frederic Jameson, *Postmodernism, or, the Cultural Logic of Late Capitalism* (Durham, NC: Duke University Press, 2003), 305. Cf. Will Norman, *Nabokov, History, and the Texture of Time* (New York: Routledge, 2012).

CHAPTER 21

Popular Culture

Nassim Winnie Balestrini

Despite Nabokov's persistent refusal to acknowledge any cultural, literary or historical influence on his art, his novels rework and integrate elements of the popular cultures of his time, including his fictionalisations of Berlin in the 1920s and 1930s and his narrative transformations of American and Soviet film aesthetics. Equally interesting is the reverse movement of popular culture adapting Nabokov's work. Almost a hundred years on, Nabokov's oeuvre has proven to be fertile ground for a wide range of re-workings, especially in popular culture. Indeed, ever since his *succès de scandale* with *Lolita* (1955), Nabokov's works have become a veritable treasure trove for allusions, adaptations and appropriations. Besides films, Nabokov's works have been adapted for musical theatre, dance and spoken drama; they have been absorbed into fashion, into the visual personae of singers and into popular song lyrics.[1] Within pornographic texts of all media and in journalism, Lolita has become synonymous with sexually precocious females. Japanese Lolita fashion paradoxically ranges from eroticised schoolgirl outfits to clothing promoted by the desexualised modesty movement. While also some of his other narrative texts have been adapted into film,[2] *Lolita* has had the strongest impact on popular culture and has become a stand-in for Nabokov's entire oeuvre in the popular imagination. Adaptations of *Lolita* in novels, films and popular music demonstrate that generations of readers and critics have either succumbed

[1] See lyricist Alan Jay Lerner and British composer John Barry's musical *Lolita, My Love* (1971); Edward Albee's 1981 drama adaptation of *Lolita*; Rodion Shchedrin's opera *Lolita* (premiered in Stockholm in 1994); Oliver Reese's theatrical monologue *Lolita* (premiered in Berlin in 2003); the 1998 radio play, directed by Walter Adler, *Lolita: Hörspiel* (Munich: Der Hörverlag, 2009).

[2] Film adaptations include *Laughter in the Dark* (dir. Tony Richardson, 1969); *Bend Sinister* (dir. Herbert Vesely, 1970); *Invitation to a Beheading* (dir. Horst Flick, 1973); *King, Queen, Knave* (dir. Jerzy Skolimowski, 1972); *Despair* (dir. Rainer Werner Fassbinder, 1978); *Maschenka* (dir. John Goldschmidt, 1986); *Mademoiselle O* (dir. Jérôme Foulon, 1994); 'An Affair of Honor' (dir. Valentin Kuik, 1999); *The Luzhin Defence* (dir. Marleen Gorris, 2000); 'Skazka'/'A Nursery Tale' (dir. François Lossier, 1997); 'Christmas' (dir. Serge Gregory, 2000).

to Humbert Humbert's manipulative prose by adopting his perspective on Lolita's victimisation, or they have attempted to depict Lolita through her own or through her creator's eyes.[3] Stanley Kubrick's 1962 film uses irony to undermine Humbert's self-centred narrative, while Adrian Lyne's 1997 movie draws Humbert's emotional world in a more sympathetic light. In popular music, Humbert's perspective also clearly dominates. Attempts to assume Lolita's perspective are contradictory and less frequent. They either depict a young woman who equates sexual precociousness with empowerment, or they combine sexually charged visual representations with lyrics that deny her putative role as seductress. Stereotypical depictions of Lolita simply use the protagonist's first name (perhaps in the hope of attracting readers who associate it with underage pornography), while more complex representations demonstrate in-depth knowledge of Nabokov's novel and/ or situate Lolita within more contemporary aesthetics of youthfulness, sexuality and individual agency.

Lolita According to Kubrick and Lyne

In his introduction to the 1974 publication of his *Lolita* screenplay, Nabokov pinpoints the different exigencies of a novelist and a film-maker as well as the impossibility of adapting without interpreting: 'When adapting *Lolita* to the speaking screen [Kubrick] saw my novel in one way, I saw it in another – that's all, nor can one deny that infinite fidelity may be an author's ideal but can prove a producer's ruin' (*Lolita Screen*, 676). Nabokov's screenplay clearly sides with Lolita and condemns Humbert. For instance, Nabokov first included but then excluded the famous epiphany scene at the end of the novel in which Humbert claims that he was pained by not hearing Lolita's voice among other children's voices. Nabokov may have been concerned that such a filmic moment could make the rapist's remorse appear more convincing than the novelist may have intended.

In addition to the challenge of producing a film about a paedophile within the legal restrictions regarding what can be shown on the screen, any adapter of *Lolita* faces two central problems. First, the filmic medium requires representing not Dolores Haze but rather a figment of Humbert's imagination, that is, the Lolita refracted through his mental

---

[3] Novelistic spin-offs include Pia Pera's *Lo's Diary* (1995) and Emily Prager's *Roger Fishbite* (1999). Nabokov's work as a lepidopterist inspired a poem by William Matthews ('Nabokov's Blues', *Poetry* [August 1989], 250–52).

prism and literary style with the intention of exculpating himself.
Rendering this imaginary 'nymphet' through a flesh-and-blood actress
creates an illusion of mimesis based on her tormentor's vision.[4] Second, a
film's chronology of images, words and sounds, which is somewhat analogous to the novel's sequence of narrative development and linear presenta-
tion on the page, goes against Nabokov's aesthetics of creating patterns
embedded in superimposed layers which aim at dissolving strict temporal
chronology and spatial separation.

Kubrick certainly could not solve the problem of having to have an
actress embody Lolita, but the director managed to imitate Nabokov's
narrative aesthetics through filmic means. Not surprisingly, the visual and
corporeal rather than any other features of Kubrick's Lolita character had a
particularly long-lasting impact on the popular imagination and, thus, on
subsequent depictions of Nabokov's fictional 'nymphet'. Actress Sue
Lyon's heart-shaped sunglasses, lollipop and furtive glance above the
upper rims of the sunglasses have become an iconographic shorthand for
Lolita as underage seductress. However, rather than focusing on Humbert
and Lolita's highly problematic sexual relationship, Kubrick foregrounds
Humbert's murder of Clare Quilty. The film's narrative focuses on the
reasons behind the murder. The crime against Lolita recedes into the
background – a strategy supported by raising her age from twelve (in
the novel) to fourteen and through heavy doses of 'silly or ribald humor'
that 'sublimat[ed] the serious sexual themes'.[5]

Lyne's *Lolita* never achieved the visibility and popularity of Kubrick's
film. For two years, Lyne's version lacked a North-American distributor.
Following its Showtime premiere (2 August 1998), the film utterly failed in
the cinema. Stephen Schiff's screenplay for Lyne relies on 'the character-
driven aspects of cinematic realism', which permit 'viewers [to] probe more
into the hearts and minds of the characters'.[6] The film privileges – largely
through voice-over narration – Humbert's perspective; thick layers of
nostalgia and declarations of suffering conceal his similarities to Quilty
and his predatory sexual behaviour. Ennio Morricone's lush score and
the predominance of soft colours, only occasionally interrupted by the use
of the colour red, support this effect. Joan Driscoll Lynch argues that the
'film places the incestuous father figure in a sympathetic position, the

---

[4] See Lara Delage-Toriel, 'Shadow of a Double: Taking a Closer Look at the Opening of Kubrick's
Lolita', *Miranda*, 3 (2010), 6.
[5] Ken Burke, 'Novel to Film, Frame to Window: The Case of *Lolita* as Text and Image', *Pacific Coast
Philology*, 38 (2003), 19.
[6] Burke, 'Novel to Film', 21.

victim of his uncontrollable urges and a seductive child-woman. Their sexual relationship proceeds in four phases that could be labeled "the construction of a nymphet": objectification, the child as tease, the complicity of the victim, and the "incested" child-woman as whore'.[7] Implicating Lolita in her own sexual abuse ignores her position of dependency. While Lyne's narrative is constructed from Humbert's perspective, Kubrick plays with recurring near-identical features that question unambiguous explanations.

Although decades have passed since both films were released, critical debate about their implications continues. The slogan on one of the posters advertising Kubrick's film, 'How did they ever make a film of *Lolita*?', still appears in scholarship about any adaptation's success or failure. Kubrick's version lives on in popular culture, particularly in lyrics and music videos, more tenaciously than does Lyne's film. The two versions exemplify two principal trends in *Lolita* adaptations: Kubrick transforms the novelist's doubts about solid and solitary truths into a film; Lyne advances a Humbert-centred reading of the novel.

Nabokov and Popular Music

Nabokov's works first appeared in popular music in the early 1970s. Except for David Bowie's 'I'd Rather Be High' (2013), whose description of Nabokov in Berlin-Grunewald evokes Fyodor Godunov-Cherdyntsev sunbathing in Nabokov's last Russian novel, *The Gift* (1937–38), ('Nabokov is sun-licked now / Upon the beach at Grunewald / Brilliant and naked just / The way that authors look'), popular songs have centred on *Lolita* to this day. Lyrical depictions of Lolita's physical features often derive not from verbal description in the novel but rather involve a triangulation that includes seductresses imagined in erotic images and sensational journalism as well as Kubrick's film and its promotional materials. For instance, M.I.A.'s '10 Dollar' (2005), links the racist stereotype of oversexed Asian seductresses with Lolita as 'a man-eater' who 'sucked on a lollipop', reminiscent of the images of Sue Lyon wearing heart-shaped glasses and holding a lollipop between her lips.

The history of popular music appropriations of *Lolita* commenced in France, where the novel was first published in 1955. In his 1971 rock concept album *Histoire de Melody Nelson*, Serge Gainsbourg relates how a middle-aged man driving a Rolls Royce crashes into a teenager on a bicycle,

---

[7] Joan Driscoll Lynch, 'Incest Discourse and Cinematic Representation', *Journal of Film and Video*, 54/2-3 (2002), 44.

Melody Nelson (portrayed by Jane Birkin), with whom he subsequently becomes sexually involved. Video clips for the seven tracks were issued as a half-hour television film (dir. Jean-Christophe Averty) in the same year. The highly acclaimed album was later re-released on CD and on DVD (with a documentary), and other artists have continued to perform its music. The title cover shows a topless woman hugging a rag doll to cover her breasts. Wide-eyed, with reddish cheeks and half-open mouth, she epitomises the stereotype of Lolita as both child-like and seductive. Neither the cover art nor Jane Birkin's impersonation of Melody Nelson in the TV film depicts the Lolita character as a 'nymphet'. According to the lyrics, she is fourteen and, at the end, dies in a plane crash on her way to 'Sunderland', lost in a Papua New Guinean jungle.

The lyrics objectify Melody Nelson into a 'poupée' (doll) and an '[a]imable petite cone' (lovable little idiot) who, according to the speaker, provokes ridiculous behaviour in the male protagonist. Nevertheless, her visual representation in the film, despite her revealing clothes and seductive dancing, does not make her a pre-teen seductress. It is the clearly visible age difference of eighteen years between the lovers, rather than Birkin's age (she was 25 years at the time), which provides the link to *Lolita*. Although reducing her verbal contribution to whispering her name makes her a cardboard character, in the overall visual strategy she acquires more depth. Except for the authentic car and bicycle, the protagonists move in a thoroughly artificial environment, walking through collages of paintings by Salvador Dalí, Paul Delvaux, Max Ernst, Félix Labisse, René Magritte and Henri Rousseau. Surrealism, love goddesses and paintings of nudes place the love affair within imaginary worlds marked by physical desire and the passing of time. In the last third of the film, Melody's death by drowning is suggested by her mermaid-like twirling, ascending and descending against a background of documentary footage of indigenous Papua New Guineans combined with a painted world of jungle scenes and underwater effects. The latter element evokes Poe's 'Annabel Lee', the literary character on which Humbert models Lolita. The film references precisely this relationship of intertextual appropriation by showing two copies of Melody moving in the underwater world in the final scenes. The ending takes up the lyrics of the opening song, in which the Venus figurine on the Silver Ghost Rolls Royce merges with Melody, thus completing the female character's surreal objectification.

Lolita the novel and Lolita the character continue to figure in popular music. In 1975, Jane Birkin released the album *Lolita Go Home*. The Police referred to Humbert's obsession in 'Don't Stand So Close to Me'

(1980), a song about a teacher's sexual attraction to his teenage pupil: 'It's no use he sees her / He starts to shake and cough / Just like the old man / in the book by Nabokov'. Numerous songs take up the dominant bad-girl cliché.[8] The Red Hot Chili Peppers' song 'Funny Face' (2006) transforms Lolita into some kind of fairy ('You're my angel baby / You're my darling / You're my star / Lo lo lo Lolita / Let her see me deep in love'), while Céline Dion uses the Lolita trope to assert young women's ability to love deeply ('Lolita [Trop jeune pour aimer]' [1987]). The persona of Katy Perry's 'One of the Boys' (2008) reads Nabokov's novel and concludes that she wants to be treated properly by her potential lover. Billy Joel's 'No Man's Land' (1993) addresses sensationalist reporting about drugs and sex ('This morning's paper says our neighbor's in a cocaine bust / Lots more to read about, Lolita and suburban lust'), thus alluding to journalists who dubbed Amy Fisher, a woman who attempted to murder her lover's wife, the 'Long Island Lolita'. Representing Humbert's perspective, MC Lars' 'Lolita' (2011) projects Nabokov's novel onto rapper Marshall B. Mathers III/Eminem's lyrical renderings of his falling-out with his ex-wife. The speaker of MC Lars' lyrics clearly knows Humbert's definition of nymphets, alludes to the role of teachers in the novel and transposes Lolita into the present by citing her enthusiasm for *Twilight* posters. The lyrics thus depict the novel as a potential prism through which one might analyse contemporary sexual relations.

A sustained treatment of *Lolita* occurs in Lana Del Rey's recent lyrics and videos.[9] In 'Lolita', a hedonistic adolescent asserts her ability to manipulate 'boys'. But the music video, which combines clips from Kubrick's and Lyne's *Lolita* movies and from Walt Disney's *Fantasia* (1940) with sequences of the singer's performance in a Lolitaesque outfit and hairstyle inspired by Kubrick's film, indicates that the speaker's views are built on the treacherous ways in which romantic love has been marketed to American children for decades. In the excerpts from *Fantasia*, passages from Ludwig van Beethoven's Pastoral Symphony accompany

---

[8] See Aerosmith, 'Shame on You' (1985); Shania Twain, 'Whose Bed Have Your Boots Been Under?' (1995); Alizee, 'Moi ... Lolita' (2000); Master P, 'Ghetto Model' (2004); Prince, 'Lolita' (2006); Ghostface Killah, 'Shakey Dog Starring Lolita' (2007); Cobra Starship, 'Scandalous' (2007); Miley Cyrus, 'Permanent December' (2012); The Veronicas, 'Lolita' (2012); Wavy Spice, 'Versace Hottie' (2013); Father, 'Nokia' (2014).

[9] Among the songs discussed in this section, the tracks 'Lolita', 'Off to the Races', and 'Diet Mountain Dew' are part of Del Rey's 2012 album *Born to Die*. '1949' was recorded in 2008 but never released as part of an album. 'Put Me in a Movie' is a 2010 release. For an extended discussion of Del Rey's use of Nabokov's Lolita as part of her artistic persona, see Nassim W. Balestrini and Silke Jandl, 'Lolita and Lana in the Age of Internet Memes', *Nabokov Online Journal*, X–XI (2016), 1–18.

images of desexualised figures inspired by Greek mythology. Even though
the scene dramatises a Bacchanal and the courtship of half-human creatures, the unclad females are breastless. While *Fantasia* infantilises courtship, the clips from the *Lolita* films imply that the protagonist of Del Rey's
video may have a more realistic sense of the nature of sexual relationships
between underage girls and adult men.

Another example of misleading mass culture characterises the mental
world of '1949', whose Lolita-like speaker indicates how consumerism can
encourage teenagers to romanticise abusive relationships. A similar kind of
disconnect occurs in 'Off to the Races', which contrasts Lolita's supposed
immorality with being ostensibly idealised and loved. The lyrical I of 'Put
Me in a Movie' seems to address Quilty, whereas Humbert's voice dominates 'Diet Mountain Dew', which again references the heart-shaped
sunglasses from Kubrick's film.

In the opening and closing monologues of 'Ride', which was released as
part of *Born to Die* (2012), Del Rey goes beyond such clearly identifiable
references and rather uses a Lolita-meme-inflected adult persona in order
to explore the grey zone between asserting individual liberties (in the
domains of interpersonal relationships, sensuality and risk-taking behaviour) and courting social ostracism and even death. While the larger web
of Lolita-related references in Del Rey's oeuvre leaves no doubt for the
viewer that 'Ride' touches upon popular *Lolita* discourse, it takes up the
Lolita meme rather than the novel or its title character in a strict sense.
The extended music-video version is framed by the song's protagonist's
musing about her rootlessness and about looking for 'her people', who are
presented in the music video as – from the perspective of the protagonist's
age group – older men who figure as both father figures and lovers, as
members of a motorcycle gang and as partners in risk-taking behaviour. In
her epilogue, the rather nihilistic lyrical I defiantly claims that she can only
indulge in her 'darkest fantasies' because she claims her 'freedom' – a time-
honoured 'American' political ideal – and accepts her own madness.

Nabokov's *Lolita* is a textbook example of the ubiquity of adaptation
and of the ways in which narratives, motifs and images travel across cultural
borders and generations. The aesthetic and thematic distance between
Nabokov's novel and the ever-proliferating images of Lolita-seductresses
and suffering Humbert's parallels similar careers of fictional characters
like Washington Irving's Rip Van Winkle and Nathaniel Hawthorne's
Hester Prynne that assumed lives of their own as continuously evolving
cultural memes. Two strands of popular culture adaptations coexist,
irrespective of a given artistic medium: those concerned with

translating particular features of Nabokov's text into new works and those concerned with responding to emblematic interpretations of Lolita and Humbert that have developed independently of Nabokov's novel. As a result, cultural consumers may recognise them as versions of *Lolita* without exposure to the novel per se. The relation between Nabokov and popular culture must therefore be studied with an open eye for how individual artists take up and modify either Nabokov's aesthetics or how a variety of tropes have dominated the reception history of his best-known literary creation.

PART IV

Ideas and Cultures

CHAPTER 22

Science

Stephen H. Blackwell

Readers tend to think of Nabokov's science as something separate from his art, and his butterflies – the ones in his fiction – as little more than tokens of his love of Lepidoptera. But Nabokov believed in an artistic side to science (*LL*, 3), in the 'precision of poetry' (*SO*, 10) and in 'the free interchange of terminology between any branch of science and any raceme of art' (*SO*, 79). For Nabokov, science and art are deeply related, and he challenges his readers to care about discovery the way a scientist should, and to bring that passion to their encounters with both artwork and the world. In its convergence with his art, Nabokov's entomological research demonstrates a way to think of science as part of a larger whole embracing all facets of human knowledge. Nabokov helps us see science within a larger context, one that includes art.

The precision of Nabokov's science also reminds us what is at stake in the precision of his art. He connected the study of literature and science in a lecture to his students at Wellesley:

> Whichever subject you have chosen, you must realize that knowledge in it is limitless. Every subject brims with mysteries and thrills, and no two students of the same subject discover a like amount of delight, accumulate exactly the same amount of knowledge . . . Suppose a schoolchild picks up the study of butterflies for a hobby. . . . He will not even suspect the fascinating variety of inner organs, the varying shapes of which allow the scientist not only unerringly to classify them, often giving the lie to the seeming resemblance of wing patterns, but also to trace the origin and development and relationship of the genera and species, the history of the migration of their ancestors, the varying influence of the environments on the developments of the species and forms, etc. etc. etc.; he will not [have] even touched upon other mysterious fields, limitless in themselves, of for instance mimicry, or symbiosis. This example applies to every field of knowledge, and it is very apt in the case of literature. . . . And if by luck you hit upon some scrap of knowledge referring to your subject that has not yet become common knowledge, then will you know the true felicity of the great adventure of

learning, and your years in this college will become a valuable start on a road of inestimable happiness.[1]

That he made these comments about the study of *literature* demonstrates clearly that he considered works of art to be analogous to complex phenomena in nature. Thus, the way we come to understand Nabokov's scientific work and attitudes provides a vital perspective for efforts to understand his art.

Nabokov began his scientific journey as a seven-year-old butterfly collector, became a professional lepidopterist and curator at Harvard's Museum of Comparative Zoology in the 1940s, and left scientific research after he started teaching at Cornell University, though he continued his summertime collecting and worked for years on a guide to the butterflies of Europe (which he eventually abandoned when the publisher lost interest). The early years were ambitious ones, characterised by a passion to discover a new species of butterfly. Despite a near miss at the age of thirteen, he kept pursuing this goal, which remained a driving force behind his collecting during the 1910s, 20s and 30s. His first scientific publications – in 1920 and 1931 – were locality reports about collecting expeditions, giving useful information to scientists who might study these ecosystems in the future. When his entomological pursuits took a more professional turn, soon after his arrival in the United States, Nabokov started out still entranced by the prospect of becoming a 'first describer', something he achieved quickly but fleetingly in the New World using two of his 1938 catches from Moulinet, France – which he named *Lysandra cormion* Nab. (1941) and commemorated with the poem 'A Discovery' (1943).[2] A year later he found two new species and three subspecies, rearranging the genus *Neonympha*.[3] During the next six years, Nabokov described several new species and genera, but meanwhile his scientific priorities shifted, perhaps because discovering new species was not terribly difficult once one had access to Harvard's large collection of poorly organised Blue butterflies. As early as 1945, he was writing to fellow scientist John Dos Passos that another colleague 'was merely interested in giving names to things and was far from possessing the true scientific spirit'.[4] That spirit blossomed in the process of dissection

[1] *Nabokov's Butterflies*, ed. Brian Boyd and Robert Michael Pyle (Boston, MA: Beacon Press, 2000); 398–99.
[2] Ibid., 273–74. The species eventually turned out to be a hybrid and was 'sunk'. See Dieter E. Zimmer, *A Guide to Nabokov's Butterflies and Moths*, Web Version, 2012. URL: www.d-e-zimmer.de/eGuide/Lep1.htm#Lep1.1.
[3] See Zimmer, *Guide*. URL: www.d-e-zimmer.de/eGuide/SciPapers.htm#Lep5.
[4] *Nabokov's Butterflies*, 347.

and analysis of the insects' minute genitalia, where not just new species, but never-before-seen mechanisms and structures of nature could be discovered: as he wrote to his sister in December of that same year, 'to know that no one before you has seen an organ you are examining, to trace relationships that have occurred to *no one* before, to immerse yourself in the wondrous crystalline world of the microscope, where silence reigns, circumscribed by its own horizon, a blindingly white arena – all this is so enticing that I cannot describe it'.[5] For Nabokov, the 'true scientific spirit' is found in expanding the limits of human perception; he therefore took greater pride in the new structures he identified and named than he did in new species themselves. Yet these taxonomic discoveries, he soon came to realise, might not be as immortal as he originally hoped they would be. He told Edmund Wilson in 1944 that the results of his major reclassification work might stand for twenty-five years or so, to be superseded by later studies.[6]

Although his work was admired by many scientists with whom he collaborated, his most important contributions, in the area of Latin American Blues, were neglected for decades by subsequent systematists. Yet Nabokov's research proved both innovative and largely correct. He was working at a time when taxonomic systematics was still developing its methodologies, which in the 1940s remained fairly imprecise. Nabokov's profound grasp of morphological variety and change in the Old and New Worlds enabled him to estimate, accurately, the evolution of specific forms across millions of years, resulting in his radical and surprising hypothesis regarding the multi-wave pattern of Blues' dispersal from Asia to North and South America (recently confirmed by genetic analysis).[7] Nabokov tended to imagine *seeing time* in the objects around him, as if time itself could be manipulated as easily as space. This habit, combined with his extensive knowledge of Old World fauna from his many visits to European collections in the 1920s and 1930s, led him to the verge of one of the greatest leaps of twentieth-century science: the discovery of phylogenetic systematics, a taxonomy that sought to establish and describe actual evolutionary relationships, as opposed to the then-dominant practice of describing groups as if external appearance were more important than genetics.

---

[5] *Nabokov's Butterflies*, 387.
[6] *Nabokov's Butterflies*, 346.
[7] Roger Vila et al., 'Phylogeny and palaeoecology of Polyommatus blue butterflies show Beringia was a climate-regulated gateway to the New World', *Proceedings of the Royal Society B*, 278/1719 (22 September 2011), 2737–44 [doi: 10.1098/rspb.2010.2213]

Nabokov had arrived independently at an approximation of this method in his 1949 article on the genus *Lycaeides*, before the complete breakthrough was published in 1950 by Willi Hennig (in German). Now known as cladistics, Hennig's approach has dominated systematics since the late 1970s.[8] Nabokov was probably just a step or two behind Hennig in his methodological innovations, and he left active work in the field before he could bring these insights to full fruition. Today, Nabokov's work from the 1940s is recognised as near the vanguard of its field, if not visionary in quality.

More controversial has been his attitude towards mimicry. Throughout the late 1930s, and into the 1940s, Nabokov famously argued that mimicry and protective disguise must represent exceptions to natural selection, because frequently, he thought, 'a protective device was carried to the point of mimetic subtlety, exuberance, and luxury far in excess of a predator's power of appreciation' (*SM*, 465). As it turned out, he significantly underestimated predators' (especially birds') visual acuity. One of the remaining mysteries concerns what happened to his completed article on mimicry, which he handed to William de Vane for *The Yale Review* in 1941. Regardless of its long-term viability, Nabokov's thinking about mimicry is another example of his scientific independence, his willingness to push the limits of existing scientific explanation. Yet his famed artistic comments about mimicry may have added to later scientists' reluctance to take his research seriously, a neglect that endured until the mid-1980s and was not fully overturned until the 2011 confirmation of Nabokov's hypothesis for the diversity of South American *Plebejinae*.

Although butterflies were his only field of actual scientific research, Nabokov's first decades as a writer paralleled the emergence of major developments in other areas of scientific inquiry, and they left their traces clearly throughout his art. Physics, in particular, was in revolutionary flux from 1919 and attracted increasing public interest. Albert Einstein's relativity in large-scale physics, Niels Bohr's complementarity and Werner Heisenberg's uncertainty principle on the quantum scale fascinated the educated public throughout the 1920s and 1930s (there was a riot in New York City among a crowd trying to get into a lecture by Einstein in 1930).[9] The temporal implications of relativity worked their way into *The Gift*

---

[8] The book's English publication in 1966 precipitated the method's eventual wide acceptance: *Phylogenetic Systematics*, translated by D. Davis and R. Zangerl (Urbana: University of Illinois Press, 1966 [1950]).

[9] See 'Khronika', *Rul'*, 11 January 1930, 3.

(1937–38), and other hints at Einstein's work may appear as early as the first page of Nabokov's first novel, *Mary* (1926). But the essence of time was Nabokov's main concern in those years (the mid-1920s), 'when Time [was] in fashion', as his protagonist Fyodor puts it in Nabokov's last Russian novel (*Gift*, 26). The era's fascination with time was also driven by at least two other sources, Proust's *À la recherche du temps perdu* (1913–27), and Henri Bergson's writings on memory and on the concept of duration (la durée), written mainly in 1889 and 1896. Nabokov read both in the 1920s. According to his memoir, as a college student he saw the walls of Cambridge as if perceiving temporal depth the same way one perceives a visual field: '[n]othing one looked at was shut off in terms of time, everything was a natural opening into it' (*SM*, 590). He created narrators with this exact ability in his late novel *Transparent Things* (1972). In *The Gift*, clocks occasionally run backwards, and Fyodor's progression through time is affected not by near-light-speed travel, of course, but by his excited state of mind:

> He thought he was keeping his pace to a dawdle, yet the clocks that he came across on the way (the emergent giants of watchmakers' shops) advanced even more slowly and when, almost at his destination, he overtook in one stride Lyubov Markovna, ... he understood that he had been borne along throughout his journey by his impatience, as by an escalator that transforms even a motionless man into a runner. (*Gift*, 29)

Perhaps these early musings were based on a not quite accurate understanding of Relativity, for when Nabokov returned to it while writing *Ada* (1969) in the 1960s, his attitude appears highly sceptical: 'While not having much physics, I reject Einstein's slick formulae' (*SO*, 116). What made him decide to take a public stance opposed to one of the twentieth century's most revered theoretical physicists? One must always treat comments in Nabokov's interviews cautiously, but we can speculate that he may have played with this contrarian idea because he found Relativity's treatment of time to be unattractively restrictive. Nabokov read many works on relativity during those years, and his note cards demonstrate in a lively fashion his effort to challenge, or to imagine challenging, Einstein's theory. Among other things, he explored the idea that the time dilations suggested by relativity indicate 'the elasticity of mathematics and not that of Time'.[10] In his notes he, or a persona he imagines, also resists the idea that information cannot travel faster than light (for example, on the note cards with the titles

---

[10] VN Berg, 'Notes for the Texture of Time: Simultaneous Events 6'.

'Relativity 4' and 'Simultaneous Events 7'). More interesting than Nabokov's opinion here is the reasoning behind his efforts. Perhaps because relativity allowed travel into the future but not into the past, he rebelled against the inflexibility of its picture of time.[11] He wanted to believe in the possibility of pure time – time that could be torn away from space or 'space-time' and explored freely by an appropriately equipped consciousness. Although such ambitions are redolent of science fiction, it should be no surprise to learn that, here too, Nabokov was exploring the outer edges of the most advanced scientific theories, looking for explanations and possibilities that others might not have noticed. He probably studied these matters rather superficially in the 1920s and 1930s, and only while working on *Ada* decided to examine the ideas as completely as he could. We may regret that he did not find a flaw in relativity that would allow for faster-than-light travel and the freedom to move around in time at will. These extensive notes deserve a much more careful examination by someone well versed in both the physics and the philosophy behind Nabokov's musings: the story of exactly what he was doing, or trying to do, remains to be told.

The same 'Notes for the Texture of Time' also show extensive engagement with popularised quantum theory and particle physics, but we find reflections of these new theories at least as early as *The Gift*, probably in *Invitation to a Beheading* (1935–36), and prominently in 'Ultima Thule' (1942) and *Bend Sinister* (1947). In fact, the narrative structure of both *The Gift* and *The Real Life of Sebastian Knight* (1941) may deliberately embody an interpretation of the wave-particle duality of matter (Bohr's *Complementarity*, published in 1927, the idea that subatomic particles exhibit the properties both of matter and of waves), Heisenberg's uncertainty principle (also 1927, relating to insuperable problems in the simultaneous measurement of the speed and location of subatomic phenomena), or both. Uncertainty is modelled in the short story 'Ultima Thule' as if it were a horse race (*Stories*, 519). The narrative instability evident in every novel Nabokov wrote between 1934 and 1962 may have been partially inspired by these theories. We know such things were on his mind, because he wrote in his lecture on Chekhov's works (most likely written in 1940–41) that in them, 'we get a world of waves instead of particles of matter, which, incidentally, is a nearer approach to the modern scientific understanding of the universe' (*LRL*, 262). Although professing to be an 'indivisible monist' (*SO*, 85), Nabokov was clearly attracted to this dual essence of the physical

---

[11] Nabokov's interest in the possibility of multidirectional time is clear from his dream experiments following J. W. Dunne. See Blackwell, *Quill*, 161 and 182, and discussion of Dunne, in this chapter.

world: more than likely, he was drawn to it for its non-material, anti-causal implications, which he refers to explicitly in another lecture, 'The Tragedy of Tragedy'.[12] As a whole, these engagements with revolutionary physical theories demonstrate not only Nabokov's fascination with discovering new details of the observable world, but also his passion to glimpse 'the under-side of the weave' of reality (*PF*, 446).

This 'reality' (Nabokov's scare-quotes) comes to us subject to the con-tingencies of our senses and consciousness, and, ever aware of this media-tion, Nabokov was committed to exploring the intricacies of the mind. Having read William James' *Principles of Psychology* at twelve or thirteen,[13] and believing that '[a]ll novelists of any worth are psychological novelists' (*SO*, 174), Nabokov may have felt that writers really *are* psychologists, after a fashion. In public perceptions, concepts of psychology and psychoanalysis were often muddled. Nabokov clearly opposed Freudian psychoanalysis as popularly conceived, but he also objected to some directions of research in psychology proper, particularly behaviourism (which receives a brutally parodic treatment in *Bend Sinister*). Although he read extensively in psycho-logical literature (as we can tell, especially, from his notes taken while writing *Pnin* [1957] and *Lolita* [1955]), as a *theme* in his work this topic is divided between parody, as in research articles pulled from real journals and ascribed to Victor Wind in *Pnin* ('Group Psychotherapy Applied to Marriage Counseling', a fictitious study originating in the real article 'Group Therapy in Sexual Maladjustment'),[14] and the direct work of psychological portrayal – for example, Luzhin in *The Defense* (1929–30), Hermann in *Despair* (1934), Fyodor in *The Gift* and Humbert Humbert in *Lolita*. All of Nabokov's major characters have complex motives, complex relations with reality and, usually, complex problems. A vital component of reading his novels involves tracing the ramifications of individual psychology across multiple layers of textual significance.

Committed though he was to the scientific method, Nabokov was also acutely aware of its limitations; in fact he may even have chafed at the bridle imposed by the norms of empirical science upon the human quest for knowledge. A regular reader of the *Journal of the Society for Psychical Research*, he was, at a minimum, curious about what it might look like to

[12] Vladimir Nabokov, *The Man from the USSR and Other Plays* (San Diego, New York and London: Bruccoli Clark, Harcourt Brace Jovanovich Publishers, 1985), 326; 327.

[13] See Brian Boyd, *Vladimir Nabokov: The Russian Years* (Princeton: Princeton University Press, 1990), 90–91.

[14] See Alexander Stone and Lena Levin, *American Journal of Psychiatry*, 107 (1950–51), 195. Notes on this article appear in VN Berg, 'Notes on Various Subjects.'

explore phenomena not amenable to traditional empirical study. During a two and a half month stretch in 1964, he followed J. W. Dunne's method in *An Experiment with Time* (1927), writing down the dreams he could remember and later comparing them with subsequent events in the hope of detecting predictive episodes.[15] The dreams did not give him much evidence for an alternative temporal flow, and of course his method did follow some empirical guidelines (Gennady Barabtarlo suggests that some of the dreams *do* have the vague appearance of predicting the future).[16] One can't help feeling that Nabokov would have liked more scientific tools for exploring the uncanny.

An extended look at Nabokov's scientific profile highlights his insatiable curiosity – an attribute that leads his parenthetical definition of art: 'curiosity, tenderness, kindness, ecstasy' (*Lolita*, 296). His scientific publications also demonstrate intellectual modesty, even as he works with confidence in his acuity and methods: his research articles acknowledge both his own weaknesses and the inexhaustibility of the subject under study. 'Modesty' is not a word often associated with Nabokov's art; more often, readers note his haughtiness, his studied superiority and his tyranny, primarily in his interviews and forewords. There has been a steady attention to his desired control over his texts, over his characters whom he called 'galley slaves' (SO, 95) and over his readers, who are enjoined to avoid Freudian and other symbolic interpretations. And yet, if we examine Nabokov's own approach to the world around him – curious, detailed, passionate, iconoclastic and playful – it seems highly unlikely that he wished his art to engender a predictable, static, controlled realisation among its audiences. It is true that he presents a controlling persona, in dramatic and entertaining fashion. But just as he believed (as quoted previously) that 'no two students of the same subject discover a like amount of delight' in the puzzles of nature, so also no two readers will solve the puzzles of his texts in exactly the same way.

[15] See Vladimir Nabokov, 'Textures of Time. A Dream Experiment', introduced by Gennady Barabtarlo, *The Times Literary Supplement*, 31 Oct 2015, 13–15.
[16] Ibid., 13.

CHAPTER 23

Darwinism

David M. Bethea

Nabokov's engagement with Darwinism was life-long. Indeed, it could be argued that as time went on classical Darwinism, much more than Freudianism, was the perfect stalking horse for the Nabokov who saw art and science in productive dialogue. Initially, with the young Vladimir's avid butterfly hunting and his passion to find an example of a new species (cf. 'A Discovery' [1943]), the Darwinian framework of modern evolutionary biology was a constant in the background (*SM*, 462–65). However, as Nabokov grew into a mature artist and experienced the vagaries of exile and personal loss the lessons of Symbolism, first and foremost the notion of other worlds existing in this one, stayed with him. Beginning in the early 1930s, with his work on *The Gift* (1937–38) and its uncompleted addendum 'Father's Butterflies' (2000), Nabokov sparred directly with concepts central to Darwinian thinking, including mimicry, species concept and 'survival of the fittest'. This dialogue then continued, but on the side of 'science proper', through the 1940s with Nabokov's tenure as research fellow-lepidopterist at the Harvard Museum of Comparative Zoology (MCZ). In his final decades and period of greatest fame, and after he had given up his microscope for good, Nabokov returned to Darwinist musings, most vividly in *Speak, Memory* (1967). But the return was also an advance, as Nabokov, child of the Symbolist era to the end, came to see his own life as part of a larger pattern, one that he created but also one that was created in him. This chapter will begin by filling in some relevant Symbolist period background to the 'early career' Nabokov, then proceed to the sustained dialogue between Darwinian theory and Nabokovian art and science in 'mid-career', and conclude with the 'later career' Nabokov's uncanny anticipation of recent developments in evolutionary theory and artificial intelligence.

Nabokov was born into a set of circumstances that inclined him to look at the world, including the natural world, in a certain way: the unconditional love of both parents that pervaded all aspects of childhood; a

mother's interest in the occult and *potustoronnost'* ('otherworldliness') that
would eventuate, inter alia, in metaphors of pupation;[1] a father's firm
domestic hand, his exemplary behaviour as legal scholar with ties to the
'neo-idealist'[2] movement, and his advocacy of the less fortunate (to be
coded in later work as art's case for 'survival of the weakest');[3] the sense that
the father's reserve was an expression of secret knowledge, a belief that his
end was written into a pattern whose limits pierced the present from the
future not unlike the way a 'nymphalid ground plan' shapes a butterfly's
wing design; the cognitive coalescing in the child's mind around a family
tendency to catch the 'butterfly bug' and to experience it as a euphoric glow
associated with the pursuit and capture of constantly morphing natural
beauty; last but not least, a happy childhood on a sprawling suburban
estate that provided endless summertime opportunities for the bug to
spread and deepen.

The 'Darwin' phenomenon was very much present, but mostly at a
secondary remove, in young Vladimir's formative years. By the turn of the
century the Russian intelligentsia had been absorbing the lessons of
Darwinian thinking for several decades, and many had come to see such
thinking, the basis of which was in science, as a powerful engine for
mobilising social and political forces. As with so much else, this merging
of empirical science and progressive social thought went back to Nikolai
Chernyshevsky, the unquestioned leader of the radical generation of the
1860s, whose publications dominated the periodic press precisely at the
time when *On the Origin of Species* (1859) was undergoing its original
reception in Russia. 'Scientific socialism', as argued by Marx and Engels
and applied by radical groups to the Russian context in the decades leading
up to Nabokov's birth, took its scientific authority first and foremost from
Darwin. Others – Comte, Buckle, Moleschott – were cited as foundational
voices in discussions of positivism, empiricism and scientific materialism,
all crucial conceptual frameworks of nineteenth-century progressive
thought, but underlying them all, framing the frameworks, was Darwin
and natural selection. The death of the great naturalist in 1882 brought his
legacy into focus at a time of *fin de siècle* flux and re-evaluation.

---

[1] Cf. the short story 'Christmas' (1925), in which Nabokov describes the terrible grief of a father, Sleptsov, who has come to the family estate at Christmastime to bury his beautiful butterfly-catching son and, overcome by despair, comes upon his son's summertime find, hidden in a biscuit tin – a great Attacus moth (*nochnaia babochka*) that breaks from its cocoon and spreads its wings in an expression of liberation and happiness.

[2] See Dana Dragunoiu, *Vladimir Nabokov and the Poetics of Liberalism* (Evanston, IL: Northwestern University Press, 2011), 49–53.

[3] Stanislav Shvabrin, 'Berlin', in present volume, 93.

Enter Vladimir Solovyov, the hugely influential philosopher, poet and 'father' of Russian Symbolism. In 1885, the Moscow Psychological Society, principal hatchery of Russian neo-idealist thought, was founded at Moscow University. Solovyov's ideas played a seminal role in the movement's inception and his articles featured prominently in its leading journal, *Questions of Philosophy and Psychology*. In a real sense, Solovyov, the anti-Chernyshevsky, was the filter through which Russian philosophy absorbed Darwinian science. No rational person would dispute the connection between the shapes of finches' beaks, the separate island locales where the beaks had to forage, and the idea that species adapt over time (i.e. are not created once and immutably by God) in order to survive. However, to apply that concept proleptically all the way up through the animal taxa to *homo sapiens* as something called 'Social Darwinism' – the leap Darwin himself was beginning to make as he moved from the ideas in *On the Origin* to those in *Descent of Man* (1871), 'sexual selection' in humans being foremost – is to fall into a trap that neither Darwinian science as then understood nor the Russian cultural space into which that science penetrated could avoid.

In Solovyov the 'Silver Age' search for other worlds – what the young Nabokov would experience most powerfully in the mesmerising poetry of Alexander Blok – and the neo-idealist concern to define mankind as more than an always partial subset of empirical data come together. He was the era's great synthesiser. His long essay entitled 'Beauty in Nature' (1889), which examines the emergence of the beautiful (design, coloration, euphony, etc.) in different species all the while parsing meticulously, and approvingly, Darwin's findings, appears simultaneously with the Society's early flowering. Furthermore, with its implied Symbolist message of another force ('Sophia'[4]) working through matter to spiritualise it and with its interest in beauty or form as a catalyst of nature 'thinking itself forward', this is a text that the 'early career' Nabokov would have found congenial. For Solovyov, the nightingale's song and the randy tomcat's urgent cries contain a difference: both involve a call to mating but in the former that urge is transformed into an 'excess' of enchanting sound that is more than it needs to be for mere reproduction and survival.

---

[4] Sophia was Solovyov's, and the Symbolist generation's to follow, expression for the 'Eternal Feminine' and 'Divine Wisdom'. Sophia could be the idea of a material world perfectly spiritualised as well as the idea of that same world in the process of becoming spiritualised. The 'before' and the 'after' of Sophia's entry into the world were often conflated and difficult to pin down in the thought of the mystical Solovyov.

Nabokov at 'mid-career' (1930s–1950s) extends his early Symbolist leanings. Now he writes with his special flair about mimicry and nature's ability to disguise herself artistically, but does so at a time when the great Darwin-Mendel synthesis of the 1930s–1940s is taking place – a synthesis which brought into fruitful contact Darwinian natural selection with Mendel's understanding of modern genetics – and the Watson-Crick discovery of the helical structure of DNA is soon to happen. Earlier notions of Solovyovian beauty (and its incompletely formed twin 'ugliness'/*bezobrazie*) as the organic world's expression of 'intelligence' become complicated by discoveries in biochemistry, microbiology and population genetics. It is this Nabokov that makes his well-known statement in favour of what today would be termed, in most cases pejoratively, as 'intelligent design' (ID). Here, in *The Gift*, he describes how Konstantin Kirillovich passes down to Fyodor his special knowledge of mimicry in butterflies:

> He told me about the odours of butterflies – musk and vanilla; about the voices of butterflies; about the piercing sound given out by the monstrous caterpillar of a Malayan hawkmoth, an improvement on the mouselike squeak of our Death's Head moth. ... He told me about the incredible artistic wit of mimetic disguise, which was not explainable by the struggle for existence (the rough haste of evolution's unskilled forces), was too refined for the mere deceiving of accidental predators, feathered, scaled and otherwise (not very fastidious, but then not too fond of butterflies), and seemed to have been invented by some waggish artist precisely for the intelligent eyes of man. (*Gift*, 108)

While modern-day naturalists like Charles Lee Remington and Stephen Jay Gould might argue that Nabokov's hero is overplaying his hand in this passage, we should note for the record that the 'ID' Fyodor is recollecting has nothing doctrinally 'Christian' about it. We should also note that the text in which Nabokov's hero is praising nature's intelligence ('incredible wit of mimetic disguise') is itself *artistic*. Nabokov the research fellow-lepidopterist would not indulge in such conceptual overreach in one of his scientific papers written while at the MCZ.

One of the most powerful theories in the history of evolutionary biology involves a metaphor, Sewall Wright's notion of 'adaptive landscape'. For Wright, an organic population is best described in terms of hills and valleys, the higher points being areas of greater Darwinian fitness and the lower points or valleys being areas of declining fitness. Wright's special insight entailed what happens when smaller subpopulations located along the downslopes and border areas of fitness 'hills' branch out and descend into 'valleys' of diminishing viability, only then to ascend another fitness 'peak'.

In this way, 'genetic drift functioned in a "shifting balance" with natural selection to generate new species through alternating periods of genetic restriction (or "bottlenecks") and expansion'.[5] The question seemed to ask itself: why don't the fit simply become more fit? Why don't those trending to the less fit *automatically* disappear?

Wright's theory is arguably pertinent for the Nabokov of the 1930s in the following way. The Russian geneticist and evolutionary biologist Theodosius Dobzhansky, who emigrated to America in 1927, became enamoured by Wright's adaptive-landscape metaphor when hearing him at a genetics congress in 1932. Thereafter, he collaborated with Wright and developed his ideas further. Dobzhansky's first major book, *Genetics and the Origins of Species*, appeared in 1937, as Nabokov was completing *The Gift* but before he wrote 'Father's Butterflies'. Not only was he one of the major players (the so-called 'four horseman') in the evolutionary synthesis of the 1930s–1940s but Dobzhansky was also a world leader in refining the concept of species through greater taxonomic and morphological precision – one of Nabokov's keenest interests once he joined the MCZ in 1941. His signature stance of foregrounding the vast genetic diversity within a given species, so that recessive genes and alleles become significant in their own right in determining aspects of speciation, surely appealed to the Nabokov who opposed the domination of the predictably unfit by the predictably fit ('the rough haste of evolution's unskilled forces' [*Gift*, 108]). Nabokov corresponded with Dobzhansky in 1954, though how much previous to that he knew the celebrated scientist's work we can only speculate.

As we know, Nabokov's core interest as a scientist was more in the accurate naming of biological form, especially the microscopically observed genitalic features of his beloved Blue butterflies, than in entering into metaphysical debates about an 'intelligence' that put that form there in the first place. 'Harvard's lepidopterists [at the MCZ in the 1940s] complained that he prioritised "description" over "synthesis".'[6] It could be argued, however, that it was the 'inverse cause' situations, where the function of something is understood only after the fact of its appearance, and where that appearance could not be predicted beforehand, that most fired Nabokov's imagination. According to this line of thought, there are phenomena of resemblance in nature that are not explainable strictly in terms of adaptation and directionality. These are those knight's moves ('nature's rhymes') that so appealed to

---

[5] Edward Larson, *Evolution* (New York: Modern Library, 2004), 230.
[6] Robert Michael Pyle, 'Between Climb and Cloud', in *Nabokov's Butterflies*, ed. Brian Boyd and Robert Michael Pyle (Boston, MA: Beacon Press, 2000), 63.

Nabokov the artist. To take an example from 'Father's Butterflies', a natural selection process that does *not* take place when we expect it to but that still eventuates in survival is the caterpillar of the Siberian Owlet moth found on the chumara plant: the colouring of the insect's fetlocks and dorsal shape appears at the end of summer, while the lookalike shrub blooms in May. Following the logic of adaptation, 'nature [has] defrauded one of the parties' (*Gift*, 390).

But more to the point: how is nature's ability to create patterned surprises 'mimicked' in Nabokov's play with ingenious feedback loops in his greatest art, including *The Gift*? To begin with, the very structure of the novel, its blurring in and out of the 'I' and 'he' narrators, its tying-up of the plot with an Onegin stanza, itself a pseudo-genetic map for creating infinite meanings out of a single string (rhyme scheme), its merging of personal and literary history ('from Pushkin Avenue to Gogol Street'[7]) – all this challenges the reader to understand such patterning as 'open' or 'closed', or somehow both (i.e. a feedback loop). Is this structure an optical illusion à la Escher, a Moebius strip modelling space as 'outside' and 'inside' simultaneously?[8] Or is it, through some ancient deep-seated psychic trace, the 'memetic' (as in 'meme') reproduction of that double helix of chemically paired on-off switches whose codes and mappings can store information indefinitely without physically transcending themselves (genetics)? (Recall how Richard Dawkins famously defined his cultural equivalent of the gene: 'The new soup is the soup of human culture. We need a name for the new replicator, a noun which conveys the idea of a unit of cultural transmission, or a unit of *imitation* . . . Examples of memes are tunes, ideas, catch-phrases, clothes fashions, ways of making pots or of building arches'.[9]) Do the spirals and spheres that imbed themselves in Nabokov's speculations about time – 'The spiral is a spiritualized circle. In the spiral form, the circle, uncoiled, unwound, has ceased to be vicious; it has been set free. . . . A colored spiral in a small ball of glass, this is how I see my own life' (*SM*, 594) – trace back to Andrey Bely and Symbolist notions of cosmic return, to Bergson's cloud of 'creative evolution', or to some other cognitive version of 'nymphalid ground plan'?

---

[7] This is how Nabokov blends and blurs Fyodor's change of residence at the end of chapter 2 with the shift in focus of the new literary history he is now writing with himself as a/the central hero and returning avatar.

[8] For more on the Moebius strip in Nabokov see Irena and Omri Ronen, '"Diabolically evocative": An Inquiry into the Meaning of a Metaphor,' in *Slavica Hierosolymitana: Slavic Studies of the Hebrew University*, 6–7 (1981), 378.

[9] Richard Dawkins, 'Memes: The New Replicators', in *The Selfish Gene* (Oxford: Oxford University Press, 2006; first edn. 1976), 192.

Fyodor says of his father's prose, which he gets closer to by reading Pushkin, that

> the very body, flow, and structure of the whole work [i.e. *Butterflies and Moths of the Russian Empire*] touches me in the professional sense of a craft handed down. I suddenly recognize in my father's words the wellsprings of my own prose: squeamishness toward fudging and smudging, the reciprocal dovetailing of thought and word ... and I doubt that the development of these traits under my frequently willful pen was a conscious act. (*Gift*, 377)

The process is presented as virtually *physiological*, which again recalls Solovyov and his 'spiritualization of matter' and of nature, even human nature, 'thinking itself forward'. Perhaps the 'body, flow, and structure' of a cultural construct are not simply figures of speech. As animal behaviourist N. K. Humphrey puts it,

> Memes should be regarded as living structures, not just metaphorically but technically. When you plant a fertile meme in my mind you literally parasitize my brain, turning it into a vehicle for the meme's propagation in just the way a virus may parasitize the genetic mechanism of a host cell. And this isn't just a way of talking – the meme, say, for 'belief in life after death' is actually realized physically, millions of times over, as a structure in the nervous systems of individual men the world over (cited Dawkins, *The Selfish Gene*, 192).

This is what we mean in modern parlance by 'going viral'. Nabokov, for his part, was trying to get at this idea *avant la lettre*, but in his own writing, in a deeply personal, deeply cultural sense.

In 'Father's Butterflies', we learn further that Fyodor is fascinated by the exceptional flora and fauna of Russia that *gets left out* ('the unfit') of popular German editions of butterfly atlases. The fact that Konstantin Kirillovich fills this lacuna with *The Butterflies and Moths of the Russian Empire*, itself a fiction, is Nabokov's attempt to reverse the dumbing-down of history that was the Soviet regime and the tragedy that was the death of Fyodor's (and Nabokov's) father. 'Father's Butterflies' ends with Fyodor's voice saying that 'The bitterness of interrupted life is nothing compared to the bitterness of interrupted work: the probability that the former may continue beyond the grave seems infinite when compared to the inexorable incompletion of the latter' (*Gift*, 402). The future is secretly embedded in one's work: that is why the latter is so crucial. In Fyodor's reading, Pushkin and Konstantin Kirillovich sense the future ('fate') in their lives and through their work. Thus, the difference between a meme à la Dawkins and the pattern Nabokov is invoking revolves around what Dawkins calls 'imitation', the cultural version of replication, and what the hero of *The Gift* experiences as artistic growth and innovation, as culture's flow in and through him, as an explosion of new and powerful energy. 'Imitation', 'meme', 'memeplex' may be sufficient from the scientific side to explain the clusters of meaning in *The Gift*, but from the artistic side they are woefully inadequate when it comes to understanding, or measuring, the 'personality', the 'aura', responsible for the cultural construct. The feedback loop formed in *The Gift* (Pushkin + poetry + Konstantin Kirillovich + butterflies + science + fatedness + art-in/as-life) is not one that can be simply 'copied'. To be authentic it must be *lived* in a new way.

Biological evolution works by trial and error. To cite Gould's famous example of the panda's thumb, the enlarged radial sesamoid is 'good enough' to serve as an opposable digit.[10] Perhaps cultural evolution does as well? Fyodor fears writing about his father because the words may not do justice to the unique intersection of life and work. The replication may not turn out to be distinctive enough to turn the circle into a spiral. Let us conclude this section with some speculation about where Nabokov was going with 'Father's Butterflies', one of the last things he wrote before emigrating to America. The issue comes down to the strikingly close *metaphorical* parallels between the Wright-Dobzhansky concepts of 'adaptive landscape' and 'genetic drift' and Konstantin Kirillovich's theory of 'spherical classification'.

First a portion of the text, whose 'weave' is too dense to avoid quoting at length:

> By 'species' he [Konstantin Kirillovich] intends the original of a being, nonexistent in our reality but unique and definite in concept, that recurs ad infinitum in the mirror of nature, creating countless reflections; each one of them perceived by our intelligence, reflected in that self-same glass and acquiring its reality solely within it, as a living individual of the given species. An aberration, or chance deviations are but the consequence of less 'faithful' areas of the mirror, while the recurrent falling of a reflection on one and the same flaw may yield a stable local race, the idea of which tends toward the periphery of the circle, the center of which, in turn, is the idea of species. These races remain on the circumference of the species insofar as the spatial link (i.e., one with a locus on earth at a given point in time) between the type (i.e., the most precise sample at a given moment) and a local variant is supported by intermediate variations (that can manifest themselves as

---

[10] Stephen Jay Gould, 'The Panda's Peculiar Thumb', in *The Panda's Thumb: More Reflections in Natural History* (New York: W. W. Norton, 1980).

local races or chance deviations), in other words, so far as the species circle remains unbroken (*Gift*, 384).

What is most fascinating about this passage is that we are witnessing the mind of a genius trying to get to the future via metaphor but not yet possessing, as it were, sufficient 'population genetics' rocket fuel for lift-off. The writer of these lines is feeling his way towards the 'hills' of fitness and the 'valleys' of unfitness Wright first brought to the world's attention as genetic landscape. For starters, the 'original of a being, nonexistent in reality' sounds too much like a Platonic idea. On the other hand, he seems to get important things right: those individuals with traits that mutated ('chance deviations') tend to migrate to the periphery of the circle (Wright would say they 'drift' into 'valleys'). And the 'spatial link' joining peripheral members to the 'original' in the centre (i.e. the members closest to the ideal for Nabokov, but simply more 'fit' for Wright) through 'intermediate variations' is also close. The 'mirror of nature' with its 'countless reflections' sounds like some *Naturphilosophie* hocus-pocus, but here too we can give the author a partial pass because he is trying to come up with a more vivid, less pedestrian-sounding version of 'replicate'. The main impasse arises, however, from the very meaning of species. One can speculate that 'the development of variational distinctions is subordinate to the circle enclosing the species' (*Gift*, 385), but one can never *prove scientifically*, because one cannot *predict unerringly*, that the variation has been caused by the over-arching pattern. One can painstakingly describe a butterfly's genitalia through a microscope, as Nabokov did at the MCZ in the 1940s, but showing those parts in the process of *morphing from a subspecies into a new species* is another story. Here we are caught between art and science, the wave and the particle.

The author of *Pale Fire* (1962), *Speak, Memory* and *Ada* (1969) has left his microscope behind and, while still continuing his, mostly critical, conversation with classical Darwinism (see, e.g., *SM*, 460–65), no longer seems interested in proving the artistry of nature (unprovable in any event) from a scientific vantage. This Nabokov does not try to join a piece of empirical reality to an over-arching pattern that explains how the piece attaches to the puzzle. He knows one cannot get there through logic or language. In this, as in his butterfly systematics, he anticipates again the future.[11] He would be on the side of modern-day epigeneticists, who study the role of phenotypic trait variations caused by *environmental* factors that switch genes on and off, which brings us back not only to Darwin, but also

[11] See Carl Zimmer, 'Nonfiction: Nabokov Theory on Butterfly Evolution Is Vindicated', *New York Times*, 25 January 2011.

Lamarck. Expert in artificial intelligence Douglas Hofstadter argues forcefully that the 'simm' (his playful model of a neuronal impulse bouncing
around the cranium/'careenium' like a bumper car) and the 'simmbol' (his
model of groups of neuronal impulses in the game of bumper cars) cannot
be understood simply by looking at the one or the other (again, the wave
and the particle). The 'gobs of detailed knowledge' compiled by neuro-
scientists '[block] deep understanding'.[12] And neuropsychologist and
Nobel Prize winner Roger Sperry makes an equally powerful case when
he writes

> In the brain model proposed here, the causal potency of an idea, or an ideal,
> becomes just as real as that of a molecule, a cell, or a nerve impulse. Ideas
> cause ideas and help evolve new ideas. They interact with each other and
> with other mental forces in the same brain, in neighboring brains, and
> thanks to global communication, in far distant, foreign brains. And they
> also interact with the external surroundings to produce *in toto* a burstwise
> advance in evolution that is far beyond anything to hit the evolutionary
> scene yet, including the emergence of the living cell.[13]

This is also where Nabokov, in his context, leaves us – somewhere between
the gene, the meme and 'ideas having sex'.[14] Darwinism is a nonpareil
heuristic framework, but its orthodoxies can and should be challenged.
With his answering vector – 'We are right in saying quite literally, in the
human, cerebral sense, that nature grows wiser as time passes' (*Gift*, 387) –
Nabokov was and is a worthy opponent.

---

[12] Douglas Hofstadter, *I am a Strange Loop* (New York: Basic Books, 2007), 45–50; 204–6.
[13] Roger Sperry, 'Mind, Brain, and Humanist Values', in John R. Platt (ed.), *New Views on the Nature of Man* (Chicago: University of Chicago Press, 1965).
[14] The phrase is Matt Ridley's (*The Rational Optimist: How Prosperity Evolves* [New York: HarperCollins, 2010]), but could just as easily be teased out of Solovyov.

CHAPTER 24

Psychoanalysis

Michal Oklot and Matthew Walker

If psychoanalysis has always been identified with the name of its founder, Sigmund Freud, during the latter half of the twentieth century Vladimir Nabokov became synonymous with the resistance to it, at least in fiction. One unsympathetic observer has summed up Nabokov's campaign against the 'Viennese Witch Doctor' as 'an unprecedented war on psychoanalysis', even crediting him with the invention of 'a new art form, psychiatry baiting',[1] but Nabokov surely has predecessors, in Karl Kraus for instance, or D. H. Lawrence, who denounced psychoanalysis as 'the serpent of sex coiled around the root of all our actions'.[2] Yet in an age when critics such as Harold Bloom have wagered on the impossibility of rejecting Freud, 'the greatest and most pervasive of modern imaginations',[3] few writers have demanded the impossible so insistently as Nabokov. On this he is unequivocal: 'I reject completely', he declares in the first paragraphs of his autobiography, 'the vulgar, shabby, fundamentally medieval world of Freud, with its crankish quest for sexual symbols (something like searching for Baconian acrostics in Shakespeare's works) and its bitter little embryos spying, from their natural nooks, upon the love life of their parents' (*SM*, 370). We might think Nabokov doth protest too much, but as far as he was concerned one could not protest enough.

We possess little exact data regarding how much of Freud's work Nabokov actually read. In interviews, Nabokov claims 'bookish familiarity' (*SO*, 23) with his works, and though he may have only known them in English, elsewhere he insists (albeit in jest) they must be read in German. His acquaintance with Freud certainly goes beyond casual: in the correspondence with Edmund Wilson, for instance, Nabokov refers directly to a

---

[1] Jeffrey Berman, *The Talking Cure: Literary Representations of Psychoanalysis* (New York: New York University Press, 1985), 211; 213.
[2] D. H. Lawrence, *Psychoanalysis and the Unconscious* (New York: Thomas Seltzer, 1921), 9.
[3] Harold Bloom, 'Introduction', in Harold Bloom (ed.), *Vladimir Nabokov's Lolita* (New York: Chelsea House, 1987), 3.

passage from Freud's letters to Wilhelm Fliess where Freud describes 'a young patient who masturbated in the w.c. of an Interlaken hotel in a special contracted position so as to be able to glimpse . . . the Jungfrau'. In a scholium that distils Nabokov's contempt for Freudian 'poetics', wherein every proper meaning is always at the mercy of common ones, Nabokov adds, 'He should have been a young Frenchman in a Wyoming motel with a view of the Tetons' (*NWL*, 334). Beyond this instance and a few others, however, most speculation about Nabokov's specific knowledge of the Freudian corpus has to remain just that. Yet, in contrast to some of his modernist counterparts (e.g. Joyce, Woolf), there are no fluctuations of opinion to measure or riddles to resolve when it comes to Nabokov and psychoanalysis: Nabokov loathed Freud, at all points of his career – the only thing that really wants clarifying is *why* he loathed him.

In taking up this question, we should first note that what may now strike us as an excessive, almost neurotic, obsession with Freud perhaps only seems that way because we have forgotten that Nabokov's rise to fame as a novelist coincides historically with a larger obsession with Freud in the American popular imagination during the twentieth century. Indeed, far from being the marginal discourse it mostly is today, from the end of the Second World War into the 1970s psychoanalysis wove itself into the very warp and woof of everyday existence in the United States. Writing in *The New York Times Magazine* in 1956, Alfred Kazin gives us an inkling of how mainstream Freud was: 'No other system of thought in modern times, except the great religions, has been adopted by so many people as a systematic explanation of individual behavior . . . to those who have no other belief, Freudianism sometimes serves as a philosophy of life.'[4] Furthermore, Kazin writes, 'It is impossible to think of the greatest names of literature without realizing our debt to Freud's exploration of dreams, myths, symbols and the imaginative profundity of man's inner life.'[5] However, alongside a clear reverence for his subject, Kazin also draws a distinction between Freud's thought and 'Freudianism' as a cultural cliché: a lazy comfort for the middle-class, 'the cunning use' of Freudian terms in advertising, and crass bowdlerisations of psychoanalysis on stage and screen.[6] It might seem enough then to assume that popular Freudianism offended Nabokov's sensibilities in the same way that the copy of Van Gogh's 'Arlésienne' hanging in the Haze home offends Humbert Humbert in *Lolita* (1955) – because it was a commonplace and a commodity.

---

[4] Alfred Kazin, 'The Freudian Revolution Analyzed', *New York Times Magazine*, 6 May 1956, 22.
[5] Ibid., 22.
[6] Ibid, 37.

Yet Freud clearly riles Nabokov more than most bourgeois enthusiasms: the stakes are somehow higher, something has to be defended. '[A]ll my books should be stamped Freudians, Keep Out' (*BS*, 168–69), he writes in the 1963 foreword to *Bend Sinister* (1947), and similar injunctions against the 'Viennese Delegation' become the rule in the prefaces to the English translations of his Russian novels as they appear in print from the late 1950s onwards. Likewise, Freudian-minded literary critics come in for particular abuse in his American novels. Early appraisals of *Lolita* identified one of its implicit targets as Marie Bonaparte's grotesquely Freudian *Life and Works of Edgar Allan Poe* (1933), which besides a foreword from Freud himself features a reading of 'Annabel Lee' that manages to tease from its title acrostics of the names of both Poe's mother *and* sister (Elizabeth and Rosalie), and an interpretation of 'Pit and the Pendulum' as a 'womb phantasy' that casts the narrator as an embryo in its 'cell' (cf. Nabokov's bitter spy in its 'natural nook').[7] *Pale Fire* (1962) is more explicit when it treats us to a scene in which the poet John Shade and his mad commentator Charles Kinbote sample the fruits of the method together, chuckling over Oskar Pfister, who decodes a child incessantly picking his nose as sublimated lust, and Erich Fromm reading Little Red Riding Hood as 'a symbol of menstruation'. Kinbote wonders: 'Do these clowns really *believe* what they teach?' (*PF*, 635).[8] Some readers of Nabokov reading Freudians here (Jeffrey Berman, and more recently the astute Jean-Michel Rabaté)[9] maintain that Fromm and Pfister's claims sound less absurd in their own context (and of course rightly note that Kinbote is insane), but they are nevertheless undeniably typical of the rote, epigonic nature of second-generation Freudian criticism, which, as Rabaté himself concedes, at its worst devolved into 'a hunting ground for loose symbols, indiscriminate projections, and wild allegorizations', so that 'we can only laugh' when we read it today.[10]

For Nabokov, however, psychoanalysis as such is more than just a source of 'good fun'. Freud, in the section of his 1925 'Autobiographical Study' devoted to artistic creation, writes that what interests the psychoanalytic critic above all in the artist is his 'mental constitution and the instinctual

---

[7] Marie Bonaparte, *The Life and Works of Edgar Allen Poe* (London: Imago, 1949), 125–32; 578; 590. On Nabokov and Bonaparte, see Elizabeth Phillips, 'The Hocus Pocus of Lolita,' *Literature and Psychology*, 10/2 (1960), 97–101.

[8] See Oskar Pfister, *The Psychoanalytic Method* (New York: Moffat, Yard, 1917), 79; Erich Fromm, *The Forgotten Language* (New York: Rinehart, 1951), 240.

[9] See Berman, 220–23; Jean-Michel Rabaté, *The Cambridge Introduction to Literature and Psychoanalysis* (New York: Cambridge University Press, 2014), 1.

[10] Rabaté, *Cambridge Introduction to Literature and Psychoanalysis*, 2; 1.

impulses at work in it – that is to say, that part of him which he shares with all men'.[11] This remark more than any lays out what is antithetical to Nabokov in Freud, for the former consistently valorises that part of the artist's consciousness that is shared with *no one* – the singular genius, the sovereign imagination, holding the general at bay for the sake of the particular. If Freud's game is myth, Nabokov believes every work of art should be a new and singular cosmogonic act, unrelated and unrelatable to any archetypal reference. Consider the following, from his *Lectures on Literature* (1980):

> Time and space, the color of seasons, the movements of muscles and minds, all these are for writers of genius ... not traditional notions which may be borrowed from the circulating library of public truths but a series of unique surprises which master artists have learned to express in their own unique way. (*LL*, 2)

Reading Nabokov's novels, we may of course legitimately ask more questions of them than Nabokov asks here about the fate of the particular in art: after all, *Lolita*, with its 'safely solipsized' (*Lolita*, 55) heroine, arguably points to the tragedy of the particular as much as to its redemption. In any case, from Nabokov's general conception of art it follows that even if he is willing to draw a relation between creative writing and daydreams,[12] he will assert the right to produce the one and interpret the other without templates or conventions, on his own terms and with his own imagination. In one late interview, Nabokov's response to the more or less de rigueur question on Freud begins precisely here, with dreams: 'Why should I tolerate a perfect stranger at the bedside of my mind? ... I've no intention to dream the drab middle-class dreams of an Austrian crank with a shabby umbrella' (*SO*, 115–16). For Nabokov, to read, write or dream via the 'standardized symbols of the psychoanalytic racket' (*Lolita*, 268) means to succumb to yet another form of *poshlost*',[13] one that consigns consciousness to a 'third-class carriage of thought'; more than that though, it means losing one's freedom and surrendering to a form of determinism, to a 'police state of sexual myth' (*SM*, 619). Thus psychoanalysis becomes compatible with 'Ekwilism', the ideology of the common denominator that animates the totalitarian regime in *Bend Sinister* (where the image of 'Dr. S. Freud' and his signature briefly appears

[11] Sigmund Freud, 'An Autobiographical Study', *The Standard Edition of the Complete Psychological Works of Sigmund Freud*, vol. XX, tr. James Strachey (London: Hogarth Press, 1953–74), 64.

[12] See Freud, 'Creative Writers and Daydreaming', *Standard Edition*, vol. IX, 141–54.

[13] When asked by an interviewer to 'pin down *poshlost* in contemporary writing', Nabokov cites Freudian symbolism first (*SO*, 101). On *poshlost*', see *NG*, 63–74.

floating on the bottom of a toilet bowl), and thus it is also directly connected with Nazism in *Ada*, where Freud pops up again as 'Dr. Sig Heiler' (*Ada*, 27). When Freudian symbols do manage to make their way up out of the third-class carriage and into Nabokov's fiction, they only do so in the most eviscerated way, as parodies or feints. In an oft-cited passage from *Lolita*, Humbert, having already admitted his fondness for trifling with psychiatrists, teases us with excerpts from his diary advertising the symptoms of a castration complex, and 'John Ray Jr.'s' preface to the novel, which he predicts will become 'a classic in psychiatric circles' (*Lolita*, 5), is a more sustained version of the same joke, as, arguably, is *Lolita* taken as a whole, with the parodically perverted Oedipal triangle at the centre of its plot.

Not all dreams in Nabokov's work operate purely as parody, of course. When it comes to 'genuine', a-Freudian ones, these can be presented either as resolutely concrete – say, the dream at the end of chapter 4 in *Pnin* (1957), where Nabokov's hapless émigré professor sees himself once again on a desolate beach somewhere in Russia with a long dead friend, fleeing the Bolsheviks – or they can appear as nonsensical, made up of seemingly random, inchoate detail, like Klara's laconic dream in Nabokov's first novel *Mary* (1926): '[S]he seemed to be sitting in a tramcar next to an old woman extraordinarily like her Lodz aunt, who was talking rapidly in German; then it gradually turned out that it was not her aunt at all but the cheerful marketwoman from whom Klara bought oranges on her way to work' (*Mary*, 37) – or, more often, they can be a combination of both. Incidentally, in the 1970 foreword to *Mary*, Nabokov expressly warns Freudians away from Klara's dream: 'Although an ass might argue that "orange" is the oneiric anagram of *organe*, I would not advise members of the Viennese delegation to lose precious time analyzing Klara's dream at the end of Chapter Four'.[14] Nabokov, one may surmise, would rather have the attentive reader simply recall the bag of oranges that Klara is inconspicuously holding as we glimpse her at the same chapter's opening. Yet if we take such dreams as miniature models for Nabokov's creative art, we see they would maintain a certain unstated syntax, a 'dream logic' (or as Nabokov elsewhere insists, a 'nightmare' logic),[15] but nevertheless a logic that remains non-determinist, strictly unique to the subjects that dream it, while all the while preserving a certain mystery regarding the true nature of their organisation. Dreams are not where myth is encoded and expressed, but where the particular is preserved. That said though, in the case of *Mary*, Nabokov

---

[14] Vladimir Nabokov, *Mary* (New York: Vintage International, 1989), xv.
[15] *The Man from the USSR and other Plays* (San Diego, New York and London: Bruccoli Clark, Harcourt Brace Jovanovich Publishers, 1985), 327.

obliquely acknowledges how Freudian 'word association' or paronomasia might permit another, alien logic to creep in. If this semantic slippage is a local problem in Nabokov's first novel, by *Bend Sinister* it has become endemic. In the foreword to the later work, Nabokov informs us that 'Paronomasia is a kind of verbal plague, a contagious sickness in the world of words', and that this is especially so in Padukgrad, 'where everybody is merely an anagram of everybody else' (*BS*, 166). Both Paduk and Krug turn out to be inter-lingual anagrams of one another, a detail which might well reveal a higher pattern, but it may also hold out the possibility that Nabokov's avatar of free consciousness is nothing more than the recto of its negation, the verso being not simply a totalitarianism of *poshlost'*, but the materiality of inscription as such, that abstract level of language that is necessarily 'common to all men'. The rub, so to speak, is this: what the regime that governs *Bend Sinister* would confront us with is not actually an absolute determinism of meaning, but the arbitrary play of the signifier, one that threatens the intelligibility of both creative writing and dream-work, and, for that matter, the integrity of the 'aesthetic' as a category and the very project of psychoanalysis as such, if that be the Delphic 'know thyself'.

We see this problem already at work in Nabokov's earliest sorties against Freud, the 1931 feuilleton 'What Should Everyone Know?' a satirical advertisement hawking 'Freudianism for Everyone':

> Wherever we cast our eyes or gaze, there we find the sexual principle [*polovoe nachalo*]. Let us turn to the well-known professions – it's everywhere: an architect builds a house [*stroit dom*] (read: courts women [*stroit kury*]); a cameraman cranks (read: with such and such); a lady doctor takes care of [*ukhazhivaet za*] a patient (read: the patient recovers and chases after [*ukhazhivaet za*] the lady doctor). . . . Compare also 'tavern waiter' [*traktir-nogo polovogo*] or 'floor rag' [*polovuiu triapku*] with 'the sexual question' [*s polovym voprosom*]. Also relevant here are the words 'half a year' [*pol-goda*], half a fathom [*pol-sazheni*], col-onel [*pol-kovnik*], etc.[16]

Meaning slips absurdly between lexemes, from *pol* ('sex') to *pol* ('half') or from 'waiter' or 'of-a-floor' (*polovoi*) to 'sexual' (*polovoi*). Thus conceived, Freudianism foolishly seeks to establish the unconscious 'sexual principle' as an ordering 'author' upon a random field of writing. It is for this reason that Nabokov in *Speak, Memory* (1967) associates psychoanalysis with the search for 'Baconian acrostics' in Shakespeare, and it is also why we might even perhaps accuse Nabokov – and certainly some strands of Nabokov

---

[16] 'Chto vsiakii dolzhen znat'?', *Sobr. soch.*, 3, 697–99. Nabokov here oddly anticipates some of his current neo-Freudian critics. See Eric Naiman, *Nabokov, Perversely* (Ithaca, NY: Cornell, 2010).

criticism – of occasionally aping just such a vulgar hermeneuticism. Nabokov, of course, actively encourages this kind of 'hunt for the author' in stories like 'The Vane Sisters' (1958), with the acrostic buried in its last paragraph, even as he discourages it elsewhere, and some of the more inventive critical readings of works like 'Signs and Symbols' (1948) tend in the same direction, even if the story itself perhaps does not. Kinbote, with his knack for drawing his would-be assassin Gradus out of the most unexpected places – in the 'Tana*gra dust*' of an alleged variant to Shade's poem, or in 'Lenin*grad us*ed to be Petrograd?' (*PF,* 606) – would perhaps be the ultimate emblem in Nabokov of this desire for meaning versus its proliferation in a madness of writing.

From this standpoint, the Freudian project is not just a 'climate of thought', something Nabokov quite accurately described as 'unspeakably spooky' (*SO,* 128). It is also an all too material question of reading, one that both Nabokov and Freud would try and at times have us fail to negotiate. This is one place where Freud and Nabokov undoubtedly cross paths. There are others too, and to recognise them is to realise that, strangely enough, there may still be no reading Nabokov *without* Freud. After all, if *Speak, Memory,* exemplifying all the positive poles of Nabokov's art, is a meditation on childhood, on the origins and patterns of personality, on the workings of memory itself, then it trespasses upon a good number of Freud's own themes as well. Likewise, if the plots of *Lolita, Pale Fire* and *Ada* are structured around sexual 'perversions', then they cannot but nod to the genre we recognise as the Freudian case study, where perversions are always allegories of something else. But if we agree with Lionel Trilling, who long before Jacques Lacan identified psychoanalysis as 'a science of tropes',[17] then what Nabokov's parodies of Freud show us is how easily figural language and knowledge part ways, or how they might even exclude one another altogether. The question then is whether this is solely a Freudian problem, or ultimately a Nabokovian one as well.

Writing in 1984, Jenefer Shute suggested that the aim of Nabokov's injunctions against psychoanalysis is to erect barricades against a hermeneutic rival, or to wrest contested territory from a powerful precursor.[18] This is a scenario that, at least for a critic of influence like Bloom, would neatly end up situating Nabokov back within the Freudian 'family romance', with Freud as castrating father and Nabokov as the rebellious

---

[17] Lionel Trilling, 'Freud and Literature', *Horizon,* XVI/92 (1947), 197.
[18] See Jenefer P. Shute, 'Nabokov and Freud: The Play of Power', *Modern Fiction Studies,* 30/4 (Winter 1984), 637–50, and her entry 'Nabokov and Freud', in Vladimir Alexandrov (ed.), *The Garland Companion to Vladimir Nabokov* (New York and London: Garland, 1995), 412–20.

son, although one can easily turn the tables and propose that it is Nabokov, in his decisive, blanket rejection of 'influence' as such, that poses just such a threat to Bloom. This, in any case, is one more way to read the trope of Nabokov reading Freud: Nabokov's parody of psychoanalysis is transformed into a symptom that confirms the validity of what it mocks. Yet it might be time to try to think beyond the usual dichotomies of Nabokov's resistance to Freud and Freud's resistance to Nabokov. There is more to read here than duelling intentions – the monuments of artistic genius on the one hand, or the symptoms of the universal myths or neuroses purveyed by classical psychoanalysis on the other – for what comes between them is a resistance to the manifestation of each that we might just as well diagnose as a symptom of something else: literature.

CHAPTER 25

Faith

Sergei Davydov

When a *Playboy* interviewer asked him, 'Do you believe in God?', Nabokov answered in typical arcane manner:

> To be quite candid – and what I am going to say now is something I never said before, and I hope it provokes a salutary little chill – I know more than I can express in words, and the little I can express would not have been expressed, had I not known more. (*SO*, 45)

In this essay, I will speculate about what Nabokov 'might have known' and what his metaphysical allegiances might have been.

The turn of the last century in Russia saw an unprecedented outburst of esoteric religious philosophies. Vladimir Solovyov, Nikolai Berdiaev, Pavel Florensky, Nikolai Lossky, Vasily Rozanov, Lev Shestov, to name a few, combined in their works the tenets of Christian Orthodoxy with mystical, theosophical, anthroposophical, deist, gnostic and other heterodox concepts in an attempt to renegotiate the relationship between man and God. Since Nabokov was of a different generation, their spiritual speculations touched him, at best, tangentially. He was a poet *par excellence* whose response (if there was one) to these religious trends can be seen in his fondness for the sensation of a plausible 'transcendental object' evoked by purely rhetorical means, such as in the opening lines of his autobiography: 'The cradle rocks above an abyss, and common sense tells us that our existence is but a brief crack of light between two eternities of darkness'. Of the two, Nabokov faced the 'prenatal abyss with more calm than the one he [was] heading for (at some forty-five hundred heartbeats an hour)' (*SM*, 369).

In the posthumous edition of his Russian poems, Nabokov's widow Véra claimed that the theme of 'the beyond' (*potustoronnost*) runs 'like a water-mark' through most of her husband's writing (*Stikhi*, 'Foreword'). Following her lead, a score of scholars set out to explore that realm and returned with the conviction that alongside the frivolous puppet master and word wizard there lived an old-fashioned moralist and an earnest seeker of some transcendental truth.[1] The more inquisitive among Nabokov's characters, too, probe into that mystery and its hieroglyphs, including Cincinnatus in *Invitation to a Beheading* (1935–36), Fyodor in *The Gift* (1937–38), Sineusov in 'Ultima Thule' (1942), the narrator V. in *Real Life of Sebastian Knight* (1941), Krug in *Bend Sinister* (1947), Pnin in *Pnin* (1957) and Kinbote and Shade in *Pale Fire* (1962). But unlike them, Nabokov seems more 'optimystic' (spelled preferably with a 'y') about mortality's 'chance to peer beyond its own limits', believing that, along that way 'there is somehow the blissful feeling that one is looking in the right direction' (*SM*, 396).

But let us start at the opposite end – with the 'cradle'. Nabokov was born to Christian parents in the last year of the nineteenth century. He was baptised according to Eastern Orthodox rites, but his religious upbringing was scanty at best. The Nabokov children were taught to pray, went to church at Lent and Easter, and their father would read out to them the 'Twelve Evangels'. When Vladimir complained that church services bored him, his father allowed him not to go. Nabokov's mother was of a sectarian (Old Believer) background, but her dislike for the atmosphere of the Russian Orthodox Church, including the occasional venality of its priests, seems unrelated to her schismatic background.

> She found a deep appeal in the moral and poetical side of the Gospels, but felt no need in the support of any dogma. The appalling insecurity of an afterlife and its lack of privacy did not enter her thoughts. Her intense and pure religiousness took the form of her having equal faith in the existence of another world and in the impossibility of comprehending it in terms of earthly life. (*SM*, 387)

Later in life she found solace in Christian Science, which evoked in Nabokov a benevolent smile.[2]

Notwithstanding the sketchiness of Nabokov's religious upbringing, the images of God, angels, Christ on and off the cross, Resurrection, Peter at the heavenly gates and other Edenic paraphernalia permeate his early poetry between 1918 and 1925. Angels were his favourites, and he dedicated to each of their nine orders (Seraphim, Cherubim, Thrones, Dominions, Virtues, Powers, Principalities, Archangels and Angels) a solemn poem (*Stikho*, 134–41). More often, however, a distinctly terrestrial and humorous thread weaves itself through the celestial fabric of these poems: an angel

---

[1] For relevant works by these scholars see 'Further Reading'. Andrew Field, *Nabokov: His Life in Part* (New York: Viking, 1977), 85; Brian Boyd, *Vladimir Nabokov: The Russian Years* (Princeton: Princeton University Press, 1990), 354.
[2] Field, *Nabokov: His Life in Part*, 85; Boyd, *Russian Years*, 354.

with 'a splinter in his foot', Peter 'smelling of fish'.[3] In the poem 'Na Golgofe' ('On Golgotha' [1921]), the Son of God thinks on the cross not of his heavenly Father but of the *earthly* one: the carpenter's shop, the floor covered with wood shavings (*Stikho*, 164). In the poem 'Mat'' ('The Mother' [1925]) we perceive the crucifixion through the eyes of a grieving *earthly* mother rather than the Mother of God. This poem can be seen as a watershed in Nabokov's spiritual quest, for it is here that the poet crosses the boundary of traditional Orthodoxy and, with a firmness worthy of Ivan Karamazov, 'returns his ticket' to the Christian God:

> Mary, what are to you the fantasies
> of fishermen? Over your grief days skim
> insensibly, and neither on the third
> nor hundredth, never will he heed your call
> and rise, your brown firstborn who baked mud sparrows
> in the hot sun, at Nazareth.   (*PP*, 32–33)

The Son of God may rise, but Maria's swarthy boy *will not*. Nabokov wrote this poem in April 1925, a few days after his civil marriage to Véra Slonim, who was Jewish. From that moment on, the Christian topoi all but vanish from the poet's repertoire and Nabokov will later dismiss them as mere stylistic exercises in 'Byzantine imagery' which were 'mistaken by some readers for an interest in "religion"' (*SO*, 160; *PP*, 13–14). Still, Nabokov's quest for 'the beyond' continued, although it would be pursued strictly on his own idiosyncratic terms.

> Since, in my metaphysics, I am a confirmed non-unionist and have no use for organized tours through anthropomorphic paradises, I am left to my own, not negligible devices when I think of the best things in life. (*SM*, 614)

What were these 'not negligible devices' that shaped the metaphysics of the 'fetterless soul in a world that is swarming with godheads', as he referred to himself in the 1942 poem 'Slava' ('Fame', *PP*, 111)?

A closer look at Nabokov's Christian and quasi-Christian poems reveals a heterodox streak which ranges from the light-hearted, humorous and exotic, to the bizarre, macabre and outright blasphemous. In a 1921 poem dedicated to Dostoevsky, Christ and his disciples stumble upon a dead dog. The Apostles avert their noses and curse the carcass teeming with worms, but Christ points out to them the beauty of the dog's 'pearl-like teeth' (*Stikho*, 65). The poem mocks Dostoevsky, who, according to Nabokov, lacked the ability to perceive beauty. In addition, Nabokov's apocryphal

---

[3] See *Stikho*, 284, 273; Boyd, *Russian Years*, 233–34.

poem comes courtesy of the twelfth-century Persian poet Nizami, known for esoteric and gnostic interpretations of Quranic verses. Goethe too translated Nizami's 'dead dog' poem in his *West-Östlicher Divan*.[4] The image of the swarthy boy 'baking mud sparrows in the hot sun in Nazareth' was borrowed from the *Infancy Gospel* attributed to the gnostic Apostle Thomas. Here the five-year-old Jesus, playing in the mud on the Sabbath, has moulded twelve clay sparrows. When Joseph chides him for defiling the Sabbath (by using his hands), the boy simply claps and the birds fly away.[5] The *Infancy Gospel* is full of similar, and sometimes quite mischievous, miracles perpetrated by the boy Jesus.

In many respects, Nabokov's deviations and eventual apostasy from Christianity remind one of the gnostic heresy, various elements of which found their way into his early poetry, where they form a rudimentary 'gnostic' plot: the deity has abandoned the universe but the poet is inextricably linked to some 'silent, secret God' with whom he shares something: 'My god and I, we know better'. While languishing on Earth in 'the shirt of flesh', the poet gradually learns how to respond properly to the summons from his secret god. At the moment of death, the poet will be released from the world and admitted to some Paradise-like eternity (*Stikho*, 100, 273, 288–89).

The most explicit reprise of the gnostic myth in Nabokov can be found in *Invitation to a Beheading* (1935–36), whose hero is condemned to death for the rare crime of 'gnostical turpitude' (*IB*, 51). On the metaphysical level, Cincinnatus exposes the false creator (the Demiurge), mocks the nature of his sham prison and, remaining faithful to his true god, ultimately prevails. On the level of metafiction, Cincinnatus exposes the author, whose 'demiurgic' nature requires that the hero, a poor actor in the farce, must die in the end. But Cincinnatus correctly responds to the summons from 'outside' and gradually becomes an inspired writer himself who now attempts to 'write off' the horror of death. The character succeeds because his metaphysical intuition and inspired art are now worthy of his author. In chapter 8, 'composed' entirely by Cincinnatus, his art comes very close to Nabokov's mastery. At the end of the novel, 'the author-cum-demiurge' beheads with one hand the 'turpid gnostic' who has declined the gallant invitation and thus brought about the novel's

---

[4] See Omri Ronen, 'Nabokov and Goethe', in Gennady Barabtarlo (ed.), *Cold Fusion: Aspects of the German Cultural Presence in Russia* (New York, Oxford: Berghahn Books, 2000), 241–51.

[5] 'The Infancy Gospel of Thomas' (II, 1–5), in *The Apocryphal New Testament*, translation and notes by M. R. James (Oxford: Clarendon Press, 1924). See also Nabokov's other Christian apocrypha: 'Evangelie Iakova Evreia', 'Pavliny', 'Legenda o starukhe', 'Ochki Iosifa' (*Stikho*, 95, 154, 255, 261).

collapse, but with his other hand 'Vladimir-the-redeemer' (Nabokov liked to point out that his first name rhymed with that word) rescues his clever hero from the scaffold and from the debris of the collapsing novel and allows him to join the 'beings akin to him' (*IB*, 180). The character returns to his creator and secures his well-earned share of immortality promised in the novel's epigraph: '*Comme un fou se croit Dieu, nous nous croyons mortels*' (As the madman believes himself to be God, we believe ourselves to be mortal). Nabokov ascribed this sophism to the 'melancholy, extravagant, wise, witty, magical, and altogether delightful Pierre Delalande' (*IB*, viii). This French sage, whom Nabokov cheerfully invented, will offer more insights into ultimate matters in Nabokov's last Russian novel.

The Gift (1937–38) is Nabokov's 'portrait of an artist as a young man'. In it the author traces three years of his hero's poetic apprenticeship during which Fyodor creates within Nabokov's novel his own works in verse and prose. The classic Russian theme of 'fathers and sons' is at the centre of *The Gift* because on his path to becoming a genuine artist Fyodor has to identify the true father figures and purge the impostors (such as the radical critic of the 1860s Nikolai Chernyshevsky).[6] Fyodor attains a perfect rapport with the 'true fathers': his biological father, his artistic ones (Pushkin and Gogol) and, most importantly, his creator Nabokov, whose transcendentally reassuring presence Fyodor feels and gratefully accepts:

> with a kind of relief – as if the responsibility for his soul belonged not to him but to someone who knew what it all meant – [Fyodor] felt that all this skein of random thoughts, like everything else as well . . . was but the reverse side of a magnificent fabric, on the front of which there gradually formed and became alive images invisible to him. (*Gift*, 326)

In return for Fyodor's trust, taste and literary talent, and for his guardianship of the patrimony of his 'true fathers', Fyodor is generously rewarded: he finds love, becomes a genuine artist, reunites with his father who briefly returns from the dead and, by the novel's close, receives the ultimate gift from his creator. Nabokov's last paragraph, camouflaged as a Pushkinian Onegin stanza, sends us back to the novel's beginning, so that upon our second reading of *The Gift* we recognise it as a novel written by Fyodor. During the brief hiatus between the novel's closure and its second beginning – the Möbius juncture – Fyodor miraculously slips from the 'reverse side' onto the front side of that 'magnificent fabric'.

[6] See Monika Greenleaf, 'Fathers, Sons and Imposters: Reading Pushkin's Trace in Nabokov's *The Gift*', *Slavic Review*, 53/1 (1994), 140–58.

Fyodor is the only protagonist who is allowed to step from the pages of Nabokov's book to its cover and thus become its 'legitimate' author. This last 'gift' adds a transcendental dimension to the covenant between the creator and his creature (Fyodor means the 'gift of god' in Greek). In the metamorphosis of the inner text into the outer text, of the character into the author, lies the key to Nabokov's 'metapoetic theology'. For Fyodor, the transition is tantamount to a transcendental leap from art to life, a *salto vitale* into a new modality of being, while for Fyodor's creator that moment is just as dramatic. Having bequeathed his last and best Russian novel to his favourite hero, Nabokov leaves the Old World for the New, abandons his docile tongue (he will never write another novel in Russian), and in a new 'installment of his serial soul' (*LL*, 377), becomes an American writer. In American works, the gnostic theme and the metaphysical/metafictional model disappear. However, conjectures on immortality will remain a staple of many of his characters in his American period.

From the Metapoetical to the Foolscap Device

To what extent, then, does the metapoetic model derived from Nabokov's novels have any bearing on Nabokov himself, on his hypothetical metaphysical creed? In the 1928 poem 'Tolstoy', for example, Nabokov envisioned the following covenant between the artist and the creator:

> ... That's how the Lord
> confers to the chosen one
> His primeval and beatific license
> to create worlds and instantly to breathe
> into the new-made flesh one-and-only spirit
>
> (*Stikho*, 342; my translation)

This pact enjoins 'the chosen one' (created, presumably, in His image and likeness and thus endowed with a smattering of His creative spirit) to engage in *imitatio Dei*. Shortly after Nabokov had finished his first novel *Mary* (1926), he described in a letter to his mother a coy version of such a covenant:

> I understand how God as he created the world found this a pure, thrilling joy. *We* are translators of God's creation, his little plagiarists and imitators, we dress up what he wrote, as a charmed commentator sometimes gives an extra grace to a line of genius.[7]

---

[7] Nabokov to Elena Nabokov, 13 October 1925, quoted in Boyd, *Russian Years*, 245.

In a lecture on Dostoevsky, Nabokov told his Cornell students that 'art is a divine game. . . . It is divine because this is the element in which man comes nearest to God through becoming a true creator in his own right. And it is a game, because it remains art . . . it is all make-believe . . .' (*LRL*, 106). The shrewder among Nabokov's characters suspect that above their inferior world (and text) there exists some supreme world (and text) of their author, who is playing games with them, and that their own make-believe lives are perhaps just a page from his book. In the poem 'Neokonchennyi cherno-vik' ('Unfinished Draft' [1931]), the poet muses that 'human days are only words on a page ripped out from who knows where' (*Stikhi*, 245). A minor character in *The Gift* ruminates before death: 'Funny that I have thought of death all my life, and if I have lived, I have lived only in the margin of a book I have never been able to read' (*Gift*, 323). The narrator of *Real Life of Sebastian Knight* (1941) suggests that human life is 'a page in a book' where 'mountains and forests, and fields, and rivers are disposed in such a way as to form a coherent sentence' and that 'the intricate pattern of human life' can be disentangled from 'the interwoven letters' (*RLSK*, 139). In 'Ultima Thule', the artist Sineusov claims 'that everything – life, patria, April, the sound of a spring or that of a dear voice – is but a muddled preface, and that the main text still lies ahead' (*Stories*, 520–21). In *Pale Fire* (1962), the poet jots down a 'Note for further use': '*Man's life as commentary to abstruse / Unfinished poem*' (*PF*, 482). Taken together, these metaphors suggest that our earthly life is only a preliminary 'text' ('a page, a note, a preface'), while 'the abstruse poem, the main text ahead' stands for some supreme *magnum opus* from which our page was torn. Nabokov concluded the 'Tolstoy' poem with this conjecture about death:

> I know that death is just a kind of border;
> I see death as a single image:
> the final page has been written,
> and the lamp over the writing desk goes off.
>
> (*Stikho*, 343; my translation)

If 'death' is not the final destination, could it be that the 'border' is the crossing point through which the 'final page' of one's life returns to the original volume?

Just as Nabokov judged his characters and chose for them their next destination according to the merits of their writing and their metaphysical 'politesse', some supreme authority might arbitrate one day whether Nabokov's oeuvre is worthy of crossing the 'border'. However, to simply proffer on the day of reckoning a well-crafted page is not enough, for in order to be admitted (and to receive the royalties from the 'publishing houses of Paradise') the page has to share with that supreme *magnum opus* some very specific 'watermark'. In the poem 'Smert'' ('Death' [1924]), for example, death lifts the poet's soul like a 'letter' (*pis'mo*), brings it 'into the light' and inspects its 'watermark', the indelible hallmark of Eden. The dying poet is sure that his page has the right imprimatur, hence his parting from this world is 'smooth and bright' (*Stikho*, 293–4). In *Speak, Memory* (1967), Nabokov searches for the origins of the 'watermark' that runs through his 'page of life':

> Neither in environment nor in heredity can I find the exact instrument that fashioned me, the anonymous roller that pressed upon my life a certain intricate watermark whose unique design becomes visible when the lamp of art is made to shine through life's foolscap. (*SM*, 374)

The choice of words here is deliberate: 'foolscap' is a brand of writing paper with a watermark depicting – appropriately – a fool in a cap. As far as Nabokov is concerned, he was, to return to our beginning, 'optimystic' that his personal page bears the right 'fool's cap' and that immortality is viable:

> That human life is but a first installment of the serial soul and that one's individual secret is not lost in the process of earthly dissolution, becomes something more than an optimistic conjecture, and even more than a matter of religious faith, when we remember that only commonsense rules immortality out. (*LL*, 377)

This sophism is worthy of Pierre Delalande, the cheerfully invented sage whose lack of common sense (*'Comme un fou se croit Dieu, nous nous croyons mortels'*) and playful irreverence towards death Nabokov and Fyodor found so delightful. In the finale of *The Gift*, Nabokov has Fyodor translate a passage from Delalande's *Discours sur les ombres*:

> there was once a man ... he lived as a true Christian; he did much good, sometimes by word, sometimes by deed, and sometimes by silence; he observed the fasts; he drank the water of mountain valleys ...; he nurtured the spirit of contemplation and vigilance; he lived a pure, difficult, wise life; but when he sensed the approach of death, instead of thinking about it, instead of tears of repentance and sorrowful partings, instead of monks and a notary in black, he invited guests to a feast, acrobats, actors, poets, a crowd of dancing girls, three magicians, jolly Tollenburg students, a traveller from Taprobana, and in the midst of melodious verses, masks and music he drained a goblet of wine and died, with a carefree smile on his face. (*Gift*, 363)

Illustration 5 The Nabokovs' grave at Clarens

Nabokov too died outside of religion, without holy sacraments. He was cremated to the tunes of two arias from Puccini's 'La Bohème' played on an organ. No Byzantine symbols mark the bluish marble slate at the Vevey cemetery in Switzerland. In the end, the bright feast to which the wise man invites his guests are his works. The immortality part remains a mystery; the fact of the works does not.

CHAPTER 26

Jewishness as Literary Device in Nabokov's Fiction

Leonid Livak

Receiving the inaugural issue of the émigré review *Novyi zhurnal*, Nabokov fired off a letter to the co-editor, Russian-Jewish writer Mark Aldanov, blasting Aleksandra Tolstaia's novella, *Fog before Dawn* (*Predrassvetnyi tuman*), as 'pogrom-style trash' whose Jewish personages came from the Nazi press. A demurring Aldanov saw no such thing in Tolstaia's text, but Nabokov's missive triggered his musings on Jewish representation, from Pushkin to Proust. As the dialogue went on, the writers switched roles, confirming the issue's complexity. Aldanov wanted to censure a Judeophobe passage in Alexander Blok's *Retribution* (*Vozmezdie*, 1910–21), whereas Nabokov thought that the poem should appear in full, to give Blok his just deserts as a gifted poet but a worthless thinker.[1] This exchange shows Nabokov's sensitivity to the discourse about the Jewish Other and frustration with extant models of Jewish representation. Nabokov had few tools at his disposal for creating Jewish characters that met his aesthetic and ethical standards, while remaining recognisable to his readers, in whose conditioned imagination the marker of Jewishness turned a literary character into a type informed by two millennia of Christian and post-Christian myth-making.

The daunting task was to normalise Jewish personages rather than engage in a Judeophile exercise that, like its Judeophobe opposite, 'set Jews apart as people radically different from all the others, needing separate concepts to describe and comprehend them'.[2] Caught between the imaginatively appealing but unethical Judeophobe model and its patronising, saccharine opposite, Russian artists often opted for a third way, dubbed *asemitism*, evacuating the subject of Jewishness from fiction into the extra-artistic

---

[1] Bakhmeteff Archive, Columbia University, Mark Aldanov Collection, Box 6, Nabokov to Aldanov, 21 January, 6 May and 20 May 1942; Aldanov to Nabokov, 23 January, 13 and 31 May 1942.
[2] Zygmunt Bauman, 'Allosemitism', in Bryan Cheyette (ed.), *Modernity, Culture and 'the Jew'* (Stanford, CA: Stanford University Press, 1998), 143–48.

discourse.[3] Nabokov was no exception to this rule. The paucity and marginality of Jews in his art, prior to *The Gift* (1937–38), was inversely proportional to the place of Jewish topics in his life.

Biographers stress Nabokov's ties to the Russian-Jewish intelligentsia and opposition to anti-Semitism. They trace the writer's attitude to his father's liberal politics, which included the advocacy of Jewish civic equality, and to Nabokov's marriage to Véra Slonim – a Russian-Jewish woman with a mostly reactive Jewish identity, brought out by expressions of prejudice in Europe and America, to which her husband was equally sensitive.[4] Such biographical circumstances stimulate the reading of Nabokov's art through the lens of the 'Jewish question', with some scholars claiming that his oeuvre sports 'a series of remarkable Jewish characters' and 'a mediated impact of Judaic religious philosophy'.[5]

In the context of traditional Jewish representation in European art, one is hard-pressed to find evidence supporting such claims. Although Nabokov's writings grew more attentive to the subject of Jewishness in response to Nazism, and then to the Holocaust, Nabokov's Jewish characters remained conventional and reliant on Judeophile clichés. More importantly, Nabokov was aware of lacking the imaginative language for depicting Jews in ways that departed from hackneyed models – hence his resort to *asemitism* until that expedient broke down when Nazi racial laws threatened his Berlin-based family. Coinciding with his work on *The Gift*, the personal urgency of the 'Jewish question' turned Nabokov's *asemitism* from a solution into a problem. From the mid-1930s onwards, his need to engage the topic of Jewishness clashed with the lack of suitable imaginative tools, all the more glaring for a writer who avoided open political commentary in art.

Nabokov made virtue of necessity. He found a solution by approaching Jewishness not as a topic *sui generis* but as a problem whose contemplation could be inscribed into the larger poetics of his mature oeuvre. Jewishness thus became a device mediating key facets of Nabokov's *ars poetica* – allusiveness, metareflexivity, and preoccupation with the ethics of creative activity. Nabokov's is a case study from a series of similar imbroglios, whereby good intentions collide with cultural conditioning that leaves Gentiles and assimilated Jews alike no imaginative lexicon to treat Jewishness in a way that

---

[3] See Vladimir Zhabotinskii, 'Asemitizm' (1909), *Izbrannoe* (Jerusalem: Aliia, 1978), 73–79.

[4] See Brian Boyd, *Vladimir Nabokov: The Russian Years* (Princeton: Princeton University Press, 1990); Brian Boyd, *Vladimir Nabokov: The American Years* (Princeton: Princeton University Press, 1991); Stacey Schiff, *Véra (Mrs. Vladimir Nabokov)* (New York: Random House, 1999).

[5] Maxim Shrayer, 'Jewish Questions in Nabokov's Art and Life', in Julian W. Connolly (ed.), *Nabokov and His Fiction* (Cambridge: Cambridge University Press, 1999), 73–91.

convinces the reader, meets high aesthetic standards and proves ethically acceptable. Nabokov instrumentalised this tension between literary means and ends as a device laying bare his overall artistic philosophy. By problematising Jewish representation, he made it not so much about Jews as about his art. Nabokov's treatment of Jewishness both reflected and exposed the aesthetic and ethical evolution of his writing from a *poetics of understatement*, on display in *The Gift*, to a *poetics of absence*, fully developed in his first successful American novel, *Pnin* (1957).

Avoiding open declarations on 'the Jewish question', Nabokov inscribes clashing political and ethical stances within one's capacity to be a 'good' or a 'bad' reader. The cornerstone of his *poetics of understatement*, intertextuality sorts readers by their ability to place a situation in the 'right' network of literary texts yielding further interpretive possibilities. *The Gift* self-consciously comments on this aspect of Nabokov's poetics by framing the problem of Jewish representation within a Tolstoyan comparison of unhappy émigré families – the Chernyshevskys, whose Berlin literary salon is frequented by Fyodor, the novel's hero, and the Shchyogolevs, Fyodor's landlords and parents of his beloved, Zina Mertz.

At first, *The Gift* lulls its readership with familiar forays into Jewishness. Alexander Yakovlevich and Yasha Chernyshevsky sport qualities codified as Jewish in the Wagnerian critique of modernity and inscribed in the father's patronymic and the son's name, evocative of patriarch Jacob, alias Israel. Jewishness brings to the common denominator Alexander's insanity and spiritual restlessness (his grandfather was baptised into Orthodoxy, but he is a Protestant), and the neuroticism, homosexuality and unoriginality of the poet-suicide Yasha. For émigré Wagnerians, who held against Nabokov his ties to the Jewish intelligentsia, Yasha symbolised Russian literature's alleged colonisation by Jews. But bringing Fyodor into Zina's family strife, Nabokov changes the rules of the game. Gone are helpful markers, like the mention of baptism in the Chernyshevskys' past or their names. Showing the Shchyogolev family for the first time, Nabokov does not describe Zina as Jewish. Instead, he tests our capacity to unravel the scene's intertextuality. Pondering the undisclosed reasons for the tensions in the Shchyogolev household, one confronts the aesthetic and ethical implications of Nabokov's decision to withhold information. Intertextual decryption thus evolves into meta-literary reflection.

At lunch, Shchyogolev urges his step-daughter: 'Come on, eat, Aïda' (*Gift*, 156). A jocose Jew-baiter, as we learn with a calculated delay (*Gift*, 182–84), Shchyogolev splits in half Zina's full name – Zinaida. The result is a pun on the Yiddish for a Jew (*a Id*), hinting at Zina's half-Jewishness, from her late father's side. But the joke is on Shchyogolev, who cannot see the pun's full meaning, as befits a 'bad' reader. 'Good' readers are expected to notice another pun, produced by the routine typographic omission of diacritics in Russian: *poesh'* (eat) could as easily read *poësh'* (you are singing), enhancing Shyogolev's inadvertent allusion to Giuseppe Verdi's *Aida* (1871), an opera about an Ethiopian princess enslaved in Egypt – a subtext with biblical resonance for Zina's home life (Jews in Egyptian slavery).

Describing Zina's situation, the narrator says 'unhappy' (*neschastna, neschast'e*) twice in one sentence (*Gift*, 186 / *Sobr. soch.*, IV, 368), both invoking the opening line of *Anna Karenina* and prodding us to recognise in the confluence of Jewishness and music the main literary subtext of Zina's filial strife – Ivan Turgenev's Judeophile story 'Neschastnaia' ('The Hapless Girl' [1869]). Like Zina, Turgenev's Susanna is artistically sensitive and proud of her half-Jewish origins. Like Zina, she lives in the vulgar Christian household of her step-father, Ratch, who besets Susanna with Judeophobe innuendos. The reader's ability to recognise Ratch the jocose raconteur with questionable ethics in Zina's step-father holds the key to the operatic dimension of Shchyogolev's pun. Composer and musician Ratch rants about music's decline and the Jewish role therein, spoofing Richard Wagner, whose crusade against 'Jewishness in music' motivated Turgenev to turn his story into a medium for dealing with rumours about the Jewishness of his life companion, opera singer Pauline Viardot.[6] The subtext is pregnant with meaning for Nabokov, who, like Turgenev, lives in Germany at a time of intensified Jew-baiting which he associates with Wagner: witness the elevator-attendant 'oddly resembling Richard Wagner' (*Stories*, 588) who takes the hero of Nabokov's story 'Double Talk' (later renamed 'Conversation Piece, 1945' [1945]) to a party featuring an array of anti-Semites.

The Gift thus reframes the problem of Jewish representation, which becomes not about Jews, but about Russian literature and its 'good' and 'bad' readers. Zina's ethical antipode, Shchyogolev, also represents the opposite of her 'absolute pitch' in art (*Gift*, 174). Her Jewishness thereby becomes a challenge to those who bemoan the prominence of the Jewish intelligentsia in the current literary process; for, even the table talk of Zina's Jewish relatives is about 'illnesses, weddings and Russian literature' (*Gift*, 186). Treating émigré writing as the only living contemporary

---

[6] Alexandre Zviguilsky, 'Ivan Tourguéniev et le problème juif', *Annales du C.E.S.E.R.E.*, I (1978), 77–97.

Russian literature, *The Gift* implicitly challenges Russian Wagnerians when it recasts in positive light their claim that émigré literature is 'half-Jewish'.[7] Fyodor's love poem – partly to Zina and partly to Russian literature – rewrites Shchyogolev's pun by similarly splitting in half the heroine's full name and turning its bipartite structure into a metaphor for his vision of both addressees:

> Kak zvat' tebia? Ty polu-Mnemozina, polumertsan'e v imeni tvoem, –
> i stranno mne po sumraku Berlina s poluviden'em stranstvovat' vdvoem
> (*Sobr. soch.*, IV, 337–38)
> What shall I call you? Half-Mnemo*syne*? There's a half-shim*mer* in your surname too. In dark Berlin it is so strange to me to roam, oh, my half-fantasy, with you (*Gift*, 154; italics in original)

Fyodor's polemical rewriting of Shchyogolev's pun was unlikely to be lost on *The Gift*'s original readers. In a case of life imitating art, poet Anatolii Shteiger called émigré literature 'half-Jewish' and conveyed to Zinaida Shakhovskoy, a Judeophobe critic of Nabokov's marriage, his Wagnerian disgust with the public at a Berlin soirée where Nabokov read excerpts from *The Gift*. But Shteiger also admitted that 'without this [Russian-Jewish] milieu not a single line in Russian would have appeared in exile', and that Nabokov's novel was brilliant.[8]

Shchyogolev's slur and its subversion in Fyodor's poem, written with a certain readership in mind, are easily lost in translation. Hence Nabokov's attempt to highlight his *poetics of understatement* in the foreword to *The Gift*'s English edition, explaining that the novel's heroine is 'not Zina, but Russian literature', and that the 'real hub' of the third chapter is 'the love poem dedicated to Zina' (*Gift*, viii). But Anglophone readers still had to connect Zina's Jewishness to her role as an allegory of Russian literature and confront *The Gift*'s intertextuality, transforming Jewish representation from a trite procedure into a problem. Finally, readers were expected to rise above the 'Jewish question', which made the problem of Jewish representation too parochial and politicised. They could do this through the process of inter-textual decryption, which elevated readers to the status of co-creators of the novel's meaning and forced them to contemplate that process as an element in and a commentary on the novel's *ars poetica*. The readers decrypting the

---

[7] Vladimir Varshavskii, *Nezamechennoe pokolenie* (New York: Chekhov, 1956), 227–28.
[8] Anatoly Shteiger to Zinaida Shakhovskoy, 5 July, 9 December 1935, in Zinaida Shakhovskoy, *Otrazheniia* (Paris: YMCA, 1975), 88, 97–98. Shakhovskoy censored the second letter, which called émigré literature 'half-Jewish', omitting Shteiger's remark about her own anti-Semitism. See Amherst Center for Russian Culture, Schakovskoy Family Papers, Series I, Box 1, Folder 41.

intertext 'correctly', that is, those who identified the Judeophile (Turgenev) rather than Judeophobe (Wagner) model of Jewish representation in *The Gift*, were vindicated ethically and aesthetically, since anti-Semitism was synonymous with Shchyogolev's bad artistic taste. The foreword, then, functioned as Nabokov's self-exegetical paratext, priming foreigners to heed Jewish personages as mediators for *The Gift*'s moral and artistic structure.

This self-exegesis suggests that transition to a foreign readership compromised the basic tool of Nabokov's *poetics of understatement* – intertextual suggestiveness – contingent on shared cultural competency. A corollary of Nabokov's painful linguistic transition, this loss of cultural connection to the reader coincided with the news of the Holocaust. Nabokov, whose family had narrowly escaped the Nazis, experienced this news as a personal loss and a blow to Russian literature. 'It is painful to think', he wrote Aldanov, 'about the killing of so many people whom I knew, whom I encountered at literary soirées (and who, when I look back now, strike me as somehow celestially pure)'.[9] The urgency of the 'Jewish question' was thus reinforced at the time when Nabokov was dealing with the poor suitability of his poetics in the American literary field. This was nowhere more obvious than in the intertextuality and punning deployed in *The Gift* to speak about Jewishness. Not only was this exercise inaudible to American readers, but its solipsistic complexity appeared vain in light of news from Europe, at least judging by Nabokov's remark in a 1946 letter to his sister:

> As much as I may want sometimes to hide in my little ivory tower, there are things that wound too deeply – like the German atrocities, the burning of children in crematorium ovens, children as delightful and precious as yours and mine. I retreat into myself but there I find such hatred for the Germans, for concentration camps, for the tyranny of all kinds that as an escape *ce n'est pas grand'chose*.[10]

Nabokov never abandoned intertextuality, but its role in his poetics diminished, becoming offset by irony reflective of the fact that too much was lost in cultural translation and too many 'good' readers had been left behind in another language or murdered on another continent. Nabokov's American novels most reputed for intertextual allusiveness also poke the most fun at it. *The Gift*'s serious exercise in literary erudition devolves into the ravings of a lunatic annotator in *Pale Fire* (1962) and a contest of motel-hopping

---

[9] Bakhmeteff Archive, Aldanov Collection, Box 6, Nabokov to Aldanov, 8 December 1945.
[10] Vladimir Nabokov, *Perepiska s sestroi* (Ann Arbor, MI: Ardis, 1985), 41.

paedophiles in *Lolita* (1955). *Absence* – from linguistic, cultural and personal losses – becomes a leitmotif in Nabokov's post-war art, displacing *understatement* at the centre of his method. *Lolita's* title character exists as a significant absence. She is a discursive projection by her tormentor and jocose raconteur, Humbert Humbert; unlike Zina, who is physically present in *The Gift*, alongside her own tormentor and jocose raconteur nursing Humbert-like paedophile fantasies.

This evolution in Nabokov's poetics is mediated by the problem of Jewish representation, on display in his story 'Signs and Symbols' (1948), which mocks the author's former reliance on the reader in the decryption of hermeneutic indices. Contracting the 'referential mania' of the story's absent hero, who is confined to a mental hospital, readers go to great interpretive lengths to find a Holocaust parable in a narrative that keeps mum about the Jewishness of its protagonists, surmised from onomastic hints and a mention of murdered European relatives – a silence made meaningful by absence.

Nabokov does not avoid the subject of Jewishness. Instead, he eschews Jewish representation, whose absence, rooted in the lack of adequate imaginative language, finds new meaning in the destruction of European Jews and in its ethical implications for art. Yet one is hard pressed to assimilate this interplay of ethics and aesthetics to Theodor Adorno's statement that 'to write poetry after Auschwitz is barbaric'.[11] The Marxist critic is selective in his attention to suffering, keeping silent about Soviet terror. Nabokov, in contrast, treats the Holocaust as a touchstone for all suffering – in Germany and in 'another torture house, [Russia]' (*Pnin*, 395). But the topic is best handled through evocative silence. Hence Nabokov's classification of 'Signs and Symbols' among the texts 'wherein a second (main) story is woven into, or placed behind, the superficial semitransparent one' (*Letters*, 117). We cannot recreate the hidden (Jewish) story in 'Signs and Symbols' the way we intertextually reconstruct it in *The Gift*. The author makes us speculate in a hermeneutic vacuum, deriding overzealous interpretation. Nor is this a one-time event in his American fiction: witness the endless debates around *Pnin*, *Lolita* or *Pale Fire*.

In *Pnin*, the unresolved critical quarrel concerns the narrative 'I' and his relation to the author. The novel presents a series of episodes from the life of an émigré who, like Nabokov, teaches literature to American college students after spending the interwar years in Europe. The narrative is ruled

---

[11] 'Cultural Criticism and Society' (1949), *Prisms*, tr. Samuel Weber (Cambridge, MA: MIT Press, 1981), 34.

by loss and absence: "'I haf nofing,'" wailed Pnin ... "I haf nofing left, nofing, nofing!'" (*Pnin*, 340). Cultural and linguistic uprootedness and conjugal misfortunes are exacerbated for the Gentile hero by his first love's tragic fate: Mira Belochkin died in the Holocaust. Writing *Pnin*, Nabokov modified his initial conception. The planned phasing out of the likable but maladapted hero by the renowned Russian-American author-narrator Vladimir Nabokov – at this time, a wish-fulfilment fantasy – yielded to a three-way dynamic between the title character, the invisible but palpable authorial persona and his visible but unreliable near-namesake narrator. Tension between the novel's 'superficial semitransparent' story about Pnin's misadventures and its 'second (main) story' was laid bare in the novel's original cover design, which Nabokov tightly controlled (see *Letters*, 190–91). Here we see Timofei Pnin holding a book that reiterates, in Russian, the information given to us in English by the physical book in our hands.

In *Pnin*, the kinship of narrative approaches to the problems of authorship and Jewish representation makes the latter a primer for the former. Readers' ability to recognise the premise behind the novel's *poetics of absence* – its ubiquitous yet invisible author – is contingent on their attention to the story of Mira, which haunts Pnin the hero in the same way that hidden authorial presence haunts the readers of *Pnin* the novel.

Like 'Signs and Symbols', *Pnin* eschews ethnonyms and erases distinction between Jewish and Gentile personages, save for onomastic signs and the story of Mira, whose death occasions the rare appearance of the word 'Jewish' (*Pnin*, 394). A system of puns prompts us to identify the missing Mira as the centre of the novel's 'second (main) story'. Pnin's heart seizures – a condition doctors call 'a shadow behind the heart' (*Pnin*, 388) – are intertwined with recollections of Mira and framed by encounters with squirrels. The animal's Russian name, *belka*, furnishes the root of Mira Belochkin's surname, while Pnin points out that its Greek name means 'shadow tail' (*Pnin*, 360). The homophonic pun – tail vs. tale – locates the hidden (shadow) source of Pnin's suffering in Mira's fate. The novel's *poetics of absence* are literalised in Mira's haunting absence, whereas the reason for this absence – Jewishness – functions as a device that lays bare the text's narrative and ethical principles.

'[I] pared my material to the bone, eliminating everything that was not strictly justified in the light of art', wrote Nabokov (*Letters*, 178). Consider the absence of detail in Mira's story. Mira is doubly absent by virtue of being Pnin's vague memory related by the untrustworthy narrator. This absence transforms the problem of Jewish representation into a meta-literary device

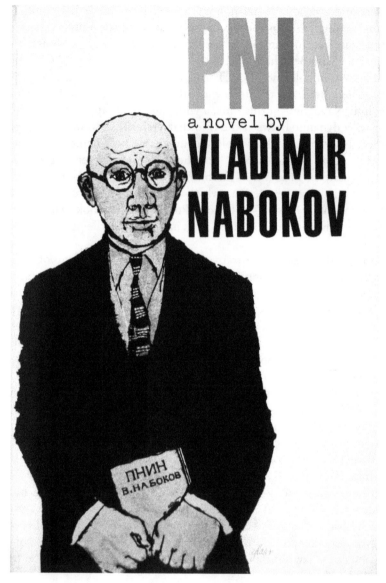

Illustration 6 Book cover of *Pnin* (Doubleday, 1957).

that draws attention to the significance of absence in the novel's larger poetics. For instance, the squirrel leitmotif is linked to the 'evil designer' who haunts Pnin's life and 'conceal[s] the key of the pattern' (*Pnin*, 313), a key that can help us rise from the narrator's cognitive level to that of the author. This key is hidden in Mira's surname, making Jewishness a device that mediates the novel's core aesthetic concern, namely, the reader's ability to identify and interpret hidden authorial design, and thus distinguish between *Pnin*'s narrator and the ubiquitous yet invisible authorial presence belying the narrator's reliability.

The diminutive suffix *chk* in Mira's surname is a marker of Jewishness (in contrast to Russian-sounding Belkin) – a procedure tested in 'Signs and Symbols', which invoked a Solovei*chik*, not a Russian-sounding Solov'ev. In Mira's surname, this suffix does double duty, also alluding to the Russian for glasses, *ochki*, and thereby incorporating Belo*chki*n in the novel's leitmotif of vision – a meta-commentary on *Pnin*'s poetics that require us to *see* past apparent absences. Russian word play in a novel for Anglophone readers encapsulates Nabokov's dilemma of cultural comprehensibility. It signals that a Russian writer's story is 'woven into' the 'semitransparent' English text, as suggested by the book's original cover design. Such targeting of two linguistic communities at once makes Mira's story both a meta-literary device drawing attention to the novel's *poetics of absence* and a locus of authorial anxiety. The reader capable of seeing the full meaning of Mira's 'shadow' tale behind Pnin's comic vicissitudes should also be able to see another tragic story ostensibly absent from the novel, that of a Russian writer who has lost his native language and many 'good' readers.

Characteristically, 'the evil designer' concealing in Mira's surname the key to the problem of authorial presence reveals that key during a Jew-baiting incident that is both an aesthetic and an ethical test for the reader. We cannot hear the joke a German guest tells at Pnin's party, but Nabokov expects his 'good' reader to heed Pnin's reaction as a rebuttal of anti-Semitism.[12] Readers who pass the test are 'good' enough to *see* a simultaneous development in another corner of the room, where professor Clements, the only male character who truly appreciates Pnin, finds a 'stunning likeness' of himself in a *Flemish Masterpieces* album (*Pnin*, 414). We identify the painting by recalling a previous scene, wherein Clements '[held] his glasses in one hand, . . . accentuat[ing] his striking resemblance, somewhat *en jeune*, to Jan van Eyck's ample-jowled, fluff-haloed Canon van der Paele' (*Pnin*, 408). *Pnin*'s original readers, unfamiliar with

---

[12] Nabokov's letter to Katharine White, quoted in Boyd, *American Years*, 279.

Nabokov's appearance prior to *Lolita*'s success, were unlikely to notice the writer's own 'stunning likeness' to the Canon in Jan van Eyck's *Madonna and Child with Canon van der Paele*. Authorial presence thus materialises in *Pnin*, like in the convex mirror the narrator mentions among the devices the Northern Masters used to tell stories within stories. Ever sceptical about the reader's ability to *see*, Nabokov later laid bare the device, posing with a pair of glasses like the Canon's; as if to mock the 'referential mania' of his readers who overanalysed the role of van Eyck's painting in *Pnin* without noticing what was hidden in plain sight.

Illustration 7 Detail of Jan van Eyck, *Madonna and Child with Canon van der Paele* (1436).

Illustration 8 Vladimir Nabokov in Montreux (1967).

The absent author of *Pnin*, then, was present all along, distinct from his evil-twin narrator, just as the absent Mira Belochkin was present in Timofei Pnin's life throughout the novel, no matter how hard he tried to forget her in order to go on living. But if Mira's is indeed the 'second (main) story' behind the 'superficial, semitransparent' story of Pnin's American adventures, then the same cannot be said about its narrative status in the larger novel that frames Pnin's story like in the book's original cover design. In that novel, the 'main' story is made up of meta-reflection on the *poetics of absence*, which has aesthetic and ethical resonance for Nabokov; whereas Jewishness is only a device pointing readers in the direction of the hidden tale about the Anglophone novel's Russian author. Since Jewishness cannot be represented in art without violating ethical standards, it becomes a figure of silence helping Nabokov speak of other unspoken things, including his modernist conviction about art's inability – no matter how unethical for a writer so concerned with ethics – adequately to represent anything but itself and its creator.

CHAPTER 27

Liberalism

Dana Dragunoiu

Recently arrived at Cambridge University, twenty-one-year-old Nabokov participated in a debate hosted by Trinity College's Magpie and Stump Debating Society. He did so by ventriloquizing a lecture his father had written and delivered under the title 'Soviet Rule and Russia's Future' a few months earlier at King's College, London. In his autobiography, Nabokov describes this modest foray into political activism as a disaster: 'the (victorious) apologist was a man from *The Manchester Guardian*; I forget his name, but recall drying up utterly after reciting what I had memorized, and that was my first and last political speech' (*SM*, 513).

Though strikingly anomalous in the career of a writer who prided himself on his 'supreme indifference' (*BS*, 164) to socio-political matters, this event serves as a valuable interpretive tool for understanding Nabokov's relationship to the political domain. Most conspicuously, it confirms what Nabokov was the first to admit about himself: that is, his lack of aptitude for political advocacy and debate (*SM*, 511–12). But it also shows how closely Nabokov's political views were entangled with those of his father. This is something Nabokov eagerly acknowledged: when asked in the 1960s about his political commitments, he asserted that he was 'an old-fashioned liberal' like his father (*SO*, 96).

Nabokov's father, V. D. (Vladimir Dmitrievich) Nabokov (1870–1922), was one of the most respected leaders of the liberal opposition against tsarist autocracy in late-imperial Russia. After studying law at the University of St Petersburg, he taught criminal law at the Imperial School of Jurisprudence and became an eminent criminalist. A leading member of the Constitutional Democratic (Kadet) Party, he served on its Central Committee and was elected to the First State Duma, Russia's short-lived elected national legislative assembly. Between the 1917 February Revolution and Lenin's seizure of power on October 25/November 7 of the same year, he served as the head of the Chancellery of the Provisional Government. In Crimea, where he sought refuge with his family after the Bolshevik takeover, he occupied the post of

Minister of Justice in the (also short-lived) Crimean Regional Government. After settling with his wife and three younger children in Berlin, he became the leader of the Kadet Party's conservative wing.

Given the vast distance separating V. D. Nabokov's political career from his son's depiction of himself as 'supremely indifferent' (*BS*, 164) to socio-political concerns, it might seem difficult to credit Nabokov's claim that his own politics had much in common with those of his father. Yet the paradox between Nabokov's self-styled 'old-fashioned liberalism' and his unwillingness to sign petitions and join political parties can be understood in several mutually reinforcing ways. The first of these has to do with an insight we find in the work of François Billacois and Hayden White, who remind us that history operates not only as a science but also as poetry.[1] Nabokov was intimately acquainted with the poetic side of history: as he tells us in his memoir, he experienced the political activities of his famous father 'through a prism of my own, which split into many enchanting colors' (*SM*, 518). These enchanting colours constitute Nabokov's liberal poetics and become refracted in his fiction in unexpected ways.

Nabokov's ambivalence about political activism can be understood as a facet of liberal thought. As a theory primarily concerned with the protection of personal freedom, liberalism extends that protection to those who seek freedom *from* political participation. Nabokov seems to have fully absorbed this central liberal premise. In an interview from 1963, for instance, he defined his 'political creed' in terms that subordinate political arrangements to civil freedoms: 'Freedom of speech, freedom of thought, freedom of art. The social or economic structure of the ideal state is of little concern to me' (*SO*, 34–35). He also expressed his awareness that only liberal structures can provide a haven for the apolitical individual when he invoked the nineteenth-century Russian radicals who 'advocated freedom and equality' but 'contradicted their own creed by wishing to subjugate the arts to current politics' (*LRL*, 5).

And finally, the apparent paradox of Nabokov's anti-activist politics ceases to be a paradox at all when considered in light of the milieu in which Nabokov came of age. Though Nabokov is best known for insisting upon the uniqueness of his genius, he wrote Edmund Wilson that he was 'a product' of the Russian Silver Age and that he 'was bred in that atmosphere' (*NWL*, 246). The 'Russian Cultural Renaissance', as Nabokov's

[1] See François Billacois, *The Duel: Its Rise and Fall in Early Modern France*, ed. and trans. Trista Selous (New Haven, CT: Yale University Press, 1990), 242; Hayden White, *Metahistory: The Historical Imagination in Nineteenth-Century Europe* (Baltimore, MD: Johns Hopkins University Press, 1973), x–xi.

friend and literary scholar Gleb Struve referred to it, occurred in the first
decade and a half of the twentieth century and encompassed developments
across many disciplines – arts, letters, philosophy, religion and political
thought. Marking a broad revolt against the positivism of the 1860s and
1870s radical intelligentsia, Russian Silver Age culture championed individualism, aestheticism and religious and philosophical idealism as the
natural allies of progressive thought.[2]

The history of the Russian Cultural Renaissance and the liberal theories
and struggles that convened under that name can no longer be said to be as
uncharted as they were in Nabokov's lifetime. V. D. Nabokov's closest
friends and allies authored a vast corpus of liberal writings on moral
philosophy, legal theory and the philosophy of science. These writings
enable us to see the legacy that Nabokov inherited from these men and the
extent to which his thinking about matters ranging from art to Darwin,
from freedom to national security, remains locked in the foreign tongue of
pre- and post-revolutionary Russian liberalism.

Russian Liberalism and *lichnost'*

The liberal principles championed by the Kadets differed from those of
their Western counterparts. Most significantly, Russian liberalism was not
guided by the economic interests of the bourgeoisie and consequently did
not develop a consistent defence of property rights and the free market. In
the Russian context, the inalienable rights of classical liberalism applied to
religious affiliation, press, assembly, association and free speech. As Pavel
Novgorodtsev wrote in *Pravo* (the juridical weekly co-edited by V. D.
Nabokov), the Kadets' work in the First Duma aimed to transform Russia
into a state 'founded on the respect for personhood, on the strict guarantee
of personal rights'.[3] Though many Kadets were positivists (such as, for
instance, Pavel Miliukov, Alexander Kizevetter and Sergei Muromtsev),
the idealists among them sought to give a metaphysical dimension to the
idea of personhood invoked by Novgorodtsev. The landmark essay collection *Problems of Idealism* (*Problemy idealizma* [1902]) contributed to liberal
political theory a metaphysically inflected conception of *lichnost'*, a Russian
term that signifies 'personhood', 'person', 'personality,' 'individual' or
'individuality'. Drawing inspiration from Kant, symposium contributors

[2] See Gleb Struve, 'The Cultural Renaissance', in Theofanis George Stavrou (ed.), *Russia Under the Last Tsar* (Minneapolis: The University of Minnesota Press, 1969), 183.

[3] Paul [Pavel] Novgorodtsev, 'Zakonoproekt o neprikosnovennosti lichnosti' ['Draft Legislation on the Inviolability of Personhood'], *Pravo*, 29 (1906), 2409.

argued that human subjectivity cannot be reduced to naturalistic explanations and that, as ends-in-themselves, people are bearers of an unconditional value and dignity. The uniquely human capacity to act upon deontological (rule-based) moral principles was proof of autonomy, and liberalism was seen as both the natural defender of this autonomy and a protest against deterministic accounts of social progress such as Marxism.[4] In his own attacks on Marxism, Nabokov invoked the same logic that guided the objections levelled by Russia's idealist philosophers against Marxist determinism. In *Speak, Memory* (1967), for instance, he celebrates 'the essentially human urge to reshape the earth, to act upon a friable environment (unless [man] is a born Marxist or a corpse and meekly waits for the environment to fashion *him*)' (*SM*, 621).

Although V. D. Nabokov did not ground his political activism in a metaphysical worldview, he agreed with the key idealist claim that it is impossible to explain the human individual by empirical observation alone and that this impossibility is bound up with the concept of self-determination.[5] Like his teacher and mentor, the legal scholar Nikolai Tagantsev (1843–1923), he also opposed positivist approaches to crime by arguing that they denied the existence of free will and, by extension, individual responsibility.[6]

By the time Nabokov made his first and last political appearance at Trinity College, the Kadets' efforts to establish the liberal structures that would have defended the rights associated with the idea of *lichnost'* – constitutionalism, civil liberties and the rule of law – had ended in defeat. This was the subject of the talk authored by V. D. Nabokov and delivered by his son at Cambridge; 'Soviet Rule and Russia's Future' describes what Nabokov much later describes as 'the terrible betrayal of the cause of liberty in the deepest sense of the word engendered on principle by the *earliest* Bolshevists' (*Letters*, 485). To the very end of his life, Nabokov blamed the Bolsheviks for extinguishing his father's and his father's colleagues' dreams of a free Russia, but his fiction also suggests that he may have held liberalism itself partially to blame for this failure. Contemporary accounts of Kadet activities during Russia's second revolutionary period and the

---

[4] See Randall A. Poole, 'Editor's Introduction: Philosophy and Politics in the Russian Liberation Movement', in Randall Poole (ed.), *Problems of Idealism: Essays in Russian Social Philosophy* (New Haven, CT: Yale University Press, 2003), 1–83.

[5] V. D. Nabokov, 'Soderzhanie i metod nauki ugolovnago prava' ['The Science of Criminal Law: Contents and Method'], *Sbornik statei po ugolovnomu pravu [A Collection of Articles in Criminal Law]* (St Petersburg: Tipografiia Tovarishchestva 'Obshchestvennaia Pol'za', 1904), 18; 19.

[6] V. D. Nabokov, 'Soderzhanie', 2.

subsequent civil war underscore the self-defeating nature of liberal values. In *The Provisional Government*, an admired account of the revolutionary months preceding Lenin's seizure of power, V. D. Nabokov recalls with anguish how the ministers of the Provisional Government allowed Lenin free passage into Russia because they had no legally sanctioned reasons to keep him out.[7]

More poignant still are V. D. Nabokov's self-recriminations regarding his work as Minister of Justice in the Crimean Regional Government. Fellow Kadets Maxim Vinaver and Daniil Pasmanik describe, respectively, the civil-liberties legislation drafted by V. D. Nabokov and his staunch refusal to impose martial law at a time when the Crimean Regional Government's fidelity to rule-of-law principles was seen as playing into Bolshevik hands. Friends, colleagues and White Army commanders censured him bitterly for allowing the peninsula's freedoms of press, assembly and movement to undermine their anti-Bolshevik efforts. Though Nabokov spent most of his time in Crimea collecting butterflies, he was also aware that his father ('in constant friction with trigger-happy elements in Denikin's army') was caught up in a hopeless struggle to preserve what he wryly referred to as 'minimal justice' (*SM*, 511).

Personal Inviolability, *Lolita* and the Cold War

The liberal values that animated V. D. Nabokov's and his colleagues' hopes and defeats lie at the heart of *Invitation to a Beheading* (1935–36) and *Lolita* (1955) – the two novels Nabokov singled out as inspiring in him 'the greatest esteem' and 'the most affection', respectively (*SO*, 92). Both are organised around a trope that Nabokov is likely to have encountered in the intellectual 'thick' émigré journal *Sovremennye zapiski* (*Contemporary Annals*). At the same time as it was publishing Nabokov's own work and the work of his favourite writers, the journal published a series of articles on 'rule-of-law' socialism by Nabokov's acquaintance and Kantian idealist philosopher of law Sergei Hessen (1887–1950). The principal aim of these articles was to establish a socialist political model capable of underwriting what Hessen called liberalism's 'eternal idea' (*vechnaia ideia*), which he summed up as the 'impenetrability of an individual by another person, including the state' [*nepronitsaemost' lichnosti dlia drugogo litsa, v tom chisle*

---

[7] *V. D. Nabokov and the Provisional Government*, 1917, tr. and ed. Virgil D. Medlin and Steven L. Parsons (New Haven, CT: Yale University Press, 1976), 143–44.

i gosudarstva].[8] Drawn from the classical liberal concept of personal inviolability, the trope of impenetrability was used by Hessen to insist upon the need to insulate the individual from state intrusion and social pressures.

Hessen's impenetrability trope makes visible the ways in which political thought is translated into art in Nabokov's fiction. It also provides a crucial link between Nabokov's Russian-language and English-language work. Humbert's dream of total penetration in 1950s America ('My only grudge against nature was that I could not turn my Lolita inside out' – *Lolita*, 154) signals Nabokov's return to a trope that had first absorbed him in Berlin when he interrupted his work on *The Gift* (1937–38) to write *Invitation to a Beheading*. Cincinnatus C., the protagonist of the latter novel, is condemned to death because he is impenetrable to the gaze of others. Like Cincinnatus, Dolly in *Lolita* possesses a kernel of inviolable personhood that Humbert cannot penetrate, but, unlike Cincinnatus, her body is repeatedly violated.

Invitation to a Beheading champions liberal values by making tyranny incompatible with Cincinnatus' nature (his 'gnostical turpitude' in the novel's terminology). *Lolita*, by contrast, examines liberal values from the inside – that is, from within the borders of a modern liberal state. In this second return to Hessen's trope for liberalism's 'eternal idea', Nabokov reflects upon the self-undermining nature of liberal ideals during a time when the United States was engaged in its own conflict with the Soviet Union. As a novel about a foreigner's sexual exploitation of a young American girl, *Lolita* can be read as both an anguished tribute to liberal values and a meditation on the vulnerability that a liberal commitment to pluralism and freedom engenders.

Humbert's description of his colleague and fellow paedophile Gaston Godin encapsulates *Lolita*'s ambivalent nature as both tribute to and critique of American liberalism during the Cold War. Gaston successfully conceals his crimes not only because he is good at deceiving his neighbours, but also because his neighbours do not automatically assume the worst of foreigners. His ignorance of the English language and his refusal to assimilate are in themselves no reason for suspicion. Like Humbert and Quilty, Gaston escapes detection because he lives in a country that protects the privacy of its citizens and is organised around the legal principle of presumed innocence. As Dolly reminds Charlotte, '[t]his is a free country' (*Lolita*, 42).

---

[8] Sergei Hessen, 'Problema pravovogo sotsializma' ['The Problem of Rule-of-Law Socialism'], *Sovremennye zapiski*, 22 (1924), 279; 278.

Though child abuse is not limited to liberal societies, Humbert is protected from the kind of interference that Nabokov's earlier fiction associates with political tyranny. In *Bend Sinister* (1947), for example, spies masquerade as nannies in Paduk's regime. Significantly, no such spying interferes with Humbert's sexual enslavement of Dolly. Though he often feels that he and Dolly 'lived in a lighted house of glass, and that any moment some thin-lipped parchment face would peer through a carelessly unshaded window' (*Lolita*, 169), his anxiety springs from paranoia rather than from a nosy neighbour's intrusion into his personal life. Though it is difficult to condone Charlotte's invasion of Humbert's privacy when she breaks into his desk and reads his diary, it is also important to remember what she uncovers. The swiftness of her subsequent death diverts attention from a lesson that Nabokov must have found both repellent and instructive: that is, being a snoop can expose criminal intentions.

As Ellen Pifer has noted, Humbert's crimes against Dolly are not only sexual but also political.[9] In his afterword to *Lolita*, Nabokov prepares the ground for Pifer's insight when he labels Humbert 'a foreigner and an anarchist' (*Lolita*, 296). Penned at a time when blacklists, FBI investigations and criminal prosecutions of the American left dominated the nation's political life, the conjunction of 'foreigner' and 'anarchist' was likely to raise the spectre of communism. This would have been especially true for Nabokov in relation to the term 'anarchy': the primary documents that chronicle the turbulent events surrounding Russia's second revolutionary period consistently invoke the term 'anarchy' to refer to the chaos, violence and lawlessness in the aftermath of the Bolshevik revolution. Communism's rejection of law as an autonomous and binding mechanism of social order justifies these associations.

Nabokov's most self-consciously 'American' novel can be read as a meditation on the promises and blind spots of liberal politics. The tolerant, unsuspicious Americans who fail to notice Humbert's crimes against Dolly recall the ministers of the Provisional Government whose fidelity to the country's newly established liberal provisions allowed Lenin free passage into Russia. For Nabokov in particular, they might also have brought to mind the ministers of the Crimean Regional Government – with his father foremost among them – whose commitment to civil freedoms allowed the Bolsheviks to flourish in their midst. Though *Lolita* is no coded account of

[9] Pifer, 'Nabokov's Discovery of America: From Russia to *Lolita*', in Mario Materassi and Maria Irene Ramalho de Sousa Santos (eds.), *The American Columbiad: "Discovering" America, Inventing the United States* (Amsterdam: VU University Press, 1996), 411.

the Cold War conflicts and anxieties that coincided with its composition, it is nonetheless guyed into what Boyd refers to as the one political issue that excited Nabokov throughout his life: that is, 'the attitude those outside the country should take toward the Soviet Union'.[10]

Blok's Smoky Iris and the Apolitical Writer

The man whose words Nabokov borrowed for the sake of influencing his Cambridge colleagues' attitude towards the Soviet Union was murdered two years after the debating fiasco at Trinity College. During a Kadet event sponsored by V. D. Nabokov himself, assassins from an extreme reactionary Russian émigré organisation sneaked into Berlin's Philharmonia Hall with the purpose of killing Miliukov. In Iosif Hessen's account of the events that followed, one of the assassins opened fire during a break in Miliukov's lecture. While Miliukov was being taken to safety, V. D. Nabokov and Avgust Kaminka threw themselves on the gunman in an attempt to disarm him. In the scuffle that followed, another gunman came to his partner's rescue and fatally wounded V. D. Nabokov.[11]

When Hessen telephoned with news of the tragedy, Nabokov was reading Blok's Italian poems to his mother. Elena Nabokov had just expressed her admiration for Blok's botanical evocation of Florence: 'How splendid that is. Yes, yes, exactly: a smoky iris', her son recalled her saying to him.[12] This was neither the first nor the last time that political events forced themselves upon the Nabokovs' domestic life. The great calamities of Nabokov's biography – the loss of homeland, the death of his brother Sergei in a Nazi concentration camp, the abandonment of his 'natural idiom, my rich, infinitely rich and docile Russian tongue, for a second-rate brand of English' (*SO*, 15) – were all forged in the crucible of history and politics.

'My pleasures', Nabokov said in an interview from 1962, 'are the most intense known to man: writing and butterfly hunting' (*SO*, 3). But life taught him that intense pleasures are also intensely fragile, and his work frequently stages the violent intrusion of the political into lives that are concerned with decidedly non-political matters. Nabokov's fiction is an

[10] Brian Boyd, *Vladimir Nabokov: The American Years* (Princeton: Princeton University Press, 1991), 84.

[11] Iosif V. Hessen [Gessen], *Gody izgnaniia: Zhiznennyi otchet* [*The Years of Exile: An Autobiographical Account*] (Paris: YMCA, 1979), 134–35.

[12] Quoted in Brian Boyd, *Vladimir Nabokov: The Russian Years* (Princeton: Princeton University Press, 1990), 191.

earnest attempt to lend dignity to those who yearned for a world in which
the political could not intrude upon a scientist's drawing of a butterfly
('Dvoe' ['*The Two*']), a philosopher and a scholar's abstruse reflections on
Hamlet in *Bend Sinister*, or his and his mother's dreamy late-night idyll
with Blok's smoky iris. If he seemed to privilege the iris over the violence of
the political, it is not because he underestimated the power of the latter.
Rather, it was because he saw himself as a 'ridiculous cacologist' capable of
convincing no one of anything when he used the language of political
discourse (*SM*, 512). By dwelling instead on the iris and its cognates,
Nabokov sublimated the political into the poetical. This is the energy
that bubbles up from under the surface of his last two great novels, *Pale Fire*
(1962) and *Ada* (1969). Kinbote's capacity to spin the poetic Zembla out of
Russia's political misfortunes finds its analogue in Antiterra, a planet where
'America' and 'Russia' have preserved their territorial distinctions but only
as 'poetical' – and emphatically not 'political' – domains (*Ada*, 19).

CHAPTER 28

Totalitarianism

Olga Voronina

Nabokov's exposure to the twentieth century's most brutal European totalitarian regimes – Soviet and Nazi – was allegedly limited and unharrowing: he fled the first and managed to have years of contented and robustly creative life within the second. Refusing to admit the possibility of his being a victim of history, he often toned down the impact of the escapes from Bolshevik Russia and National Socialist Germany on his life and was uniformly adamant in denying his involvement in politics. 'I am not "sincere", I am not "provocative," I am not "satirical." I am neither a didacticist nor an allegorizer. Politics and economics, atomic bombs, primitive and abstract art forms, the entire Orient, symptoms of "thaw" in Soviet Russia, the Future of Mankind, and so on, leave me supremely indifferent' (BS, 164), Nabokov wrote in the 1963 introduction to his ardently anti-totalitarian novel Bend Sinister (1947). In a 1968 interview for The New York Times, he again tried to disassociate himself from the theme, speaking of 'the brutal farce of totalitarian states' sarcastically, rather than apprehensively, and pointing out 'the absolute abyss yawning between the barbed-wire tangle of police states and the spacious freedom of thought we enjoy in America and Western Europe' (SO, 113). It was as if Nabokov's individualism in all matters related to politics aimed to refute Hannah Arendt's ideas on the futility of artistic effort in totalitarian societies[1] or challenge George Orwell's famous pronouncement: 'The fallacy is to believe that under a dictatorial government you can be free inside.'[2] This author was one such believer. For him, what was fallacious was not artists' or thinkers' attempts to be free, but their acceptance of totalitarian power's vigour and permanence.

---

[1] See Hannah Arendt, The Origins of Totalitarianism (Cleveland, OH, and New York: The World Publishing Company, 1958), 339; 429; 494.
[2] George Orwell, The Complete Works of George Orwell, vol. 16 (London: Secker and Warburg, 1986), 170.

Arendt defined totalitarianism as a form of government that exercised absolute power over citizens by means of ideological control, extreme use of terror and 'conspicuous disdain of the whole texture of reality'.[3] Orwell, who addressed the subject of the nature of totalitarianism almost a decade earlier, saw in it a state hierarchy that physically and psychologically endorsed egalitarianism whose population was split into those being equal and those being 'more equal than others'.[4] For these two thinkers, as well as for such divergent analysts of dictatorships as Karl Popper, Carl Friedrich and Zbigniew Brzezinski, Soviet Russia and National Socialist Germany were similar in their dependence on authoritarian leadership, one-party governance and state control of mass media. Twentieth-century totalitarian systems differed from the earlier forms of tyranny, Arendt suggested, because they claimed that they had a hold over the past, present and future of mankind. But for her as well as for others, what brought the two regimes together most forcefully were their atrocious crimes against humanity: the imprisonment, torture and execution of enemies of the Bolshevik state and the German concentration camps. Closer to the end of the century, however, the intellectuals' outlook changed. To many of them, the Nazi regime that exterminated its enemies on the grounds of race appeared more felonious than the Soviet state that purged its citizens according to the class principle. This provided Susan Sontag with a rationale to accuse the left of misunderstanding the nature of communism and becoming susceptible to its 'angelic language'.[5] In 1982, when she notoriously called communism 'Fascism with a human face', she provided a 'verbal adjustment' to Western intelligentsia's attitude to the crimes of Stalinism.[6]

Neither as a thinker nor as a writer did Nabokov accentuate the differences between National Socialist Germany and the Soviet State, preferring to replace specific references to either one with a sweeping expression of disdain for 'dictatorships and police states' prone to 'regimentation of thought, governmental censorship, racial or religious persecution, and all the rest of it' (SO, 47–48). In fiction, his vicarious experience of the Soviet regime as well as his encounters, in the 1930s, with the realities of Hitler's Germany, brought into being a nationally unspecific image of an oppressive society ruled by a power- and blood-thirsty minority. The horrors of Zoorland imagined by Martin Edelweiss and Sonia Zilanov in Glory (1931)

---

[3] Arendt, 'Preface to the First Edition', The Origins of Totalitarianism, viii.
[4] George Orwell, Animal Farm (New York: Harcourt, Brace, 1946), 112.
[5] Quoted in 'Susan Sontag Provokes Debate on Communism', The New York Times, 27 February 1982, 27.
[6] Phillip Lopate, Notes on Sontag (Princeton: Princeton University Press, 2009), 217–19.

find their continuation in the 'dark, zoological, Zoorlandic ideas' of 'Tyrants Destroyed' (1938) where a 'wildflowery country' is transformed into an evil land replete with slavery, veneration of bloodshed and a cult of a single personality – 'a pigheaded, brutal, and gloomy vulgarian full of morbid ambition' (*Stories*, 440, 441). Except for the German-singing villains in 'Cloud, Castle, Lake' (1941), his totalitarian societies are patchwork representations of political terror that knows no national borders: their dictators share a number of universally ludicrous characteristics, while the majority of their citizens represent a complacent mass perfectly suited for the role of tyrants' accomplices. In *Bend Sinister*, even the language everyone speaks cannot be attributed to a single linguistic source. Formed of Indo-European morphemes, it is a metaphor of totalitarianism's widespread influence in Nabokov's day.

This fusion alone invalidates Nabokov's claim that his Berlin experience – including all of its ominous political shadows – did not affect him either personally or as an artist (see *SO*, 189; *SM*, 594–95). In fact, his visceral hatred of Germany (in *Nikolai Gogol* [1944], he confessed that 'one . . . would like to see it destroyed to the last beer-mug and last forget-me-not' [NG, 65]) could be attributed to the fact that the country allowed him an immediate knowledge of wide-scale capitulation to political control, which he and other Russian émigrés had been spared due to their fortuitous escape from Bolshevik Russia. Yellow pansies in Berlin's parks reminded Nabokov of 'little Hitler faces' (*LTV*, 391), but he had no recollections of Bolshevik leaders' portraits in Leningrad's offices and on public buildings. Likewise, although he heard about the NKVD's interrogation techniques from those who escaped the Gulag (*LTV*, 288; 416), it was the deaths in German concentration camps of his brother Sergei, Ilya Fondaminsky, Mother Maria, Khodasevich's third wife Olga Margolin and many others he knew in Berlin and Paris that turned mass murders of innocent citizens into his personal concern. After Hitler appointed Sergei Taboritsky, one of V. D. Nabokov's murderers, second-in-command to the director of Germany's émigré affairs, Nabokov reacted by seeking a job in the United States or the UK. On Véra's prompt, he left for Paris in January 1937 to prepare the family's move to France.[7] Cincinnatus C. is convicted to be executed because of his opacity among translucent individuals. Now the author of *Invitation to a Beheading* (1935–36) was becoming liable to 'Cincinnatus's basic illegality' (*IB*, 17). Other characters he created around that time – Lik ('Lik' [1939]),

---

[7] Brian Boyd, *Vladimir Nabokov: The Russian Years* (Princeton: Princeton University Press, 1990), 428–30.

Vasiliy Ivanovich ('Cloud, Castle, Lake') as well as the earlier Romantovski ('The Leonardo' [1933]) – strive to keep their discreet, unassuming selves intact and unpolluted by an alien uncaring touch, monstrous curiosity or hideous cruelty. None of them succeeds.

Nabokov, who saw in National Socialist Germany a 'dull beastly farce' (*IB*, vii), did not experience Nazi totalitarianism directly. The Bolshevik Soviet Union, however, remained for him both hostile and tangible – the land of his childhood fouled by the new regime's brutality and marred by its 'barbed-wire tangle' (*SO*, 113). It would be incorrect to say that he had received no scars and bore no grudges when, as a twenty-one-year-old, he departed Russia already engulfed in Civil War. He knew from the start about the horrors of the Russian revolution, 'the growls, the howls, the whistles and the senseless visions, / assassinated horses' vitreous eyes, / the sinuous streets, the evil-auguring constructions' ('Revolution', *Poems*, 6). His city had been taken over by authoritarians and his father's colleagues and acquaintances had perished, while V. D. Nabokov himself, having providentially sent the entire family away in late 1917, barely avoided being executed as one of the leaders of the Kadet party and, thus, an 'enemy of the people'. In *Speak, Memory* (1967), his getaway would have formed an entertaining vignette – 'my father followed a dim corridor, saw an open door at the end, walked out into a side street and made his way to the Crimea' (*SM*, 511) – had the autobiographer not prefaced the briskly paced adventure-story excerpt with a reference to the revolution's 'gory course' (*SM*, 511). At that time, the Red Terror was pressing forward inexorably and fast. In 1917–19, when the Nabokovs resided in Gaspra and Livadia, up to 140,000 people became its victims.[8] After they had left the Crimea, the Red Army executed 50,000 refugees, earning Sebastopol the name of 'the city of hangmen'.[9] The Whites retaliated by targeting Bolshevik sympathisers and the Jewish population. The echoes of the post-revolutionary chaos sounded not only in Nabokov's earlier works, but can still be heard in a work as late as *Ada or Ardor: A Family Chronicle* (1969), where the peninsula's Tatar villages contribute to the name of Tartary, the land of political oppression run by 'Khan Sosso and his ruthless Sovietnamur Khanate' (*Ada*, 272).[10] The 'Crimean War' fought in *Ada* is bloody, and there is no escape from 'Sovereign Society

[8] See Anna Geifman, 'Red Terror in Soviet Russia, 1917-1921', in Brett Bowden and Michael T. Davis (eds.), *Terror: From Tyrannicide to Terrorism* (Brisbane: University of Queensland Press, 2008), 166–67.
[9] See Jörg Baberowski, *Krasnyi terror: Istoriia stalinizma* (Moscow: Rossiiskaia politicheskaia entsyklopediia, 2007), 38.
[10] 'Sosso' was one of Iosif Dzhugashvili's party nicknames.

of Solicitous Republics' (*Ada*, 272), except for a nearly impossible flight over the 'Golden Curtain' (*Ada*, 145).

It was Nabokov's perception of the Soviet Union as a 'torture-house [with a] blood-bespattered wall' (*SM*, 584) that led to his confrontation with 'fellow-traveler' types at Cambridge and other supporters of the Soviet regime in Berlin, Paris, Boston and New York.[11] Nabokov, this politically 'indifferent' man, would not speak to any Bolshevik sympathiser or even the prized Soviet belle-lettrist, Aleksey Tolstoy (see *SO*, 85–86), skipped a meeting at the Pen-Club when Ivan Maysky, the Soviet ambassador to Great Britain, was to give a talk there (see *LTV*, 307) and refused to consider the Soviet victory in the Second World War an absolution of Stalin's crimes. Both in 'Conversation Piece, 1945' (1945) and in *Pnin* (1957), he portrayed those who admired the Soviet allies as philistine dupes, unable to tell one fact of history from the other and susceptible to totalitarian indoctrination. 'The great Russian people has waked up and my country is again a great country. We had three great leaders. We had Ivan, whom his enemies called Terrible, then we had Peter the Great, and now we have Joseph Stalin. . . . Today, in every word that comes out of Russia, I feel the power, I feel the splendor of old Mother Russia', Colonel Melnikov says to a group of Nazi sympathisers in the story 'Conversation Piece, 1945', initially titled 'Double Talk' (*Stories*, 594–95). In *Pnin*, the title character is watching what his gullible colleagues present as 'an impressive Soviet documentary film, made in the late forties. It was supposed to contain not a jot of propaganda, to be all sheer art, merrymaking, and the euphoria of proud toil' (*Pnin*, 354). Of course, the film turns out to be a prime example of Soviet brain-washing. Incredulously, Pnin follows the procession of 'unkempt girls' on the screen, celebrating 'an immemorial Spring Festival with banners bearing snatches of old Russian ballads such as "*Ruki proch ot Korei*", "*Bas les mains devant la Corée*", "*La paz vencera a la guerra*", "*Der Friede besiegt den Krieg*"' (*Pnin*, 354). The reiteration of Soviet-style slogans in four languages is the medium of Nabokov's satire. The onscreen rally denounces the American involvement in the Korean War, fought, in essence, by the Soviet Union and the People's Republic of China against the United States and its allies in 1950–53. Here, the author's singular vision exposes the puerility of American left intellectuals who fail to recognise totalitarian underpinnings of Soviet political propaganda.

---

[11] Boyd, *Russian Years*, 168.

One of the most telling examples of Nabokov's opposition to the American liberals' sympathy for the great 'Socialist experiment' is his skirmish, in November of 1949, with *The New Yorker* about the publication of 'Student Days', which would soon become chapter 13 of *Speak, Memory*. Katharine White, who edited most of Nabokov's submissions to the magazine, insisted that his outbursts against the Bolsheviks had made the essay unreadable. Citing *The New Yorker*'s editor-in-chief Harold Ross, she chided her favourite author for the lack of his 'usual detachment when talking about the revolution'.[12] Ross himself was even more specific in his requirement that Nabokov 'tone down' the essay. Saying that Nabokov's bitterness 'destroy[ed] the nostalgic and reminiscent mood of the piece', Ross suggested that, 'without being an apologist for Lenin, one could find considerable differences between his views and those of the present regime, and that there was some reason for Western liberals of the '20s to have hope, at least, for the outcome of the revolution'.[13] Nabokov's response to this reprimand was quick and categorical: 'It is really not my fault that Americans knew so little about former Russia. . . . I am frank but not bitter.'[14] He withdrew the piece and, in 1951, published it in *Harper's Magazine*.[15]

The 1940s were an especially trying time for Nabokov's avowed political apathy. Explicated by Soviet defectors and provoking heated debates in the US Congress,[16] totalitarianism became a more pronounced subject not only of US media discourse, but also of Nabokov's poetry and prose. In the poem 'No Matter How', written in late 1943, Nabokov affirms his 'loathing' of Soviet Russia as the land of 'filth, brutality, and boredom / of silent servitude' (*Poems*, 118). In 'On Rulers', dated 1944, his wrath is directed against all kinds of 'cronies' excited by 'the trench-coated wolf / in his army cap with a German steep peak, / hoarse-voiced, his face all distorted, / speaking from an immobile convertible' (*Poems*, 120). 'The Art of Literature and Commonsense', which he presented to American universities and colleges as a lecture from the early days of his arrival in the States, contains similarly adamant pronouncements against tyranny and its dim-witted supporters. Just like 'Tyrants Destroyed', however, 'Commonsense' explicates the problem and at the same time offers a possible solution to it. Laughter, Nabokov insists, is the artist's most effective weapon

[12] VN Berg, Vladimir Nabokov's Correspondence with *The New Yorker*, Folder 24, Katharine White to Vladimir Nabokov, 8 November 1949.
[13] Ibid.
[14] VN Berg, Vladimir Nabokov's Correspondence with *The New Yorker*, Folder 24, Vladimir Nabokov to Katharine White, 9 November 1949.
[15] Vladimir Nabokov, 'Lodgings in Trinity Lane', *Harper's Magazine*, 202 (January 1951), 84–91.
[16] See Lee Edwards, 'Congress and the Origins of the Cold War: The Truman Doctrine', *World Affairs*, 151 (1989), 131–33.

against oppression. Commenting on the 'twinkle in the author's eye as he notes the imbecile drooping of a murderer's underlip' and suggesting that it is that twinkle that 'punishes your man more surely than the pistol of a tiptoeing conspirator' (*LL*, 376), he is already paving the way not only for his fish-eyed Paduk, but also for Gradus, the inarticulate and inept assassin from *Pale Fire* (1962). Dispatched by Zembla's new rulers to kill 'King Charles', Gradus instead shoots the poet of genius, John Shade. Nabokov was well aware that a totalitarian state would aim to do both.

Shortly after he began lecturing American students on literature, Nabokov wrote *Nikolai Gogol* – a whimsical biography of one of Russia's most eccentric writers. He placed Gogol's ability to ridicule philistine vulgarity (for which he used the Americanised Russian word *poshlust*) way above his social caricatures, noting that in the Gogolian 'upside down world' all kinds of miracles were possible, including the enchantment by laughter of '[t]he Supreme Censor, the One above all, ... the radiant, totalitarian Tsar Himself' (*NG*, 36). Although a literary biography, *Nikolai Gogol* expresses political concerns and ideas which converge with the political analysis of several influential works on totalitarian thinking, behaviour and government structure which were released at the same time. In *The Open Society and Its Enemies* (1945), Karl Popper juxtaposed 'open' and 'closed' societies on the grounds of their ability to favour an individual over a group or vice versa and denounced oppressive states for their partiality to abstract social entities and disregarding the needs of actual individuals. In the same way, F. A. Hayek's *The Road to Serfdom* condemned socialism for its neglect of economic competition, while Isabel Paterson's *The God of the Machine*, Ayn Rand's *The Fountainhead* and Rose Wilder Lane's *The Discovery of Freedom*, all published in 1944, deplored collectives that could not appreciate the virtues of individualism. These voices resonated in Nabokov's denunciation of totalitarianism. When he told his American readers that Gogol appeared in Russian literature already run by 'a flock of quacks' exercising the 'civic minded literary criticism which was to result finally in the ineptitudes of Marxism and Populism' (*NG*, 29), or when he complained, in a letter to Edmund Wilson of 26 March 1944, that the former 'Russian Socialists' had published, in 'the special ritualistic cautious manner of reference', one of his poems as an anonymous 'forbidden poem' (*NWL*, 142), he was revealing what he saw as the shortcomings of the old Russian intelligentsia's thinking and political behaviour as well as what he considered the deeply flawed foundations of the current Soviet dictatorship. Three years down the road, *Bend Sinister* would appear: there, the philosopher hero Adam Krug refuses to cooperate with Paduk's government exactly because, as a believer in the power of individual intellect, he cannot accept 'that the State was bigger and wiser than any mortal could be' (*BS*, 289).

It was intellectual resilience, rather than political resistance, that Nabokov advocated in his novels and lectures, poems and interviews. Highly responsive to what Arendt called the 'sensual vindictive cruelty of Stalin'[17] or what the French philosopher Étienne Balibar referred to as the 'extreme violence' of Nazism,[18] he chose, according to his son Dmitri, 'contempt for cruelty' (*Stories*, xiv) as his main theme and cultivated a new type of individualism – that of the readers who, as the enlightened companions of 'good writers' (see *LL*, 2–3), were willing to let a work of fiction fascinate and inspire them. Nabokov's artistically sophisticated, linguistically coded and otherwise 'estranged' portrayals of dictatorships condemn despotic regimes and make their leaders look absurd and vulnerable. But it is the act of Nabokovian reading that destroys tyrants while empowering those whom tyrannies abhor: the introspective, the eccentric and the nonconformist. By taking the readers to 'other states of being where art (curiosity, tenderness, kindness, ecstasy) is the norm' (*Lolita*, 296), it creates an impenetrable boundary between critically minded individuals endowed with artistic sensibility and political systems that aim to take their freedom away.

---

[17] Arendt, *The Origins of Totalitarianism*, 327.
[18] Balibar, 'Outline of a Topography of Cruelty: Citizenship and Civility in an Era of Global Violence', in his *We, the People of Europe? Reflections on Transnational Citizenship* (Princeton: Princeton University Press, 2003), 115–32.

CHAPTER 29

The Cold War

Will Norman

Strong Opinions was the apposite title Nabokov gave to the collection of non-fiction writings and interviews he published in 1973. He included in that volume an interview conducted for *Paris Review* in 1966, in which he declared, 'In foreign policy, I am definitely on the government's side. And when in doubt, I always follow the simple method of choosing that line of conduct which may be the most displeasing to the Reds and the Russells' (*SO*, 98). Bertrand Russell, the British philosopher and intellectual, was at that time one of the most prominent public opponents of the Vietnam War and the escalation of the nuclear arms race. In an example of the binary thinking long associated with American Cold War ideology, for Nabokov that made him complicit with the Reds. Even if James Mason once gave him a Christmas gift of an Uncle Sam tie with 'Fuck Communism' written on it, the hyperbolic caricature of Nabokov as the red-baiting Yankee was as much a performance of his own making as it was an image devised by others. Behind it lay a life-long opposition to communism, which was deeply rooted in historical experience and became woven into the texture of his aesthetic theory and practice. Nabokov was a Cold Warrior before the fact, in the sense that his witnessing of the Bolshevik revolution of 1917, his subsequent exile in Europe and his mourning of the destruction of Russian culture helped to shape a critique of communism as fundamentally incommensurable with liberal values. In this regard, he both participated in the anti-Bolshevik consensus that defined the Russian émigré community in Europe during the interwar period, and anticipated in several respects the dominant currents of thought among US intellectuals and policy makers during the late 1940s and 1950s. Indeed, one of the most influential of those policy makers, George F. Kennan, spent several years at the University of Berlin during the 1930s under the tutelage of liberal, anti-Bolshevik Russian émigrés, an experience that profoundly impacted his developing views on communism. Viewed from this perspective, Nabokov's emigration to the United

States brought about an encounter between two related chronologies – that of Nabokov's virulent opposition to the Soviet Union from its birth, corresponding to the notion of a 'long Cold War' starting in 1919, and that of the Cold War proper of US-Soviet hostility. This latter is conventionally dated as beginning in 1947, with the announcement of the Truman Doctrine and the adoption of George Kennan's well-known 'containment' thesis in US foreign policy regarding the Soviet Union.

In order to make sense of Nabokov's writing career in the context of the Cold War, we might divide it into four parts. In the first, 1919–1940, Nabokov lived in European exile and wrote mainly in Russian, his politics shaped largely by the liberalism of his father, who had been a prominent member of the Constitutional Democratic Party before the Revolution. But it was only in the mid-to late 1930s that Soviet tyranny began to manifest itself in his fiction, albeit in veiled and displaced forms. Socialist realism was installed as the official state aesthetic in 1934 and in the years to follow, Stalin's purges took their toll both in the general population and among the literary intelligentsia. In partial response, in the novel *Invitation to a Beheading* (1935–6) and the short story 'Tyrants Destroyed' (1938), Nabokov began to blend the themes of fascist and communist incarceration, violence and repression in a way that anticipated the alignment of Nazism and Stalinism under the banner of 'totalitarianism' in one of the defining moves of the early Cold War in the late 1940s. The short second period, from his arrival in the United States in 1940 to the dramatic decline of US-Soviet relations in 1947, is one of the most interesting and least studied of Nabokov's career, characterised as it is by a disjunction between American public perception of Stalin as an ally in the fight against fascism and Nabokov's unrelenting insistence on the fundamentally unacceptable values of the Soviet regime. When his novel *Bend Sinister* (1947) is read alongside his study *Nikolai Gogol* (1944) and the series of reviews he wrote for the *New York Sun* and the *New Republic*, it becomes clear that Nabokov understood his role at this time as a critical source of historical experience able to disabuse naïve American intellectuals of their faith in a communist state and to warn them of the dangers of complicity.

The third period, including the composition of the novels *Lolita* (1955) and *Pnin* (1957), corresponds to the first phase of the Cold War proper, in which Nabokov's long-held opposition to the Soviet Union finally resonated with mainstream public opinion and government policy. This harmony goes some way to explaining the relative ease with which Nabokov was received by the American cultural establishment and entered the canon of American writers in the 1950s, despite the difficulties surrounding the search for an American publisher for *Lolita*. Publishing regularly in the *New Yorker* as well as in more highbrow periodicals such as *Partisan Review*, Nabokov's views on the need for vigorous defence of creative freedom and liberal values in the face of communist threats eventually harmonised with those of the New York Intellectuals, from whom he garnered a series of laudatory reviews. Finally, the fourth period of Nabokov's Cold War chronology presents the paradox of pairing his grandest declarations of American patriotism and support for military interventionism with the fact that he lived in Switzerland from 1961 until his death in 1977, barely setting foot in the nation he claimed as his intellectual home. His novels of the 1960s, *Pale Fire* (1962) and *Ada* (1969), both present pastoral motifs and geopolitical reconfigurations that can only be grasped under the rubric of a distinctive spatial imagination corresponding to Cold War ideology. Nabokov's stance in this last period remained in step with conservative hawks such as William F. Buckley, Jr., who visited him in Switzerland, but left him isolated both geographically and ideologically from growing protest and social unrest in the United States at the conduct of the Cold War through interventions in Cuba, Vietnam and elsewhere.

What is at stake in reading Nabokov's fiction in the context of the Cold War? The Cold War is not only the name we give to the era in which he wrote much of his work and forged his reputation, but also the ideological structure within which his most foundational ideas about aesthetic autonomy and the nature of creativity were formed, expressed and understood. Perhaps Nabokov's clearest articulation of his aesthetics is the 1942 essay 'The Creative Writer', an extraordinary defence of the power of the irrational imagination in the face of tyrannical demands for conformity. 'At times of special political stress', he claims, 'earnest people are apt to try and discover the exact whereabouts of a writer in relation to the national or universal community, and writers themselves begin to worry and wonder about their duties and rights.'[1] Writing in the midst of the Second World War at a time when Allied victory was far from assured, Nabokov advocates the ivory tower as 'a fixed address' for the writer.[2] 'The Creative Writer' already sets out the terms under which Nabokov's cultural Cold War was to be fought. The United States was to provide both a physical and an ideological home for culture, free from state interference,

---

[1] Vladimir Nabokov, 'The Creative Writer', *Bulletin of the Northeastern Modern Languages Association*, 4/1 (1942), 21.

[2] Ibid., 21

offering not simply 'the snuggest nook of an unshelled country' from which to write, but also guaranteed protection for creative idiosyncrasy and individualism.[3] In a foretaste of the Manichean rhetoric that was to come in the Cold War proper, Nabokov ends the essay on a note of violence. Common sense, the 'fundamentally immoral' impulse towards orthodoxy, 'must be shot dead'.[4]

'The Creative Writer' needs to be read alongside Nabokov's other essays and lectures from this period, during which he further elucidated for an American audience the perils of 'common sense' as they had materialised in Soviet literature and culture. This process was Nabokov's bourgeoisification of communism, in which he appropriated the pejorative term 'bourgeois' from Marxist-Leninist discourse and inverted it, turning it against Soviet culture, just as in 'The Creative Writer' he had borrowed the structure of a polemic against common sense from Marx and Hegel and transformed it into a perverse defence of liberalism. As he put it in one lecture, '[the] term *bourgeois* I use following Flaubert, not Marx. *Bourgeois* in Flaubert's sense is a state of mind, not a state of pocket. A bourgeois is a smug philistine, a dignified vulgarian' (*LRL*, 309). He explained in a review for the *New Republic* in 1944 that Soviet literature, far from being experimental and progressive, as some were claiming, 'never despised the oldest bourgeois clichés, (the avant-garde touch being of course automatically supplied by political enlightenment)'.[5] Nabokov's most important statement on bourgeois taste, however, came in his *Nikolai Gogol*, in which he first explained his notion of 'poshlust', an anglicised version of the Russian *poshlost'*, that he roughly translated as philistinism, 'cheap, sham, common, smutty, pink-and-blue, high falutin', in bad taste' (*NG*, 64). Though 'poshlust' was a transhistorical, 'beautifully timeless' (*NG*, 64) term, Nabokov saw it emerging in particular forms in different periods and nations. Given the wartime context in which he was writing, it is perhaps unsurprising that in *Nikolai Gogol* he suggests that 'poshlust' has a special relationship to German romanticism, though he also sees glimpses of it in contemporary American advertising. Elsewhere in his lectures, however, it becomes clear that Nabokov saw the true contemporary home of 'poshlust' in the Soviet Union: 'The Russia of today, a country of moral imbeciles, of smiling slaves and poker-faced bullies, has stopped noticing *poshlism* because Soviet Russia is so full of its special brand, a blend of despotism and pseudo-culture' (*LRL*, 313).

---

[3] Ibid., 21.
[4] Ibid., 29.
[5] Vladimir Nabokov, 'Cabbage Soup and Caviar', *The New Republic*, 17 January 1944, 92–93.

Nabokov's notion of 'poshlust', defined in its distinction from authentic culture, resonated with the culture critiques mounted in the same period by American intellectuals such as Clement Greenberg and Dwight Macdonald. In particular, Greenberg's 1939 article 'Avant-garde and Kitsch' made a similar manoeuvre in distinguishing between the modernism of Pablo Picasso and the kitsch realism of the Russian painter Ilya Repin, much admired during the early years of the Soviet regime. 'The encouragement of Kitsch', Greenberg argued, 'is merely another of the inexpensive ways in which totalitarian regimes seek to ingratiate themselves with their subjects'.[6] Both Greenberg and Macdonald, as ex-Trotskyists, took Marx more seriously than Nabokov did, but by reading them together we can see how Nabokov's own views participated in a growing consensus that understood the aesthetics of popular realism to be not only illegitimate in its aspirations to constitute authentic culture, but also politically corrupt following its prescription by repressive regimes, and in particular the Soviet Union. This assumption was to become one of the cornerstones of the cultural Cold War fought throughout the 1940s and 50s by a coalition of American intellectuals and CIA-funded institutions such as the Congress for Cultural Freedom (CCF). Nabokov himself, who harboured a deep antipathy to the idea of belonging to any organisation, was not a member of the CCF, though his cousin Nicolas was its president.

Nabokov's 1947 novel *Bend Sinister* should be understood as part of this cultural Cold War, broadly conceived. In its most accessible dimensions it portrays the deep complicity between mass bourgeois taste and totalitarian ideology, a dystopian world in which the banalities of 'light music' and cartoon funnies harmonise with brutal violence and political repression. However, in its alienating metafictional conceits and jarring prose style, bristling with arcane language and erudite allusion, it also manifests itself as an autonomous world of the creative imagination, capable of staging and then subsuming the insubstantial realities of tyranny and oppression. *Bend Sinister* presents a paradox in its genre, then, which Nabokov was well aware of: a dystopian political novel that disclaimed politics as a determining force in its own world. 'The story in *Bend Sinister* is not really about life and death in a grotesque police state', Nabokov declared in his 1963 introduction to the novel, despite admitting to borrowing 'bits of Lenin's speeches, and a chunk of the Soviet constitution, and gobs of Nazist pseudo-efficiency' (*BS*, 164–65). This apparent contradiction is resolved through the startling metafictional conceit with which the novel

[6] Clement Greenberg, 'Avant-Garde and Kitsch', *Partisan Review*, 6/5 (1939), 47.

concludes, as what Nabokov described as an 'anthropomorphic deity impersonated by me' (*BS*, 169) intercedes to save its protagonist Krug from execution at the hands of the regime. The disclosure by this super-natural author figure that 'death [is] but a question of style' (*BS*, 358), and the subsumption of Krug's political fate by an aesthetic one, confirms the metaphysical power of the imagination as the determining force in the novel. This staged encounter between individual creativity and political oppression finds a structural echo in the ideology of the cultural Cold War, whereby autonomous aesthetics must always present itself as universal and apolitical in distinction to the world of totalitarian unfreedom, even while it performs the most political of functions by virtue of its social and institutional framing by the cultural institutions of the Cold War. This is what Giles Scott-Smith in his study of the cultural Cold War calls 'the politics of apolitical culture', according to the logic of which, authentic artistic accomplishments could only be achieved under the 'free' condi-tions of liberal capitalism, and were marshalled as proof of the United States' cultural and moral superiority over the Soviet Union.[7] Whether Nabokov was aware of it or not, the Chekhov Publishing House in New York, with which he published the first full text of *Dar* (*The Gift*) in Russian in 1952, the Russian version of his autobiography *Drugie berega* ('Other Shores') in 1954 and his short story collection *Vesna v Fial'te* (*Spring in Fialta*) in 1956, received large sums of money from the CIA as part of its efforts to promote the United States to the world as the new home for the great Russian literary tradition.[8] Artistic freedom had its political uses.

By the late 1940s and early 50s, when Nabokov began to compose *Lolita* and *Pnin*, his views on the Soviet Union were no longer controversial. In 1948, he noted to Edmund Wilson with some irritation that American intellectuals had finally woken up to what he had known all along – that Soviet communism represented 'an unchanging black abyss of oppression and terror' (*NWL*, 223). As anti-communism became orthodoxy during the second 'red scare', so the subject receded from Nabokov's fiction. This is not to say that the Cold War is irrelevant to these novels. On the contrary, it is precisely because anti-communism and Cold War ideology had become orthodox for both Nabokov and for American public discourse that they became less prominent as content. *Lolita* can nevertheless be read

[7] Giles Scott-Smith, *The Politics of Apolitical Culture: The Congress for Cultural Freedom and the Political Economy of American Hegemony 1945–1955* (London: Routledge, 2002).

[8] See Frances Stonor Saunders, *The Cultural Cold War: The CIA and the World of Arts and Letters* (New York: The New Press, 2013), 118–19.

as constituting in one sense a deliberate test-case for American liberalism, which explores the potential costs incurred in absolutising the freedom of the private individual to pursue happiness and the ways in which such 'inalienable rights' might be cynically exploited.[9] It is only when seen from the wider perspective offered by the Cold War that we can realise how the ambivalent probing of liberal values such as tolerance, privacy and the pleasures of consumption in Nabokov's 1950s fiction was itself an assumed privilege made possible by the relative hegemony of American liberalism, which in theory if not practice included robust self-examination among its constituent virtues. When the assumption of that privilege was questioned, Nabokov was quick to respond. Following charges that *Lolita*'s treatment of cultural vulgarity made it 'anti-American', he answered in print that 'this is something that pains me considerably more than the idiotic accusation of immorality . . . I am an American writer and claim only the same rights that other American writers enjoy.'[10] Appropriately enough, the journal in which he printed this essay was *Encounter*, another project funded by the CIA.[11]

In 1961, during the composition of his masterpiece *Pale Fire*, Nabokov left the United States and settled for the remainder of his life in Switzerland. This movement marked the beginning of an important stage in his relationship to the Cold War, during which he uncoupled the idea of America from its material geography and rendered it an abstract ideal. In a sense, this process had been underway ever since, in 'The Creative Writer', he had insisted that the essential, irrational goodness of humanity existed as a universal and not just 'in the snuggest nook of an unshelled country'. By 1966, he was able to proclaim 'I am as American as April in Arizona' (*SO*, 98), having left it for good. It is worth pondering on this lyrical phrase, which empties the United States of its contents in order to suggest a benign, bright and 'historyless' space, a rhyming musical atmosphere and an ideological vacuum. It is an American space that contains nothing of America in it. Nabokov's two novels of the 1960s are more properly Swiss than American works in that the move to Switzerland enabled Nabokov to erase the gradual breakdown of domestic consensus over the conduct of the Cold War from his distant visions of the United States as the end of history.[12]

---

[9] See Dana Dragunoiu, *Vladimir Nabokov and the Poetics of Liberalism* (Evanston, IL: Northwestern University Press, 2012), 82–141.

[10] Vladimir Nabokov, 'On a Book Entitled *Lolita*', *Encounter* (April 1959), 76.

[11] See Saunders, *The Cultural Cold War*, 138–58.

[12] On the breakdown of consensus over the conduct of the cultural Cold War in the 1960s, see Saunders, *Cultural Cold War*, 320–42.

Read together, *Pale Fire* and *Ada* dramatise the tension between two dominant American perspectives on geopolitical space in the Cold War. On one hand, the notion of containment, with its attendant metaphors of infiltration and infection, presented a pristine homeland constantly in danger of corruption from subversives penetrating from outside. This, of course, is the logic of *Pale Fire*'s paranoid assassination plot, with an East Coast campus figured by Kinbote as a pastoral 'Arcady' infiltrated by an insidious agent. It also figures transparently in the suspense-thriller synopsis that Nabokov sent to Alfred Hitchcock in 1964, about a defector from behind the Iron Curtain who comes to the United States only to be betrayed by Americans who 'would turn out to belong to certain pro-Soviet organizations' (*Letters*, 366). On the other hand, a more global outlook inverts this domestic focus by transforming the rest of the 'free' world into an abstract extension of the American *imperium*. 'If Europe and America are coming to resemble each other more and more', Nabokov noted in 1964, 'why should I be discouraged?' (*SO*, 49).

The fullest expression of this latter spatial regime came with the publication of *Ada* in 1969, in which he created an entirely reconfigured global geography around the idea of 'Estotiland', a peaceful nation blending aspects of America, France and pre-Revolutionary Russia, while transforming the Soviet bloc into 'Tartary', an 'independent inferno' (*Ada*, 20) separated from the civilised world by the 'Golden Curtain' (*Ada*, 145). *Ada* finds the correlative of its multilingual play and transnational fantasies in the elite cosmopolitanism of Nabokov's Swiss life, where his milieu included other residents such as Denis de Rougemont and Peter Ustinov, both ardent Federalists deeply suspicious of the nation state (the former also presided over the Executive Committee for the Congress for Cultural Freedom and authored one of *Lolita*'s most favourable early reviews).[13] When Ada wonders in jest 'isn't Switzerland in Washington State, sort of, *après tout*' (*Ada*, 447), she gives oblique expression to a Cold War cosmopolitan fantasy in which Western culture is simultaneously Americanised and deterritorialised as an abstract universal. Nabokov's repeated invocations in his 1960s fiction of Cold War history as burlesque should not then be understood as in any sense freeing him from its structural confines into an ideology-free zone. As J. M. Coetzee noted of *Pale Fire*, 'by incorporating the exegesis into the fiction we do not escape history, we merely pre-empt

---

[13] See Schiff, *Véra*, 329–39; Brian Boyd, *Vladimir Nabokov: The American Years* (Princeton: Princeton University Press, 1991), 422; 423 and passim.

its first stage'.[14] Though Nabokov frequently took occasion to deny the impact of what he called 'the intrusions of history' (*Eye*, 2) on his fiction, it is now clear enough from the vantage point of the twenty-first century that such declarations of autonomy were themselves deeply historical, and that Nabokov's long Cold War had always been hiding in plain sight.

[14] J. M. Coetzee, 'Nabokov's *Pale Fire* and the Primacy of Art', *UCT Studies in English*, 5 (1974), 6.

CHAPTER 30

The Long 1950s

Andrea Carosso

Nabokov's time in America coincides roughly with the so-called 'Long 1950s', a period starting in the early Cold War years at the end of the Second World War and coming to an end around the time of Kennedy's assassination in 1963. The Long 1950s define an almost mythical period of American prosperity, coinciding with the economic boom of the post-war era, and are characterised by a remarkable expansion of the American middle class, concomitant with a growing social emphasis on family and domestic values, normative sexuality, obsessive fears of communism at home and abroad, threats of nuclear annihilation and increasing US influence in the world within the context of third-world de-colonisation. Nabokov's interest in sexuality and its social and political function in his novels written during this time and beyond – *Bend Sinister* (1947), *Lolita* (1955), *Pnin* (1957), *Pale Fire* (1962) and *Ada* (1969) – reflect ongoing cultural debates of the Long 1950s and explicitly challenge conventional moral norms of the early Cold War period.

At least four of these novels emphasise so-called sexual subversion as they plot sexual behaviour that lies beyond the normative middle-class conventions of the age. *Lolita* is a tale of paedophilia; homosexuality plays a key role in both *Bend Sinister* and *Pale Fire; Ada* is a story of brother-sister incest. This explicit interest in sexually non-conformist behaviour can be read as Nabokov's historically conscious response to some of the central preoccupations in American society and culture at that time, an interest on Nabokov's part to articulate, and capitalise on, some of early Cold-War society's apparently most repressed anxieties.

In the Long 1950s, masculinity and femininity appeared rigidly contained within specific and narrowly defined gender roles, and sexuality was predicated upon an assumed moral purity of womanhood, i.e. a series of social expectations that Betty Friedan famously defined, in her 1963 bestseller, as the 'feminine mystique'.[1] Another bestseller of the period, Dr Benjamin Spock's *The Common Sense Book of Baby and Child Care* (1946), encouraged women to 'focus on motherhood', putting an end to the larger sexual and economic freedom women had experienced in war-time (when many had worked and earned real money). According to Dr Spock's orthodoxy, the aim of contemporaneous education was for girls and boys from early onwards to follow rules and control emotions (the latter a euphemism for sexual desires) which his book completely ignored. In the Long 1950s, fears of a nuclear catastrophe seemed to reinforce the already strong tendency to form stable families in which men and women held specific gender roles. Deviation from norms of any kind, especially in the realm of sexuality, was not only frowned upon, but even regarded as dangerous to the body politic. Gender roles were strictly reinforced by the media, especially television, whose images of wholesome, nuclear, essentially de-sexualised suburban families became all-pervasive.

In a decade when popular literature mostly shied away from frank discussion of sexual matters, one of the most widely sold books was *A Marriage Manual: A Practical Guidebook to Sex and Marriage* by Hannah and Abraham Stone. First published in 1935 and completely revised for its 1952 edition, *A Marriage Manual* is a useful Baedeker to prevailing attitudes to sexuality during the decade. It discussed sexuality strictly as a function of procreation within marriage, and viewed female sexuality and female orgasm as ultimately irrelevant. The Stones' suggestion that a woman's sexual impulse 'may normally remain dormant for a long period' was concomitant with their functional idea that sex was nothing more than a practicality aimed at the larger goal of engendering a healthy family nucleus. When, in the final pages of *Lolita*, Humbert pleads to the 'frigid gentlewomen of the jury', Nabokov's sarcasm is both a reflection of 1950s light-hearted misogyny and a tongue-in-cheek commentary on sexual orthodoxy in the early Cold War era.

Another popular family planning manual of the decade, Eustace Chesser's *Love without Fear: How to Achieve Sex Happiness in Marriage*, took a slightly more progressive view than the Stones' book. Originally published in Britain in 1940 (and acquitted of obscenity charges in 1942), *Love without Fear* came out in the United States in 1947, selling three-quarter of a million copies in its first hardcover edition. The paperback edition did even better. Chesser's book suggested that pre-marital sex might in fact be beneficial to produce what the author called a 'mature

---

[1] Betty Friedan, *The Feminine Mystique* (New York: Norton, 1963).

marriage'. Nevertheless, it depicted sexual promiscuity among women as being wholly opposed to a 'woman's true feminine nature',[2] reflecting a wariness that, if unleashed under the wrong circumstances outside marriage, female sexuality would become difficult to control. Hence, Chesser stressed, like the Stones, the need for its rigid containment within the boundaries of marriage and reproduction.

As these manuals made clear, sexual activity outside marriage was at least problematic, if not outright illegal. During the Long 1950s, adultery was outlawed in most American states, and even its depiction was clearly limited by the Hollywood Production Code – the great enforcer of morals in twentieth-century America – which stipulated that extra-marital affairs, while sometimes necessary as plot material, 'must not be explicitly treated, or justified, or presented attractively'.[3] Homosexuality was punished harshly in the United States (in many states, well into the twenty-first century): prior to 1962, sodomy was a felony in every state, and homosexuals were socially stigmatised as sick individuals, both physically and mentally.

But if, on the one hand, during the Long 1950s, repressive public norms contributed to define subjectivity as constructed in rigidly normative sexual behaviour, empirical research showed that the private sexuality of Americans diverted significantly from its mainstream representations. Alfred Kinsey's *Sexual Behavior in the Human Male* (1948) and *Sexual Behavior in the Human Female* (1953), better known as the 'Kinsey Reports', made headlines as they challenged some of the orthodoxies of American sexual mainstream culture in the 1950s. Kinsey's work contested the notions that women were generally not sexual and presented evidence that the sexual behaviour of Americans not infrequently transgressed the sacred boundaries of marriage. Even more controversially, Kinsey claimed that one in three Americans had had homosexual experiences at some point in their lives. Moreover, he devoted parts of his studies to the taboo topic of child rape: based on interviews with educators, parents as well as convicted child molesters, Kinsey provided detailed evidence of hundreds of cases of sexual abuse of children by adults. In other words, Kinsey's studies exposed a country swarming with 'sexual subversives', which Cold War orthodoxy read as evidence of an ongoing attack on America's founding values.

---

[2] M. E. Melody and Linda M. Peterson, *Teaching America about Sex: Marriage Guides and Sex Manuals from the Late Victorians to Dr. Ruth* (New York: New York University Press, 1999), 124.
[3] Jody W. Pennington, *The History of Sex in American Film* (Westport, CT: Praeger, 2007), 153.

Although there is no evidence that Nabokov ever read either of the 'Kinsey Reports', *Lolita* contains at least two references to Kinsey's work. In the Foreword, the fictional editor John Ray, Jr., PhD, remarks that Humbert is one of 'at least 12% of American adult males . . . [who] enjoy yearly, in one way or another, the special experience "H.H." describes with such despair' (*Lolita*, 4). A little later on in the novel, Humbert cites sexology statistics and makes reference to 'writers on the sex interests of children' (*Lolita*, 39). As Alfred Appel, Jr. has pointed out, these puns explicitly 'poke fun at the work of Alfred Kinsey'.[4] In fact, they do more than that: they establish a wider link between Nabokov and Kinsey and by extension to the whole era of early Cold War culture which also includes J. D. Salinger's *The Catcher in the Rye* (1951), the Beats and Grace Metalious' lowbrow sensation *Peyton Place* (1956) – each in their own way interested in exploring sexual subversion in the American 1950s.

Youth, and adolescence in particular, was a problematic locus of subversion in early Cold War culture, when teenagers emerged for the first time as a sociologically distinct category, endowed with specific social roles, as well as specific rights, mostly derived from their newly acquired power in influencing consumption choices during the post-war boom.[5] This new social group emerged in a cultural space that was radically different from the narrowly defined social and sexual roles of the immediate post-war era. American teenagers during the early Cold War years were cast as inherently subversive, their rebellion inscribed in the emergence of youth movements that denied the orthodoxies of American culture, and yet were given currency in the Long 1950s. The rise of rock 'n' roll, James Dean's rebellion 'without a cause', Brando's misfit bikers, as well as the proliferation of 'bad girls' and 'tomboys' in popular movies and novels of the period, are evidence of a decade in which American culture had to come to terms with, and to a certain extent appropriate, non-normative behaviour.

The 'deviant girl' phenomenon is, of course, particularly relevant to Nabokov's work. In *Lolita*, Humbert's deceptive and self-delusional construction of Lolita as a tomboy presents the ideal cover-up for his perversion. In the second part of the novel, Humbert reveals that he is very careful to rearrange the bed sheets in every motel he and Lolita visit in order to conceal his serial rape of a minor. Before room service arrives, Humbert makes the bed 'in such a way as to suggest the abandoned nest of a restless

---

[4] Vladimir Nabokov, *The Annotated Lolita*, ed. Alfred Appel, Jr. (London: Penguin, 1991), 324.
[5] See Leerom Medovoi, *Rebels: Youth and the Cold War Origins of Identity* (Durham, NC: Duke University Press, 2005).

father and his tomboy daughter, instead of an ex-convict's saturnalia with a
couple of fat ole whores' (*Lolita*, 130). Lolita matches even more closely the
other model of psycho-politically independent femininity of the 1950s, the
'bad girl', whose anti-domestic rebellion turns her into easy prey for sexual
exploitation by male predators.[6] Lolita, the 'bad girl', closely resembles
other prototypes of female delinquency in 1950s culture, including Silver in
Mamie Van Doren's *Girls Town* (1959) and Sarah Jane in Douglas Sirk's
seminal film *Imitation of Life* (1959), cultural texts that posit sexual exploration as rebellious behaviour, frequently leading to ultimately self-inflicted
sexual violence and exploitation.[7]

It appears legitimate to speculate that the *Lolita* theme appealed to
Nabokov also for commercial reasons. Once in the United States, he had
made it a point to seek a wider circulation for his novels – if nothing else,
for mere financial gain. Even before *Lolita* was written, he told Edmund
Wilson that he had 'decided to welcome all kind and manner of publicity
from now on', and declared himself 'sick of having [his] books muffled up
in silence like gems in cotton wool' (*NWL*, 292). And although, in his
letters to Maurice Girodias, Nabokov indicated distress at the prospect of a
succès de scandale (*Letters*, 175), *Lolita*'s direct challenges to prevailing moral
conventions (e.g. Lolita the 'bad girl' who initiates the sexual encounter
with HH in Humbert's contestable representation) placed the novel in a
perpetual dialectic between serious art and voyeuristic fetish. Lionel
Trilling has argued that in writing *Lolita*, Nabokov explicitly sought to
shock his readers by breaking 'one of our unquestioned and unquestion-
able sexual prohibitions', the taboo of 'the sexual inviolability of girls of a
certain age', compounded by 'what amounts to [impious] incest'.[8] Praising
the novel as great literature, Trilling emphasised its vision of love as based
on passion and erotic pleasure, and opposed to the practical, contractual
relationship of bourgeois marriage. Writing in 1959, Trilling in other words
celebrated what he saw as Nabokov's liberating subversion of the Cold War
canon of sexual normativity. Within this perspective, it is not surprising
that, in *Lolita*, subversive sexuality is enacted not directly, but rather
through the mediation of the confessing pervert, whose penance functions
as a tongue-in-cheek ploy to re-enact the pleasure of that very subversion
he is atoning for. Taken literally, the atoning pervert allows *Lolita* to tread
the delicate space between Cold War normativity (in John Ray's farcical

---

[6] See Medovoi, *Rebels*, 265–316.
[7] Ibid., 270.
[8] Lionel Trilling, Review of *Lolita* (1958), in Norman Page (ed.), *Nabokov: The Critical Heritage*
(London: Routledge and Kegan Paul, 1982), 92.

'Preface', the claim is made that *Lolita* is 'a tragic tale tending unswervingly to nothing less than a moral apotheosis' – *Lolita*, 4) and pornography, a space which would prove crucial to the book's success.

Despite Nabokov's well-known abhorrence of psychiatry and psycho-analysis – whose logic and authority the novel constantly seeks to under-mine – the whole of *Lolita* appears framed (albeit in language whose satirical thrust cannot be eluded) within the standards and norms of Cold War notions of psychological propriety and sanity, thereby dismiss-ing the events it reports as a tale of 'horrible', 'abject' and, ultimately, 'abnormal' (John Ray's words) sexual behaviour. In so doing, it exposes the distinct limits of a Cold War discourse on sexuality which denies the existence of sexual behaviour (even if criminal) that transgresses societal norms: Humbert is not jailed for rape – his 'unspeakable' crime becoming public only upon the posthumous publication of *Lolita* – but for the murder of Claire Quilty, a rival paedophile. And in noting that if he were his own jury, he would dismiss his murder charge and sentence himself to thirty years for rape, Humbert acknowledges that the problem with Cold War America lies in its inability even to acknowledge sexual subversion. Read from this perspective, *Lolita* anticipates concerns of Nabokov's subsequent novels of the Long 1950s: the contestation of Cold War culture's unremitting pathologising of sexual deviance, which becomes most explicit in *Pale Fire*, his postmodernist *tour de force*.

Like *Lolita*, *Pale Fire* is organised around the theme of sexual subversion. Despite having long been read as an old-world aesthete's opus of wordplay and allusion, some scholars have recently shifted the emphasis from the novel's presumed aesthetic focus onto Nabokov's interest in the 'cultural narratives that prescribed the limits of mid-century reality'.[9] In *Pale Fire*, Nabokov confronts homophobia and its political translation into anti-communism in the early Cold War era. Although the Kinsey Reports had shocked the nation by revealing that homosexuality was not uncommon in America, the public debate over that perceived 'heinous abnormality' raged on during the early Cold War. And while the topic of male–female sexuality was avoided in public debate and representations (in 1950s movies, for example, married couples slept in separate beds), homosexu-ality turned out to be the perfect site to turn social stigma into a matter of public discourse. In the McCarthy years, America's leading newspapers played a crucial role in orchestrating a homophobic campaign aimed at

[9] Steven Belletto, *No Accident, Comrade: Chance and Design in Cold War American Narratives* (Oxford and New York: Oxford University Press, 2012), 62.

alleged communist sympathisers working in the State Department which intersected with the wider crusade against Soviet spies who had allegedly infiltrated the US government. Beginning in 1950, the 'Perverts on the Potomac' campaign – as the media dubbed it – was instrumental in demonising homosexuals not only as 'perverts', but also as a threat to national security. Homosexuals were described as emotionally unstable, immoral and hence 'very susceptible to Communism',[10] and thus targeted, along with communists, in the same category as other enemies of the nation. Nabokov held strong opinions regarding both. His blatant homophobia, as both his biographers and his correspondence unequivocally document,[11] was further complicated by his ambivalent relationship with his gay brother Sergei, who had died in a Nazi concentration camp. *Conclusive Evidence* (1951) failed to even acknowledge Sergei's existence, while in only three chapters before the end of *Speak Memory* (1967) did Nabokov finally tackle the subject, confessing how 'inordinately hard' it was for him to speak about his younger brother (*SM*, 580). On the anticommunist front, Nabokov's autobiography had plenty to say, and his eager embrace of Joseph McCarthy's crusade, if not for its methods, at least because he believed that there was merit in the senator's fierce anticommunism, was no surprise.

It is within this national, as well as Nabokov's personal, short-circuit of homophobia and anti-communist patriotism that *Pale Fire* must be situated. In the novel – or better, in one possible reading of it – King Charles the Beloved is Kinbote, a flamboyantly gay man, displaced from his kingdom of Zembla following a Bolshevik-style revolution and hiding out in the US northeast in order to evade an 'extremist' assassin. The story (or at least its 'present' portion in Appalachia, a fictional proxy for New England or upstate New York) is set between 1958, when King Charles arrives in the United States, and 1959, when John Shade, whose 999-line poem is the subject of Kinbote's preposterous explication, is assassinated in lieu of Kinbote. Although Kinbote is far from being a communist sympathiser, the novel's themes of closeted homosexuality, illicit infiltration, disguised identities and paranoia are reflections of the cultural climate in which the book was written. Steven Belletto and Andrea Pitzer have recently pointed

---

[10] Rodger Streitmatter, *From "Perverts" to "Fab Five": The Media's Changing Depiction of Gay Men and Lesbians* (New York: Routledge, 2009), 8–11.

[11] See Andrew Field, *Nabokov: His Life in Art: A Critical Narrative* (Boston, MA: Little Brown, 1967); Brian Boyd, *Vladimir Nabokov: The Russian Years* (Princeton: Princeton University Press, 1990), 73; 106; 396; and Brian Boyd, *Vladimir Nabokov: The American Years* (Princeton: Princeton University Press, 1991), 261.

out *Pale Fire*'s allusions to Cold War-era real-life events (Nova Zembla, for example, was actually a Soviet test site for atomic bombs, discussed as it was in several *New York Times* articles at the turn of the 1960s), which make it first and foremost a sly commentary on the Cold War.[12]

If *Pale Fire* can be read as an engagement with leading Cold War concerns of anti-communist paranoia and homophobia, it remains to be seen where exactly Nabokov positioned himself on the issue. In *Bend Sinister*, the novel Nabokov was working on when he learned of Sergei's death in 1945, the hero – like Sergei – pays with his life for speaking out against a brutal and repressive regime. However, to reveal Nabokov's conflicting feelings towards his brother, in *Bend Sinister* it is not the hero who is gay, but rather the tyrant who orders his death. In this regard, *Bend Sinister* is textbook Cold War material. In *Pale Fire*, however, this paradigm is upended. Having established Kinbote/King Charles as a homosexual from the book's very foreword (beginning with Kinbote's repulsion towards a 'pulpous pony-tailed [waitress]' working in the college faculty lounge; *Pale Fire*, 449), the commentary goes on to integrate homosexuality and Cold-War politics in a non-normative way. The 'lithe youths diving into the swimming pool' that King Charles observes from afar while in captivity after being dethroned by the revolution (*PF*, 521) create one of several moments in the novel where the sexually 'deviant' individual is cast as the victim, not the agent, of a totalitarian regime. The same dynamics applies in America, where King Charles/Kinbote finds himself compelled to keep a low profile – not only sexually but also politically. He is clearly not a communist, but his somewhat effeminate posturing, unknown identity (making him a potential spy within the Cold War paranoia about possible infiltration) and illicit behaviour (Kinbote steals Shade's manuscript, which he then publishes with his own commentary) all come together to make him the object of persecution by a Cold War community whose sinister conflation of sexual and political subversion Nabokov now appears finally ready to confront. As Belletto has put it, 'in his capacity as both sexual subversive and Cold Warrior, Kinbote challenges what the homophobic narrative claimed a homosexual person could do'.[13]

In spite of Nabokov's repeated claims for political neutrality, his novels of the Long 1950s display an active engagement in the politics of the Cold

---

[12] See Belletto, *No Accident, Comrade*; Andrea Pitzer, *The Secret History of Vladimir Nabokov* (New York and London: Pegasus, 2013).
[13] Belletto, *No Accident, Comrade*, 67.

War, and sexual subversion appears to be his chosen mode to mimetically reflect those concerns. If *Lolita* shook Cold War America in its presumed social and sexual suburban conformity, *Pale Fire* intervened in that era's blurring of sexual and political normativity as a precondition for the integrity of the body politic.

CHAPTER 31

Transnationalism

Rachel Trousdale

Vladimir Nabokov's life is a long history of exile. The decisive moment is his flight from Russia in 1919, but his subsequent moves across Europe and then the Atlantic, like his decision to write in English rather than Russian, entail continual uprooting, displacement and recontextualisation. These upheavals provide much of the subject matter of his writing. But despite his awareness of the specific practical challenges faced by the émigré, Nabokov treats exile as a universal condition: we are all exiles in time, if not in space or culture, cut off from childhood, the past and the world of the dead.

Nabokov's childhood was cosmopolitan – he says that he grew up a 'perfectly normal trilingual child' (*SO*, 43), fluent in English, French and Russian, and travelled in Europe with his family. He was, however, profoundly attached to Vyra, his family's country estate south of St Petersburg. While his multilingual upbringing prepared him for a nomadic life in Europe and America, the loss of Russia, and especially of Vyra, is central to his fiction. His physical exile from Russia is intertwined throughout his writing with his temporal exile from an idyllic childhood; the lost country and the lost era are equally impossible to regain.

When Nabokov's family left Russia in 1919, they settled in Berlin, and Nabokov joined them there after finishing Cambridge. He began his writing career within the city's Russian émigré community, which would provide the setting for most of his Russian-language novels.

Nabokov's second major displacement after leaving Russia was his decision to write in English, beginning with *The Real Life of Sebastian Knight* (1941). This move was motivated by his desire to find work in England or America. It was a wrenching choice, and for the rest of his life he regretted abandoning 'my natural language, my natural idiom, my rich, infinitely rich and docile Russian tongue, for a second-rate brand of English' (*SO*, 15). With his switch in languages and his move to America in 1940, while he continued to write about Russian émigrés, his main characters began to have more peculiar hybrid backgrounds, from Humbert Humbert's pan-European origins in *Lolita* (1955) to Van Veen's childhood in an alternate-history Amerussia in *Ada* (1969). The Nabokovs' final move back across the Atlantic to Montreux, Switzerland, is emblematic of their life in exile: they spent their last years living in permanent transience at the Montreux Palace Hotel.

Nabokov's work offers many approaches to resolving the incongruities of emigration, but in the end, he treats exile as a chrysalid stage of development: the exile, rather than being someone who has lost his country, is someone who has not yet created it. *Pnin* (1957), *Pale Fire* (1962) and *Speak, Memory* (1967) show how Nabokov educates readers in the experience of exile, drawing them into his own peculiar state of cultural and linguistic displacement and teaching them to create alternate worlds in which those displacements are no longer a loss.

Nabokov's distinctive stylistic techniques are central to this work. Narrative developments presented as asides, unexplained multilingual puns and unheralded incongruities train readers in a process of interpretation and adaptation that mirrors the education undergone by the exile. Like émigrés, Nabokov's readers experience an initial disorientation, but re-readers gain fluency within his worlds and a richer set of associations within their own. Nabokov's writing draws readers into a community of displaced persons by showing how the exile's accretion of resonances and double exposures blurs the boundaries between places, times and metaphysical states.

Nabokov's narratives frequently refer to the most obvious traumas of exile – the danger of arrest, torture or execution at the hands of a revolutionary government, and the crossing of borders to escape them – only obliquely, leaving us to infer the details of real-world physical perils. *Speak, Memory*, for example, has major omissions that require the reader to deduce how historical events affected the family. Most strikingly, when the news that Nabokov's father has been killed initially reaches them, Nabokov reports it only as an interruption to a conversation 'when the telephone rang' (*SM*, 394). An attentive reader will see that the date Nabokov assigns to the passage (28 March 1922) is the day of his father's death reported in the next chapter, but the memoir's programmatic privileging of individual experience over geopolitics means that the text deals with such major events almost indirectly.

This apparent avoidance of historical context is misleading. Real-world events are a pressing concern to Nabokov and his characters, especially once Western Europe becomes dangerous.[1] The perils of exile become more visible when Nabokov describes his flight from Europe to America:

> The season was May – mid-May, 1940. The day before, after months of soliciting and cursing, the emetic of a bribe had been administered to the right rat at the right office and had resulted finally in a *visa de sortie* which, in its turn, conditioned the permission to cross the Atlantic. (*SM*, 612)

Switching from 'the season was May' to 'mid-May, 1940' shifts the text's location from a romantic springtime to France immediately before the Nazi occupation, when Nabokov, his Jewish wife and their son were again in danger. But Nabokov does not dwell on their situation, instead discussing how his 'relief' at obtaining the visa lets him write his best chess problem. Other memoirists might take self-preservation as the central problem of exile; Nabokov treats it as a component of the process of composition. Readers are required to work out the gravity of his situation on their own.

Nabokov also handles such real-world dangers at a remove in his fiction. The tragicomic émigré professor Pnin mourns the deaths of his parents, former fiancée and friends, but the only hint we have that he himself may have faced danger comes during 'one of those dreams that still haunt Russian fugitives, even when a third of a century has elapsed since their escape from the Bolsheviks' (*Pnin*, 375). Once again, Nabokov requires readers to deduce the real roots of Pnin's dreamed 'escape' and thus enter into the problem of crossing borders.

The haunting trauma of exile is developed in *Pale Fire*. Charles Kinbote, the novel's mad narrator, who believes himself to be the exiled king of a country called Zembla, lives in a continual state of paranoia:

> Often, almost nightly, throughout the spring of 1959, I had feared for my life . . . I would lie awake and breathless – as if only now living consciously through those perilous nights in my country, where at any moment, a company of jittery revolutionists might enter and hustle me off to a moonlit wall . . . Would they shoot me at once – or would they smuggle the chloroformed scholar back to Zembla, Rodnaya Zembla, to face there a dazzling decanter and a row of judges exulting in their inquisitorial chairs? (*PF*, 503–4)

Nabokov here treats the real perils he and his fellow émigrés have fled as fantasy.

---

[1] Leona Toker, 'Nabokov's Worldview', in Julian W. Connolly (ed.), *The Cambridge Companion to Nabokov* (Cambridge: Cambridge University Press, 2005), 232–47 [244].

Whatever the threats faced by characters as they flee their native countries, exile itself becomes a kind of death in Nabokov's fiction – not because it marks the end of a life but because it is a transfiguration. Exile, like death, is a one-way trip that changes the traveller's reality. Kinbote imagines such a transformation in which he turns into Nabokov:

> God will help me, I trust, to rid myself of any desire to follow the example of two other characters in this work. I shall continue to exist. I may assume other disguises, other forms, but I shall try to exist. I may turn up yet, on another campus, as an old, happy, healthy, heterosexual Russian, a writer in exile, sans fame, sans future, sans audience, sans anything but his art. (*PF*, 657)

This prophecy is self-fulfilling. As Nabokov tells Alfred Appel, Jr. in an interview (*SO*, 74), Kinbote commits suicide. But his suicide begins well before the end of the book, with his arrival in the United States and transformation from King Charles the Beloved of Zembla to Charles Kinbote. His name, he explains, means 'regicide'; he adds that 'a king who sinks his identity in the mirror of exile is in a sense just that' (*PF*, 632). 'Kinbote' as a person comes into existence at the moment that the King touches American soil, as indicated by a shift in pronouns halfway through Kinbote's narration of the event:

> he descended by parachute from a chartered plane ... near Baltimore whose oriole is not an oriole ... Fain would I elucidate this business of parachuting but (it being a matter of mere sentimental tradition rather than a useful manner of transportation) this is not strictly necessary in these notes to *Pale Fire*. While Kingsley, the British chauffeur, an old and absolutely faithful retainer, was doing his best to cram the bulky and ill-folded parachute into the boot, I relaxed on a shooting stick he had supplied me with (*PF*, 617).

Like the Baltimore oriole, 'Kinbote' is a new species, an American rather than a European animal. But he is not discovered on the new continent; he is created by it. His arrival by parachute avoids the bureaucratic difficulties faced by the Nabokovs in their flight from France in order to elucidate the nature of exilic transformation as Nabokov imagines it during his residence in America.

For all its echoing losses, this transformation is also fundamentally comic. Kinbote has already imagined jumping from an aircraft as the best way to commit suicide: 'The ideal drop is from an aircraft, your muscles relaxed, your pilot puzzled, your packed parachute shuffled off, cast off, shrugged off – farewell, *shootka* (little chute)!' (*PF*, 598). Kinbote's Zemblan word hints at his 'real' origins: *shootka* is Russian for 'joke,' and as we

ive reading, Kinbote is 'really' a Russian émigré named
okes and identity alike suggest, our education in exile
o laugh not just at multilingual puns but with delight

, characters are far more likely to experience problems
orientation in the unfamiliar American landscape than they
to encounter difficulties with their passports. As we have seen, Kinbote
complains that Baltimore's 'oriole is not an oriole'; he also laments the
'suburban impostor' Americans call a robin (*PF*, 486). The fact that the
birds of North America share names with European birds increases his sense
of alienation and reminds us that those names carry a long history of exile,
stretching back to the first European settlers: the birds Kinbote resents for
their dissimilarity to their European counterparts echo America's history as a
country of immigrants, and show that American language has already
adapted to the species and conditions of a new continent.

Nabokov repeatedly returns to the apparent similarity and actual difference between American and European nature. This phenomenon is particularly evident during Pnin's visit to The Pines, a country house where
members of the Russian émigré community gather. Pnin, who appears
absurd in day-to-day America, is suddenly in his element: an eloquent
speaker, an accomplished scholar and a formidable croquet player. But the
American natural world reminds us that this is a temporary respite.
A fellow guest, Varvara Chateau, demonstrates the danger of projecting
familiar European nature on alien surroundings:

> Its birches and bilberries deceived her into placing mentally Lake
> Onkwedo ... on the parallel of ... Lake Onega in northern Russia,
> where she had spent her first fifteen summers, before fleeing from the
> Bolsheviks to western Europe ... More fabulous than pictures in a bestiary
> were to her the tremendous porcupines ... She was nonplused and
> enchanted by the number of plants and creatures she could not identify,
> mistook Yellow Warblers for stray canaries, and on the occasion of Susan's
> birthday was known to have brought, with pride and panting enthusiasm,
> for the ornamentation of the dinner table, a profusion of beautiful poison-
> ivy leaves, hugged to her pink, freckled breast. (*Pnin*, 383–84)

The continuity Varvara perceives between Russia and America leaves her
vulnerable to uncomfortable, comic errors, the physical parallel to Pnin's
verbal misadventures. Like Pnin's English, too, Varvara's vision of America
asks the reader to share in her disorientation, shifting the latitude of
familiar places, recontextualising familiar animals in 'fabulous' medieval
books and imagining indigenous birds as lost (and thus vulnerable) exotic

pets. Her errors turn the New England woods into an alien location ᵥ
for its native inhabitants.

Nabokov emphasises the unfamiliarity of American nature throughout
his fiction, and in *Speak, Memory*, he writes of 'yearn[ing] after an ecological niche' (*SM*, 419). The memoir contains a very different treatment of
the two continents' natural worlds from that of the novels, however: in his
fiction, American nature is irreducibly unfamiliar, but in Nabokov's
memoir, it provides continuity between the continents, which makes
possible a resolution to exile's incongruities, as marked by a swallowtail
butterfly that escapes from his wardrobe in 1906 to fly

> over timber and tundra, to Vologda, Viatka and Perm, and beyond the
> gaunt Ural range to Yakutsk and Verkhne Kolymsk, and from Verkhne
> Kolymsk, where it lost a tail, to the fair Island of St. Lawrence, and across
> Alaska to Dawson, and southward along the Rocky Mountains – to be
> finally overtaken and captured, after a forty-year race, on an immigrant
> dandelion under an endemic aspen near Boulder. (*SM*, 460)

Kinbote's slip into Russian suggests another of the primary attributes of
Nabokov's work: linguistic hybridity, what George Steiner calls the 'poly-
linguistic matrix' of translations of his own and others' work.[2] Nabokov's
multilingual prose mimics the experience of exile for readers through both
its difficulty and its rewards.

Failure to adapt to the local language can be catastrophic. Pnin's terrible
English makes him a comic figure to Americans. But it also gives readers
insight into his position. When his friend and landlady Joan Clements tries
to explain a *New Yorker* cartoon to him, Pnin objects that the picture is
unrealistic:

> 'So small island, moreover with palm, cannot exist in such big sea.'
> 'Well, it exists here.'
> 'Impossible isolation,' said Pnin.   (*Pnin*, 339–40)

Pnin wants to say that the island depicted in the cartoon is physically
impossible – but his use of 'isolation' conflates the Germanic derivation of
the word 'island' with the French derivation of 'isolation', 'isolé', from the
Latin *insula*. His mistake offers as much insight into his own loneliness as
that of the comic's castaway. The error also reveals the potential for linguistic
hybridity: when we understand the full meaning of 'impossible isolation', we
gain access to a pan-European fluency in which the boundaries between

---

[2] George Steiner, *Extraterritorial: Papers on Literature and the Language Revolution* (New York:
Atheneum, 1976), 7.

language groups become porous as the Romance and Germanic words for island are reunited. But the insights he offers are not available to his interlocutors: only the reader sees how his malapropisms and inadvertent puns accrete into a rich new language.

Kinbote's Zemblan takes the reader's education in exile several steps further. In his commentary to *Pale Fire*, Kinbote immerses the reader in all things Zemblan, so that we experience cultural and linguistic disorientation comparable to his own. His Zemblan phrases slowly increase our fluency in his invented language, composed of an unlikely fusion of Slavic and Germanic roots.[3] In re-reading – which, Nabokov says, is the only way to read a novel – [4] we find that we are closer to Kinbote's position than to Shade's: we can now laugh at his multilingual puns and see the double exposures of American and Zemblan life.

In *Speak, Memory*, Nabokov writes that Russia and Europe are the thesis and antithesis in his life, and America 'a synthesis – and a new thesis' (*SM*, 594). This synthesis ends Nabokov's period of exile: while he can no more return to Russia than to childhood, his work blends America and Russia more completely than the overlaps Pnin's fellow exile Varvara perceives. Nabokov learned this mnemonic blending from his mother, who retains the essence of her former life: 'As a company of traveling players carry with them everywhere, while they still remember their lines, a windy heath, a misty castle, an enchanted island, so she had with her all that her soul had stored' (*SM*, 395). Elena Nabokov overcomes exile through sheer power of memory, but as the comparison to Shakespearean actors shows, memory collaborates with artistic invention, and Nabokov combines fact and fancy in his mnemonic reclamation of Russia. In a passage describing years of butterfly hunting, Vyra gives way to Colorado:

> After making my way through some pine groves and alder scrub I came to the bog ... I knew I would find here quite special arctic butterflies ... over the flower spikes of the fragrant bog orchid (the *nochnaya fialka* of Russian poets), a dusky little Fritillary bearing the name of a Norse goddess passed in low, skimming flight ... Still unsated, I pressed forward. At last I saw I had come to the end of the marsh. The rising ground beyond was a paradise of lupines, columbines, and pentstemons. Mariposa lilies bloomed under Ponderosa pines. In the distance, fleeting cloud shadows dappled the dull

---

[3] See Ronald E. Peterson, 'Zemblan: Nabokov's Phony Scandinavian Language', *Vladimir Nabokov Research Newsletter*, 12 (1984), 29–37; John R. Krueger, 'Nabokov's Zemblan', *Linguistics*, 31 (1967), 44–9; and Priscilla Meyer, *Find What the Sailor has Hidden* (Middletown, CT: Wesleyan University Press, 1988), 87–98.

[4] See *LL*, 3.

green slopes above timber line, and the gray and white of Longs Peak. (*SM*, 478–79)

Plants and butterflies linguistically marked as distinctively Northern European (a butterfly named for a Norse goddess, the *nochnaya fialka*) blend seamlessly with plants marked as North American (Mariposa lilies, Ponderosa pines). The landscapes are different (a bog, mountains) but continuous, joined in the narrative by a journey on foot and in Nabokov's biography by his life-long hunt for a new species of butterfly or moth. His success in this hunt makes the familiar unfamiliarity of American nature the goal of his quest: the new species he discovers is one of the family of Pugs, the same 'tiny moths' he hunted at Vyra. The novelty of North American terrain makes it possible for him to achieve his childhood wish. Unlike the 'imposter' robin, Nabokov's Pug is a genuinely new species, but still belongs to the same family as its European counterparts. While for his characters, the landscapes of America and Russia are misleadingly similar, Nabokov's scientific precision and powerful memory make sense from the variety of species, and it is the continents' differences that are misleading.

Nabokov's fusions of Russian and American landscapes perform the same function as his multilingual puns and his oblique historical references: they teach the reader to find not just commonality between unfamiliar cultures but the potential for new discoveries in the conjunction of old and new worlds. Exile, for Nabokov, turns out not to be a loss after all: it is the beginning of a process of recombination and invention that makes the world anew, revealing deep-seated continuities across space and time.

Further Reading

The Russian and American Years

Boyd, Brian, *Vladimir Nabokov: The American Years* (Princeton: Princeton University Press, 1991).
Vladimir Nabokov: The Russian Years (Princeton: Princeton University Press, 1990).
Grayson, Jane, *Illustrated Lives: Vladimir Nabokov* (London: Penguin, 2001).
Schiff, Stacey, *Véra (Mrs. Vladimir Nabokov)* (New York: Random House, 1999).
Wyllie, Barbara, *Vladimir Nabokov* (London: Reaktion, 2010).

Childhood

Clayton, J. Douglas, *Pierrot in Petrograd: Commedia dell'Arte/'Balagan' in Twentieth Century Russian Theatre and Drama* (Montreal & Kingston, ON: McGill-Queen's University Press, 1993).
Goscilo, Helena and Stephen M. Norris (eds.), *Preserving Petersburg: History, Memory, Nostalgia* (Bloomington and Indianapolis, IN: Indiana University Press, 2008).
Kelly, Catriona, *Children's World: Growing Up in Russia, 1890–1991* (New Haven, CT and London: Yale University Press, 2007).
Pyman, Avril, *A History of Russian Symbolism* (Cambridge and New York: Cambridge University Press, 1994).
Rendle, Matthew, *Defenders of the Motherland: The Tsarist Elite in Revolutionary Russia* (Oxford and New York: Oxford University Press, 2010).
Shapiro, Gavriel, *The Tender Friendship and the Charm of Perfect Accord: Nabokov and His Father* (Ann Arbor, MI: University of Michigan Press, 2014).
Smith, Douglas, *Former People: The Final Days of the Russian Aristocracy* (New York: Picador, 2013).

Women

Blackwell, Stephen, *Zina's Paradox: The Figured Reader in Nabokov's Gift* (New York: Peter Lang, 2000).
Herbold, Sarah, '"(I have camouflaged everything, my love)": Lolita and the Woman Reader', *Nabokov Studies*, 5 (1998/1999), 71–98.

Larmour, David H. J., 'Leaving Eurydice in the Dark: The Absent Woman in Nabokov's Early Fiction', *The McNeese Review*, 43 (2005), 1–16.

Nabokov, Vladimir, *Letters to Véra*, ed. and tr. Olga Voronina and Brian Boyd (London: Penguin, 2014).

Rakhimova-Sommers, Elena (ed.), *Nabokov's Women: The Silent Sisterhood of Textual Nomads* (Lanham, MD: Lexington Books, 2017).

Shrayer, Maxim, 'Vladimir Nabokov and Women Authors', *The Nabokovian*, 44 (Spring 2000), 52–63.

Friends and Foes

Berberova, Nina, *The Italics Are Mine*, tr. Philippe Radley (New York: Knopf, 1992).

Karlinsky, Simon (ed.), *Dear Bunny, Dear Voldoya: The Nabokov-Wilson Letters, 1940–1971*, revised edition (Berkeley: University of California Press), 2001.

Nabokov, Vladimir, *Selected Letters 1940–1977*, ed. Dmitri Nabokov and Matthew J. Bruccoli (London: Weidenfeld and Nicolson, 1990).

Shrayer, Maxim, *Bunin i Nabokov: Istoriia sopernichestva* (Moscow: Al'pina non-fikshn, 2014).

Academia

Lodge, David, 'Nabokov and the Campus Novel', *Cycnos*, 24/1 (2007), 223–46.

Moseley, Merritt (ed.), *The Academic Novel: New and Classic Essays* (Chester: Chester Academic Press, 2007).

Nicol, Charles, 'Teaching', in Vladimir E. Alexandrov (ed.), *The Garland Companion to Vladimir Nabokov* (New York and London: Garland, 1995), 705–9.

Smith, Wilson and Thomas Bender (eds.), *American Higher Education Transformed, 1940–2005: Documenting the National Discourse* (Baltimore, MD: Johns Hopkins University Press, 2008).

Wetzsteon, Ross, 'Nabokov as Teacher', in Alfred Appel, Jr. and Charles Newman (eds.), *Nabokov: Criticism, Reminiscences, Translations, and Tributes* (Evanston, IL: Northwestern University Press, 1970), 240–46.

Authorial Persona

Connolly, Julian W., 'From Biography to Autobiography and Back: The Fictionalizing of Narrative Self in *The Real Life of Sebastian Knight*', *Cycnos*, 10/1 (2008), 39–46.

Dolinin, Alexander, *Istinnaia zhizn' pisatelia Sirina: raboty o Nabokove* (St Petersburg: Akademicheskii proekt, 2004).

Field, Andrew, *Nabokov: His Life in Part* (New York: Viking, 1977).

Malikova, Maria, *Nabokov: avtobiografiia* (St Petersburg: Akademicheskii proekt, 2002).

Tammi, Pekka, *Problems of Nabokov's Poetics: A Narratological Analysis* (Helsinki: Suomalainen Tiedekatemia, 1985).

Volkov, Kirill, *Biografiia pisatelia v tvorchestve V. V. Nabokova 1930-kh – nachala 1940-kh godov ("Dar", "Istinnaia zhizn' Sebast'iana Naita", "Nikolai Gogol")*, PhD Thesis, Russian State University for the Humanities, Moscow, 2013.
'From Text to Work: Vladimir Nabokov's Novel *The Real Life of Sebastian Knight* and Its Interpretations', *Social Sciences*, 43/2 (2012), 44–60.

St Petersburg

Annenkov, P. V., *The Extraordinary Decade: Literary Memoirs*, trans. Irwin R. Titunik (Ann Arbor, MI: University of Michigan Press, 1968).
Antsiferov, N. P., *Dusha Peterburga* (Petrograd: Brockhaus-Efron, 1922).
Day, Jennifer Jean, *Memory as Space: The Created Petersburg of Vladimir Nabokov and Iosif Brodskij* (Bloomington: Indiana University Press, 2001).
Giroud, Vincent, *St. Petersburg: A Portrait of a Great City* (New Haven, CN: Beinecke Rare Book & Manuscript Library, Yale University, University Press of New England, 2003).
Lilly, Ian K. (ed.), *Moscow and Petersburg: The City in Russian Culture* (Nottingham: Astra, 2002).
Tammi, Pekka, 'The St Petersburg Text and Its Nabokovian Texture', *Cycnos*, 10 (1993), 123–33.

Cambridge

Brooke, Christopher, *The History of the University of Cambridge, 1870–1990* (Cambridge: Cambridge University Press, 1993).
Trevelyan, George Macaulay, *Trinity College: An Historical Sketch* (Cambridge: Cambridge University Press, 1943).

Berlin

Dolinin, Alexander, '"The Stepmother of Russian Cities": Berlin of the 1920s Through the Eyes of Russian Writers', in Gennady Barabtarlo (ed.), *Cold Fusion: Aspects of the German Cultural Presence in Russia* (New York, Oxford: Berghahn Books, 2000), 225–40.
Engel-Braunschmidt, Annelore, 'Die Suggestion der Berliner Realität bei Vladimir Nabokov', in Karl Schlögel (ed.), *Russische Emigration in Deutschland 1918 bis 1941: Leben im europäischen Bürgerkrieg* (Berlin: Akademie Verlag, 1995), 367–78.
Naumann, Marina Turkevich, *Blue Evenings in Berlin: Nabokov's Short Stories of the 1920s* (New York: New York University Press, 1978).
Shvabrin, Stanislav, 'Nabokov and Heine', *Russian Literature*, LXXIV (III–IV) (2013), 363–416.
Williams, Robert C., *Culture in Exile: Russian Émigrés in Germany, 1881–1941* (Ithaca, NY: Cornell University Press, 1972).
Zimmer, Dieter E., *Nabokovs Berlin* (Berlin: Nikolai, 2001).

Paris

Beaujour, Elizabeth Klosty, *Alien Tongues: Bilingual Russian Writers of the 'First' Emigration*, Studies of the Harriman Institute (Ithaca, NY, and New York: Cornell University Press, 1989).

Benjamin, Walter, *The Arcades Project*, Rolf Tiedemann (ed.), trans. Howard Eiland and Kevin McLaughlin (Cambridge, MA, and London: Belknap Press, 1999).

Casanova, Pascale, *The World Republic of Letters*, trans. M. B. Debevoise, (Cambridge, MA, and London: Harvard University Press, 2004).

Gretchanaia, Elena, *'Je vous parlerai la langue de l'Europe. . .': La francophonie en Russie (XVIIIe-XIXe siècles)* (Brussels: P.I.E. Peter Lang, 2012).

Higonnet, Patrice, *Paris: Capital of the World*, trans. Arthur Goldhammer (Cambridge, MA, and London: Belknap Press, 2002).

Milne, Anne-Louise (ed.), *The Cambridge Companion to the Literature of Paris* (Cambridge: Cambridge University Press, 2013).

East to West Coast

Haegert, John, 'Artist in Exile: The Americanization of Humbert Humbert', in Harold Bloom (ed.), *Lolita* (New York: Chelsea House, 1993), 120–33.

Manolescu, Monica, *Jeux de mondes : L'ailleurs chez Vladimir Nabokov* (Bordeaux: Presses universitaires de Bordeaux, 2010).

Roper, Robert, *Nabokov in America: On the Road to Lolita* (New York: Bloomsbury, 2015).

Sweeney, Susan Elizabeth, '"By Some Sleight of Land": How Nabokov Rewrote America', in Julian W. Connolly (ed.), *The Cambridge Companion to Vladimir Nabokov* (Cambridge: Cambridge University Press, 2005), 65–84.

Switzerland

Bankowski, Monika, Peter Brang, Carsten Goehrke and Robin Kemball (eds.), *Fakten und Fabeln: Schweizerisch-slavische Reisebegegnung vom 18. bis 20. Jahrhundert* (Basel and Frankfurt am Main: Helbing & Lichtenhahn, 1991).

Beaujour, Elizabeth Klosty, 'Devenir Nabokov', *Revue de littérature comparée*, 342 (2012), 139–54.

Lanne, Jean-Claude, 'L'autobiographie chez Vladimir Nabokov: poétique et problématique', *Revue des Études Slaves*, 72 (2000), 405–13.

Shishkin, Mikhail, *Russkaia Shveitsariia: Literaturno-istoricheskii putevoditel'* (Zürich: Pano Verlag, 2000).

Vincent, Patrick, *La Suisse vue par les écrivains de langue anglaise* (Lausanne: Presses polytechniques et universitaires romandes, 2009).

Wood, Michael, 'Nabokov's Late Fiction', in Julian W. Connolly (ed.), *The Cambridge Companion to Nabokov* (Cambridge: Cambridge University Press, 2005), 200–12.

The Russian Literary Canon

Connolly, Julian W., *Nabokov's Early Fiction: Patterns of Self and Other* (Cambridge: Cambridge University Press, 1992).

Dolinin, Alexander, *Istinnaia zhizn' pisatelia Sirina: raboty o Nabokove* (St Petersburg: Akademicheskii proekt, 2004).

'Nabokov as a Russian Writer', in Julian W. Connolly (ed.), *The Cambridge Companion to Nabokov* (Cambridge: Cambridge University Press, 2005), 49–65.

Karlinsky, Simon, 'Nabokov and Chekhov: The Lesser Russian Tradition', in Alfred Appel, Jr. and Charles Newman (eds.), *Nabokov: Criticism, Reminiscences, Translations and Tributes* (Evanston, IL: Northwestern University Press, 1971), 7–16.

Tammi, Pekka, *Russian Subtexts in Nabokov's Fiction: Four Essays* (Tampere: Tampere University Press, 1999).

The Western Literary Canon

Bloom, Harold, *The Western Canon: The Books and Schools of the Ages* (New York: Riverhead Books, 1995).

Coetzee, J. M., 'What is a Classic?' in *Stranger Shores: Literary Essays 1986–1999* (London: Vintage, 2002).

Guillory, John, *Cultural Capital: The Problem of Literary Canon Formation* (University of Chicago Press, 1993).

Hirsch, E. D., *Cultural Literacy: What Every American Needs to Know* (New York: Vintage, 1988).

Kermode, Frank, *The Classic: Literary Images of Permanence and Change* (Cambridge, MA: Harvard University Press, 1983).

Wood, Michael, *The Magician's Doubts: Nabokov and the Risks of Fiction* (London: Pimlico, 1994).

Russian Émigré Publishing

Bethea, David M., *Khodasevich: His Life and Art* (Princeton: Princeton University Press, 1983).

Bethea, David M. and Siggy Frank, 'Exile and Russian Literature', in Marina Balina and Evgeny Dobrenko (eds.), *The Cambridge Companion to Twentieth-Century Russian Literature* (Cambridge: Cambridge University Press, 2011), 195–213.

Johnston, Robert H., *New Mecca, New Babylon: Paris and the Russian Exiles, 1920–45* (Kingston and Montreal: McGill-Queen's University Press, 1988).

Livak, Leonid, *How It Was Done in Paris: Russian Émigré Literature and French Modernism* (Madison, WI, and London: University of Wisconsin Press, 2003).

Mel'nikov, N. G. and O. A. Korostelev (eds.), *Klassik bez retushi: Literaturnyi mir o tvorchestve Vladimira Nabokova* (Moscow: Novoe literaturnoe obozrenie, 2000).

Morard, Annick, *De l'émigré au déraciné : la "jeune génération" des écrivains russes entre identité et esthétique (Paris, 1920–1940)* (Lausanne: L'Âge d'Homme, 2010).

Rubins, Maria, *Russian Montparnasse: Transnational Writing in Interwar Paris* (Basingstoke: Palgrave, 2015).

Schlögel, Karl (ed.), *Russische Emigration in Deutschland: Leben im europäischen Bürgerkrieg* (Berlin: Akademie Verlag, 1995).

American Publishing

Rainey, Lawrence, *Institutions of Modernism: Literary Elites and Public Culture* (New Haven, CT: Yale University Press, 1998).

Turner, Catherine, *Marketing Modernism Between the Two World Wars* (Amherst: University of Massachusetts Press, 2003).

White, Duncan, *Nabokov and his Books: Between Late Modernism and the Literary Marketplace* (Oxford: Oxford University Press, 2017).

Wicke, Jennifer, *Advertising Fictions: Literature, Advertisement and Social Reading* (New York: Columbia University Press, 1988).

Detective Fiction

Auden, W. H., 'The Guilty Vicarage: Notes on the Detective Story, by an Addict', in *The Dyer's Hand and Other Essays* (New York: Random House, 1962), 146–58.

Hoffmann, Josef, *Philosophy of Crime Fiction*, trans. by Carolyn Kelly et al. (Harpenden: No Exit Press, 2013).

Merivale, Patricia and Susan Elizabeth Sweeney (eds.), *Detecting Texts: The Metaphysical Detective Story from Poe to Postmodernism* (Philadelphia: University of Pennsylvania Press, 1999).

Panek, LeRoy L., *Watteau's Shepherds: The Detective Novel in Britain 1914–1940* (Bowling Green, OH: Popular Press, 1979).

Priestman, Martin, *Detective Fiction and Literature: The Figure on the Carpet* (Basingstoke: Macmillan, 1990).

Routley, Erik, *The Puritan Pleasures of the Detective Story* (London: Gollancz, 1972).

Theimer Nepomnyashchy, Catharine, 'Revising Nabokov Revising the Detective Novel: Vladimir, Agatha, and the Terms of Engagement', in Mitsuyoshi Numano and Tadashi Wakashima (eds.), *Revising Nabokov Revising: The Proceedings of the International Nabokov Conference* (Kyoto: The Nabokov Society of Japan, 2010), 163–68.

Samizdat and Tamizdat

Kind-Kovács, Friederike, *Written Here, Published There: How Underground Literature Crossed the Iron Curtain* (Budapest-New York: CEU Press, 2014).

Kind-Kovács, Friederike and Jessie Labov (eds), From *Samizdat to Tamizdat: Transnational Media During and After Socialism* (New York: Berghahn Books, 2013).

Komaromi, Ann, *Uncensored: Samizdat Novels and the Quest for Autonomy in Soviet Dissidence* (Evanston, IL: Northwestern University Press, 2015).

Paperno, Slava and John V. Hagopian, 'Official and Unofficial Responses to Nabokov in the Soviet Union', in George Gibian and Stephen Jan Parker (eds.), *The Achievements of Vladimir Nabokov* (Ithaca, NY: Center for International Studies, 1984), 99–117.

Proffer, Ellendea, 'Nabokov's Russian Readers' in Alfred Appel, Jr. and Charles Newman (eds.), *Nabokov: Criticism, Reminiscences, Translations and Tributes* (Evanston, IL: Northwestern University Press, 1970), 253–60.

Zverev, Alexei, 'Literary Return to Russia', in Vladimir E. Alexandrov (ed.), *The Garland Companion to Vladimir Nabokov* (New York and London: Garland Publishing, 1995), 291–305.

Film and Painting

Appel, Alfred Jr., *Nabokov's Dark Cinema* (Oxford: Oxford University Press, 1974).

Bozovic, Marijeta, *Nabokov's Canon: From Onegin to Ada* (Evanston, IL: Northwestern University Press, 2016).

Leving, Yuri, 'Filming Nabokov: On the Visual Poetics of the Text', *Russian Studies in Literature*, 40/3 (Summer 2004), 6–31.

Shapiro, Gavriel, *The Sublime Artist's Studio: Nabokov and Painting* (Evanston, IL: Northwestern University Press, 2009).

Trubikhina, Julia, 'Struggle for the Narrative: Nabokov and Kubrick's Collaboration on the *Lolita* Screenplay', *Ulbandus*, 10 (2007), 149–72.

Vries, Gerard de, and D. Barton Johnson, *Nabokov and the Art of Painting* (Amsterdam: Amsterdam University Press, 2006).

Wyllie, Barbara, *Nabokov at the Movies: Film Perspectives in Fiction* (Jefferson, NC: McFarland, 2003).

Popular Culture

Balestrini, Nassim W. (ed.), *Nabokov Online Journal*, X [special issue: 'Nabokov and Popular Culture'] (2016).

Leving, Yuri, and John Bertram (eds.), *Lolita: The Story of a Cover Girl: Vladimir Nabokov's Novel in Art and Design* (Blue Ash, OH: Print Books, 2013).

Martiny, Erik (ed.), *Lolita: From Nabokov to Kubrick to Lyne* (Paris: Éditions Sedes, 2009).

Norman, Will, 'Nabokov's Dystopia: *Bend Sinister*, America and Mass Culture', *Journal of American Studies*, 43/1 (2009), 49–69.

Pifer, Ellen, 'The *Lolita* Phenomenon from Paris to Tehran', in Julian W. Connolly (ed.), *The Cambridge Companion to Nabokov* (Cambridge: Cambridge University Press, 2005), 185–99.

Stringer-Hye, Suellen, 'Vladimir Nabokov and Popular Culture', in David H. J. Larmour (ed.), *Discourse and Ideology in Nabokov's Prose* (London: Routledge, 2002), 150–59.

Vickers, Graham, *Chasing Lolita: How Popular Culture Corrupted Nabokov's Little Girl all Over Again* (Chicago: Chicago Review Press, 2008).

Science

Blackwell, Stephen H., *The Quill and the Scalpel: Nabokov's Art and the Worlds of Science* (Columbus: Ohio State University Press, 2009).

Blackwell, Stephen H. and Kurt Johnson, 'Introduction', in their (eds.), *Fine Lines: Vladimir Nabokov's Scientific Art* (New Haven, CT: Yale University Press, 2016), 1–28.

Johnson, Kurt and Steven L. Coates, *Nabokov's Blues: The Scientific Odyssey of a Literary Genius* (Cambridge, MA: Zoland Books, 1999).

Nabokov's Butterflies ed. Brian Boyd and Robert Michael Pyle (Boston, MA: Beacon Press, 2000).

Zimmer, Dieter E., *A Guide to Nabokov's Butterflies and Moths*, Web Version, (2012). URL: www.d-e-zimmer.de/eGuide/PageOne.htm.

Darwinism

Beer, Gillian, *Darwin's Plots: Evolutionary Narrative in Darwin, George Eliot, and Nineteenth-Century Fiction*, 3rd edn. (Cambridge: Cambridge University Press, 2009).

Bethea, David M., 'The Evolution of Evolution: Genes, Memes, Intelligent Design, and Nabokov', *The Superstitious Muse: Thinking Russian Literature Mythopoetically* (Boston, MA: Academic Studies Press, 2009), 127–48.

Boyd, Brian, 'Nabokov, Literature, Lepidoptera' (2000), in *Stalking Nabokov* (New York: Columbia University Press, 2011), 73–99.

Levine, George, *Darwin the Writer* (Oxford: Oxford University Press, 2011).

Todes, Daniel P., *Darwin Without Malthus: The Struggle for Existence in Russian Revolutionary Thought* (New York and Oxford: Oxford University Press, 1989).

Vucinich, Alexander, *Darwin in Russian Thought* (Berkeley: University of California Press, 1988).

Psychoanalysis

Berman, Jeffrey, *The Talking Cure: Literary Representations of Psychoanalysis* (New York: New York University Press, 1985).

Bloom, Harold, *Anxiety of Influence: A Theory of Poetry*, 2nd edition (Oxford and New York: Oxford University Press, 1997).

Couturier, Maurice, *Nabokov's Eros and the Poetics of Desire* (New York: Palgrave Macmillan, 2014).

Green, Geoffrey, *Freud and Nabokov* (Lincoln: University of Nebraska Press, 1988).

Hale, Nathan G. Jr., *The Rise and Crisis of Psychoanalysis in the United States: Freud and the Americans, 1917–1985* (New York: Oxford University Press, 1995).

Meisel, Perry, *The Literary Freud* (London and New York: Routledge, 2006).

Naiman, Eric, *Nabokov, Perversely* (Ithaca, NY: Cornell University Press, 2010).

Shute, Jenefer P. 'Nabokov and Freud: The Play of Power', *Modern Fiction Studies*, 30/4 (Winter 1984), 637–50.

Faith

Alexandrov, Vladimir E., *Nabokov's Otherworld* (New Haven, CT: Yale University Press, 1991).

Boyd, Brian, *Nabokov's Ada: The Place of Consciousness* (Ann Arbor, MI: Ardis, 1985).

Nabokov's 'Pale Fire': The Magic of Artistic Discovery (Princeton: Princeton University Press, 1999).

Connolly, Julian, 'The Otherworldly in Nabokov's Poetry', *Russian Literature Triquarterly*, 24 (1991), 329–39.

Davydov, Sergei, *'Invitation to a Beheading'*, in Vladimir E. Alexandrov (ed.), *The Garland Companion to Vladimir Nabokov* (New York and London: Garland, 1995), 188–203.

"Teksty-Matreški" Vladimira Nabokova (Munich: Otto Sagner, 1982).

Johnson, D. Barton, *Worlds in Regression: Some Novels of Vladimir Nabokov* (Ann Arbor, MI: Ardis, 1985).

Jewish Themes

Diment, Galya, *Pniniad: Vladimir Nabokov and Marc Szeftel* (Seattle: University of Washington Press, 1997).

Leving, Yuri (ed.), *Anatomy of a Short Story: Nabokov's Puzzles, Codes, "Signs and Symbols"* (New York: Continuum, 2012).

Livak, Leonid, *The Jewish Persona in the European Imagination: A Case of Russian Literature* (Stanford, CA: Stanford University Press, 2010).

Shrayer, Maxim, 'Jewish Questions in Nabokov's Art and Life', in Julian W. Connolly (ed.), *Nabokov and His Fiction: New Perspectives* (Cambridge: Cambridge University Press, 1999), 73–91.

Liberalism

Dragunoiu, Dana, *Vladimir Nabokov and the Poetics of Liberalism* (Evanston, IL: Northwestern University Press, 2011).

Nethercott, Frances, *Russian Legal Culture Before and After Communism: Criminal Justice, Politics, and the Public Sphere* (London: Routledge, 2007).

Pipes, Richard, *Struve: Liberal on the Left, 1870–1905* (Cambridge, MA: Harvard University Press, 1970).

Struve: Liberal on the Right, 1905–1944 (Cambridge, MA: Harvard University Press, 1980).

Rosenberg, William G., *Liberals in the Russian Revolution: The Constitutional Democratic Party, 1917–1921* (Princeton: Princeton University Press, 1974).

Walicki, Andrzej, *Legal Philosophies of Russian Liberalism* (Notre Dame, IN: University of Notre Dame Press, 1992).

Totalitarianism

Borejsza, Jerzy W. and Klaus Ziemer (eds.), *Totalitarian and Authoritarian Regimes in Europe: Legacies and Lessons from the Twentieth Century* (New York: Berghahn Books, 2006).

Connolly, Julian W., *Nabokov's 'Invitation to a Beheading': A Critical Companion* (Evanston, IL: Northwestern University Press, 1997).

De la Durantaye, Leland, *Style is Matter: The Moral Art of Vladimir Nabokov* (Ithaca, NY: Cornell University Press, 2007).

Geyer, Michael and Sheila Fitzpatrick (eds.), *Beyond Totalitarianism: Stalinism and Nazism Compared* (New York: Cambridge University Press, 2009).

Larmour, David H. J. (ed.), *Discourse and Ideology in Nabokov's Prose* (London and New York: Routledge, 2002).

Nafisi, Azar, *Reading 'Lolita' in Tehran: A Memoir in Books* (New York: Random House, 2003).

Cold War

Belletto, Steven, *No Accident, Comrade: Chance and Design in Cold War American Narratives* (Oxford: Oxford University Press, 2012).

Isaac, Joel and Duncan Bell (eds.), *Uncertain Empire: American History and the Idea of the Cold War* (Oxford: Oxford University Press, 2012).

Kennan, George F., *American Diplomacy*, expanded edition (Chicago: University of Chicago Press, 1984).

Nadel, Alan, *Containment Culture: American Narratives, Postmodernism and the Atomic Age* (Durham, NC: Duke University Press, 1995).

Norman, Will, *Nabokov, History and the Texture of Time* (London: Routledge, 2012).

Piette, Adam, *The Literary Cold War: 1945 to Vietnam* (Edinburgh: Edinburgh University Press, 2009).

Saunders, Frances Stonor, *The Cultural Cold War: The CIA and the World of Arts and Letters* (New York: The New Press, 2013).

Scott-Smith, Giles, *The Politics of Apolitical Culture: The Congress for Cultural Freedom, the CIA and Post-war American Hegemony* (London: Routledge, 2002).

The Long 1950s

Carosso, Andrea, *Cold War Narratives: American Culture in the 1950s* (Bern: Peter Lang, 2012).

Centerwall, Brandon S., 'Hiding in Plain Sight: Nabokov and Paedophilia', *Texas Studies in Literature and Language*, 32/3 (1990), 468–84.

Goldman, Eric, '"Knowing" Lolita: Sexual Deviance and Normality in Nabokov's *Lolita*', *Nabokov Studies*, 8 (2004), 87–104.

Melody, Michael Edward and Linda Mary Peterson, *Teaching America About Sex: Marriage Guides and Sex Manuals from the Late Victorians to Dr. Ruth* (New York: New York University Press, 1999).

Pitzer, Andrea, *The Secret History of Vladimir Nabokov* (New York and London: Pegasus Books, 2013).

Whiting, Frederick, '"The Strange Particularity of the Lover's Preference": Paedophilia, Pornography, and the Anatomy of Monstrosity in *Lolita*', *American Literature*, 70/4 (1998), 833–62.

Transnationalism

Foster, John Burt, Jr., *Nabokov's Art of Memory and European Modernism* (Princeton: Princeton University Press, 1993).

Levie, Sophie, 'Exile and Assimilation', *Arcadia: Internationale Zeitschrift für Literaturwissenschaft*, 44/2 (2009) 400–19.

Meyer, Priscilla, *Find What the Sailor Has Hidden* (Middletown, CT: Wesleyan University Press, 1988).

Norman, Will and Duncan White (eds.), *Transitional Nabokov* (London: Peter Lang, 2009).

Trousdale, Rachel, *Nabokov, Rushdie, and the Transnational Imagination: Novels of Exile and Alternate Worlds* (New York: Palgrave Macmillan, 2010).

Index

Titles of Nabokov's works are double-posted as main headings and grouped as subheadings under 'Nabokov, Vladimir Vladimirovich (works of)'.

Titles of Russian works are given in English. Transliterated Russian titles from the text are given as main headings with a *See* reference to the English title.

Depending on context, 'Nabokov family' may refer either to Nabokov and his ancestors or to Nabokov, his wife and son.

Illustrations are indicated by page numbers in *italics*.

'About the Contemporary State of Russian Symbolism' (Blok), 128–29
academia. *See also* Cornell University; Harvard University; Stanford University; Trinity College; Wellesley College
overview, 58
academics' interpretations of Nabokov, 122–23
in *Ada*, 23, 53, 57–58
in *Bend Sinister*, 51, 55, 56–57
benefits of, 55–56, 102
the campus novel genre and, 53–56
colleagues categorized in, 56–57
diminishing importance of, 57
in 'An Evening of Russian Poetry', 55
in *Look at the Harlequins!* 57–58
Nabokov's American experience and, 53
Nabokov's need for freedom from, 153
Nabokov's writing experience and, 53–56
in *The Original of Laura*, 58
in *Pale Fire*, 23–24, 51, 52, 54–55, 93
in *Pnin*, 23–24, 51, 53, 54–57, 234–35
protagonists in, 58
in *Speak, Memory*, 57–58
Ada (*Ada, or Ardor*) (Nabokov)
academia in, 23, 53, 57–58
Bruder und Schwester and, 92
the Cold War in, 264
vs. commercialised publishing, 156
corpses presented in the beginning of, 163
death in, 114–15
as detective fiction, 163

emigration and, 275–76
exploration theme in, 106
film practices appropriated in, 180
films as subject matter in, 175, 179–80
Freud in, 217
Hollywood parodied in, 24
Lake Geneva and, 114
in the Long 1950s, 264
multiple media references in, 176, 178
Nabokov's modernism in, 181
Nazism in, 214
over-sexualisation in, 26
photography in, 179
print culture hypertext and, 177–78
psychoanalysis in, 214
relativity theory and, 197, 198
Russian literature and, 25, 127–28
the Russian Revolution in, 252–53
sexual freedom in, 26
Switzerland in, 111
unequal creative partnership, 38–39, 41
US as extension of free world in, 264
US reconfigured in, 104, 105
women in, 38–39, 41
Adamovich, Georgii, 18, 45–46, 121, 125, 142, 144
adaptive landscape, 204–5
'The Admiralty Spire' (Nabokov), 41
Adorno, Theodor, 179–80, 234
Adrian, E. A., 81
Aerosmith (Rock Group), 187n8

'An Affair of Honor' (Nabokov), 182n2
Aikhenvald, Yuli, 17, 36, 146
Aizenberg, Mikhail, 167, 172–73
À la recherche du temps perdu (Proust), 97–98, 197
Aldanov, Mark, 21, 51–52, 140, 146, 228
Alice B. Toklas (Stein), 153
Alizee (singer), 187n8
American literature (overview). *See also* publishing; United States publishing culture; *individual American publishers* , 150–57
Amis, Martin, 27
The Anchor Review (literary journal), 154–55
'Annabel Lee' (Poe), 186
Anna Karenina (Tolstoy), 5–6, 122, 124, 127–28, 231
anti-Semitism. *See The Gift*; Jewishness; *Lolita*; Nazism; Paris; *Pnin*; Shakhovskoy, Zinaida; Wagner, Richard
Appel, Alfred, Jr., 25–26, 49–50, 179, 269
Ardis Publishers, 167, 168–69, 170, 171, 172
Arendt, Hannah, 249–50
Arnheim, Rudolph, 177
'The Art of Literature and Commonsense' (Nabokov lecture), 254–55
asemitism, 229
The Atlantic (*The Atlantic Monthly*) (magazine), 22, 48
Aucassin and Nicolette (French chantfable), 85
Auden, W. H., 155
audition colorée. See synaesthesia
'The Aurelian' (Nabokov), 92, 106
Austen, Jane, 23, 39–40, 121–22
authorial persona
  overview, 59–67
  biography conflicting with, 64–67
  in English-language texts, 59–60
  in *The Gift*, 61–62
  in *The Gift*'s abandoned sequel, 62–63
  in literary biography, 4–5, 59
  manifestations of, 59
  in *Pnin*, 235, 238
  of the post-*Lolita* Nabokov, 64–65
  of Pushkin, 59, 142
  in *The Real Life of Sebastian Knight*, 63–64
  Russian-language origins of, 61–62
  as self-invention, 4–5
  in *Speak, Memory*, 65–66
  in *Speak On, Memory*, 59
  younger émigré writers' interest in, 142
'Autobiographical Study' (Freud), 213–14
'Avant-Garde and Kitsch' (Greenberg), 151, 261
Aveling, Eleanor Marx, 40

'A Bad Day' (Nabokov), 47
Bakhtin, Mikhail, 4, 65, 172n21
Bakst, Leon, 29–30
Bakunina, Ekaterina, 140, 141–42
Balestrini, Nassim Winnie, 6, 182–89
Balibar, Étienne, 256
Balmont, Konstantin, 13, 128–29
Balzac, Honoré, 94–95, 131, 132–33
Barabtarlo, Gennady, 5, 71–79, 200
Barzun, Jacques, 155
The Bath of the Nymphs (Hayez painting), 178
Baudelaire, Charles, 35, 100, 131, 154
Beach, Sylvia, 154
Beat Generation, 269
Beaujour, Elizabeth, 95–96
'Beauty in Nature' (Solovyov), 203
Beckett, Samuel, 26, 132, 181
Been Down So Long, It Looks Like Up to Me (Fariña), 54
Belletto, Steven, 272–73
Bely, Andrey, 14–15, 32–33, 76–77, 206
Bend Sinister (Nabokov)
  academia in, 23, 51, 55, 56–57
  American publication of, 152, 153
  behaviourism parodied in, 199
  the bourgeoisie in, 261–62
  the Cold War and, 261–62, 273–74
  communazist regime in, 22
  communism in, 261–62
  Don Quixote and, 134
  film adaptation of, 182n2
  freedom from pain and, 136
  Freud in, 213, 214–15, 216
  homosexuality in, 266, 272–73
  in the Long 1950s, 266
  mortality questioned in, 220
  Nazism in, 88, 261–62
  novels of ideas and, 97
  paronomasia in, 216
  psychoanalysis in, 214–15
  sexual subversion in, 266
  spies in, 246
  Tate as advocate for, 153
  totalitarianism in, 249, 250–51, 255–56, 273
Benjamin, Walter, 94
Benois, Alexandre, 29–30
Berberova, Nina, 40, 47, 139, 170
Berdiaev, Nikolai, 121, 219
Bergson, Henri, 197, 206
Berkman, Sylvia, 47
Berlin
  overview, 87–93
  in *The Gift*, 87, 123, 144–45
  Hitler's rise to power in, 87
  King, Queen, Knave and, 91

Berlin (cont.)
  Nabokov coming of age in, 16, 95
  Nabokov family in, 5, 16–17, 19,
    20–21, 51
  Nabokov's attitudes toward, 87
  Nabokov's father assassinated in, 32
  Nabokov's income sources in, 17, 31–32, 51
  Nabokov's literary activities in, 16–18, 19, 143
  Nabokov's observational powers in, 92–93
  Nabokov's pre-WW I memories of, 88
  publishing culture in, 6
  Rul' published in, 45
  as Russian emigration centre, 16–17, 89,
    95
  Sirin and, 91
  Soviet Union and, 16–17
  in *Speak, Memory*, 88, 182
  Third Reich's rise in, 5, 19–20
Berman, Jeffrey, 213
Bethea, David M., 1–8, 201–10
Billacois, François, 241
'Biology' (Nabokov), 83–84
Birkin, Jane, 186
Bishop, Morris and Alison, 22, 47, 57
Bitov, Andrey, 27, 167
Blackwell, Stephen H., 7, 193–200
Bleak House (Dickens), 39–40
Bloch, Ernst, 163
Blok, Alexander
  'About the Contemporary State of Russian
    Symbolism', 128–29
  'Dead End', 71–72, 73
  Jewishness represented by, 228
  Nabokov's admiration for, 13, 32–33, 203
  poem of 1 September 1914 by, 77–78
  smoky iris image of, 247–48
  The Stranger, 178
  Symbolism and, 13
  'The Twelve', 15, 77–78
Bloom, Harold, 131–32, 136, 176–77, 217–18
Bobbs-Merrill (publishing house), 152
Body (Bakunina), 141–42
Bohr, Niels, 196–97, 198
Bolshevism. *See also* Russian Revolution
  Blok and, 15
  in the Crimea, 14, 244
  crimes against humanity and, 250
  Nabokov family's direct experience with,
    252–54, 257
  Nabokov's escape from, 1
  Nabokov's hatred of, 252–54
  Nabokov's refusal to speak to sympathisers
    of, 253
  Nazism's similarities with, 250
  October coup of, 14, 240–41

in *Pnin*, 215
  Russian culture destroyed by, 257
  Russian émigré community vs., 257
  Russian liberalism defeated by, 243–44, 257
  US policies against, 257
Bolter, Jay David, 176–77
Bonaparte, Marie, 213
Borges, Jorge Luis, 26, 132
Born to Die (Del Rey), 187n9
Bosch, Hieronymus, 178
bourgeoisie
  in *Bend Sinister*, 261–62
  communism and, 260
  in Flaubert, 260
  Freud and, 212–13
  in *Lolita*, 212–13
  Nabokov's views of, 260
  in *Nikolai Gogol*, 260
  poshlost' of, 260
  Russian liberalism and, 242
  Soviet literature embracing clichés of, 260
Bowers, Fredson, 159
Bowie, David, 185
Boyd, Brian, 11–18, 19–27
  Field's errors critiqued by, 66–67
Bozovic, Marijeta, 6, 174–81
Brando, Marlon, 269
'Breaking the News' (Nabokov), 89–90
Breughel, Pieter, 178
Brier, Evan, 153
Briusov, Valery, 13, 32–33, 71–72, 128–29
Brodsky, Joseph, 170
The Bronze Horseman (Pushkin), 72, 73n3
Brooke, Rupert, 15–16
The Brothers Karamazov (Dostoevsky), 122–23
Bruder und Schwester (Frank), 92
Brzezinski, Zbigniew, 250
Buckle, Henry Thomas, 202
Buckley, William, Jr., 259
Bunin, Ivan
  aestheticism of, 141
  in *The Gift*, 125
  vs. modernism, 47
  Nabokov and, 51–52, 66–67, 144, 146
  Russian émigré literature and, 140
  the Russian literary canon and, 129–30
  Slovo as publisher of, 146
  V. D. Nabokov and, 46–47, 51–52, 66–67, 146
Burnett, Frances Hodgson, 80
Butler, Judith, 41–42
butterflies (Lepidoptera). *See also* Harvard
    Museum of Comparative Zoology; moths
  in 'The Aurelian', 92
  as authorial persona codes, 59
  continuities in exile provided by, 280

'Father's Butterflies', 201, 205, 206, 207, 208
in France, 194n2
Lolita and, 105
mimicry in, 7, 53, 193, 196, 201, 203–4
Nabokov as world expert in, 22–23
Nabokov on, 193–94
'Nabokov's Blues' inspired by, 183n3
Nabokov's collection of, 115
Nabokov's contributions rediscovered, 27,
195, 196
as Nabokov's passion, 12, 32
in St Petersburg, 73n4
species discovered by Nabokov, 22–23, 102–3,
194, 195, 201
in Switzerland, 111, 115
in the US, 22–23, 102–3
in Vyra, 5

Callier, Jacqueline, 36
Cambridge (Massachusetts). *See also* Harvard
University, 23
'Cambridge' (Nabokov essay), 82
Cambridge (University of Cambridge, England).
See also Trinity College, 15–16, 51, 80–86, 253
Camera Obscura (*Kamera Obscura*) (Nabokov).
See also Laughter in the Dark, 19, 124,
152, 175
Caravaggio, Michelangelo Merisi da, 178
Carosso, Andrea, 8, 266–74
'The Cart of Life' (Pushkin), 128
Carver, Beci, 5, 80–86
Casanova, Pascale, 94
The Catcher in the Rye (Salinger), 269
Catherine II (Catherine the Great) (Empress), 13,
95–96
Cerf, Bennet, 154
Cervantes, Miguel de, 131
Chabon, Michael, 27
Chaliapin, Feodor, 29–30
Cheever, John, 24
Chekhov, Anton, 5–6, 29–30, 124, 130, 132–33, 198
Chekhov Publishing House, 147–48, 168, 171, 262
Chernyshevsky, Nikolai
empirical socialism of, 202
in *The Gift*, 19–21, 66, 95, 123, 125–26, 142,
223
in the Russian literary canon, 127
social commitment in art and, 19–20
Solovyov vs., 203
Chervinskaia, Lidiia, 140
chess. *See also The Defense* (*The Luzhin Defense*),
14–15, 31–32, 59–60
Chesser, Eustace, 267–68
Chesterton, G. K, 159, 164, 165
Cheyney, O. H., 150

childhood (Nabokov's childhood)
overview, 28–29
cosmopolitan nature of, 275
early education in, 12, 13
early scientific interests in, 194
'paying-it-forward' patrimony of, 4
religion in, 220
in Russia, 11–14
sexuality in, 88
Chisla (Numbers) (literary journal), 46, 142, 144
Chorny, Sasha (pseudonym for Alexander
Glikberg), 44–45
Chretién de Troyes, 85
Christie, Agatha, 160
'Christmas' (Nabokov), 182n2, 202n1
Chronicle of Current Events (samizdat bulletin),
170–71
CIA (Central Intelligence Agency), 169, 261,
262, 263
cinema. *See* films and film-making
cladistics (phylogenetic systematics), 195, 196n8
'Cloud, Castle, Lake' (Nabokov), 91–92, 93,
250–52
Cobra Starship (pop music group), 187n8
Coetzee, J. M., 264
Cold War
overview, 257–65
Ada and, 264
apolitical aesthetic culture in, 261–62
artistic accomplishment and capitalism in,
261–62
Bend Sinister and, 261–62, 273–74
Chekhov Publishing House and, 171
CIA cultural funding in, 169, 261,
262, 263
communism and, 257, 258–59, 262
as cultural war, 261–62
homosexuality in era of, 270–71
in *Lolita*, 246–47
Nabokov as Cold Warrior, 7–8, 257–58
Nabokov's aesthetics formed during, 259
Nabokov's alleged political indifference and,
264–65
Nabokov's books available in Russia during,
171–72
Nabokov's views on, as mainstream,
258–59, 262
Nabokov's views on, from Switzerland,
259, 263
Nabokov's writing sequence in, 258–59
1919 origins of, 257–58
Pale Fire and, 264, 272–73
sexual orthodoxy in, 271
sexual subversion during, 270–71
US ideology of, 257

Cold War (cont.)
  as US-Soviet hostility, 257–58
  Vietnam War protests in, 259
Commedia dell'arte (Italian theatrical genre),
  29–30
The Common Sense Book of Baby and Child Care
  (Spock), 267
communism
  American intellectuals' views of, 246,
    258–59, 261
  in *Bend Sinister*, 261–62
  as bourgeois, 260
  the Cold War and, 257, 258–59, 262,
    271–73
  in *Invitation to a Beheading*, 258
  Lolita and, 246
  in the Long 1950s, 266, 271–73
  Nabokov's anti-communism, 7–8, 16–17,
    23–24, 26, 47–48, 257, 272
  in *Pale Fire*, 273–74
  publishing issues and, 171
  Sartre and, 96–97
  Sontag on, 250
  in 'Tyrants Destroyed', 258
  US complicity with, 258
  US intellectuals' views of, 250, 262
Complementarity (Bohr), 198
Comte, Auguste, 202
Conclusive Evidence (Nabokov), 62, 152, 272
Confessions (Rousseau), 100
Congress for Cultural Freedom (CCF), 261
Connolly, Julian W., 4–5, 43–50
Conrad, Joseph, 121–22
Constitutional Democratic (CD) Party. *See also*
  Kadet Party, 12, 14, 15, 16, 240–41, 258
Contemporary Annals. See Sovremennye zapiski
contexts of Nabokov (overviews), 1–8, 11–18,
  19–27
'Conversation Piece, 1945' (Nabokov), 91–92,
  231, 253
Cooper, James Fenimore, 44
Cornell University
  Dostoevsky lecture at, 224–25
  Dr. Jekyll and Mr. Hyde lectures at, 158
  Nabokov's professorship at, 22–23, 47–48,
    52–53, 56, 102, 134
  Nabokov's resignation from, 57, 155–56
  Nabokov tenure at, 52
  Pnin and, 54, 57
  professional scientific research abandoned
    at, 194
  students at, vs. Nabokov's sexism, 40
cosmic synchronisation, 33
La Course du fou (French translation of *The
  Defense*), 152

Covici, Pascal, 22
'The Creative Writer' (Nabokov essay),
  259–60, 263
Crimea
  Bolshevism in, 244
  butterfly hunting in, 244
  German army and, 14, 15
  Nabokov family into exile from, 15, 74, 78
  Nabokov family's refuge in, 14
  Nabokov's youth in, 14–15
  Red Army in, 14, 15, 252–53
  Sergei Nabokov in, 14–15
  V. D. Nabokov in Provisional Government of,
    15, 240–41, 244, 246–47
  Yalta Massacre in, 14, 15
Crime and Punishment (Dostoevsky), 73
'Criticism Inc.' (Ransom), 151
Cubism, 99
cultural evolution, 208
cultural meliorism, 13
'Le Cygne' (Baudelaire), 100
Cyrus, Miley, 187n8

Dante Alighieri, 132
Dar. See The Gift
Darwinism. *See also* adaptive landscape
  overview, 201–10
  artistry of nature and, 204, 206, 209
  cultural evolution and, 208
  Darwin-Mendel synthesis, 204
  Descent of Man (Darwin), 203
  The Gift and, 201, 204
  human species advancement and, 210
  intelligent design and, 204, 205
  inverse cause paradigm in, 205–6
  Nabokov's engagement with, 201–10
  On the Origin of Species (Darwin), 202, 203
  in Russia, 202
  Social Darwinism evolving from, 203
  Solovyov and, 202–3
  in *Speak, Memory*, 201
  Symbolism and, 7, 203–4, 206
Davenport, Guy, 135
Davet, Yvonne, 40
Davydov, Sergei, 7, 219–27
Dawkins, Richard, 206, 207–8
'Dead End' (Blok), 71–72, 73
Dead Souls (Gogol), 63, 124
Dean, James, 269
'Death' (Nabokov), 226
Dedalus, 178
'A Defence of Detective Novels'
  (Chesterton), 165
The Defense (*The Luzhin Defense*) (Nabokov)
  Berberova on, 139

chess as dominant theme in, 31–32
film adaptation of, 182n2
French translation and publication of, 152
Iosif Hessen as publisher of, 45, 146
Nabokov's place in Russian literature secured
   by, 19
Paris serialisation of, 95
photo of, *148*
psychological portraiture in, 199
Russian émigré community and, 139
St Petersburg in, 75, 77
Sovremennye zapiski serialisation of, 18, 147
Tolstoy and, 124
Delage-Toriel, Lara, 4, 35–42
de la Mare, Walter, 15–16, 85
Del Rey, Lana, 187, 188
Depression, 19, 150
Descent of Man (Darwin), 203
Despair (Nabokov)
   British publication of, 152
   character portrayal in, 91, 199
   as detective fiction, 6, 20, 162–63
   film adaptation of, 182n2
   French publications of, 152
   human document genre parodied by, 142
   Pushkin in, 125
   Sarthe's review of, 96–97
   the Russian classic tradition in, 122
   Russian Symbolism in, 128
   samizdat editions of, 171
   women in, 41–42
detective fiction. See also *Ada*; *Despair*; *The Eye*;
      Lolita; *The Real Life of Sebastian Knight*
   overview, 158–65
   and the *Bildungsroman*, 165
   blame and guilt in, 161
   crime and investigation as separate elements
      in, 162–65
   'A Defence of Detective Novels', 165
   Dr. Jekyll and Mr. Hyde and, 158–59
   false art vs. true art in, 161–62
   genre automatisms from, 160–61
   in *Lectures on Literature*, 159
   literary style and, 6, 158–59, 165
   modernist evaluations of, 162–63
   Nabokov's attitudes toward, 6, 159–60
   Pale Fire as, 163–64
   as *poshlost*', 158
   Sherlock Holmes and, 159
   Sherlock Holmes detective stories, 159
   and socialist realism, 160–61
   Stein on, 162–63
   'The Typology of Detective Fiction', 162–63
   Wilson on, 160, 161
The Devils (Dostoevsky), 97

Diaghilev, Sergei, 29–30, 129–30
Dickens, Charles, 23, 31, 39–40, 132, 134, 136
'Diet Mountain Dew' (Del Rey), 187n9, 188
Dion, Céline, 187
Discours sur les ombres (Delalande), 226
'A Discovery' (Nabokov), 194, 201
The Discovery of Freedom (Lane), 255
Disintegration of the Atom (Ivanov), 141–42
Disney, Walt, 187–88
Divan Japonais (Toulouse-Lautrec), 178
DNA, 204
Döblin, Alfred, 87
Dobuzhinsky, Mstislav, 29–30
Dobzhansky, Theodosius, 205, 208
Doctor Zhivago (Pasternak), 155
Dolinin, Alexander, 5–6, 62, 121–30, 144–45, 172
Don Quixote (Cervantes)
   Cervantes' artistic sense in, 135
   freedom from pain and, 136
   Nabokov's *Don Quixote* lectures, 133–38
   pain and cruelty in, 134–35
   Shakespeare vs., 135–36
   as three different works, 134–35
'Don't Stand So Close to Me' (The Police),
      186–87
Dos Passos, John, 194
Dostoevsky, Fyodor
   American vs. Russian views of, 133–34
   The Brothers Karamazov, 122–23
   Crime and Punishment, 73
   The Devils (Dostoevsky), 97
   The Double, 122–23
   at Lake Geneva, 113–14
   Nabokov lecture on, 224–25
   Nabokov's indebtedness to, 130
   Nabokov vs., 131
   The Possessed, 122–23
   in the Russian classic tradition, 122–23, 126
   St Petersburg and, 72
   White Nights, 73
   women in, 35
   as writer of literature of ideas, 96–97, 122–23
   younger émigrés adoption of, 141
The Double (Dostoevsky), 122–23
'The Double-Bass Romance' (Chekhov), 124
Doubleday (publishing house), 22, 152,
      154–55
double helix structure, 206
'Double Talk' (Nabokov), 91–92, 231
Doyle, Arthur Conan, 113–14, 159–60
'The Dragon' (Nabokov), 89
Dragunoiu, Dana, 7, 240–48
Dr. Jekyll and Mr. Hyde (Stevenson), 158–59
Drugie berega. See Other Shores
Dunne, J. W., 199–200

East Coast to West Coast. *See Lolita*; *Pale Fire*;
    Pnin; United States
Eberling, Alfred, 71n1, 79
Economic Survey of the Book Industry 1930–31
    (Cheyney), 150
Éditions de la Seine (publishing house), 168
Éditions Victor (publishing house), 168
Einstein, Albert. *See also* relativity theory, 196–98
Eliot, George, 121–22, 131
Eliot, T. S., 24, 126
Emerson, Ralph Waldo, 106
emigration. *See* Berlin; exile; Paris; Russian
    émigré literature; Russian Revolution;
    Switzerland; United States
Eminem (Marshall B. Mathers III), 187
The Empyrean Path (Nabokov), 44–45
The Enchanter (Nabokov), 21n3, 98, 157
Engels, Friedrich, 202
English culture, 19, 20–21, 31, 80–81, 82–83
English language (general)
    bedtime stories in, 36
    Nabokov as a tutor in, 17, 51
    Nabokov's ability to write in, 12
    as refuge from political extremism, 80
    sonorousness of, in Nabokov's poetry, 83
    un-Russianness of, 80
English language (Nabokov's switch to)
    advantages of, 147–49
    as cultural betrayal, 143
    as displacement, 275
    France and, 5, 19
    Nabokov becoming an American writer
        and, 224
    and Russian émigré literature, 145
    the Russian literary canon and, 127–28
    Sirin's disappearance and, 60–61
    in the US, 22
English language (Nabokov's writings in). *See
    also Ada*; *Bend Sinister*; *Glory*; *Lolita*; *Look at
    the Harlequins!*; *Pale Fire*; *Pnin*; *The Real
    Life of Sebastian Knight*; *Speak, Memory*
    authorial persona in, 59–60
    Field's interest in, 49
    impenetrability trope and, 242–45
    male perspective developing in, 42
    Nabokov's control over, 156
    Nabokov's distance from narrators in, 181
    Nabokov's English fluency in, 174
    the Russian classic tradition and, 127–28, 130
    scholarship in, 49
    at Trinity College, 80, 82–83
English literature
    Ada and, 25
    English literary culture, 19
    the great tradition in, 121–22

Nabokov's reading of, 15–16, 30, 31, 32
Nabokov's study of, at Trinity, 84–85
Epstein, Jason, 22, 154–55
Ergaz, Doussia, 36, 154
Eugene Onegin (Pushkin)
    in 'On a Book Entitled *Lolita*', 129
    feedback loops in, 206
    in *The Gift*, 206
    Nabokov's translation and commentary, 22,
        25, 48–49, 52, 95–96, 123, 128, 130
    Repin's painting and, 175
    the Russian literary canon and, 130
    Tchaikovsky's opera of, 175
'An Evening of Russian Poetry' (Nabokov), 55
Evreinov, Nikolai, 29–30
'The Execution' (Nabokov), 71–72, 73
exile. *See also* Berlin; Paris; Russian émigré lit-
    erature; Switzerland; United States
    advantages of, for Nabokov, 116, 276
    comic aspects of, 278–79, 280–81
    continuities in, 279–80, 281–82
    dangers of, 276–78
    as death, 278
    as disorienting in the US, 279–80
    displacement ending in Paris, 100
    Elena Nabokov in, 147, 281
    in *The Gift*, 74, 89–90
    in *Invitation to a Beheading*, 89–90
    linguistic disorientation in, 280–81
    linguistic hybridity and, 280–81
    in *Mary*, 89
    Nabokov's denationalised stance on, 114–15
    Nabokov's indirect presentations of, 276
    in *Pale Fire*, 275–76, 277–79, 281
    in *Pnin*, 89, 275–76, 277, 279–80
    Sirin in, 139
    in *Speak, Memory*, 89, 275–76, 279–82
    as a universal condition, 275
    Vyra estate and, 275
An Experiment with Time (Dunne), 199–200
Eyck, Jan van, 237–38, *238*
The Eye (Nabokov), 19, 125, 164–65

faith
    overview, 219–27
    the cradle image and, 219
    dead dog poem and, 221–22
    in 'Death', 225–27
    death and, 225–27
    dual eternities and, 219
    and the foolscap device, 226–27
    and the gnostic heresy, 222–23
    in God, 219
    God/artist interaction and, 224–25
    life as text and, 225

metapoetic theology in *The Gift*, 224
mud sparrow poem and, 221, 222
Nabokov's apostasy, 222
Nabokov's childhood and, 220
Nabokov's conceptions of, 219–27
Nabokov's death outside of religion, 227
Nabokov's heterodoxy, 221–23
Nabokov's writings' immortality and, 226–27
religious philosophies in Russia, 219
in 'Tolstoy', 224–25
'Fame' (Nabokov), 34
Fantasia (Disney), 187–88
Fariña, Richard, 54
fascism. *See also* Hitler, Adolph; Nazism, 16, 87–88, 91–92, 250, 258
Father (rapper), 187n8
Father Brown detective stories, 159, 164
'Father's Butterflies' (Nabokov), 201, 205, 206, 207, 208
Faulkner, William, 24
Feigin, Anna, 19
Felski, Rita, 2, 4
Fel'zen, Iurii, 140
feminism, 26
Fet, Afanasy, 22, 32–33, 92
Field, Andrew, 4–5, 25, 49, 59, 61, 64, 67
films and film-making. *See also* Kubrick, Stanley; *Lolita*; Lyne, Adrian; popular culture
competing with other media, 175
film adaptations of Nabokov's works, 182n2
as international language, 175
literature and, 175n3
Nabokov's direct involvement with, 179
Nabokov's utilisation of, 178–80, 182
Nabokov's visual imagination and, 175
in Nabokov's writing, 175
photography and, 179
self-referentality in, 179–80
silent films, 179–80
twentieth-century impact of, 176, 178–79
Vertov on, 175
'First Love' (Nabokov), 100–1
Fisher, Amy, 187
Flaubert, Gustave
aestheticism of, 121–22
bourgeois state of mind in, 259–60
Don Quixote in, 136
irony and pathos combined in, 138
Joyce and, 132–33
Lolita and, 42
Madame Bovary, 5–6, 53, 97–98, 133, 154
Nabokov as a Flaubertian, 122–23
Nabokov's canon and, 132–33
in Nabokov's Cornell curriculum, 23
Nabokov's Harvard lectures on, 134

Nabokov's reading of, 32, 94–95, 97–98
obscenity charges against, 154
Proust and, 132–33
as stylist, 42, 97, 121–22
in the Western canon, 5–6
Fleishman, Lazar, 168n9
Les Fleurs du Mal (Baudelaire), 154
Florensky, Pavel, 219
Fog before Dawn (Tolstaia), 228
Fondaminsky, Ilya
concentration camp death of, 95, 251
Nabokov supported by, 146
in Paris with Nabokov, 5, 95, 143
as *Sovremennye zapiski* editor, 18, 46, 145
Formalism (Russian Formalism), 162
Forsythe-Grant, Vera Kathleen, 84
Foster, John Burt, Jr., 5, 94–101
Foster, Michael, 83–84
The Fountainhead (Rand), 255
France. *See also* Paris
butterfly species discovered in, 194n2
Lolita popular music appropriations in, 185–86
Nabokov family in, 17–18, 21
Nabokov's attempts to establish himself in, 20
Nabokov's escapes from, 21, 102
in *Pale Fire*, 115
Frank, Leonhard, 92
Frank, Siggy, 1–8, 139–49
French language, 111
Aucassin and Nicolette and, 85
'Lance' and, 15–16
'Mademoiselle O' written in, 111
Nabokov as tutor in, 51
Nabokov writing in, 94–96
Nabokov writings translated into, 95–96
Swiss governess as teacher of, 96, 100, 112
French literature. *See also* Balzac, Honoré; Beckett, Samuel; Flaubert, Gustave; Proust, Marcel; Robbe-Grillet, Alain; Rousseau, Jean-Jacques; Sartre, Jean-Paul; Stendahl, Maurice, 12, 15–16, 25, 51, 96, 141–42
Freud, Sigmund. *See also* psychoanalysis
in *Ada*, 217
in the American popular imagination, 212
'Autobiographical Study', 213–14
Bloom's support of, 132, 211
in English-language translations of Nabokov, 213
Freudianism, 16, 201, 212–13
Freudian literary critics, 213–14, 216n16
Freudian symbols, 214n13, 215
in German intellectual discourse, 92
Kazin's support of, 212
in *Lolita*, 217

Freud, Sigmund (cont.)
    Nabokov's fame arising simultaneously
        with, 212
    in Nabokov's fiction, 217
    Nabokov's knowledge of, 211–12
    Nabokov's rejection of, 7, 64, 159, 199, 200,
        211, 213
    Pale Fire and, 213
    reading Freud, 217–18
    in *Speak, Memory*, 217
Friedan, Betty, 266–67
Friedrich, Carl, 250
friends and foes
    overview, 43–50
    academics as, 47–48, 51–52, 121
    biographers as, 49, 59, 61, 64, 67
    critics as, 18, 45–46, 48–49, 97, 121, 125, 126
    family and relatives as. See *individual family
        members*
    in *The Gift*, 46
    in 'Lips to Lips', 46
    Lolita and, 49
    at Montreux, 25–26, 49–50
    The Real Life of Sebastian Knight and, 48
    in *The Song of Igor's Campaign* translation,
        47–48
    writers and poets as, 18, 45–47, 51–52,
        61–62, 121
From England at War (V. D. Nabokov), 170
Fromm, Erich, 213
From the Other Shore (Herzen), 74n5
'Funny Face' (The Red Hot Chili Peppers), 187

Gaertner, Eduard, 87
Gainsbourg, Serge, 185–86
Gallimard (publishing house), 152
Garnett, Constance, 40
Gazdanov, Gaito, 140
Genetics and the Origins of Species
    (Dobzhansky), 205
geographical invention in Nabokov's writing,
    103–4
German literary expressionism, 92
Germany. See also *fascism; Hitler, Adolph;
    Nazism; Wagner, Richard*
    the Depression in, 19
    escape from, 100
    Nabokov avoiding travel in, 20
    Nabokov's hatred of, 251
    Nabokov's observational powers in,
        88, 91
    pre-WW I, 88
    in *Speak, Memory*, 93
    Turgenev in, 231
    Véra's insistence on leaving, 20, 251

'Ghetto Model' (Master P), 187n8
Ghostface Killah (rapper), 187n8
The Gift (abandoned sequel to) (Nabokov), 4–5,
    60–61, 62–63
The Gift (Nabokov)
    Adamovich hoaxed in, 46
    anti-Russian sentiments in, 92
    anti-Semitism in, 230–33
    authorial persona in, 61–62
    Berlin in, 87, 123, 144–45
    Bunin in, 125
    The Butterflies and Moths of the Russian Empire
        (fictitious work) in, 207–8
    Chekhov Publishing House publication of,
        147–48
    Chernyshevsky's biography in, 19–21, 66, 95,
        123, 125–26, 223
    Darwinism in, 201, 204
    Delalande in, 226
    double helix space models and, 206
    the elsewhere in, 31
    English translation of, 149
    Eugene Onegin stanza in, 206
    exile theme in, 74, 89–90
    exploration theme in, 106
    fathers and sons theme in, 223
    'Father's Butterflies' addendum to, 201, 205,
        206, 207, 208
    feedback loops in, 206, 207–8
    the future considered in, 207–9
    German culture in, 93
    Gogol in, 125, 223
    great literary traditions in, 125–27
    homosexuality in, 230
    human document genre parodied by, 142
    intelligent design and, 201, 204, 205, 206
    intertextuality in, 230, 232–34
    Invitation to a Beheading in, 31
    Jewishness in, 228–29, 230–34
    Joyce and, 19–20
    life as text and, 225
    metapoetic theology in, 224
    mimicry in, 204, 206
    modernism in, 20
    Moebius strip space models and, 206n7,
        206, 223
    mortality questioned in, 220
    Pilsky's attack on, 126
    poetics of understatement in, 230, 232–33
    in popular music, 185
    Proust challenged by, 19–20
    psychological portrayal in, 199
    Pushkin and, 19–21, 63, 123–24, 125–27,
        207–8, 223
    quantum/particle theory and, 198

relativity theory and, 196–97
Russia in, 74
Russian émigré literature and, 139, 144–45, 149, 231–32
the Russian literary canon and, 125–27
samizdat editions of, 168, *169*, 170
Soviet science and, 207–8
Sovremennye zapiski and, 95, 142, 166
species identity/variations in, 208–9
Symbolism in, 125
as tamizdat, 166, 168
Tolstoy and, 124, 229–30
V. D. Nabokov's death and, 207–8
Vyra estate and, 62
wave-particle duality in, 198–99
women in, 37–38
Gippius, Zinaida, 46, 140
Girls Town (film), 270
Girodias, Maurice, 49, 154, 155, 270
Glikberg, Alexander (Sasha Chorny, pseudonym), 44–45
Glory (Nabokov)
Chekhov and, 124
the elsewhere in, 31
Hitler and, 250
medieval Russian and, 15–16
memories of Russia in, 33–34
samizdat editions of, 171
success of, 19
Switzerland in, 111, 115–16
totalitarianism in, 41, 250–51
women in, 250–51
gnostic heresy, 222–23
The God of the Machine (Paterson), 255
Goethe, Johann Wolfgang von, 93, 221–22
Gogol, Nikolai
Dead Souls, 63, 124
Don Quixote in, 136
in *The Gift*, 125, 223
at Lake Geneva, 113–14
Nabokov as translator of, 22
Nabokov compared with, 122
Nabokov on, 121
Nabokov's Harvard lectures on, 134
Nabokov's indebtedness to, 130
Nabokov's literary style and, 142
Gorianin, Alexander, 166, 168, 170
Gorky, Maxim (Aleksei Maximovich Peshkov), 129
Goudy, Alexander, 85
Gould, Stephen Jay, 204, 206, 208
Government (V. D. Nabokov), 243–44
Graff, Robert de, 150
Grani (publishing house), 45
Grayson, Jane, 59–60

Great Depression, 19, 150
Greenberg, Clement, 151, 261
Grinberg, Roman, 112
The Groves of Academe (Mary McCarthy), 53–54
Grusin, Richard, 176–77
Guadanini, Irina, 20–21, 37n3
'A Guide to Berlin' (Nabokov), 71n1, 89
Gumilev, Nikolai, 32–33, 72
Gutenberg Galaxy (MacLuhan), 177

Hagopian, John V., 167
'The Hapless Girl' (Turgenev), 231
happiness (inestimable happiness), 194
Harper & Brothers (publishing house), 152
Harris, James, 24, 30–31
Harrison, E., 81–82
Harvard Museum of Comparative Zoology, 22, 52, 102, 194–95, 201, 204–5, 209
Harvard University, 22, 23, 47–48, 52, 134
Hawthorne, Nathaniel, 188
Hayek, F. A., 255
Hayez, Francesco, 178
Hegel, Georg Wilhelm Friedrich, 93, 260
Heine, Heinrich, 92
Heisenberg, Werner, 196–97, 198
Hemingway, Ernest, 94
Hemon, Aleksandar, 27
Hennig, Will, 195–96
Henry Holt (publishing house), 152, 153
A Hero of Our Time (Lermontov), 52, 129, 130
Herzen, Alexander, 74n5
Hessen, Georgii, 45, 63–64, 65
Hessen, Iosif , 17, 45, 145, 146, 247
Hessen, Sergei, 244–45
Higonnet, Patrice, 94–95
Histoire de Melody Nelson (Gainsbourg), 185–86
Hitchcock, Alfred, 264
Hitler, Adolf
Czechoslovakia threatened by, 21
Glory and, 250
Nabokov's hatred of, 88, 91–92
rising to power, 16, 19–20, 87
Russia invaded by, 23
Stalin allied with, 7–8
V. D. Nabokov's assassination and, 251
Hofstadter, Douglas, 210
Hollywood Production Code, 268
Holocaust, 24, 229, 233, 234–35
'Home' (Nabokov), 80, 82
homophobia, 271–72, 273–74
homosexuality
in *Bend Sinister*, 266, 272–73
in Cold War era, 272–73
in *The Gift*, 230
in the Kinsey Report, 268

homosexuality (cont.)
in the Long 1950s, 268, 271–72
Nabokov's aversion to, 43–44, 272
in *Pale Fire*, 266, 272–73
of Sergei Nabokov, 43–44, 272
Horkheimer, Max, 179–80
Housman, A. E., 15–16, 85
human document (literary genre), 45n2,
141–42
Humphrey, N. K., 207
Hunter, Gordon, 150

Ianovsky, Vasily, 140
Icarus, 178
'I'd Rather Be High' (Bowie), 185
Imitation of Life (film), 270
impenetrability, 244–45
inestimable happiness, 194
Infancy Gospel (attributed to the Apostle
Thomas), 222
Infinite Jest (Wallace), 181
In Search of Lost Time (Proust). See *Á la recherche
du temps perdu*
intelligent design, 204, 205
intertextuality, 105–6, 130, 186, 230,
232–34
Invitation to a Beheading (Nabokov)
Commedia dell'arte influences in, 29–30
exile theme in, 89–90
film adaptation of, 182n2
in *The Gift*, 31
gnostic heresy in, 222–23
impenetrability and, 244–45
liberalism in, 245
mortality questioned in, 220
mystery as then norm in, 165
published by the Proffers, 168–69
samizdat editions of, 168–69
smuggled into the Soviet Union, 169
Soviet Union in, 20
as tamizdat, 166, 168
totalitarianism in, 251–52, 258
Irving, Washington, 188
Isolde (Odoevstseva), 46
Ivanov, Georgii, 18, 46, 121, 141–42
Ivan Riabov: An Archangel Fisherman
(Kukol'nik), 125

Jakobson, Roman, 47–48, 52
James, Henry, 24, 110, 121–22
James, William, 30, 199
Jameson, Frederic, 176, 181
Janelli, Altragracia de, 36
Jarrell, Randall, 53–54

Jewishness
overview, 228–39
anti-Semitism and, 228–29, 230–33, 232n9
asemitism and, 229
ethical standards relating to, 229–30, 234, 235,
237, 239
in *The Gift*, 228–29, 230–34
Jewish characters in Nabokov's fiction, 229
the Jewish question and, 229–30
as a literary device, 228–39
Nabokov/Aldanov debate and, 228
Nabokov's aesthetic approach to, 229–30
Nabokov's difficulties with, 7, 228–29
poetics of absence and, 230, 234, 235, 239
poetics of understatement and, 230
Proust and, 228
Pushkin and, 228
readership difficulties and, 228, 230, 231,
232–33
in 'Signs and Symbols', 234, 235, 237
of Véra, 7, 17, 19–20, 229
Joel, Billy, 187
John Long (publishing house), 152
Johnson, D. Barton, 92
Joyce, James
censorship issues, 153–54
as dilemma for Nabokov, 181
Flaubert and, 132–33
Freud and, 212
The Gift and, 19–20
modernism in, 88, 137
Nabokov's canon and, 131, 132
in Nabokov's curriculum, 23
Ulysses, 19–20, 98, 153–54, 178
in the Western canon, 5–6
'The Jubilee' (Nabokov), 90
'Junge Leiden' (Heine), 92

Kadet Party, 145, 240–41, 242, 243–44, 247, 252
Kafka, Franz, 23, 88, 132
Kahane, Jack, 154
Kamera Obscura. See Camera Obscura; *Laughter
in the Dark*
Kant, Immanuel, 242–43, 244
Karamzin, Nikolai, 113–14
Karlinsky, Simon, 25–26, 39
Karpovich, Mikhail, 47, 56
Kennan, George F., 257
Kerouac, Jack, 110
Keys to Lolita (Carl Proffer), 171, 172
Khodasevich, Vladislav
aestheticism of, 141
Berberova and, 40
'The Life of Vasily Travnikov', 46

Nabokov as translator of, 22
Nabokov's admiration of, 144, 146
as Nabokov's literary ally, 18
in Paris with Nabokov, 5, 95
on poets' awareness of their times, 1
as Russian émigré writer, 140
as *Sovremennye zapiski* editor, 45–46
wife's concentration camp death, 251
on writers portrayed in fiction, 61–62
King, Queen, Knave (Nabokov), 17–18, 38, 45, 91, 123, 146, 182n2
Kinsey, Alfred, 268–69
Kinsey reports, 268–69, 271
Kipling, Rudyard, 31
Kizevetter, Alexander, 242
Kjellström, Nils, 40
Komaromi, Ann, 6, 166–73
Korean War, 253
Koussevitzky, Serge, 29–30
Kraus, Karl, 211
Kubrick, Stanley
　Lolita screen rights acquired by, 24
　in Nabokov's dreams, 30–31
　Nabokov's narrative aesthetics imitated by, 184
　Nabokov's screenplay adapted by, 24, 155–57, 180
　Oscar nomination for *Lolita* screenplay, 156–57
　as Uncle Ruka reincarnation, 30–31
Kukol'nik, Nestor, 125
Kuzmin, Mikhail, 32–33
Kuzovkin, Gennady, 171n16

Lacan, Jacques, 217
Lady Chatterley's Lover (Lawrence), 133–34
'The Lady with the Little Dog' (Chekhov), 124
Lake Geneva, Switzerland, 5, 112, 113, 114
Lamarck, Jean-Baptiste, 209–10
'Lance' (Nabokov), 15–16, 26, 106
Landscape with the Fall of Icarus (Breughel painting), 178
Lane, Allen, 150
Lane, Rose Wilder, 255
Langley, John Newport, 84
Lanz, Henry, 51–52
Lapsley, G. T., 82
Larmour, David, 41–42
The Last and the First (Berberova), 40
'The Last Lover' (Trilling), 155
Laughlin, James, 22, 40, 152
Laughter in the Dark (Nabokov's translation of *Kamera Obscura*), 38, 111, 124, 175, 182n2
Lawrence, D. H., 121–22, 211
Leavis, F. R., 121–22

Lectures on Literature (Nabokov), 159, 165, 214
Leiris, Michel, 96
Lenin, Vladimir, 16, 240–41, 243–44, 246–47, 261
'The Leonardo' (Nabokov), 91–92, 251–52
Lepidoptera. *See* butterflies (Lepidoptera)
Lermontov, Mikhail
　Adamovich's advocacy of, vs. Pushkin, 18, 45
　ekphrasis used by, 178
　A Hero of Our Time, 52, 129, 130
　Nabokov as translator of, 22
　Nabokov's early passion for, 32–33
　Nabokov's indebtedness to, 130
　St Petersburg and, 72
　younger émigrés adoption of, 141
Levin, Harry, 47
liberalism
　overview, 240–48
　Bolshevik defeat of, 243–44, 257
　impenetrability and, 244–45
　as individual liberty, 242–43
　in *Invitation to a Beheading*, 245
　as lichnost', 242–45
　Nabokov father/son relations and, 240–41
　of Nabokov's education, 13, 28
　Nabokov's equivocal views on, 243–44
　Nabokov's fiction and, 241
　Nabokov's political ambivalence and, 241–42
　of *Rul'*, 16
　in Russia, 12, 241–44, 255
　in the US, 245–47, 253–54, 255, 262–63
　of V. D. Nabokov, 7, 11–12, 229, 240–41, 242, 258
lichnost' (personhood; individualism; individual identity), 242–45
Life and Works of Edgar Allan Poe (Bonaparte), 213
Life of Chernyshevsky. See The Gift
'The Life of Vasily Travnikov' (Khodasevich), 46
'Lips to Lips' (Nabokov), 46, 144
literary biography, 59, 255
Little Lord Fauntleroy (Burnett), 80
Livak, Leonid, 7, 228–39
Lodge, David, 54
'Lolita' (Del Rey), 187, 188
Lolita (Kubrick film)
　cinematic equivalents sought in writing of, 180
　in Del Rey's 'Lolita', 187–88
　dream interpretation in, 214
　Humbert undermined in, 182–83
　Lolita impacting the popular imagination, 184
　vs. Lyne's *Lolita*, 184, 185
　murder foregrounded in, 184
　Nabokov's screenplay for, 24, 155–56, 180, 183
　royalties from, 155–56
　success of, 185

Lolita (Lyne film)
  as box-office failure, 184
  in Del Rey's 'Lolita', 187–88
  vs. Kubrick's *Lolita*, 184, 185
  Lolita as complicit in, 184–85
  musical score of, 184–85
  screenplay of, 184
  sympathy for Humbert in, 183–85
'Lolita' (MC Lars), 187
Lolita (Nabokov), 127–28
  academia in, 51, 54–57
  anti-Semitism in, 108
  Appel's annotation of, 49–50
  Ardis edition of, 167, 172
  art/life theory in afterword to, 137–38
  automobile culture in, 108–10
  begun in Paris, 98, 134
  'On a Book Entitled *Lolita*', 129–30
  the bourgeoisie in, 212–13
  butterfly hunting and, 105
  censorship issues, 98, 154–55
  the Cold War in, 246–47
  Commedia dell'arte influences in, 29–30
  commercialised publishing and, 156
  cultural capital of, 6
  as detective fiction, 163
  emigration and, 275–76
  The Enchanter as precursor to, 98
  exploration theme in, 106
  film adaptation challenges in, 183–84
  films as subject matter of, 175, 179–80
  financial security provided by, 24, 112
  French literary influences on, 15–16
  French reception of, 98
  Freudian symbols in, 215, 217
  Girodias as publisher of, 49, 154, 155, 270
  heroes absent from, 85
  impenetrability and, 244–45
  intertextuality in, 105–6, 186
  Lolita as a meme, 188
  Lolita in popular music, 185–89, 187n8
  Lolita's perspective assumed in, 183
  in the Long 1950s, 266, 269–70
  Madame Bovary and, 133
  mothers in, 35–36
  Nabokov established as an American writer by, 23
  Nabokov on fame of, 35
  Nabokov's control over critical reception and, 145
  Nabokov's essay on, 127–28
  Nabokov's promotion of, 270
  new media representations of, 188–89
  novel spin-offs from, 183n3
  Olympia Press and, 98, 154

  Orlova's reading of, 172
  photography in, 179
  Poe's 'Annabel Lee' and, 186
  popular culture adaptations of, 182–89
  poshlost' in, 214
  psychoanalysis and, 214, 271
  psychological research for, 199
  publishers' double game with, 153, 155
  reader/author dialogue in, 172
  Russian Symbolism and, 128–29
  Russian translation of, 25, 168
  samizdat editions of, 167, 168, 169–70, 171
  sexual orthodoxy in, 267
  sexual subversion in, 266, 269–71
  stereotypes of Lolita, 183, 186, 187n8
  success of, 7–8, 24, 35, 57, 156, 182
  surrealism and, 186
  teenage delinquency and, 269–70
  theatrical adaptations of, 182n1
  tourist culture in, 107–8
  Transcendentalism and, 106
  US liberalism and, 245–47, 262–63
  US publication of, 150–51, 152
  US reception of, 24, 49, 98
  US reinvented in, 5, 103–4
  US travels and, 5, 23, 103–4, 105–6, 107–8
  victimisation in, 182–83
  women in, 35–36, 41–42
'Lolita' (Prince), 187n8
'Lolita' (The Veronicas), 187n8
Lolita Go Home (Birkin), 186–87
London. *See also* Cambridge (University of Cambridge, England); Trinity College (University of Cambridge), 20, 152, 240
Long 1950s
  overview, 266–74
  in *Ada*, 264
  in *Bend Sinister*, 266
  characteristics of, 266
  communism in, 266, 271–73
  homosexuality in, 268, 271–72
  in *Lolita*, 266, 269–70
  in *Pale Fire*, 266
  in *Pnin*, 266
  private vs. orthodox sexuality in, 268, 270–71
  sexual orthodoxy in, 266–68, 271
  sexual subversion in, 266, 268, 269, 270–71, 273
  teenagers as sociological category in, 269
Long Face (Sharshun), 141–42
Look at the Harlequins! (Nabokov)
  academia in, 57–58
  Commedia dell'arte influences in, 29–30
  Heine and, 92
  St Petersburg in, 76
  Soviet Union imagined in, 34

Speak, Memory and, 25
Switzerland in, 111, 115–16
women in, 36, 37, 41–42
Lord Byron, 113–14, 115–16
Lo's Diary (Pera), 183n3
Lossky, Nikolai, 219
Lotman, Yuri, 4
Love without Fear (Chesser), 267–68
Lowell, Robert, 25
Lukash, Ivan, 16–17, 45
The Luzhin Defense. See The Defense (The Luzhin Defence)
Lynch, Joan Driscoll, 184–85
Lyne, Adrian. *See Lolita* (Lyne film)
Lyon, Sue, 184, 185

Macdonald, Dwight, 261
MacLuhan, Marshall, 177
Madame Bovary (Flaubert), 5–6, 53, 97–98, 133, 154
'Mademoiselle O' (Nabokov), 96, 100, 111, 112, 182n2
Madonna and Child with Canon van der Paele (van Eyck painting), 237–38, *238*
Malikova, Maria, 4–5, 59–67
Malraux, André, 96–97, 99
'The Man in the Passage' (Chesterton), 164
Mann, Thomas, 131, 132
Manolescu, Monica, 5, 102–10, 116
Man's Fate (Malraux), 97
Mansfield Park (Austen), 39–40
'The Man Stopped' (Nabokov), 76n9
'The Man Who Dreamed of Fairyland' (Yeats), 86
Mare, Walter de la, 15–16, 85
Margolin, Olga, 251
A Marriage Manual (Hannah and Abraham Stone), 267
Marx, Karl, 159, 202, 259–60
Marxism, 243, 255, 261
Mary (Nabokov)
Berlin in, 87, 91
Chekhov and, 124
dreams vs. Freudian symbolism in, 215
exile theme in, 89
Freudian paronomasia in, 215–16
Iosif Hessen as publisher of, 45, 146
Maschenka film adaptation and, 182n2
as Nabokov's first novel, 17–18
published by the Proffers, 168–69
relativity theory in, 196–97
St Petersburg and, 76–77
smuggled into the Soviet Union, 169
Tolstoy and, 124
Maschenka (Nabokov). *See Mary*

Mason, James, 257
Master P (rapper), 187n8
Mathers, Marshall B., III, 187
Matthews, William, 183n3
Mayne Reid, Thomas, 31, 44
Maysky, Ivan, 253
McAfee, Mildred, 23
McCarthy, Joseph, 23, 271–72
McCarthy, Mary, 53–54, 160
McCarthy Era, 23
McDonald, Dwight, 156
MC Lars (Andrew Nielsen) (rapper), 187
MCZ. *See* Harvard Museum of Comparative Zoology
media issues. *See* visual imagination
Melville, Herman, 24
memes, 188, 206, 207–8
Memoirs of Hecate County (Wilson), 154
Mendel, Gregor, 204
Men'shov, V., 169–70
La Méprise (Despair) (Nabokov), 152
Merezhkovsky, Dmitri, 140
Mesures (literary journal), 100
Metalious, Grace, 269
metapoetic theology, 224–27
Meyerhold, Vsevelod, 29–30
M.I.A. (Mathangi Arulpragasam) (rapper), 185
Miauton, Cécile (Swiss governess). *See also* 'Mademoiselle O', 112
Michaux, Henri, 96
Miliukov, Pavel, 16, 242
mimicry, 7, 53, 193, 196, 201, 204, 206
Minden, George, 169
Minton, Walter, 40, 155
Missmann, Max, 87
modernism
in *Ada*, 181
Bunin vs., 47
commercial publishing and, 153
detective fiction and, 162–63
émigré resistance to, 145
Freud and, 212
in *The Gift*, 20
human document genre in, 141–42
in Joyce, 137
Laughlin's as publisher and, 152–53
Nabokov and, 88, 126, 181
in Proust, 137
Russian émigré literature and, 141
the Russian literary canon reinterpreted via, 141–42
Tate and, 153
un-Russianness of, 141
vs. US publishing culture, 151
Moebius (Möbius) strip, 206n7, 206, 223

'Moi. Lolita' (Alizee), 187n8

Moleschott, Jacob, 202

Montreux, Switzerland
friends and foes at, 25–26, 49–50
literary fame of, 113–14
Montreux Palace Hotel in, 5, 24, 275–76
Nabokov's last meeting with Wilson at, 48
as Nabokov's permanent residence, 5, 24,
275–76

Morard, Annick, 5, 111–17

Morricone, Ennio, 184–85

Moscow, 74, 140

Moscow Psychological Society, 203

'The Mother' (Nabokov), 220–21

moths, 36, 160, 202n1, 204, 206, 282

Multimedia Modernism (Jameson and
Murphet), 176

Muromtsev, Sergei, 242

Murphet, Julian, 176

Nabokov family. *See also* Berlin; France; Prague;
Switzerland; United States
anglophilia of, 31
Bolshevist regime's direct experience with,
252–54, 257
as butterfly enthusiasts, 202
Crimean refuge for, 14
Eastern Orthodox religion of, 220
liberalism of, 11
in London, 15–16
Nabokov as defender of, 49–50
on the *Nadezhda*, 78n15
under Nazi threat, 19–20, 21, 87–88, 229, 233
as nurturing environment, 201–2
permanent exile of, 15, 74, 78–79
St Petersburg residence of, 29, 31–32
social class and wealth of, 3, 11–12, 28–29

Nabokov, Dmitri Nikolaevich (grandfather), 12

Nabokov, Dmitri Vladimirovich (son), 19–21, 22,
24–25, 87–88, 111, 157

Nabokov, Elena Ivanovna (mother)
butterfly metaphors and, 201–2
émigré writers' books kept by, 147
in exile, 147, 281
mnemonic blending by, 281
mysticism of, 30, 201–2
Nabokov's memories and, 17, 28–34
Nabokov's relationship with, 36, 43
in Prague, 17–18, 20–21
religious faiths of, 220
social class and wealth of, 11–12
synaesthesia of, 36
WWI, service during, 13

Nabokov, Elena Vladimirovna (sister). *See*
Sikorski, Elena

Nabokov, Kirill (brother), 39, 43–44

Nabokov, Nicolas (cousin), 22, 152, 261

Nabokov, Sergei (brother)
childhood of, 12
concentration camp death of, 87, 94, 247, 251,
272, 273
in the Crimea, 14–15
early education of, 12, 28
homosexuality of, 43–44, 272
Nabokov's relationship with, 43–44
The Real Life of Sebastian Knight and, 44
'Scenes from the Life of a Double Monster'
and, 44
in *Speak, Memory*, 272

Nabokov, Véra (Véra Slonim) (wife)
dedication to Nabokov, 4, 17, 37, 39
employment during the Depression, 19
escaping Germany, 19–20
inscriptions to, 36–37
Jewish identity of, 7, 17, 19–20, 229
marriage to Nabokov, 17
as a muse, 37
as Nabokov's chauffeur, 5, 103
on Nabokov's poetry, 219
on Nabokov's Soviet readership, 168
Nabokov works published posthumously
by, 157
under Nazi threat, 19–20, 21, 87–88, 229
and Sirin, 36–37
as unequal creative partner, 38, 39
Vera Forsythe-Grant and, 84

Nabokov, Vladimir Dmitrievich (father). *See also*
Constitutional Democratic (CD) Party
as advocate for the poor, 202
assassination of, 16, 20, 32, 85, 87–88,
247–48, 276
Bunin and, 46–47, 51–52, 66–67, 146
in the Crimea, 14–15, 240–41, 243–44, 246–47
cultural meliorism concept of, 13
From England at War, 170
escaping Bolshevist Russia, 252
Government, 243–44
idealism and, 243
imprisonment of, 13
legal profession of, 11–12, 202
liberalism of, 7, 11–12, 229, 240–41,
242, 258
library of, 30, 31–32
on *lichnost's* failure, 243
Nabokov's literary interests nurtured by, 32
Nabokov's respect for, 32, 62, 202
neo-idealism of, 202
political activities of, 12, 14, 15, 243–44
The Provisional Government, 243–44
as *Rech* co-publisher, 77

as *Rul'* editor, 16, 145
Russian Jews protected by, 21
the Russian Revolution and, 14, 15, 240–41
social awareness of, 29
'Soviet Rule and Russia's Future', 240, 243
in WWI, 13, 77
Nabokov, Vladimir Vladimirovich. *See also*
  academia; authorial persona; Berlin;
  Bolshevism; bourgeoisie; butterflies; chess;
  childhood; Cold War; detective fiction;
  Freud, Sigmund; friends and foes; *individual family members*; Jewishness; liberalism;
  modernism; Nazism; Paris; popular culture;
  psychoanalysis; publishing; Russian émigré
  literature; Russian language writing;
  Russian literary canon; St Petersburg;
  samizdat; science; Soviet Union;
  Switzerland; tamizdat; women
achievements of, summarized, 22
anglophilia of, 31
athleticism of, 13, 31–32, 81
Bunin and, 51–52, 66–67, 144, 146
as a Cold Warrior, 7–8, 257–58
contempt for cruelty in, 256
contexts of, 1–8, 11–18, 19–27
cultural meliorism and, 13
death in late writings of, 114–15
domineering attitudes of, 64, 200
early education of, 12, 13, 28, 51
early romantic interests of, 13–14, 100–1
English literature read by, 15–16
faith and, 7
vs. feminism, 26
as a genius, 2
grave of, *227*, 227
heroes absent from writings of, 85
hoaxes perpetuated by, 46, 144
honour as a virtue for, 44
human document genre parodied by, 142
independence/individuality of, 11, 16–17,
  23–24, 27, 28–29, 43, 214, 249, 256
literary legacy of, 157
in the Long 1950s, 8
memories' significance to, 28–34
otherworldliness of, 7, 201
photos of, 108, *109*
political indifference of, as expressed by, 7,
  64–65, 87, 240, 241, 249
political indifference of, called into question,
  24n4, 87, 249–56, 264–65
political realities sublimated into poetics
  by, 248
readers of, good and bad, 1, 64, 229–30, 231
on reading, 166–67
residence regions and periods, summarized, 71

Russian literary influences on, 15–16
self-respect of, 49–50
on sensuous thought, 136–37
statue of, *60*
synaesthesia of, 30, 36, 174
time and space conceptions of, 33
time-vision of, 195, 197
un-Russianness of, 5–6, 121, 143, 174
as a womanizer, 13–14, 20–21, 37n3
Nabokov, Vladimir Vladimirovich (as a poet)
the beyond as theme of, 219
'Biology', 83–84
Blok and, 15, 32–33, 71–72, 73,
  203
Christian themes in, 220–21
dead dog poem by, 221–22
'A Discovery', 194, 201
early poetry of, 14–15
Elena Nabokov's dedication to, 36
in Field's biography, 66
'First Love', 100–1
first publications of, 13–14
gnostic heresy and, 222
'Home', 80, 82
'The Mother', 220–21
mud sparrow poem by, 221, 222
'No Matter How', 254–55
'On Golgotha', 220–21
'Pale Fire'. *See Pale Fire* as a main heading
'Revolution', 252
'Rulers', 254–55
Russian memories retained by, 34
Russian poetry's influence on, 32–33
'Slava', 221
'Tolstoy', 224–25
translated into English, 32
'Unfinished Draft', 225
'The University Poem', 80
'Ut Pictura Poesis', 75–76n8
Véra and, 17
Verses, 170
visual imagination of, 6, 174–81
writing poetry during gun battles, 14
Yalta Massacre and, 15
Nabokov, Vladimir Vladimirovich (works by)
*Ada, or Ardor: A Family Chronicle. See Ada, or
  Ardor* as a main heading
'The Admiralty Spire', 41
'An Affair of Honor', 182n2
'The Art of Literature and Commonsense'
  (lecture), 254–55
'The Aurelian', 92, 106
'A Bad Day', 47
Bend Sinister. See Bend Sinister as a main
  heading

Nabokov, Vladimir (cont.)
  'Biology', 83–84
  'On a Book Entitled *Lolita*' (essay), 127–28, 129–30
  'Breaking the News', 89–90
  'Cambridge' (essay), 82
  Camera Obscura, 19
  'Christmas', 182n2, 202n1
  'Cloud, Castle, Lake', 91–92, 93, 251–52
  Conclusive Evidence, 62, 272
  'Conversation Piece, 1945', 91–92, 231, 253
  'The Creative Writer' (essay), 259–60, 263
  The Defense. See The Defense as a main heading
  Despair. See Despair as a main heading
  'A Discovery', 194, 201
  'Double Talk', 91–92, 231
  'The Dragon', 89
  The Empyrean Path, 44–45
  The Enchanter, 21, 98, 157
  Eugene Onegin English translation and commentary. *See Eugene Onegin* as a main heading
  'An Evening of Russian Poetry', 55
  'The Execution', 71–72, 73
  The Eye, 19, 89–90, 164–65
  'Fame', 34
  'Father's Butterflies', 201, 205, 206, 207, 208
  'First Love', 100–1
  The Gift. See The Gift as a main heading
  The Gift (sequel to, abandoned), 60–61, 62–63
  Glory. See Glory as a main heading
  'Gogol' (essay), 124
  'A Guide to Berlin', 71n1, 89
  'Home', 80, 82
  Invitation to a Beheading. See Invitation to a Beheading as a main heading
  'The Jubilee', 90
  King, Queen, Knave, 17–18, 38, 45, 91
  'Lance', 15–16, 26, 106
  Laughter in the Dark, 38
  Lectures on Literature, 159, 165, 214
  'The Leonardo', 91–92, 251–52
  'Lips to Lips', 46, 144
  Lolita. See Lolita as a main heading
  Look at the Harlequins! See Look at the Harlequins! as a main heading
  'Mademoiselle O', 96, 100, 111, 112, 182n2
  'The Man Stopped', 76n9
  Mary. See Mary as a main heading
  'The Mother', 220–21
  Nabokov's Dozen, 98–101
  Nikolai Gogol, 52, 125, 251, 255, 258, 260
  'No Matter How', 254–55
  'Notes for the Texture of Time', 198

'On Golgotha', 220–21
The Original of Laura, 31–32, 58, 92, 157, 174–75
Other Shores, 71–72
Pale Fire. See Pale Fire as a main heading
'The Passenger', 161–62
Pnin. See Pnin as a main heading
The Pole, 106
'The Proletarian Novel' (lecture), 151
'Pushkin, or the Real and the Plausible', 64, 96
The Real Life of Sebastian Knight. See The Real Life of Sebastian Knight as a main heading
'Recruiting', 91
The Return of Chorb, 45
'Revolution', 252
'Rulers', 254–55
'A Russian Beauty', 89–90
'Scenes from the Life of a Double Monster', 44
'Signs and Symbols', 165, 217, 234, 235–37
'Skazka'/'A Nursery Tale', 182n2
'Slava', 221
'A Slice of Life', 38
'Solus Rex', 21, 62–63
The Song of Igor's Campaign (translation), 15–16, 22, 47–48, 52, 130
Speak, Memory. See Speak, Memory as a main heading
Speak On, Memory (Nabokov proposed sequel), 59
'Spring in Fialta', 98–99
'A Stroll with J.-J. Rousseau', 113n9
Strong Opinions, 89, 99, 117, 145, 159, 257
'Student Days', 253–54
'Time and Ebb', 104
'Tolstoy', 224–25
The Tragedy of Mister Morn, 17
'The Tragedy of Tragedy' (lecture), 199
Transparent Things. See Transparent Things as a main heading
'Tyrants Destroyed', 131–32, 250–51, 254–55
'Ultima Thule', 62–63, 198, 220, 225
'Unfinished Draft', 225
'The University Poem', 80
'Ut Pictura Poesis', 75–76n8
'The Vane Sisters', 217
'Vasiliy Shishkov', 144
Verses, 170
'The Visit to the Museum', 75–76n8
The Wanderers, 44–45
'What Should Everyone Know?', 216n16
Nabokov: His Life in Art (Field), 49
Nabokov: His Life in Part (Field), 61
Nabokov Museum, 169–70
Nabokov's Dozen (Nabokov), 98–101
Nadezhda (Speranza; Hope) (ship), 78n15

Narrative of Arthur Gordon Pym (Poe), 106
Nausea (Sartre), 96–97
Nazism
  in *Ada*, 214
  Balibar on, 256
  in *Bend Sinister*, 88, 261–62
  Bolshevist parallels with, 250, 258
  in 'Cloud, Castle, Lake', 91–92, 93
  extreme violence of, 256
  Fog before Dawn and, 228
  in 'The Leonardo', 91–92
  Nabokov family under threat of, 19–20, 21,
    87–88, 93, 229, 233
  Nabokov's escape from, 249
  Nabokov's experiences of, 87–88
  Nabokov's hatred of, 1
  under Nazi threat, 93
  Sergei Nabokov's death and, 44, 87, 94, 247,
    251, 272, 273
  in *Speak, Memory*, 88
neo-idealism, 7, 202, 203–4
New Directions (publishing house), 152–53
The New Republic (magazine), 22, 152, 258, 260
The New Yorker (magazine)
  Nabokov censored in, 24, 254
  Nabokov's editors at, 22, 36, 47, 254
  Nabokov's readership and, 153–54, 259
  Pnin and, 54, 134, 280
Nicol, Charles, 53
Nikolai Gogol (Nabokov), 52, 125, 251, 255,
  258, 260
'1949' (Del Rey), 187n9, 188
Nixon, Richard, 65
'Nokia' (Father), 187n8
'No Man's Land' (Billy Joel), 187
'No Matter How' (Nabokov), 254–55
nonhuman actors, 2, 3n2
Norman, Will, 7–8, 257–65
'Notes for the Texture of Time' (Nabokov), 198
La nouvelle Héloïse (Rousseau), 113–14
Novgorodtsev, Pavel, 242
nuclear arms race and warfare, 249, 257, 267

Obelisk Press, 153–54
Odoevstseva, Irina, 46
'Off to the Races' (Del Rey), 187n9, 188
Oklot, Michal, 6–7, 158–65, 211–18
Olympia Press, 98, 153–54
'On a Book Entitled *Lolita*' (Nabokov essay),
  127–28, 129–30
'One of the Boys' (Perry), 187
'On Golgotha' (Nabokov), 220–21
On the Origin of Species (Darwin), 202, 203
On the Road (Kerouac), 110
The Open Society and Its Enemies (Popper), 255

The Original of Laura (Nabokov), 31–32, 58, 92,
  157, 174–75
Orlova, Raisa, 172
Orwell, George, 249–50
Other Shores (Nabokov), 71–72, 168, *169*, 169–70

paedophilia, 26, 35, 128, 245, 266, 268, 269–70, 271
Pale Fire (Nabokov)
  academia in, 23–24, 51, 52, 54–55, 93
  America as abstract ideal in, 263
  the Cold War and, 264, 272–73
  vs. commercialised publishing, 156
  communism in, 273–74
  corpses presented in the beginning of, 163–64
  death in, 114–15
  as detective fiction, 163–64
  exile theme in, 275–76, 277–79, 281
  France in, 115
  Freud and, 213, 217
  homophobia in, 271–72, 273–74
  homosexuality in, 266, 272–73
  life as text and, 225
  in the Long 1950s, 266
  mortality questioned in, 220
  Nabokov's alleged political indifference and,
    264–65
  paronomasia in, 217
  political realities sublimated into poetical
    realities in, 248
  print culture hypertext and, 177–78
  Pushkin and, 128
  sexual subversion in, 266, 271
  Switzerland in, 111, 115–16
  totalitarianism in, 254–55, 272–73
  US reconfigured in, 104
Pamuk, Orhan, 27
Panaev, Ivan, 72
Panin (Countess Panin), 14
Paris
  overview, 94–101
  anti-Semitism in, 94
  cultural innovation in, 94
  The Defense serialised in, 95
  in 'First Love', 100–1
  Fondaminsky in, 5, 95, 143
  Khodasevich in, 5, 95
  Lolita begun in, 98, 134
  Nabokov family moving to, 21, 51, 94
  Nabokov's attitudes toward, 94–95
  in *Nabokov's Dozen*, 98–101
  Nabokov's literary activities in, 19–20,
    94–101, 152
  publishing culture in, 6, 98
  in *The Real Life of Sebastian Knight*, 94
  as Russian emigration centre, 17, 95, 100, 139–40

Paris (cont.)
Sovremennye zapiski published in, 95
Paris note (literary style), 142, 144
Parmigianino, Francesco, 178, 181
paronomasia (word interplay), 215–17
particle physics, 198–99
Partisan Review (literary journal), 151, 154, 259
Pasmanik, Daniil, 243–44
'The Passenger' (Nabokov), 161–62
Pasternak, Boris, 155
Paterson, Isabel, 255
Penguin Books (publishing house), 150
Pera, Pia, 183n3
'Permanent December' (Miley Cyrus), 187n8
Perry, Katie, 187
'*Petersburg*' (Bely), 76–77
Petty Demon (Sologub), 128–29
Peyton Place (Metalious), 269
Phaedra (publishing house), 168
phylogenetic systematics (cladistics), 195, 196n8
Pictures from an Institution (Jarrell), 53–54
Pifer, Ellen, 246–47
Pilsky, Petr, 126
Pisemsky, Alexsey, 121
Pitzer, Andrea, 272–73
Playboy (magazine), 26, 219
Pnin (Nabokov)
academia in, 23–24, 51, 53, 54–57, 234–35
Anglophone ignorance of Russia in, 22
anti-Semitism in, 237
author/character relationships in, 234–37
authorial persona in, 235, 238
automobile culture in, 108
Bolshevism in, 215
book cover of, 235, *236*
cover of, 237
dreams in, vs. Freudian symbolism, 215
Pnin as émigré, 234–35
exile theme in, 89, 104, 275–76, 277, 279–80
fascism in, 91–92
freedom from pain and, 136
the Holocaust in, 24, 234–35
irony and pathos combined in, 138
Jan van Eyck in, 235
Jewishness in, 234–39
linguistic disorientation in, 279–80
in the Long 1950s, 266
Madonna and Child with Canon van der Paele, 237–38
modern atrocity and, 138
mortality questioned in, 220
The New Yorker and, 54, 134, 280
poetics of absence in, 235, 239
psychological research for, 199
publication on, 134

readership difficulties of, 235–38
Russian classic tradition in, 127–28
sexual subversion in, 266
Soviet propaganda in, 253
US in, 103–4
US publication of, 152
women in, 41
word interplay in, 235–37
Pocket Books (publishing house), 150
Poe, Edgar Allen, 35, 106, 186, 213
The Poet (Emerson), 106
poetics of absence, 230, 234, 235, 239
poetics of understatement, 230, 232–33
Pohl, Vladimir, 14–15
The Pole (Nabokov), 106
Poplavsky, Boris, 140
Popper, Karl, 249–50, 255
popular culture (overview). *See also Lolita;*
Lolita (Kubrick film); (*Lolita*) (Lyne Film), 182–89
popular music. *See also individual recording artists, 185–89*
poshlost' (banality; philistinism; bad taste). *See also*
'Avant-arde and Kitsch', 158, 214n13, 216, 260
Poslednie novosti (Latest News) (newspaper), 46, 144
The Possessed (Dostoevsky), 122–23
Pound, Ezra, 24, 133–34, 152
Prager, Emily, 183n3
Prague, 17–18, 20–21, 88, 139–40
Priglashenie na kazn'. See Invitation to a Beheading
Prince (singer), 187n8
Principles of Psychology (William James), 199
The Prismatic Bezel (Nabokov novel within a novel), 163–64
Prisoner of Chillon (Byron), 113–14
Problems of Idealism (Russian idealist essay), 242
Proffer, Carl and Ellendea, 25–26, 49–50, 168, 170, 171, 172
'The Proletarian Novel' (Nabokov lecture), 151
Proust, Marcel
À la recherche du temps perdu, 97–98, 197
as dilemma for Nabokov, 181
Flaubert and, 132–33
The Gift and, 19–20
Jewishness represented in, 228
modernism in, 137
Nabokov's admiration of, 94–95, 131
Nabokov's canon and, 132
in Nabokov's curriculum, 23
in the Western canon, 5–6
The Provisional Government (V. D. Nabokov), 243–44
psychoanalysis. *See also* Freud, Sigmund
overview, 211–18
Kraus vs., 211

Lawrence vs., 211
in *Lolita*, 271
Nabokov's rejection of, 199, 271
as *poshlost'*, 214
as science of tropes, 217
in *Speak, Memory*, 216–17
as symptomatic in Nabokov, 217–18
as totalitarian, 214–15
in 'What Should Everyone Know?', 216
publishing. *See also* American literature; *Lolita*;
    Russian émigré literature; samizdat;
    Sovremennye zapiski; tamizdat; United
    States publishing culture
in Berlin, 6, 45
commercialised publishing, 156
commercial publishing and, 153
The Defense and, 45, 146
in France, 6, 152, 168
friends and foes in, 22, 44–45, 46, 47, 49, 155
Invitation to a Beheading and, 168
Mary and, 146, 168–69
modernism and, 151, 152–53
Nabokov's control over, 156
Pale Fire and, 156
Russian émigré literature and, 139–49
Pushkin, Alexander
Adamovich's advocacy of Lermontov vs., 18, 45
authorial persona of, 59, 142
The Bronze Horseman, 72, 73n3
'The Cart of Life,' 128
Eugene Onegin. See Eugene Onegin as a main
    heading
The Gift and, 19–21, 63, 123–24, 125–27, 206,
    207–8, 223
Jewishness represented in, 228
Nabokov's early passion for, 32–33
Nabokov's literary style and, 142
in *Pale Fire*, 128
in 'Pushkin, or The Real and the Plausible', 20,
    64, 96
'The Queen of Spades', 129
'The Rhyme', 128
Rusalka (*The Mermaid*), 124, 129
and the Russian diaspora in Berlin, 90–91
Russian literature advanced by, 13
Russian travels of, 74
St Petersburg and, 72
style of, 19–20, 123–24
in wartime, 77
women in, 35
younger émigrés rejection of, 141
'Pushkin, or the Real and the Plausible'
    (Nabokov), 64, 96
'Put Me in a Movie' (Del Rey), 187n9, 188
Putnam's & Sons (publishing house), 152, 155, 156

quantum theory, 196, 198
'The Queen of Spades' (Pushkin), 129–30
Questions of Philosophy and Psychology (neo-idealist
    journal), 202–3

Rabaté, Jean-Michel, 213
Radio Liberty (Munich), 168, 171
Ramanujan, S., 81
Rand, Ayn, 255
Random House (publishing house), 154
Ransom, John Crowe, 151
Rausch von Traubenberg, Yuri (cousin), 13–14,
    31, 44
Reader's Subscription book club, 155
'The Real and the Plausible' (Nabokov), 96
The Real Life of Sebastian Knight (Nabokov)
    authorial persona in, 63–64
    corpse/decay in, 163
    corpses presented in the beginning of, 163–64
    as detective fiction, 163–64
    as first English-language novel, 63–64,
        153, 275
    friends and foes and, 44
    life as text and, 225
    mortality questioned in, 220
    as Nabokov artwork template, 163
    Paris in, 94
    The Prismatic Bezel in, 159, 163–64
    quantum/particle theory and, 198
    Sergei Nabokov and, 44
    US publication of, 152, 153
    wave-particle duality in, 198–99
    women in, 21
'Recruiting' (Nabokov), 91
relativity theory, 7, 196–98
Remediation: Understanding New Media (Bolter
    and Grusin), 176–77
Remington, Charles Lee, 204
Repin, Ilya, 175
Retribution (Blok), 228
The Return of Chorb (Nabokov), 45
'Revolution' (Nabokov), 252
'The Rhyme' (Pushkin), 128
'Ride' (Del Rey), 188
The Road to Serfdom (Hayek), 255
Robbe-Grillet, Alain, 26
Rodenbach, Georges, 71–72
Roger Fishbite (Prager), 183n3
Ross, Harold, 254
Roth v. *United States* (US supreme court), 155
Rousseau, Jean-Jacques, 100, 113, 114
Rozanov, Vasily, 219
Rozhestveno (Nabokov's inherited estate). *See
    also* Rukavishnikov, Vasily, 74, 79
Rudnev, Vadim, 145

Rukavishnikov, Vasily (Uncle Ruka). *See also* Rozhestveno, 13–14, 30–31
Rul' (*The Rudder*) (Russian daily journal), 16, 17, 45, 46, 145
'Rulers' (Nabokov), 254–55
Rusalka (*The Mermaid*) (Pushkin), 124, 129
Russell, Bertrand, 257
Russia. *See also* Cold War; Silver Age; Symbolism
American ignorance of, 15, 22
artistic milieu of, 29–30
Darwinism in, 202
in *The Gift*, 74
in *Glory*, 33–34
Hitler's invasion of, 23
imperial culture of, 29
liberalism in, 12, 242–44, 255
male literary chauvinism in, 39
memories of, retained by Nabokov, 33–34
Nabokov family's permanent exile from, 15
Nabokov's childhood in, 11–14
Nabokov's memories of, 32, 82, 85
in *Pnin*, 22
in *Speak, Memory*, 79
in 'Spring in Fialta', 98–99
Tsars of, 12, 13
World of Art movement in, 29
'A Russian Beauty' (Nabokov), 89–90
Russian Berlin, 88–90, 91
Russian diaspora, 5, 89, 90–91, 95, 100
Russian émigré literature
overview, 139–49
anti-Soviet stances in, 140
Bunin and, 140
Chekhov Publishing House and, 147–48
cultural nationalism and, 140, 146–47
Dostoevsky and, 141
First Wave of, 139, 140
The Gift and, 139, 144–45, 149, 231–32
ideological debates on, 139, 141–43, 145–46
importance of, to émigrés, 139
modernism and, 141
Nabokov's Russian oeuvre published as, 147
Nabokov's stances toward, 142–46
Nabokov's switch to English and, 145
Paris note in, 142
publishing difficulties in, 139, 146–49, 148
Pushkin/Lermontov debates and, 141
vs. Soviet Literature, 149
'The Visit to the Museum' and, 140
writers representative of, 140
younger émigré writers' interest in, 142
Russian formalism, 162

Russian-language writings by Nabokov (general). *See also* English Language main headings
authorial identity in, 59–60
authorial persona originating in, 61–62
in European exile, 258
Field as biographer and, 49
impenetrability trope and, 242–45
innovations in, 96
language crisis and, 60–61, 95, 96
poetry in, 34
publication scandals in, 96–97
and the Russian literary canon, 121–30
Russian publications of, 147–48
samizdat editions of, 169–70
Sirin's disappearance and, 60–61
at Trinity College, 80, 82, 83–84
unpublished, 60–61
Russian-language writings by Nabokov (translated into English). *See also Despair*; *The Enchanter*; *Eugene Onegin*; *The Eye*; *The Gift*; *Glory*; *Invitation to a Beheading*; *King, Queen, Knave*; *Laughter in the Dark*; *Mary*; *The Song of Igor's Campaign*, 25, 144, 152, 156, 213
Russian literary canon
overview, 121–30
Bunin, Ivan in, 129–30
Chernyshevsky in, 127
in *Despair*, 121–23
émigré writers' adherence to, 141
émigré writers' challenges to, 141
Eugene Onegin in, 130
European writers and, 121–22
Flaubert vs., 121–22
in *The Gift*, 125–27
great traditions and, 121–23
intertextuality and, 130
modernist émigré reading of, 141–42
Nabokov in, 123, 126
Nabokov's canon and, 133
Nabokov's critique of, 125–27
Nabokov's distancing from, 176
Nabokov's knowledge of, 123
Nabokov's Russian-language writing and, 121–30
Nabokov's switch to English and, 127–28, 130
Pushkin in, 130
Russian literature
Ada and, 25, 127–28
in 'On a Book Entitled *Lolita*', 129–30
classical tradition in, 127–28
The Defense and, 19
formalism in, 162
and *The Gift*, 19–20
Nabokov as translator of, 22

Nabokov's Cornell teaching career and, 23
Nabokov's desire for a place in, 19–20
Nabokov's English-language literature and, 25
Nabokov's knowledge of, 17, 19–20
Nabokov's place in, 19
Nabokov's tributes to, 142–43
Nabokov's Trinity College studies in, 51
realism in, 141–43
Russian émigré literature, 139–49
socialist realism and, 126
Western misunderstanding of, 133
Russian Revolution. *See also* Bolshevism;
    communism; Soviet Union; Stalin, Joseph
in *Ada*, 252–53
anarchy following, 246
in the Crimea, 252–53
emigration resulting from, 139–40
Red Army vs. White Army in, 15, 139, 252–53
V. D. Nabokov and, 14, 15, 240–41
Ryan, Marie-Laure, 177

St Petersburg
overview, 71–79
Berlin and, 88–90
in *The Bronze Horseman*, 72, 73n3
butterflies in, 73n4
in *The Defense*, 75, 77
English culture and, 80
in *Look at the Harlequins!* 76
Mary and, 76–77
Nabokov born in, 79
Nabokov family home in, 31–32, 79
as Nabokov's birthplace, 11–12, 72
Nabokov's eighteen-year residence in, 71
Nabokov's knowledge of Russia limited to,
    12, 74
in Nabokov's memoirs, 75–76
in *Other Shores*, 72
portability of, in memories, 74n5, 75
in *Speak, Memory*, 76
Symbolists' interest in, 71–72
in 'Ut Pictura Poesis', 75–76n8
viewed from exile, 140
in 'The Visit to the Museum', 75–76n8
vs. Vyra, 73
Salinger, J. D., 24, 269
samizdat (self-publishing)
overview, 166–73
Chronicle of Current Events and, 170–71
of *Despair*, 171
of *The Gift*, 168, *169*, 170
of *Glory*, 171
illegality of, 166, 170, 171n16
of *Invitation to a Beheading*, 168–69
of *Lolita*, 168, 169–70, 171

Nabokov's disapproval of, 169–70
Nabokov's rediscovery in, 6
reading as self-investment and, 172–73
smuggled into the Soviet Union, 6, 168
Sartre, Jean-Paul, 96–97, 99, 116n13
'Scandalous' (Cobra Starship), 187n8
'Scenes from the Life of a Double Monster'
    (Nabokov), 44
Schiff, Stephen, 184
Schiff, Stacey, 40
Schopenhauer, Arthur, 92
Schuman, Sam, 53, 54
science. *See also* butterflies (Lepidoptera);
    Darwinism; psychoanalysis
overview, 193–200
art complemented by, 193–94, 201
limitations of, 199–200
Nabokov on, 193–94
Nabokov's curiosity and, 200
Nabokov's intellectual modesty and, 200
Nabokov's profile as a scientist, 193–200
Nabokov's scientific independence, 196
phylogenetic systematics (cladistics), 195–96
psychology in Nabokov's writing, 199
quantum-theory investigations, 196–98
relativity-theory investigations, 196–98
scientific socialism, 202
Soviet Union's standards of, 207–8
the true scientific spirit, 194–95
Scott-Smith, Giles, 261–62
Ségur, Mme de, née Rostopchine, 95–96
sensuous thought, 136–37
Sentimental Education (Flaubert), 97–98
Sevastopol (Tolstoy), 85
Sexual Behavior in the Human [*Male/Female*]
    (Kinsey), 268
sexuality. *See also* homosexuality; Long 1950s;
    paedophilia
censorship and, 98, 153–54
in Freud, 211, 214–15, 216
of Lolita in popular culture, 182–83, 184–85,
    186–88
in Nabokov's childhood, 88
sexual freedom and, 26
sexual subversion, 266, 268, 269, 270–71, 273
Shakespeare, William, 5–6, 32, 132, 172n21, 216–17
'Shakey Dog Starring Lolita' (Ghostface Killah),
    187n8
Shakhovskoy, Zinaida, 20, 36–37, 232n9
'Shame on You' (Aerosmith), 187n8
Sharshun, Sergei, 140, 141–42
Shelley, Mary, 41, 113–14
Shelley, Percy Bysshe, 113–14
Sherlock Holmes detective stories, 159
Shestov, Lev, 219

Shikhovtsev, Evgeny, 171
The Shropshire Lad (Housman), 82–83
Shulgina, Valentina, 13–14
Shute, Jenefer, 217–18
Shvabrin, Stanislav, 5, 87–93
Siewert, Svetlana, 37n3, 92
'Signs and Symbols' (Nabokov), 165, 217, 234,
    235–37
Sikorski, Elena, née Nabokov (Nabokov's sister),
    24–25, 39, 43–44, 65, 111
Silver Age, 32–33, 128, 203, 241–42
Simon & Schuster (publishing house), 150
Sirin, Vladimir (Nabokov pseudonym)
    Adamovich's attacks on, 125
    authorial persona metamorphosis from, 59,
        60–61
    Berlin and, 91
    in exile, 139
    gender structures and, 42
    literary style of, 143
    Nabokov's literary hoax and, 46
    and Nabokov's switch to English, 60–61,
        147–49
    poetry published under, 16–17, 45
    becoming Professor Nabokov, 52
    the Russian literary canon and, 130
    Slovo as publisher of, 146
    un-Russianness of, 121
    Véra and, 36–37
Sirk, Douglas, 270
'Skazka'/'A Nursery Tale' (Nabokov), 182n2
'Slava' (Nabokov), 221
'A Slice of Life' (Nabokov), 38
Slonim, Véra Evseevna. *See* Nabokov, Véra
Slovo (publishing house), 45, 146
Smith, Zadie, 27
Social Darwinism, 203
socialist realism, 126, 140, 160–61, 258
Socialist Revolutionary Party, 145
Sologub, Fyodor, 121, 128–29
Solovyov, Vladimir, 203n4, 203–4, 207, 219
'Solus Rex' (Nabokov), 21, 62–63
Somov, Konstantin, 29–30
The Song of Igor's Campaign (Medieval Russian
    Epic; Nabokov's translation), 15–16, 22,
    47–48, 52, 130
'Song of the Open Road' (Whitman), 110
Sontag, Susan, 250
Sophia (Symbolist spiritual force), 203n4
Soviet realism. *See* socialist realism
'Soviet Rule and Russia's Future' (V. D.
    Nabokov), 240, 243
Soviet Union. *See also* samizdat; tamizdat
    American ignorance of, 254
    Berlin and, 16–17

    Bertrand Russell and, 257
    dissident writers in, 170
    Elena Sikorski's visits to, 26
    emigration policies of, 16–17
    émigré literature boycotted by, 146
    émigré rejection of, 140–41
    in *Invitation to a Beheading*, 20
    Jakobson's sympathies with, 47–48
    the Korean War and, 253
    Lenin's New Economic Policy and, 16
    Lolita smuggled into, 168
    in *Look at the Harlequins!* 34
    Nabokov-samizdat/tamizdat cult in, 167
    Nabokov's distancing from Soviet readers, 168
    Nabokov's hatred of, 7–8, 23–24, 253–54
    Nazism parallels with, 250
    orthography in, 140
    as *poshlost*'s home, 260
    Russian émigré literature vs., 149
    socialist realism as official aesthetic of, 140–41,
        258, 261
    in 'Spring in Fialta', 99
    substandard science in, 207–8
    as totalitarian, 249, 255
    as US WWII ally, 23
Sovremennye zapiski (*Contemporary Annals*)
    (publishing house), 89
    The Defense serialised in, 18, 95
    Fondaminsky and, 18, 46, 95, 145
    The Gift published in, 166
    The Gift's Chernyshevsky biography rejected
        by, 95, 142
    impenetrability trope in, 244–45
    Khodasevich as editor of, 45–46
    Nabokov's later work published by, 146
    Nabokov's literary hoax in, 46
    older Russian émigrés in control of, 145
    Sirin published by, 17
Speak, Memory (Nabokov)
    academia in, 57–58
    authorial persona in, 65–66
    Berlin in, 88, 182
    continuities in exile described in, 280–82
    Darwinism in, 201
    direct address technique in, 37
    exile theme in, 89, 275–76, 279–82
    'First Love' and, 100–1
    Freud in, 217
    German culture in, 93
    Look at The Harlequins! and, 25
    'Mademoiselle O' in, 100, 113
    Nazism in, 88
    psychoanalysis in, 216–17
    Russia in, 79
    St Petersburg and, 76

Sergei Nabokov in, 272
success of, 100
watermark as life image in, 226
women in, 37
Speak On, Memory (Nabokov proposed
  sequel), 59
Sperry, Roger, 210
Spock, Benjamin, 267
'Spring in Fialta' (Nabokov), 98–99
Stalin, Joseph, 7–8, 23, 250, 253, 256, 258
Stanford University, 21, 22–23, 51–52
Stanislavsky, Konstantin, 29–30
Stein, Gertrude, 94, 153, 162–63
Steinbeck, John, 110
Steiner, George, 280–81
Stendhal, Maurice, 94–95, 131, 132–33
Sterne, Laurence, 66
Stevenson, Robert Louis, 158–59
Stone, Hannah and Abraham, 267, 268
Strachey, Lytton, 66
The Stranger (Blok), 178
'A Stroll with J.-J. Rousseau' (Nabokov), 113n9
Strong Opinions (Nabokov), 89, 99, 117, 145,
  159, 257
Struve, Gleb, 16–17, 84, 121, 241–42
'Student Days' (Nabokov), 253–54
style (literary style)
  detective fiction and, 6, 158–59, 165
  displacement techniques in, 276
  of Flaubert, 42, 97, 121–22
  of the human document genre, 141–42
  Nabokov's biography and, 65
  of Pushkin, 19–20, 123–24
  significance of, for Nabokov, 158–59
  of Sirin, 143
  of Stevenson, 158
  of women writers, 38
surrealism, 94–95, 99, 186
Sweeney, Susan Elizabeth, 4–5, 44, 51–58
Swiss governess (Cécile Miauton). *See also*
  'Mademoiselle O', 96, 100, 111, 112
Switzerland. *See also* Montreux, Switzerland
  overview, 111–17
  in *Ada*, 111
  America idealized by Nabokov in, 263
  anti-Soviet stance of, 112
  benefits of, 111–12
  butterfly hunting in, 111
  disappearance into, 115–16
  Elena Sikorski in, 24–25
  in *Glory*, 111, 115–16
  Lake Geneva and, 5, 112, 113, 114
  in *Look at the Harlequins!* 111, 115–16
  multiculturalism of, 115–16
  Nabokov's Cold War views from, 259, 263

Nabokov's early connections with, 111
Nabokov's identity and, 117
as Nabokov's permanent residence, 5,
  25–26, 112
Nabokov's visitors in, 25–26
natural beauty of, 112
nature/culture in, 113–15
in *Pale Fire*, 111, 115–16
town-name word play in, 116–17
in *Transparent Things*, 116–17
Symbolism
  'About the Contemporary State of Russian
    Symbolism', 128–29
  Blok and, 13, 71–72, 128–29
  Briusov and, 71–72
  cosmic return concept of, 206
  as cultural innovation, 29
  Darwinism and, 7, 203–4
  in *Despair*, 128
  in *The Gift*, 125
  Lolita and, 128–29
  Nabokov's adherence to, in exile, 201
  in Nabokov's early career, 201
  in Nabokov's mid career, 204
  Nabokov's otherworldliness and, 201
  Nabokov vs., 128
  Rodenbach and, 71–72
  in Russia, 29
  Solovyov as the father of, 202–3
  Sophia as spiritual force in, 203n4
  urbanism in, 71–72
  Verhaeren and, 71–72
synaesthesia (*audition colorée*), 30, 36, 59, 62, 174
Szeftel, Marc, 54

Tagantsev, Nikolai, 243
tamizdat (uncensored western publications)
  overview, 166–73
  available on loan only, 166
  book-sharing network for, 167
  The Gift as, 166, 168
  illegality of, 166, 170, 171n16
  Invitation to a Beheading as, 166, 168
  Nabokov's rediscovery in, 6
  reading as self-investment and, 172–73
  smuggled into the Soviet Union, 168
Tammi, Pekka, 65
Tatarinov, Raisa, 17, 36
Tate, Allan, 153
Tchaikovsky, Peter, 175
Tebbel, John, 150–51
10 Dollar (M.I.A.), 185
The Police (rock group), 187
The Red Hot Chili Peppers (rock group), 187
The Veronicas (pop music group), 187n8

Third Reich. *See* Berlin; Hitler, Adolph; Nazism
Thomas (apostle), 222
Three Sisters (Chekhov), 124
'Time and Ebb' (Nabokov), 104
time-vision, 195, 197
Todorov, Tzvetan, 162–63, 164–65
Tolstaia, Aleksandra, 228
'Tolstoy' (Nabokov), 224–25
Tolstoy, Aleksey, 253
Tolstoy, Leo
  absence of heroes in, 85
  Anna Karenina, 5–6, 122, 124, 127–28, 231
  'Death' (Nabokov poem) and, 226
  The Defense and, 124
  Don Quixote in, 136
  in *The Gift*, 229–30
  at Lake Geneva, 113–14
  Nabokov's admiration of, 142
  Nabokov's Harvard lectures on, 134
  Nabokov's indebtedness to, 130
  Nabokov's pantheon and, 124, 132
  Nabokov's reading of, 32
  as Proust's precursor, 97–98
  in the Russian classic tradition, 122–23, 126
  Sevastopol, 85
  'Tolstoy' (Nabokov poem), 224–25
  in the Western canon, 5–6
totalitarianism. *See also* Bolshevism; communism; Hitler, Adolph; Nazism; Soviet Union; Stalin, Joseph
  overview, 249–56
  Arendt on, 249–50
  art as barrier to, 256
  artistic activity in, 249
  in *Bend Sinister*, 249, 250–51, 255–56, 273
  characteristics of, 249–50
  in 'Cloud, Castle, Lake', 251–52
  in *Glory*, 41, 250–51
  Greenberg on, 151
  individual freedom and, 249
  in *Invitation to a Beheading*, 251–52, 258
  and Kitsch, 151, 261
  in 'The Leonardo', 251–52
  mockery as weapon against, 254–55, 256
  Nabokov's alleged political indifference and, 249–56
  Nabokov's exposure to, 214–15
  Nabokov's hatred of, 7, 249–50
  Nazi/Soviet parallels in, 250, 258
  Orwell on, 249–50
  in *Pale Fire*, 254–55, 272–73
  popular realism and, 261
  of *poshlost'*, 214–15, 216
  psychoanalysis and, 214–15
  in 'Revolution', 41, 252

in 'Tyrants Destroyed', 258
in US discourse, 253–54
Toulouse-Lautrec, Henri, 178
The Tragedy of Mister Morn (Nabokov), 17
'The Tragedy of Tragedy' (Nabokov lecture), 199
Transcendentalism, 106
transnationalism (overview), 275–82
Transparent Things (Nabokov), 33, 65, 111, 115–17, 197
Traubenberg, Yuri Rausch von (cousin), 13–14, 31, 44
'Traveller's Companion' series (Olympia Press), 154
Travels with Charley (Steinbeck), 110
Trediakovsky, Vasily, 95–96
Trilling, Lionel, 155, 217, 270
Trinity College (University of Cambridge)
  E. Harrison as tutor at, 81–82
  Nabokov's adaptation to, 81, 82–83
  Nabokov's athleticism and, 81
  Nabokov's debate at, 240, 243
  Nabokov's English-language writings at, 80, 82–83
  Nabokov's identities at, 5
  Nabokov's Russian-language writings at, 80, 82, 83–84
  Nabokov's scientific career at, 83–84
  Nabokov's writings at, 80, 82–83
  Nabokov welcomed to, 80
  overseas applicants at, 81
Triolet, Elsa, 95–96
'Trop jeune pour aimer' (Dion), 187
Trousdale, Rachel, 8, 275–82
Turgenev, Ivan, 126, 231, 232–33
Twain, Shania, 187n8
'The Twelve' (Blok), 15, 77–78
'The Typology of Detective Fiction' (Todorov), 162–63
'Tyrants Destroyed' (Nabokov), 131–32, 250–51, 254–55, 258
Tyutchev, Fyodor, 22, 32–33, 113–14

'Ultima Thule' (Nabokov), 62–63, 198, 220, 225
Ulysses (Joyce), 19–20, 98, 153–54, 178
Uncle Ruka (Vasily Rukavishnikov), 13–14, 30–31
Understanding Media (MacLuhan), 177
'Unfinished Draft' (Nabokov), 225
United States. *See also Lolita*; publishing
  butterfly species discovered in, 102–3
  continuities with Europe for exiles in, 279–80, 281–82
  exiles' disorientation in, 279–80
  free world as an extension of, 264
  Freud's reception in, 212

Hudson River School painting in, 106
idealized by Nabokov from Switzerland, 263
the Korean War and, 253
liberalism in, 245–47, 253–54, 255
linguistic disorientation of exiles in, 279–80
in the Long 1950s, 266–74
Nabokov family moving to, 22, 47
Nabokov's adaptation to, 85–86
Nabokov's anti-communist warnings to, 258
Nabokov's continued interest in, 26
Nabokov's literary connections in, 22–23
Nabokov's travels in, 5, 23, 102–10
publishing culture in, 6
purity in geopolitical space of, 264
reconfigured in Nabokov's writing, 103–4
road literature in, 110
Transcendentalism in, 106
United States publishing culture
in the Depression, 150
Nabokov's celebrity status in, 156–57
Nabokov's control over, 156
Nabokov's numerous publishing houses
and, 152
Nabokov vs. commercialised publishing in,
151–52, 153, 156
post-WWII boom in, 6, 150–51
'The University Poem' (Nabokov), 80
un-Russianness
of the English language, 80
of modernism, 141, 174
of Nabokov, 5, 121, 143
of Sirin, 121
Updike, John, 24, 27
Upton, Florence Kate, 31
'Ut Pictura Poesis' (Nabokov), 75–76n8

Van Doren, Mamie, 270
Vane, William de, 196
'The Vane Sisters' (Nabokov), 217
'Vasiliy Shishkov' (Nabokov), 144
Verhaeren, Emile, 71–72
Verne, Jules, 26
'Versace Hottie' (Wavy Spice), 187n8
Verses (Nabokov), 170
Vertov, Dziga, 175
Viardot, Pauline, 231
Vietnam War, 26, 257, 259
Viking (publishing house), 22
Vinaver, Maxim, 243–44
Vishniak, Mark, 145
'The Visit to the Museum' (Nabokov),
75–76n8, 140
visual imagination
overview, 174–81
ekphrasis and, 178, 179

film (motion-pictures) and, 175
vs. linear thinking, 177
media competition in, 177
media ecologies in, 176–77
media influences on thought and, 177
media refashioning and, 176–77
of Nabokov, 6, 174–81
Nabokov's multiple media representations in,
177–78
painters in Nabokov's works and, 174–75
transnationalism and, 174–75
Ut Pictura Poeisis concept and, 177–78
Visual Thinking (Arnheim), 177
Voloshin, Maximilian, 14–15
Voronina, Olga, 7, 249–56
Vozrozhdenie (Resurrection) (émigré
newspaper), 146
Vrubel, Mikhail, 178
Vyra (Nabokov family country home), 5, 31, 33,
62, 74, 79, 275, 281–82

Wagner, Richard, 230–33
Walker, Matthew, 6–7, 158–65, 211–18
Wallace, David Foster, 181
The Wanderers (Nabokov), 44–45
War and Peace (Tolstoy), 97–98
Ward, Hilda, 40
Watson-Crick DNA discovery, 204
wave-particle duality, 198–99, 209
Wavy Spice (hip-hop group), 187n8
Weeks, Edmund, 22
Wellesley College, 23, 47–48, 56, 102, 134, 151,
193–94
Wells, H. G., 26, 31
Western literary canon
overview, 131–38
art/life fusions in, 137–38
Don Quixote in, 133–36
modern atrocity and, 137–38
Nabokov as sceptical of, 131, 133–34
Nabokov in, 132
Nabokov's canon in, 131–33
Nabokov's *Don Quixote* lectures and, 133–38
Nabokov's selectivity in, 131
Shakespeare in, 5–6
strangeness of, 131–32
text vs. reputation in, 134–36
thrill of reading and, 136–37
West-Östlicher Divan (Goethe), 221–22
'What are Master-Pieces and Why Are There So
Few of Them' (Stein), 162–63
'What Should Everyone Know?' (Nabokov),
216n16
White, Duncan, 6, 150–57
White, Edmund, 27

White, Hayden, 241
White, Katharine, 22, 36, 47, 254
Whitehead, A. N., 81
White Mule (Williams), 153
White Nights (Dostoevsky), 73
Whitman, Alden, 33
Whitman, Walt, 110
'Whose Bed Have Your Boots Been Under?'
   (Shania Twain), 187n8
Wilde, Oscar, 31
Williams, William Carlos, 153
Wilson, Edmund
   on California, 85–86
   on detective fiction, 160, 161
   Mary McCarthy and, 53–54
   Memoirs of Hecate County, 154
   in Montreux, 48
   on Nabokov, 77
   vs. Nabokov on Malraux, 97
   Nabokov's falling-out with, 4–5, 25, 48–49
   Nabokov's introduction to, 152
   among Nabokov's literary connections,
     22–23, 24
   women novelists and, 39
women. *See also* Berberova, Nina; Callier,
   Jacqueline; Guadanini, Irina; Janelli,
   Altagracia de; *Lolita*; Nabokov, Elena
   Vladimirovna (mother); Nabokov, Véra;
   Sikorski, Elena; Tatarinov, Raisa; White,
   Katharine
   overview, 35–42
   in *Ada*, 38–39, 41
   in 'The Admiralty Spire', 41
   in *Despair*, 41–42
   in Dostoevsky, 35

   feminism and, 26
   in *The Gift*, 37–38
   in *Glory*, 41
   in *King Queen Knave*, 38
   in *Laughter in the Dark*, 38
   in *Lolita*, 35–36, 41–42
   in *Look at the Harlequins!* 36, 37, 41–42
   and misogynistic men, 41–42
   Nabokov as a womanizer, 13–14, 20–21, 37n3
   Nabokov's dependence on, 4
   Nabokov's literary sexism and, 39–42
   in *Pnin*, 41
   in Pushkin, 35
   in *The Real Life of Sebastian Knight*, 21
   in *Speak, Memory*, 37
   subjectivity of, 42
   as translators, 40
   as unequal creative partners, 37–39, 41
   Wilson and, 39
Wood, Michael, 5–6, 131–38
Woolf, Virginia, 212
Wordsworth, William, 113–14
World of Art (artistic movement), 29
World War I, 13, 78–79
World War II, 23, 95, 147, 150, 253, 259–60, 266
Wright, Sewall, 208, 209
Wyllie, Barbara, 4, 28–29, 179

Yeats, W. B., 86

Zaitsev, Boris, 140
Zashchita Luzhina. See The Defense (*The Luzhin
   Defense*)
Zhdanov, Andrey, 65
Zitzewitz, Josephine von, 171n16

CPSIA information can be obtained
at www.ICGtesting.com
Printed in the USA
LVHW050803081120
671069LV00010B/88